Kiss Your Stockbroker Goodbye

KISS YOUR STOCKBROKER GOODBYE

A Guide to Independent Investing

John G. Wells, CFA

St. Martin's Press
New York

Design by Chris Welch

Library of Congress Cataloging-in-Publication Data

Wells, John G.
    Kiss your stockbroker goodbye : a guide to independent investing / by John G. Wells.—1st ed.
      p. cm.
    ISBN 0-312-15158-6
    1. Investments—United States—Handbooks, manuals, etc.
    2. Stocks—United States—Handbooks, manuals, etc.   3. Bonds—United States—Handbooks, manuals, etc.   4. Mutual funds—United States—Handbooks, manuals, etc.   5. Investment advisors—United States—Handbooks, manuals, etc.   I. Title.
HG4921.W438   1997
332.6—dc20   96-32028
                                                              CIP

First Edition: April 1997

10 9 8 7 6 5 4 3 2 1

Dedicated to TC, Jillian, Libby, and Kip, the richest assets I have.

Acknowledgments

Many thanks go to Peter Butler, William Song, and Stephen Biggs for their assistance and diligence in gathering and organizing material for this book. A special recognition goes to Charles Foster of Blankinship & Foster for the assistance he provided regarding financial planners. And to my agent, Faith Hamlin, goes my sincere gratitude for believing in this book and in me.

CONTENTS

■ Information is obtained from sources thought to be reliable but its accuracy is not guaranteed.

■ Neither author nor publisher warrant the performance of services listed in the book; past performance is no assurance of future results.

KISS YOUR STOCKBROKER GOODBYE

INTRODUCTION

I am in a non-business. Inventory is never a problem for me, yet my inventories are unlimited. Seasons are never a problem, yet style changes in my business would give Yves St. Laurent a spastic colon. Selling my merchandise is easy because it sells itself. Dreams of glory always sell themselves. Men and women lie, cheat, steal, kill and commit suicide over my merchandise. It makes them miserable and it makes them joyous; it makes everything possible and everything impossible. . . . I'm a stockbroker and my game is greed.[1]

This passage from a 1971 exposé of the brokerage business, written by one of its own (hence, the author's pen name, Brutus), concisely sets the stage for the relationship that exists between the full-commission retail stockbroker and his clients. I am quick to distinguish between the *retail* stockbroker (salesperson) and the *institutional* salesperson. The retail broker services individual investors and the institutional broker services large clients such as pension funds, money managers, mutual funds, banks, and insurance companies. Both brokers share comparable job functions, and the objectives of both are similar: to generate income for themselves and their employers through securities transactions that throw off commissions. The institutional salesperson usually has a compensation package that includes a generous "salary," or "draw" against future commissions, with additional incentive compensation coming from commissions that exceed some predetermined target. Because of this arrangement, the institutional salesperson on a day-to-day basis is less concerned about transactions and more concerned with providing service to his institutional client. That service includes showing the client an investment concept that promises to make money. If the concept achieves that goal, then the commissions will flow, big-time. If the concept does not make money . . . well, it may be awhile before the salesperson gets another shot at it with that client. I know this because for over twenty-five years I have dealt with institutional salespeople from my capacity as a securities analyst and portfolio manager at two large banks. The distinction between the two salespeople is that the

[1]Brutus, *Confessions of a Stockbroker* (Boston: Little, Brown), 1971.

1

institutional salesperson approaches his relationship not with greed in mind but with the notion that if he is truly helpful to his client, the rewards will follow.

Through the years I have also dealt with a number of retail stockbrokers. In contrast, retail stockbrokers are locked into a compensation package that rewards them only for transactions on the books. Reinforcing that is a brokerage management mindset that promotes unit volume more than the quality of the sale or the personal service behind it. Their salespeople could just as easily be selling automobiles or encyclopedias; it makes no difference. If the stock trade makes money, great. If it doesn't, that's okay too; it's the transaction and its commission that count. When an eighty-year-old customer is being sold a thirty-year bond, it's irrelevant that the bond will outlive the customer; it's the sales commission that counts. If a young worker's individual retirement account is being sold a front-end sales load mutual fund that lops a 5 percent commission off the top of his initial investment and all subsequent contributions, not to worry; it's the sales commission that counts.

To the analytical observer, it is baffling why this system still survives and flourishes. The solution to the quandary is self-evident. As long as millions of investors are content to do business this way, business will continue to be done this way. The logical question follows, "Why do investors continue to invest through the full-commission retail stockbroker, when there are so many alternatives?" One explanation is that some investors are unaware of the alternatives available to them. Another explanation can be summarized in one word: *fear*. The fear of having to make their own investment decisions. The fear of not knowing how to invest. The fear of being wrong. The fear of making a change. The fear of having to tell the stockbroker you are not going to do business with him anymore. These, and many others, are all legitimate fears.

The question "Why do investors continue . . . ?" provided the inspiration for this book. The answers offered above, and others, are the essence of this book. For those who are simply unaware of the alternative brokers one can obtain, or for those who are bewildered by the many choices, this book will identify the alternatives and explain how to work with them. If investors are aware of the multitude of research services and newsletters but are overwhelmed by the sheer number of them, this book will alleviate the confusion.

More important, I will strive to calm the investor's fears. Fear of anything usually comes from a lack of knowledge or understanding. By broadening your knowledge base and enhancing, even in a small way, your understanding of the investment process, you can minimize the fear of investing for yourself and not rely on the advice of the stockbroker whose vested interest may be in conflict with your own. Hopefully, you will also see that investing for yourself can be fun!

Before outlining the structure of this book, let's briefly discuss what this book is *not* and what the book will *not* do. This is not a textbook. Heaven knows that I've read enough finance and investment textbooks over the years that I would never want to write one. And the reality is, another investment textbook doesn't need to be written, at least not until a truly innovative investment theory is devised or discerned. There will be no mathematics found here. Nor is this a *How I Made a Million Dollars in the Stock Market on My Summer Vacation* book. In fact, this is not really a how-to book at all, although you will have a better feel of "how to" after reading it. Most notably, this book does not profess to have all the answers. The truth is, with the dynamics of investing being what they are, *there are no answers*. There is no magic formula that works all the time. If there were, everyone would invest according to that formula and the formula would then cease to be effective. What works for one person will not work for another. The investment methodology that performs well today will not perform as well tomorrow. If you can understand and accept these premises, you are already on your way to being a better investor.

The book can be divided into two sections. The first section will describe what alternatives exist for the investor: alternative brokers, alternative information sources, alternative investment strategies and products. Perhaps the most useful part of this section is the resource guide contained in several of the chapters. There is an exhaustive listing of brokers, newsletters, on-line services, computer software, and books, as well as ideas on what to do with them. If nothing else, this section will provide you with a resource guide that can be referred to again and again, as your investment needs and information requirements change. Rather than just present a catalog of resources arranged by product type (newsletters, software, and so on), I have grouped the resources within separate chapters according to the three types of assets in which most investors invest: stocks, bonds, mutual funds. The grouping of information in this manner should provide you with maximum utility and convenience of use.

The latter section of the book is designed to assist you with finding and working with a suitable *fee-only* investment professional who is the alternative investment expert to the full-commission retail stockbroker. These practitioners include money managers, trust departments, and fee-only financial planners. Even those of you who feel comfortable selecting your own investments, and who make money doing so, will at some point need the services of a financial professional. These services might consist of establishing a trust, a family limited partnership, or some other estate-planning vehicles. Or perhaps you just need someone to help devise an overall financial plan. No matter what the situation, the worst thing to do is to turn to a commission-based salesperson for such advice. The salesman's knowledge about such topics may be as good as that of the fee-only practitioner. However, as long as their compensation is based on commissions from products sold, their advice has to be suspect. You will want to have no doubts that the strategy being pursued is the one that maximizes the benefits to you, and not the commission dollars to the broker.

One last thought before proceeding. I am a firm believer in the KISS principle: Keep It Simple, Sweetheart. Like many other human endeavors, investing has been made a complicated and convoluted process. The blame for this lies with those in my own profession. They have become purveyors of a process or processes (market timing, dividend discount models, growth investing, tactical asset allocation, to name only a few), and many have lost sight of what the real objective is: *to make money*. Their accomplices include those in academia, especially mathematicians with too much time on their hands, who attempt to formulate what essentially cannot be formulated: human emotion and behavior.

It is, after all, human emotions, primarily greed and fear, and the response to those emotions that drive up or force down the price of anything: stocks, real estate, baseball cards, tulip bulbs, and so on. Hence, my goal in every chapter is to simplify the investment process, introduce you to the tools that help to execute the investment process, and keep you focused on the real objective: making money for yourself.

Chapter 1

WHERE ARE THE
CUSTOMERS' YACHTS?

There is an old story that circulates through the investment business and beyond. Its date of origin is unknown, but it is safe to say that it is set in the early part of the twentieth century. The story tells of a client being wined and dined aboard a yacht, owned by one of Wall Street's prominent stockbrokers, cruising through New York Harbor. As the yacht glides along, the broker, hoping to impress the client with his knowledge and position on Wall Street, points to three of the yachts at anchor and proclaims, "There is J. P. Morgan's yacht; that one there is Dean Witter's yacht; and over there is E. F. Hutton's yacht."

After a moment of silent deliberation, the client, thoroughly unimpressed with the broker's recitation, responds drolly, "Yes, but where are the customers' yachts?"

This fictional anecdote summarizes what everyone already knows: stockbrokers make fortunes, in good markets and in bad markets. The customers also make money, at least in good markets when prices are rising. They fare much worse when prices are falling. Why is this? How is it that the brokers can earn such high income while the client makes do with more modest returns?

The answer is quite simple. Stockbrokers do not make money from their investment advice, good or bad. No, the advice is merely the tool used to operate the moneymaking machine: transactions. Every time a customer enters into a buy or sell transaction, the broker who facilitates the trade receives a commission. Consider how many transactions a client can enter into in the course of a year, even with a small portfolio. Now also remember that when a broker recommends something to buy, there is usually a sell transaction somewhere in the general vicinity. Hence, the broker can easily get two trades from you with each phone call: 1) buy that hot stock that the research department is so keen on; and 2) sell last month's "selection-gone-bad" to raise cash for the purchase. Each trade generates a commission. It matters not whether you made a profit on the stock being sold, or even whether or not you *will* make a profit on the new stock purchased. A commission will be paid to the broker. Consider, if you will, that money managers routinely calculate and disseminate portfolio performance for individual clients. Mutual fund managers also provide past performance of their portfolios, as do many services and newsletters. In contrast, brokers do not provide portfolio performance on their statements.

Of course, your broker wants you to make money. A broker's most loyal customer will find a new adviser if his trades do not generate profits over some period of time. At least we think he would. But on a day-to-day basis, the vested interest of the broker is to generate trades and to generate commissions. It is what he is hired to do. It is what his manager expects him to do. It is what his performance and compensation are based on. Generate trades and generate commissions.

One volume on the history of Wall Street describes a new broker's introduction to the commission game:

> In 1924 Matthew Josephson, late of Columbia University and the Paris surrealist circles, went to Wall Street and became a customer's man. Josephson admitted that he knew little of what was going on, and relied more often than not upon rumors for the advice he gave clients.
>
> "What counted for us was the business of keeping our clients trading in and out of securities, so that win or lose we gathered our broker's fees at fifteen dollars for each hundred shares. . . ."
>
> Josephson did well; everything was going up, and his clients were put into stocks which were swept along by the bull market. . . . Josephson continued to put his happy customers into stocks of which he had heard wild rumors, and for a while they went up. Then, after committing most of his accounts to a particular security, it fell sharply, wiping out many of his customers. Josephson realized that a more experienced customer's man would not have acted as rashly as he, but he was counseled not to feel sorry for his ruined clients.[2]

Brokers (of one commodity or another) have been around for millennia. You could say that it is the world's second oldest profession, one that might trace its roots back to *the* oldest profession. Although their commerce was in different goods and services than the intangibles stockbrokers handle today, the functions performed are and were the same. Stockbrokers have assumed many names during their existence. The term *stockbroker* has been most widely used over the centuries. As the preceding passage shows, the term *customer's man* was commonly used

---

[2]Sobel, Robert, *The Big Board—A History of the New York Stock Market* (New York: The Free Press), 1965.

during the 1920s and 1930s. This term left no room for the inclusion of women in the profession, which suited Wall Street just fine at the time. In the 1960s the title *registered representative* came into vogue. It is unclear who initiated this title change or why. The growing entrance of women into the sales force may be one reason. Or, could it have been brokerage house managements' attempt to differentiate their salespeople from those *unregistered representatives* whom their unprincipled competitors were employing? Perhaps it emanated from the brokers themselves in their effort to overcome one of the barriers they encounter in cold-calling prospective clients. (Prospective client upon hearing telephone sales pitch after being interrupted from dinner: "No, I don't want to buy stock through you. I already have a stockbroker." Stockbroker: "Yes, I am sure you do. However, I am a 'registered representative,' not a 'stockbroker.' ")

Today those salespeople interrupting you from your dinner are more likely to call themselves *personal financial advisers* or *investment planners*. Considering their true motivation (selling stocks, bonds, mutual funds, insurance, annuities, and other commission-rich products), such modern-day monikers are the most insidious. These names may also confuse the client into thinking the broker is a so-called *financial planner,* a professional who counsels clients as to their total financial needs and objectives, often for a fee rather than a commission. We shall discuss working with real financial planners in Chapter 7, Working with Fee-Only Professionals. The thing to remember here is that no matter what name is being used by the stockbroker, it is merely a euphemism for *salesperson*.

The true function of a real broker (not the stockbroker/salesperson we refer to elsewhere) is and has always been to facilitate the trading of whatever commodity is up for auction. This is done by:

- Maintaining the means through which buyer and seller can meet
- Keeping a record of all transactions in that commodity, so that buyer and seller have accurate information with which to make decisions
- Executing the purchase or sale and receiving a *commission* for their efforts

However, the stockbroker has, through time, evolved into a high-pitched selling machine, a peddler of products and promises whose covert mission is to create demand for new securities and services. In the wake of this evolution many brokers have forsaken the concept of meeting clients' needs and objectives. Instead they sell the mutual fund with the highest commission (called sales load), push the latest high-risk initial public offering (IPO) from the brokerage firm's underwriting desk, or hawk the office's quota of those dicey real estate limited partnerships. Thus, there often arises a conflict of interest between the stockbroker, his employer, and the client. One always has to wonder when a broker calls: "Is the transaction being proposed by the broker in my best interest, or is the call prompted by a sales quota or incentive contest?" and "Will this trade make money for me and move me closer to my investment goal, or does the broker have a mortgage payment coming due in two weeks and need the commission revenue for himself?" The answers to these and similar questions are rarely evident, at least not before the fact.

The stockbroker of today typically provides the following services:

- Counsels clients on asset allocation
- Provides clients with research on products
- Makes buy-sell recommendations to clients
- Offers price data, current and/or historic
- Buys and sells securities on clients' behalf
- Sends to clients a record (confirmation) of trades
- Offers custody of securities and cash held by clients
- Sends to clients a periodic (quarterly or monthly) statement
- Provides clients with summary data for tax preparation

For such services brokers expect and do receive compensation, as well they should. Understand, however, that it is the fifth item, buying and selling stocks, in which brokers are most interested. It is their reason for being and it is how that compensation is generated. And good compensation it is, too. According to the Securities Industry Association, the trade group for the brokerage business, the average retail stockbroker (those dealing with individual investors) earned over $123,000 from trading commissions in 1995.

We should pause here and say that most of the approximately 95,000 stockbrokers registered in the United States (and those doing business outside the U.S. as well) are decent, honest people who genuinely want to do well for their clients. In most cases they probably believe in the products they are selling, and expect that their clients will make money by investing in them. The dilemma confronting them as investment professionals is the potential conflict of interest that we referred to earlier. In other words, the broker who calls you to sell these products is merely a pawn in a selling scheme developed, nurtured, and perpetuated by her employer, the brokerage firm. The line between doing what is right for the client and putting food on one's own table is difficult to draw. The dilemma confronting you, the investor, is how to achieve your financial objectives through suitable investment vehicles, obtained at the lowest cost, free from the worry of a broker's ulterior motives.

The answer to the broker's dilemma is to do what thousands of stockbrokers have done in recent years: leave the full-commission retail brokerage firms and establish themselves as fee-only investment professionals. This conversion eliminates the inducement to act from a desire for commissions and creates for them the same vested interest that the client has: to make money for the client and build the client's portfolio. The solution to the investor's dilemma, your dilemma, is . . . well, the fact that you are reading this book means you are on your way to finding the solution.

Just as the evolution of animals did not begin or end with the dinosaurs, neither has the evolution of stockbrokers or the brokerage business ended. Millions of investors have already turned to using discount brokers and other sources that will allow them to make independent judgments that are sound and well-thought-out for their own situation. A shrinking client base will ultimately force the full-commission brokerages to change the way their service providers operate. This means that brokerage personnel will do less selling of products and more unbiased counseling to achieve clients' financial goals. Some brokerage firms now pay lip service to financial problem solving, but it is all a marketing sham. Until the sales incentive, commissions, is removed from the table, their people will continue to sell and will eschew unbiased counseling.

The solution for the brokerages is that the brokers are put on salary. A West Coast office manager of one of America's largest full-commission brokers has told me he thinks that is where the industry is headed. Salaried brokers will provide services for their clients. Incremental compensation for the broker would follow from investment performance and asset gathering, the same as it is with money managers, trust departments, mutual funds, and financial planners. This is the inevitable destiny of the brokerage industry. Those who try to defy that destiny will join the dinosaurs as evolutionary dropouts.

Review the nine services a broker furnishes on page 8. These services define what the investor basically requires in order to transact the business of investing. What will become apparent is that all of these can today be accessed without the use of a commission-based stockbroker. Armed with resources available at a reasonable cost, you the investor are better able than ever before to think and act on your own behalf. The remaining chapters will show you where and how to find and use those resources. The matrix below outlines the different resources, including fee-based professional service providers, that can be used in place of the full-commission broker.

It is often said today that we are in the middle of the Information Revolution created over the last twenty years through innovations in and the convergence of microcomputer and telecommunications technologies. Make no mistake about it, this Information Revolution is as profound a period in human development as the Industrial Revolution was 150 years ago. One hundred years from now, schoolchildren will study this era in their history classes. While the significance of

	Discount Brokers	Newsletters	On-Line Services	Money Manager	Trust Dept.	Financial Planners
Asset Allocation		X		X	X	X
Research	X	X	X	X	X	X
Recommendations		X	X	X	X	X
Price Data	X		X	X	X	X
Buy/Sell	X			X	X	X
Trade Confirms	X			X	X	X
Custody	X				X	
Statements	X			X	X	X
Tax Summary	X			X	X	X

it all will be crystal clear to them, those who are living it here and now often cannot see the relevance in their lives. To investors, the Information Revolution could not be more apparent nor more relevant than it is today.

To illustrate the point, if in 1970 you wanted a quote on a stock you could do one of two things: 1) call your broker; or 2) go into a brokerage office and read the quotes off their ticker tape (yes, they were still in use then) or gape at that electronic quote board with the letters and numbers flying by. If you wanted research on a stock, you could: 1) call your broker, again; or 2) go down to the library and shuffle through the meager data they had. When you decided to make a purchase or sale of a stock, you could: 1) yes, call the broker one more time; or 2) . . . well, there was no 2. Your favorite full-commission broker was the only way to trade. Discount brokers did not yet exist.

Let's fast-forward to today and place you at a desk with a computer terminal connected to the phone line with a modem. To retrieve quotes you simply dial any one of several services and retrieve stock quotes. To access research reports, you call up the same or similar vendors to retrieve and download to your machine data on stocks, bonds, and mutual funds. You can electronically look at research from brokers or other research sources; call up price charts; and access investment newsletters. And, of course, if you need a hard copy of any of these, you quickly print them out on your laser printer. When you decide which stock to buy or sell, you can call the *discount broker* on your computer, enter the order, and receive the trade confirmation, all electronically. If you do not own a computer, that's all right too. You can still access most of the same information over the telephone or through the mail. It will just take a little longer to use it.

It should be evident that in 1970, and for two hundred years preceding that, the stockbroker—the full-commission stockbroker—was an essential part of the investment process. The Information Revolution has rendered the stockbroker less relevant today. All nine of the broker services cited before can now be provided faster and cheaper than through the broker. The options are more plentiful than before. For example, a broker can provide you with *his* firm's research but little in the way of research from competitors. In contrast, some electronic data services and several newsletters offer research from many different sources.

Recall the old saying, "Information is power!" If you know where to look for it, today you the investor can have *information* and *power* that were undreamed of in 1970. The objective of this book is to convey to you the information, and with it the power you need to invest profitably for your future. Let's begin, then, to explore the resources that will give you the information, the power, and the freedom to kiss your stockbroker goodbye.

Chapter 2

DISCOUNT BROKERS AND
THEIR SERVICES

One of the primary goals of this book is to furnish you with information sources that will assist you in making independent investment decisions, that is, decisions that are undistorted by the static transmitted from stock-brokers. There is one aspect of the investment process, however, that you will *never* be able to do on your own: the actual buying and selling of shares in stocks and mutual funds. Performing these functions, as well as the purchase and sale of most bonds, requires the services of an intermediary (a person and/or a company) who is registered with the Securities and Exchange Commission and state regulatory bodies to buy and sell securities on behalf of customers like you. Yes, these intermediaries are called "brokers." Fortunately for investors, a new kind of broker has emerged in the last twenty years, one that bears little resemblance to its mercenary cousins at the so-called full-commission brokerage houses.

Discount brokers, as the name suggests, provide investment brokerage services to clients at fees and commissions that are significantly below those of the full-commission brokers. The extent of the discounts varies somewhat, as do the services they provide. Later in this chapter, many of the larger discount brokers currently in business will be outlined to afford you a convenient reference source. Something to keep in mind about discount brokers is that the services they provide are equivalent to or sometimes exceed those of the full-commission brokers. Once again, let's look at the services that a full-commission broker can provide to its clients, as outlined in Chapter 1:

- Counsels clients on asset allocation
- Provides clients with research on products

- Makes buy/sell recommendations to clients
- Offers price data, current and/or historic
- Buys and sells securities on clients' behalf
- Sends to clients a record (confirmation) of trades
- Offers custody of securities and cash held by clients
- Sends to clients a periodic (quarterly or monthly) statement
- Provides clients with summary data for tax preparation

Discount brokers provide most of these services—all except the first three. Discount brokers rarely counsel clients on their financial situation. Several brokers do offer brochures that treat such financial topics as estate planning, retirement accounts, and budgeting for college education. Most discount brokers do not offer research on stocks or other investment vehicles, although some do make research products available at additional expense to clients. In addition, some discount brokers send an investment newsletter to clients along with their statements. These letters may contain stock recommendations, but otherwise, discount brokers are not in the business of making stock picks. While these may seem like important functions to be lacking in discount brokers, consider this: the commission savings you will realize from trading with the discount broker can amount to hundreds or thousands of dollars each year. With those savings you can purchase a lot of expert advice.

Among the other services that either full-commission brokers or discount brokers now also provide are:

- Mutual funds traded without commissions or fees
- Checking accounts and cash management
- Securities quotations over the phone
- Orders input by phone or computer
- Insurance of client assets against broker insolvency

The lexicon of the securities industry ascribes the term "full-service" to the old-line major brokerage firms with the sales forces collectively numbering in the tens of thousands. For the latter, the only service they are certain to provide, beyond those previously listed, is the dispensing of advice designed to proactively move the investor into and out of securities. Why? In order to generate trades, of course. No trades, no commissions. No commissions, new career! This is why we shall refer to these firms as "full-commission" brokers rather than "full-service" brokers.

Some things will certainly not happen in using a discount broker. No salesperson is going to call you at odd hours of the evening trying to solicit your business. No salesperson will call you at work trying to convince you to sell shares of your favorite stock so you can buy front-end-load mutual funds or shares in a limited partnership. About all you will receive from the discount broker, aside from your account statement, is material apprising you of products or services that are available through them. The decision to use them or not is yours alone to make. No one from the discounter will prod, prompt, coach, or coerce you.

Another goal of this book is to help you identify those information resources that you will be comfortable in using to make investment decisions. When those decisions have been made, you will still require the use of a broker to actually implement the decisions. Make that broker a discount broker. Remember . . .

> ### *Use Only Discount Brokers.*

Twenty years ago there were only a handful of discount brokers in business. Several firms took the early lead in the discount broker sector, with Fidelity Investments and Charles Schwab being the two largest players. They remain the largest discount brokers today, but many other discounters have emerged whose level of service is comparable and whose commissions and fees are priced well below Fidelity's and Schwab's. It is not the intent of this chapter to endorse or critique any particular broker. Armed with information provided here, you can contact any or all of the brokers listed to learn more about them.

From there the process enters the trial-and-error mode that drives so many decisions you make. Cross-reference the information here with your own personal experiences or experiences of friends or family members who may have used one or more of the discount brokers listed. Each year in their July issue *Smart Money* magazine publishes a survey of brokerage firms and rates them by various measures. Beyond this there is little more research that can be done except to take the plunge, open an account, do some trades, and then see if the service meets your needs at the cost you anticipated. If your needs are being met, you have accomplished your goal.

Commission schedules are easy to compare; the numbers speak for themselves. The only caveat is to be aware of any hidden charges that some discount brokers are reputed to charge clients. If after doing some trades you find that there are "special fees or charges," you should be aware of them before trading with that broker any further. If the broker is assessing fees and charges that you feel they did not adequately disclose to you, you may want to change brokers.

CHANGING STOCKBROKERS

The decision to change a broker will be far more taxing than the actual procedure to change a broker. It's one of those *fears* we spoke of in the introduction. In reality, few business dealings could be any easier. The decision of which broker to select may be based on the low commission rates advertised. Perhaps the broker offers a group of mutual funds that can be bought and sold without any transaction charges. Maybe your friend has an account at a certain broker and he is pleased with that service. Or maybe a discount broker has an office two blocks from your workplace, making it seem like a convenient choice. Whatever the criteria, the important thing to remember is that if you become dissatisfied with your new broker, another broker is easily secured with a minimal amount of effort.

In the course of doing your homework on one or more brokers, you should call the toll-free phone number given in the list that follows on pages 16–18. Ask the marketing representative who answers for a new account information package. This will contain material on the broker's services, fees, and commission rates. This material can range from a few pages to a book the length of a short novel. Study the material and make your choice. If the alternatives all sound too similar, write on a piece of paper what you expect to do with your account and the assets it will contain. Call this your Investment Account Manifest. If you have several types of investment accounts, as many people do these days, create a manifest for each. If your investment strategy is to use only mutual funds and not to use individual stocks and bonds, you should be more interested in the brokers' mutual fund services and not in their commission scale. Likewise, if you expect to trade individual stocks, the commission table will be of most value to you. The following is what an Investment Account Manifest might look like for two accounts with different objectives and characteristics:

INVESTMENT ACCOUNT MANIFEST

Account Type	Objective	Securities	Account Features
IRA Rollover	Long-Term Growth	Mutual Funds	No Transaction Fee Funds
Liquid Fund	Short-Term Liquidity/ Long-Term Growth	Tax-Exempt Bonds/ Stocks/Money Market Fund	Check Writing

Included in the material sent to you by the broker will be an account application. These forms can be cumbersome, but do not be discouraged by them. Most of the information requested is self-evident. Like any form it can take awhile to complete, but do not let the inconvenience distract you from your mission. Think of the money you are about to save by making the switch to a discount broker. Somewhere on this form you will be asked if you have assets at another broker that you would like transferred. This is the most convenient part of the broker-changing process. By merely indicating the broker currently holding the assets and your account number with that broker, the new broker will contact them for you, sending them a copy of your signed instructions to transfer the assets. You do not have to initiate the transfer yourself with the old broker; you don't even have to speak to or contact the old broker if you so choose. In other words, you can kiss your stockbroker goodbye without actually saying goodbye.

Common courtesy may dictate that you at least send a brief note to the old broker apprising him or her of the change. Doing so may keep the broker from phoning you. If you want to write but find yourself at a loss for the right words, try the following:

MR. AND MRS. JOSEPH A. INVESTOR
1234 MAIN STREET
SOMEWHERE, USA 00001

Mr. Nick L. Endime
High Commission Brokerage, Inc.
10000 Wall Street
New York, NY 10000

Dear Mr. Endime:
   If you are not already aware, we are moving our brokerage account to Deep Discount Brokers, Inc. We appreciate your past efforts on our behalf.

Sincerely,

The letter need not be any longer or more involved than this. If it makes you feel better to let the broker have it with both barrels about the high commissions and losing transactions, go for it. Such catharsis may be better enjoyed over the phone, however. If the broker should call you trying to salvage your business, maintain your resolve. The easiest response you can make is simply to state that you are moving the account because the commissions at your new discount broker are a fraction of those his firm charges. This is the best single reason to offer and the one that will get him off the phone and out of your hair the fastest. The broker has no control over the commissions his firm charges. Those are established at the home office, with some latitude given to branch managers. As such, he cannot counter by saying that he will lower your commissions to be competitive. If by chance he should offer a new, lower commission schedule to you, he has now exposed himself for what he is. Where was this lower commission schedule before? Was your business not worthy of such preferential commission levels? No matter what discounted schedule they may throw at you, the full-commission broker's schedule will never come close to that of the discount brokers, and with the commission weapon in hand you can quickly and cleanly dispatch the bygone broker.

The only other chant in the broker's litany of excuses to rescue your business is the research that he or she provides. He will tell you that you will be left alone, adrift without their research recommendations. The purpose of this book is to show you the many other research sources available to you that will provide buy-hold-sell opinions unbiased by the often conflicting considerations of a broker's research department, syndicate underwriting department, trading desk, and the never-ending quest for commissioned transactions. You need not get into a debate about this with the broker. Simply explain that you are now using an investment adviser. The broker, being the aggressive salesperson that he is, will inquire who that adviser is. He is asking for one or both of two reasons: 1) he will attempt to discredit the adviser and convince you to remain with High Commission Brokers, Inc.; and/or 2) he will approach the investment adviser on his own and use various tactics to try to do business with that adviser, indirectly retrieving your business and that of others in the process. You can respond to the broker's inquiry with a polite but firm "That's none of your concern." At this point the broker, unless truly desperate for the business, will probably lose interest in talking with you. He will perceive that this is a losing cause as you disarm and repel his salesman's banter. More important, you are now cutting into the valuable time he needs to generate commissions with other clients or to prospect new clients through cold–calling on the phone. Congratulations! You have officially kissed your stockbroker goodbye.

DISCOUNT BROKERS

A listing follows of the more prominent discount brokerage firms currently in operation. Contact each firm in which you may be interested for more information. The listing is intended to be as complete as possible. However, new firms continually enter the business, and it is conceivable you will encounter a broker not listed. The listing below will assist you in comparing the new firm's commissions and services with those of brokers listed here. The asterisk (*) indicates that the firm has on–line or Internet access.

DISCOUNT BROKERS		
Broker	*Address*	*Phone*
AccuTrade*	4211 S. 102nd Street Omaha, NE 68127-1031	800-858-0406
K. Aufhauser and Co.*	112 W. 56th Street New York, NY 10019	800-368-3668
Barry Murphy and Co.	77 Summer Street Boston, MA 02110	800-221-2111
Brown and Co.*	20 Winthrop Square Boston, MA 02110	800-822-2829
E*Trade Securities*	480 California Avenue Palo Alto, CA 94306	800-786-2575
Fidelity Brokerage Svcs.*	161 Devonshire Street Boston, MA 02110	800-544-0237
R. J. Forbes Group	150 Broad Hollow Road Melville, NY 11747	800-488-0090

Broker	Address	Phone
Investex Securities*	50 Broad Street New York, NY 10004	800-822-2050
Kennedy, Cabot and Co.	9470 Wilshire Blvd. Beverly Hills, CA 90212	800-252-0090
Levitt and Levitt*	135 S. LaSalle St., Ste. 1945 Chicago, IL 60603	800-671-8505
Lombard Institutional Brokerage*	595 Market Street San Francisco, CA 94105	800-566-2273
Marsh Block and Co.	50 Broad Street New York, NY 10004	800-366-1500
Midwood Discount Brokerage*	One Battery Park Plaza New York, NY 10004	800-643-9663
National Discount Brokers*	50 Broadway, 18th Floor New York, NY 10004	800-417-7423
Olde Discount Corp.	751 Griswold Street Detroit, MI 48226	800-235-3100
J. B. Oxford and Co.*	9665 Wilshire Blvd. Beverly Hills, CA 90212	800-656-1776
Pacific Brokerage Svcs.*	5757 Wilshire Blvd., Ste. 3 Los Angeles, CA 90036	800-262-2294
PC Financial Network*	One Pershing Plaza Jersey City, NJ 07399	800-825-5723
Perelman-Carley and Assoc.	3000 Farnham Street Omaha, NE 68131	800-444-5880
Prestige Status, Inc.	271-603 Grand Central Parkway Floral Park, NY 11005	800-782-8871
Quick and Reilly*	26 Broadway New York, NY 10275-0592	800-848-8844
Regal Discount Securities	209 W. Jackson Blvd., Ste. 906 Chicago, IL 60606-9684	800-786-9000
Redstone Securities	101 Fairchild Avenue Plainview, NY 11803	800-285-3500
Charles Schwab and Co.*	333 Bush Street San Francisco, CA 94104	800-435-4000
Scottsdale Securities	12855 Flushing Meadow St. Louis, MO 63131	800-888-1980

Broker	Address	Phone
Muriel Siebert and Co.*	2020 Avenue of the Stars Los Angeles, CA 90067-4704	800-535-9652
StockCross	One Washington Mall Boston, MA 02108	800-225-6196
Vanguard Brokerage Services	Vanguard Financial Center Valley Forge, PA 19496-9906	800-992-8327
Washington Discount Brokerage Corp.	100 Wall Street New York, NY 10005	800-843-9838
Waterhouse Securities*	100 Wall Street New York, NY 10005	800-934-4410
Jack White and Co.*	9191 Towne Centre Drive San Diego, CA 92122	800-909-6777

COMMISSIONS

Until now we have spoken only generally about the high costs of trading through full-commission brokers. The time has come to show just what the incremental cost is. On the following pages is a comparison of randomly sampled full-commission brokers and commissions for all of the discount brokers listed above. We have created several hypothetical trades for stocks listed on the New York Stock Exchange or the American Stock Exchange, in order to illustrate the commission costs associated with various-sized transactions.

COMMISSION COMPARISON

	# Shares @ Price Per Share			
	200@$40	500@$40	1,000@$40	2,000@$20
Full-Commission Brokers				
Merrill Lynch	$175.35	$347.55	$592.73	$593.25
A. G. Edwards	$165.00	$367.00	$552.00	$606.00
Smith Barney	$186.00	$387.00	$605.00	$681.00
Paine Webber	$183.36	$387.18	$618.62	$694.32
Average	**$177.43**	**$372.18**	**$592.09**	**$643.64**

COMMISSION COMPARISON

	# Shares @ Price Per Share			
	200@$40	500@$40	1,000@$40	2,000@$20
Discount Brokers				
AccuTrade	$ 48.00	$ 48.00	$ 48.00	$ 60.00
Aufhauser	$ 34.00	$ 34.00	$ 34.00	$ 40.00
Barry Murphy	$ 40.00	$ 62.00	$100.00	$115.00
Brown and Co.	$ 29.00	$ 29.00	$ 29.00	$ 29.00
E*Trade	$ 19.95	$ 19.95	$ 19.95	$ 19.95
Fidelity Brokerage	$102.70	$143.50	$187.50	$187.50
R. J. Forbes	$ 35.00	$ 35.00	$ 35.00	$ 35.00
Investex	$ 30.00	$ 30.00	$ 33.00	$ 40.00
Kennedy, Cabot	$ 33.00	$ 33.00	$ 53.00	$ 63.00
Levitt and Levitt	$ 35.00	$ 35.00	$ 70.00	$ 60.00
Lombard	$ 34.00	$ 34.00	$ 34.00	$ 40.00
Marsh Block	$ 50.00	$ 50.00	$ 50.00	$ 60.00
Midwood	$ 36.50	$ 36.50	$ 36.50	$ 36.50
National Discount	$ 33.00	$ 33.00	$ 33.00	$ 33.00
Olde Discount	$ 60.00	$100.00	$125.00	$155.00
J. B. Oxford	$ 23.00	$ 23.00	$ 23.00	$ 23.00
Pacific Brokerage	$ 25.00	$ 25.00	$ 25.00	$ 35.00
PC Financial	$ 80.00	$110.00	$140.00	$140.00
Perelman–Carley	$ 29.00	$ 29.00	$ 54.00	$ 64.00
Prestige Status	$ 39.95	$ 39.95	$ 39.95	$ 39.95
Quick and Reilly	$ 79.00	$109.00	$145.00	$145.00
Regal Discount	$ 29.00	$ 29.00	$ 29.00	$ 29.00
Redstone Securities	$ 33.00	$ 33.00	$ 33.00	$ 33.00
Charles Schwab	$103.20	$144.00	$188.00	$188.00
Scottsdale	$ 40.00	$ 55.00	$ 80.00	$120.00
Muriel Siebert	$ 75.00	$ 75.00	$ 75.00	$ 75.00
StockCross	$ 42.00	$ 67.50	$110.00	$195.00
Vanguard	$ 58.00	$ 75.00	$ 90.00	$120.00
Washington	$ 28.00	$ 28.00	$ 28.00	$ 28.00
Waterhouse	$ 45.40	$ 98.40	$155.74	$174.29
Jack White	$ 39.00	$ 48.00	$ 63.00	$ 73.00
Average	**$ 44.80**	**$ 55.22**	**$ 69.89**	**$ 79.23**

Source: Telephone survey conducted January 1996.

Take a moment and compare the average discount commission shown above with that of the full-commission average on the previous page. Let's use the first trade shown in the table, an $8,000 transaction, which is not small but not particularly large either. The average savings from using a discount broker amounts to $134.30 for this transaction. Now assume that you are buying and selling just five stocks in a typical year, with each transaction amounting to our hypothetical 200 shares at $40 per share. Never forget, the broker gets you coming *and* going, so this scenario entails ten trades! By using the full-commission broker you are spending an extra $1,343 each year for the "service" afforded by the full-commission broker. Surely you can think of a better use for that money.

An acquaintance of mine who happens to be schooled in marketing told me about an axiom of marketing called "perceived value of pricing." Roughly stated, this axiom postulates that if a service provider prices goods or services at a higher price, then the buyer thinks or perceives he is receiving a better service or product; conversely, if goods or services are priced at a lower level, then it cannot possibly be worth even the lesser amount you are spending. This is the sales ploy full-commission brokers have used since discount brokers evolved. In the end it becomes a value judgment for you to determine whether such money is significant to you or not for the "perceived value of service" you are receiving.

Before leaving the "perceived value" concept, you should understand the economic reality of the brokerage business. Contrast a hypothetical 100-share transaction of a given stock with a 1,000-share transaction of the same security. The latter trade is obviously ten times larger in size than the former. However, the cost to the broker of doing the 1,000-share trade is certainly not ten times the cost of doing the 100-share trade. No additional office space has to be leased for the larger trade. No additional personnel have to be hired. Think about it. All that is involved here is people talking on a telephone and keypunching data into computer terminals. The difference in man-hours for doing each trade amounts to the difference between saying "one hundred" and "one thousand." According to my stopwatch, that difference is *zero* (0). And that, my friends, is the truth about this business. You are charged more, by most brokers, for doing the larger trade when it costs the broker no more to process that trade than a smaller one. Not until you enter the realm of the institutional block trade, somewhere in the land beyond 10,000 shares, does it cost the broker more time to execute a trade, and hence, the economics warrant more revenue to compensate them. More to the point of this discussion, when you see a broker listed here who is charging the same for a 2,000-share trade as he is for a 200-share trade, you now know how it is he can afford to do so. And he can afford to do so without any loss of service to you. So do not rush to judgment and "perceive" that a lower commission means poor service and that a higher commission means superior service.

Even among the discount brokers themselves, the tables prove the difference in commissions can be quite significant between the larger discount firms and the so-called "deep discount" firms. Having personally used both deep discount brokers and the larger discount brokers, I can shed light on the relative attraction of each type. With the large discount broker, you speak with a live person and are able to ask questions about trading activity in a particular security and inquire about your account information. The most attractive feature of these firms is that the trader at the other end of the phone line can often confirm your trade and give you details before you hang up. That is what you are paying for, and for some people this is worthwhile if they want to get the trade out of the way and forget about it so they can move on to other matters. To them spending the extra money for that feature may be money well spent.

In contrast, when dealing with a deep discounter you will probably get a recorded message that instructs you on the procedures for initiating trades or retrieving account information, all using a Touch-Tone telephone or personal computer. One of the many options listed is to speak with a person, but you may be on hold for a while. Once trades are inputted, it may be hours before someone calls you back with a confirmation of a transaction. Then again, I have been called back by deep discounters with a trade confirmation within minutes. The tradeoff of course is the commission savings. Since the difference can amount to virtually hundreds of dollars for each transaction, you have to really be desperate for human conversation and need to talk to someone live in order to forgo the savings.

So where do I trade? Well, I look separately at each of the different accounts that I have and examine their size, makeup, activity, and objectives, just as you have done in your Investment Account Manifest. For accounts where the trades are small and infrequent, I feel better-served using a large discounter to avail myself of various services such as check writing. For those accounts in which trading is active and each transaction is relatively large, I have to go with the deep discounter; the savings are simply too compelling. I recommend you review your Investment Account Manifest again and match the type of account you have against the type of discount broker that will provide the optimal service for the account. Keep in mind, if the broker you choose is not what you expect and you become dissatisfied, you can move the account with ease.

ON-LINE TRADING

Some of the discount brokers listed on pages 16–18 have an asterisk (*), indicating that they offer the ability to deal with the broker on-line through a personal computer. On-line capability could mean dialing up the broker via modem through software provided, often at a small cost, by the brokerage firm. On-line capability could also mean the brokerage firm has its own Web site on the Internet. In either case, on-line functions usually involve one or more of the following:

- Initiating or canceling a transaction
- Getting a report on a completed transaction
- Accessing account information, such as cash balances
- Obtaining market updates and securities quotes
- Pulling up research reports

Some investors may prefer using a brokerage firm with on-line capability. The chief advantage of on-line access is that it allows the client to enter orders twenty-four hours a day. When trading desks are closed, a live person will usually not accept an order and will direct the caller to call the next day during trading hours. On-line trading eliminates this problem. The same could be said for those who simply want account information, such as cash balances or asset holdings in their account.

As a time-saver, on-line trading may not be more advantageous than a live call. Frequent on-line users sometimes complain of busy signals and long waits to log on to the brokerage firm's computer. The live-call phone systems prevent this from occurring by using more elaborate phone lines complete with holding patterns and forwarding of call overloads to other offices. Another drawback to not speaking with a live trader is that you will forgo gathering the information, to be discussed later in this chapter, that will enable you to monitor the quality of the broker's fulfillment of your order. Offsetting these disadvantages is the fact that some brokers using on-line capability will discount their commission schedule to those who trade on-line. Those who like to be on the leading edge may look first to those brokers who are on-line.

EXECUTION: THE HIDDEN COST

One of the most important aspects of an investor's trading program is execution. No, we're not talking about the capital punishment you want to inflict on your old broker for those high commissions he's been charging you. Execution refers to the quality of the broker's buying or selling of shares in your account. It has two components: 1) promptness with which the trade instructions are carried out; and 2) price—as in receiving the highest possible price at the time you sell a stock, and paying the lowest possible price at the time you buy a stock. Poor performance by the broker in either of these areas will cost you money and is tantamount to a commission surcharge.

Promptness is easy to measure. As we mentioned earlier, if a broker rep you are speaking with on the phone can confirm a trade before you hang up, you know you have had prompt execution of the trade. If the rep cannot confirm the trade before hanging up, write down the time as you hang up. If a broker rep can call back within fifteen minutes with a report of the trade, then you can be reasonably assured that the trade was done promptly. A call back thirty minutes later or longer raises the question of whether the trade sat on someone's desk while other orders were completed ahead of it. If a time lag occurs, ask the rep for the time the trade was completed and compare that time with the time you noted when hanging up earlier. If the difference is more than fifteen minutes, it is not prompt execution. You should understand, however, that on any given day a stock may not trade frequently, and it will take more time to complete the trade. We will discuss how you can monitor this a little later.

Turning to the price component of execution, you do not benefit from lower commissions if your discount broker is going to trade your stocks at less than optimal prices. In other words, saving 10 cents per share on one broker's commission schedule may be negated if that broker costs you an additional ⅛ of a point, or 12½ cents per share, on each trade. All brokers, full-commission or discounters, assume you have little or no information and they proceed accordingly. Perhaps a personal anecdote will exemplify the situation. A new client of mine notified the discount broker, a small local firm that had custody of his stocks and through which the client had traded previously, that my firm would thereafter be acting as his investment adviser and would initiate trades on his behalf. The first trade I did was to submit an order to sell 5,000 shares of a certain stock at a price of $21½, no more and no less. I selected that price (referred to as a *limit order*) because the stock had traded most of its volume that day at this particular price, a price that also happened to be at about the midpoint of the day's trading range. Since the broker knew nothing about me professionally, he assumed that my information resources were less than his own. In fact, while awaiting his call back with the report, I was monitoring the price of the stock, trade by trade, on the quotation service at my desk. When I did not hear from him in one hour I phoned to inquire about the status of the order. "We have been unable to fill the order at the price you specified. The stock has been trading at twenty-one and three-eighths or less," he said. I could have unloaded on him over the phone, but instead I calmly and serenely described how the screen in front of me indicated that 47,000 shares of the stock had traded since we last spoke, and that more than half had traded at the $21½ level. I further pointed out that some shares had traded above $21½ and that we may have received an even higher price than requested. There was the proverbial moment of silence at the other end of the line, then he said, "Let me talk to our trader and I'll get right back to you." He called back within five minutes with a report of the 5,000 shares sold at $21½. Needless to say, I relayed this event to the client and I recommended a change of broker, to which he agreed.

You may be puzzled about what happened here and why. Almost all discount brokers have to run your order through a "specialist" for stocks listed on an exchange or a "market maker" who deals in unlisted stocks. Either of these is a person, or more likely a firm, whose function is to perform the actual purchase or sale of the security on the floor of the stock exchange or over the counter. The market maker is, in essence, a wholesaler who sells the stock to your broker at wholesale plus a markup for the market maker's profit. Even with the markup added, however, you are still dollars ahead to be using their services rather than the full-commission broker's. The discounter's markup would have to exceed ½ point or 50 cents per share, depending on transaction size, to make trading through a full-commission broker less expensive. In the story cited above, the broker did not shop around for a better price by showing the trade to another market maker. That particular market maker may have had orders only to buy at $21½, leaving him no profit if he bought my shares at the same price; hence, the order sat there and was not filled. Had the broker's trading desk shopped the trade with other market makers who perhaps had *market orders* or orders to buy stock at $21⅝, then the trade would have been filled more quickly. When the broker realized that the order was being monitored and could not sit there unfilled, he then scurried to execute the order. It is permissible for a discount broker to have his own specialist or market maker, although most do not. It is illegal, however, for a broker to add to the price or shave the price of the stock to you *and* also charge you a commission. He is compensated one way or the other.

TRADING THROUGH A DISCOUNT BROKER

Let's go through a hypothetical trade that you might make. The steps outlined here will help you in dealing with the broker and will ensure good execution in the process. You have decided to purchase 1,000 shares of AJZ Corporation traded on the New York Stock Exchange. When you have the discount broker's rep on the line, proceed as follows:

- Ask the rep for the *indication* on AJZ Corporation. The *indication* is simply the current price bid and the current priced asked for a stock. His response should include the current price *bid* (what potential buyers are willing to pay), current price *asked* (at what price sellers are willing to sell), and the price of the last completed trade. Write down these three prices. Example: bid $12½; ask $12¾; last trade $12⅝.
- Ask for the *price range* and *volume* so far that day and write down those numbers. Example: day's high $13; day's low $12⅜; volume 54,000 shares.
- Tell the rep the number of shares you want to buy or sell and the type of order you are placing. There are two types of trade orders that we will discuss. One type is the *market order* (buy at the lowest price the trader can obtain or sell at the highest price possible). The other type is a *limit order* (buy at the specified price and lower if possible, or sell at the specified price or higher if possible). Example, *market order:* Shares will probably be bought at $12¾, but the order may get filled at any price, even the high for the day. Example, *limit order:* Specify $12¾ limit, and it will probably be filled there although there remains the possibility that you may only pay $12⅝, the midpoint between bid and ask.
- Write down the *time* when you hang up the phone.

When the rep calls back with the report of your trade, they will say, "You bought 1,000 shares at twelve and three-quarters." Ask them for:

- The time the trade was executed
- The trading volume of AJZ Corporation at the moment you are speaking to the rep

Write these down along with the time the rep called with the report. This information is your guide to determining the level of service and trade execution that you are receiving. If the time of trade execution was thirty minutes after you placed your order and another 60,000 shares of stock have traded in that time, your order may have been lost in the heap. In fairness to the broker, they may have had trouble executing your order quickly if AJZ Corporation stock only trades another 5,000 shares in the thirty-minute time frame. Some stocks are more actively traded than others, and if your stock trades lightly on that given day, there is nothing the broker can do about it except place your order and wait for a nibble. Such is the auction marketplace.

You should also know that unlisted (over-the-counter) stocks typically have a wider spread between the bid and asked prices. So if you initiate a *limit order* and the price you specify is not right on the bid or asked prices, this may add time in filling the order. Placing a *limit order* ensures that you will ultimately get the price you think is right. The disadvantage of using a limit order is that 1) it may take longer to get the stock at that price, and 2) the stock's price may move in the wrong direction from your limit price. If the latter occurs, you will receive less than you hoped, pay more than you would like, or you may decide to abandon the order altogether. If you do not have the patience to deal with trades in this manner, then you should simply use *market orders*.

CUSTODIAL SERVICES

One of the important services that any broker, full-commission or discount, provides its clients is *custody* of the client's securities. Of all the services that a broker provides, it is the most generic. Custody is custody; one firm cannot furnish better custody than another. Getting securities into or out of custody is another matter. Depositing securities may take days for some firms and weeks for others. Withdrawing securities from your account can take even longer. Unfortunately there is no way of judging a firm's capability unless you have a reference for the brokerage firm from someone you know who himself has experienced deposits and withdrawals of securities. By the way, cash deposits and withdrawals move much faster through the system than do securities deposits and withdrawals.

Years ago brokers actually had vaults that contained their clients' stocks and bonds, at least for those clients who elected to have the broker hold them. Then again, many investors wanted to have the actual pieces of paper, their stock and bond certificates, in their possession. Today almost all securities held in custody with the broker are actually just electronic accounting entries with the Depository Trust Company (DTC) in New York. There are no pieces of paper anymore, unless one needs to be created because a client wants to receive a certificate. I am amazed to hear some investors, and even some professional financial advisers, say that they prefer to hold the certificates themselves and that it gives them peace of mind. *There are no advantages to you in holding stock and bond certificates yourself, only disadvantages.*

It is very difficult for lost or stolen securities to be negotiated by someone other than the rightful owner. Nevertheless, if your stock or bond certificates are lost, destroyed, or stolen, you are in for a real hassle to get new certificates. And while that replacement is being resolved you can forget about trading the issues. In 1995 the Securities and Exchange Commission (SEC) shortened the period for "normal settlement" from five business days to three business days. One of the reasons cited for making this change was to discourage investors from having possession of certificates. While I do not agree with some of the SEC's edicts, their motive for this one was on the mark. With only three days to settle a trade (five if the trade settlement overlaps a weekend), it is almost impossible to have certificates in your broker's possession in time to settle the trade. Also, if you have income-generating stock and bonds, as most investors do, you will be receiving all those checks, which you then have to take to your bank and quickly deposit to avoid losing reinvestment income. I have met people for whom such a ritual is, according to them, therapeutic; however, it makes no economic sense. It is far more efficient, not to mention wealth-enhancing, to have the broker receive the checks and for them to reinvest that money in interest-bearing checking or money market funds right then and there. In short,

> **Keep your securities in custody with your broker.**

To enhance your peace of mind about leaving the securities with the broker, you should understand that the brokers are covered by insurance. The Securities Investor Protection Corporation (SIPC) is a quasi-government insurance company in which all brokerage firms are enrolled. Check the broker's literature or inquire as to the firm's limits on recovering claims through SIPC, and you may also inquire what supplemental insurance a brokerage firm carries with non-SIPC providers.

SUMMARY

I hope that this chapter has heightened your knowledge of the discount broker alternative. You should have the information you need to begin selecting and trading through a discount broker. Let's review the salient points:

- Kissing your stockbroker goodbye is easy
- Moving your account to a discount broker is even easier
- Use only discount brokers
- Good execution is as important as a low commission rate
- Keep your securities in the custody of your broker

In the chapters that follow you will learn more about information resources available to you that will free you from dependence on the retail stockbroker's advice and will generate more wealth for you over time.

Chapter 3

ASSET ALLOCATION

Someone once said, "Success is a journey, not a destination." Nevertheless, most endeavors of any kind will never succeed if there is no "destination," no goal or objective being pursued. If you are embarking on a vacation trip, before you can decide whether you should fly, drive, or take a train or a boat, you first need to know where you are going. So it is with successful investing. The first step in the investment process is for you to define where you are in life, where you are headed, and how your financial assets will get you there.

Every person is different from the next person, including what their goals and aspirations are. Most people have, probably without realizing it, many diverse goals. These various goals also reside on distinctive parts of the time line. A short-term goal might be saving for the down payment on a house. Intermediate goals, those stretching out over five to ten years, might be an expensive dream vacation or that motor home or sailboat you've always wanted. Long-term goals, as you can guess, would include things like college education for children and your own retirement. In this chapter we're going to discuss how to coordinate the structure and makeup of your investment portfolio to accomplish those goals. This process is commonly referred to as *asset allocation*. Studies have shown that in a diversified portfolio of stocks, bonds, and cash, the allocation, or division, of the portfolio between the three groups is the single most important decision in determining investment results. In other words, being a good stock picker will not maximize results for you if bond or cash investments would have provided higher returns than did stocks during a given time period. That is why I dedicate an entire chapter to helping you understand and implement this critical element of investing.

There are four components in the asset allocation process:

- Establishing investment objectives
- Defining your tolerance for risk
- Determining required rate of return
- Examining other constraints

Let's examine each component in detail and suggest a methodology for putting them all together. While there are no definitive answers here, this process will enable you to approach asset allocation in a more disciplined manner.

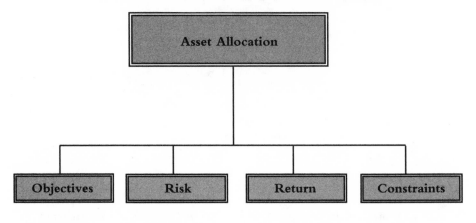

ESTABLISHING INVESTMENT OBJECTIVES

Setting your investment objectives is the first step in establishing an investment plan. As a money manager, when someone comes to me and says they have assets to invest and asks what they should do, my first response is the question "What is the objective of the portfolio?" If the same client approached the typical stockbroker, the first response would probably be something along the lines of "I have the perfect investment for you. All my clients are in it." Thus, one of the first and most important questions that should be asked of you or any investor is never asked: "What do you want to use the money for?" As we said earlier, everyone is different. You need to clarify the objectives that you want to accomplish with your portfolio.

There are several different approaches that can be taken to establish investment objectives. Here we'll use what could be called the *life stage* approach.[3] It identifies what stage of life you are in, what stage or stages of life you are preparing to enter, and what investment strategy will fulfill your needs when you are there. The life

[3]Based on material from John L. Maginn and Donald L. Tuttle, *Managing Investment Portfolios*, 2nd ed., Warren, Gorham and Lamont, 1990.

stage approach obviously has some correlation to one's chronological age. How-ever, it goes beyond chronological age. The life stage approach has the advantage of focusing on a set of probable circumstances rather than assuming that everyone of a certain age is going to be in the same circumstances and will have the same objectives. For example, many people in their late fifties will be concerned about preparing for retirement. Other people in their fifties who delayed having children may be still preparing for college education *and* planning for retirement as well. The importance of identifying and understanding the different stages is that each has distinct implications for the risk and return that the investor will be willing to incur. For the purposes of this analysis, there are four life stages to be examined:

- Accumulation stage
- Consolidation stage
- Spending stage
- Gifting stage

As its name implies, the *accumulation stage* is that period in which people are beginning to build their wealth. In the beginning of this stage the assets being accumulated are usually nonfinancial: house, home furnishings, and cars. The fi-nancial assets are often limited to insurance policies, cash savings in bank or money market accounts, individual retirement accounts (IRAs), and perhaps an employer-sponsored retirement program. If the latter is employee directed, that is, the em-ployee makes the asset allocation decision, the assets should be heavily weighted toward stocks. Since these funds are targeted for living expenses after retirement, the time horizon is far enough away to withstand the ups and downs of the stock market cycle. The same is true for IRAs and any other discretionary savings in which liquidity is not a requirement. If college educations are in the family game plan, these funds should also be earmarked for stocks, again because of the distant time horizon.

The *consolidation stage* is that period in one's career when current income growth exceeds the growth of living expenses. The result is an expanding rate of wealth accumulation in financial assets. A portfolio of stocks and bonds is established, and a program of periodic additions to that portfolio is developed. Retirement plan assets continue to grow as well. In this period, retirement is still far enough away that the asset allocation will continue to emphasize stocks over bonds. One ex-ception may be those funds earmarked for children's college expenses. Those monies are segregated and invested with a higher bond concentration, as the time of college entry approaches within a few years.

The *spending stage* is characterized by some degree of financial independence. This stage extends into the retirement years. Its hallmark is that living expenses are covered by financial assets and the cash flow they generate, rather than by earned income. This period sees a marked drop in the risk profile of the investor's stock and bond portfolio, as more emphasis is placed on the preservation of the wealth that has been accumulated. Asset allocation in the portfolio shifts primarily to bonds. Stock investments are reduced, and greater use of dividend-paying stocks prevails. Some investors feel justified in eliminating stocks from their portfolio altogether, an erroneous strategy I address later in this chapter.

In the final stage, the *gifting stage*, investors perceive that they have accumulated more assets than they can consume in the remainder of their lifetime. The strategy thus shifts from accumulating *or* spending, and proceeds to answer the question, "How, when, and to whom do I give these assets?" These people embark on programs to gift assets to people or institutions, or they establish legal vehicles, such as trusts and partnerships, to endow people or institutions both during and after the giftor's lifetime.

After reading the descriptions of these life stages, you can probably identify which stage you are in now. It is quite possible to be in more than one stage at any given time. In the sections that follow, we'll discuss in more detail the relationship between *risk* and *return*. You'll also see graphically where the life stages often rest on the risk–return scale.

DEFINING YOUR RISK TOLERANCE

As you consider risk and what, as an investor, your tolerance for it is, keep in mind what we're talking about. *Risk* is volatility in the price of and/or the rate of return on your investment. It is *not* the notion of investing your money and losing all or most of it. Many people confuse investment risk with gambling. These are two totally different concepts. Going to the racetrack and betting $10 on the favored horse to win in the fifth race is not the same as calling your discount broker and buying one share of stock priced at $10. In the first event, you're either going to receive $20 back (or whatever the odds payoff amounts to) or you will not get anything back. It's all or nothing. With the stock purchase, you can retrieve part or all of your investment, when you want it, even when the value of the stock has declined. More important, there is a good possibility that your investment will, over time, rise in value, providing you with a positive rate of return. Thus, in the investment sense, risk is the statistical likelihood of the $10 stock rising to $20 or falling to $5. In other words, risk is volatility of the asset's return.

Academic studies have come up with elaborate mathematical models that collate the risk and the return for groups of investment instruments (stocks, corporate bonds, Treasury bonds, Treasury bills, among others) as well as individual securities. In other words, they have qualified as best they can what most people know by intuition and experience: The riskier the investment you are making, a) the more that investment may rise in value, or b) the more your investment may fall in value. The academic research has also produced various products, including computer software, that allow the user to plug in certain variables. Among those are the asset groups under consideration (we'll confine ourselves here to stocks, bonds, and cash) and their historic *rate of return* and *standard deviation*, the latter being a mathematical approximation of risk or volatility. Armed with these numbers, one can move up and down the risk scale to see what combination of stocks, bonds, and cash will, within a certain probability, yield different rates of return. This process is the most "scientific" approach to asset allocation. It has not been proven, however, that the approach affords any better results over the long run than the less scientific approaches we'll soon examine. Keep in mind that this research and the resulting products were originally geared toward institutional investors, such as large pension plans. If the scientific approach did nothing else, it gave institutional investors and their money managers the satisfaction of knowing that they had approached the asset allocation exercise with statistical facts and sound reasoning. The proliferation of asset allocation software products and the decline in their cost has inspired some trust departments, money managers, and financial planners to use these tools with individual investors.

The usefulness of the software is that it numerically, and often graphically, shows the investor the tradeoff between risk and return. It also creates a set of reasonable expectations for the investor in formulating an investment strategy and asset allocation plan. More than once I have been confronted by a client who wanted, let's say, a 12 percent compounded rate of return but did not want to invest in common stocks, only bonds. Sorry, it's not going to work. Yes, there will be an occasional year or two when that return can be achieved by investing only in bonds, but over the long run, bond returns are well under 10 percent per year.

Studies of asset returns and volatility, measured over a number of decades by Ibbotson Associates, an economics research and consulting firm, show that stocks have the highest return and the highest standard deviation. These relationships are depicted in figures 3.1 and 3.2, below. To expand on *standard deviation*, it simply indicates that, although the average return of stocks has been about 10 percent per year, the standard deviation of 20 percent will move that return (within a certain probability) to a range of from −10 percent to +30 percent per year. In contrast, bonds return about 2 percent less per year, and the standard deviation is much less than that of stocks; hence, from year to year, returns on bonds will be more consistent and will occur in a narrower range than will stock returns. Finally, cash returns are lower than either stock or bond returns, and as you would guess, they also have a lower standard deviation. But don't be deceived into thinking there is no volatility in cash, just because your favorite money market fund maintains its fixed dollar value on principal. As long as the yield on the money market fund fluctuates, as it does, that *is* volatility.

An investor needs to define his objectives and assess his own comfort zone with various levels of risk. Those whose objectives are long-term in scope should lean toward the higher return and higher volatility that stocks afford. The investor can confidently do this because he is not frightened by the gyrations of stocks in any given year. He knows that if the stock market declines one year, it will regain that loss plus make more profits in the years that follow. In contrast, the risk-averse investor, or one whose objectives are short-term, is more likely to want to use more bonds and possibly cash in the portfolio, to ensure that he is not drawing upon the assets during a down portion of the stock market cycle.

VOLATILITY OF STOCK AND BOND RETURNS

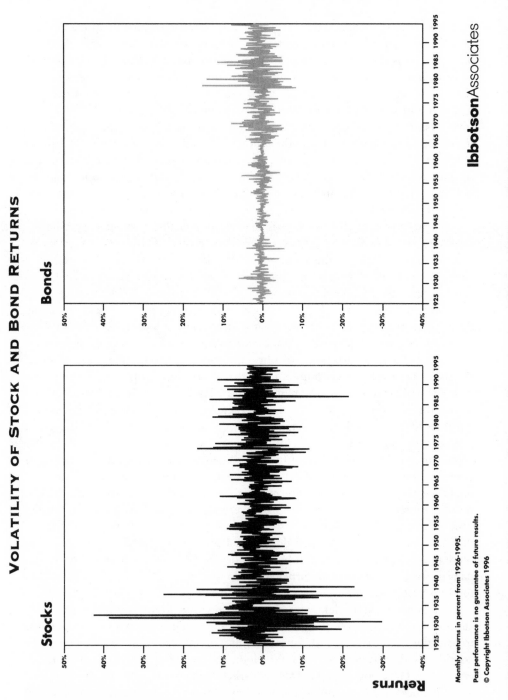

Figure 3-1

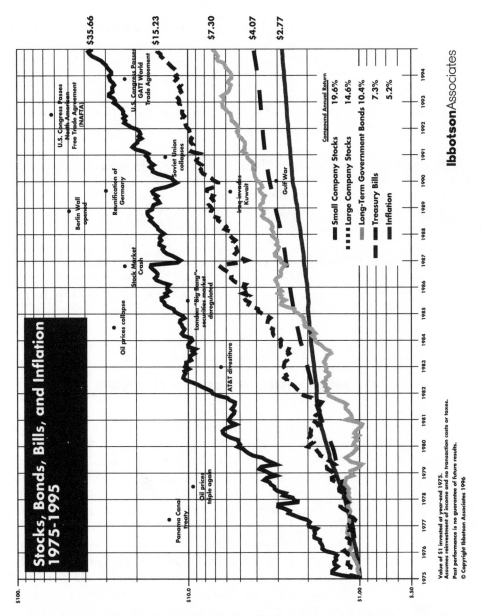

Source: © Stocks, Bonds, and Inflation 1996 Yearbook™, *Ibbotson Associates, Chicago (annually updates work by Roger G. Ibbotson and Rex. A.Sinquefield). Used with permission. All rights reserved.*

Figure 3-2

Investors who fit a short-term, minimal-risk strategy to those funds with a long-term horizon are doing themselves, and their dependents, very grave financial harm. The most explicit example of this is when someone leaves retirement funds in money market accounts or other low-volatility, low-rate-of-return investments. Many people do this, rationalizing to themselves that they know the money will be there when they need it, and they will not "lose it all in the stock market." If this sounds like you, reconsider the strategy *immediately*. Unless you now have a high six-figure portfolio, or larger, you will not have sufficient assets when you retire to maintain a comfortable lifestyle.

Before leaving the discussion of risk, we must point out that there are several different kinds of risk. Among these are:

- *Market risk:* the rise and fall of securities prices in general
- *Interest rate risk:* the rise and fall of interest rates
- *Inflation risk:* the "real" value of assets
- *Currency risk:* fluctuations in the dollar rate of exchange
- *Credit risk:* probability of default by debt issuer
- *Company-specific/industry-specific risk:* risk of unforeseen developments that negatively affect a company and/or the industry it's in.

These risks are self-evident, and as you research any investment in stocks or bonds, you should anticipate these risks and factor them into your analysis.

DETERMINING RATE OF RETURN

Rate of return (ROR) is the expression commonly used to describe, in percentage terms, what the reward is for buying and holding an investment. Many investors confuse *yield* with *rate of return*. Rate of return comprises two parts: 1) appreciation or depreciation of the assets' value; and 2) the income or yield derived from the assets. It would be an error to say that General Motors stock has a return of 5 percent simply because it pays a $2.50 dividend and the market price is $50. To the 5 percent yield must be added the percentage rise or fall in stock price from one point in time to the next, in order to have a true and accurate expression of rate of return. Thus, if GM stock rose from $50 to $55, and it paid the $2.50 dividend during the same interval, its rate of return would be the $5 plus $2.50 ($7.50), divided by the original $50 investment, for a rate of return amounting to 15 percent. Similarly, saying that you bought General Motors stock and made a profit of $7.50 per share is meaningless in and of itself. It is more useful for the investor to express that profit in relation to the initial investment of $50 per share.

Next, the time frame of your investment has to be factored into the equation. First, the overall time period in which the return is being measured must be ascertained. Second, the return for that period of time must then be converted into an *annualized* return. Annualizing returns enables you to make direct comparisons between two or more investment alternatives, and have the comparisons be valid. Returning to our General Motors example, if the 15 percent return is achieved in six months, then the annualized return is approximately 32.3 percent. The relevance of all this is that to measure your success in investing, no matter what size portfolio you're dealing with, *rate of return* is the number you will need to know. Furthermore, you must annualize that return in order to make it usable for comparison against other investments. Only by expressing the investment's profitability in terms of rate of return will you know how profitable the investment really was, and how it compared to the profitability of alternative investments you did make or otherwise might have made. This is a valid point, as well, for investments other than stocks, bonds, and cash. We'll have more detailed rate-of-return calculations in Chapter 8, Investment Performance.

Determining a suitable rate of return for a given investment objective is always tricky. First, as we've just discussed, *rate of return* is joined at the hip with *risk*. So the conundrum in answering the ROR question is that it begs the question "How much risk do I want to take?" Often it comes down to how much risk one *needs* to take in order to achieve an objective. Let's use the example of parents who have set aside $50,000 for their daughter's college education. Since the child is "gifted," she is likely to be admitted to one of the finer, and therefore more costly, universities. Furthermore, she will probably want to go to graduate school afterward. So the parents have concluded that they'll require $100,000 in the college fund ten years hence, or a 7.2 percent annual rate of return.

Accomplishing a 7.2 percent return can be accomplished handily by using a diversified stock portfolio or a portfolio of mutual funds that invest in stocks. That is premised on the historical fact that stocks' annual returns approximate 10 percent, which leaves a comfortable margin of error even if stocks underperform this expected level. Any excess return could be used for graduate school or perhaps a dream vacation for the parents when the kid is finally out of the house and supporting herself. Suppose, however, that the parents are skittish about the stock market and want nothing to do with it, at least for the time being. One of their alternative investments might be a zero-coupon Treasury note that matures in ten years; coincidentally, the rate of return on that bond just happens to be 7.2 percent per year. What this means is that they can invest $50,000 in a zero-coupon Treasury note that, when it matures, will pay them $100,000. Imagine being able to accomplish your financial goal with great ease and essentially no risk. Life is good!

As you may have discerned, there is no right or wrong answer to this situation or others like it. There can, however, be reasonable and unreasonable answers. If the scenario above was altered so that the required rate of return was 20 percent per year, then there is not a lot of room to maneuver. The reasonable response would be to 1) invest the entire portfolio in stocks or stock mutual funds, 2) start filling out those college financial assistance forms now, and 3) step up the swimming lessons in hopes of getting a water polo scholarship.

OTHER CONSTRAINTS

The three elements of asset allocation that we have examined so far are the most complex, again because there are no right or wrong responses. There is simply the reasonable response, the unreasonable response, and whatever feels best for you in the situation. The fourth element of asset allocation, *examining other constraints*, is a little easier to deal with because the constraint either enters into your situation or it doesn't. If it does, dealing with the constraint is usually a straightforward process. There could be many constraints you might be able to identify, but we'll look at the four most common constraints people encounter: time, liquidity, taxes, and legal.

Time constraints encompass circumstances like the college education scenario I just described. We've all had occasions when we knew that at or near a specific point in the future, we would need a certain amount of money for a dedicated purpose. The parents described before knew when their child would enroll in college. You can usually plan the time when you will want to buy a house and will need the money for a down payment and furnishings. People can reasonably anticipate when they will retire from their careers. All these create a time constraint on the need for your money, and hence, the time factor partially dictates how the money should be invested. For example, if you knew you would need funds within twelve months for some purpose, it would be unwise to invest that entire amount in stocks or to buy a bond maturing in ten years. There is a mismatch between the time constraint and the risk that you would be incurring. The more appropriate choice would be to weight the investment heavily toward a short-term cash instrument maturing in twelve months.

Liquidity constraints refer to the ability to convert an investment back into cash if the need arises suddenly. To use a twelve-month time horizon again, if there is even a remote possibility that you will need access to the funds before the twelve months are up, you would not want to invest in a twelve-month certificate of deposit from your local bank. With that instrument, you cannot cash out of the investment before maturity, because you will pay a penalty if you do. Investing in a twelve-month Treasury bill might be more appropriate. Examples of illiquid investments are real estate and limited partnership units.

Tax constraints vary from one individual to the next. Those people in the higher personal income tax brackets may benefit from the use of tax-exempt municipal bonds rather than taxable bonds. Changes in asset allocation may be accelerated or deferred if there are taxable capital gains that may result. Alternative minimum tax (AMT) considerations may influence the decision making, as well as estate tax planning through establishment of trusts or family partnerships.

The mention of trust and partnerships brings us to the last category, *legal constraints*. The language contained in the trust document underlying any type of trust (living trust, testamentary trust, charitable remainder trust, or others) often outlines

what investment vehicles may be used, what the income requirements of bene-
ficiaries are, when the trust is to terminate and distribute its assets, and any other
stipulation that the mind of man can conceive. The same is true for partnerships,
family or otherwise. Such legal requirements compel the people looking after the
assets to consider these things as they make investment decisions.

CREATING AN ASSET ALLOCATION PLAN

Let's try to bring together the elements we've reviewed in the previous sections.
One thing I do not address here is how to put together a financial plan or a
program of saving. In the Resource Guide for this chapter will be listed books
that may give you guidance on these and other important money matters. I also
recommend that you meet with a qualified *fee-only* financial planner (see Chapter
7) and an attorney specializing in estate planning. The financial planner can help
you map out your strategy and show you what investment vehicles are most
beneficial to you, and the attorney can advise you if a trust will be beneficial from
legal and tax standpoints.

A graphic representation of risk and return may be helpful in determining what
asset allocation you should be using. Figure 3-3 shows what the relationship between risk and return looks like:

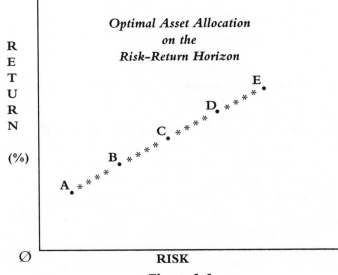

Figure 3-3

The upward-sloping line shows that as risk increases, so does the potential or
expected rate of return. Each point on the line shows some combination of asset

groups (stocks, bonds, cash) that will, based on historic results, generate the best rate of return at a given level of accepted risk. In theory there are other asset allocation combinations than those on the line, but they result in a rate of return that is too low, given the level of risk involved. Computer programs for asset allocation will mathematically calculate these optimal combinations. To illustrate the investment principles involved here, we'll look at some arbitrarily chosen asset allocations that in effect do reside somewhere on or near this line.

Point A is the "riskless" portfolio composed solely of cash instruments. Remember that our working definition of risk is "volatility." Hence, even though there may be little or no default risk with these investments, their returns can fluctuate and present interest-rate risk. That is why Point A is not positioned at zero on the left axis. As you might guess, Point E is the most volatile portfolio, made up of 100 percent stocks. It enjoys the highest expected return but also exhibits the greatest potential volatility. In between these two points lie many other asset allocation permutations. Points B, C, and D also lie on this line, and Table 3-1 below outlines these hypothetical asset allocations. As Figure 3-3 indicates, many other portfolios of assets exist as well. We'll omit any attempt at measuring the expected returns, or the volatility (standard deviation) of those returns, for each of the points shown. That exercise is better left to textbooks and asset allocation software.

TABLE 3-1
HYPOTHETICAL ASSET ALLOCATIONS

Point on Figure 3-1	Stocks	Bonds	Cash	Total
Point A	0%	0%	100%	100%
Point B	20%	30%	50%	100%
Point C	40%	40%	20%	100%
Point D	65%	30%	5%	100%
Point E	100%	0%	0%	100%

Returning briefly to Figure 3-3, the bottom axis, Risk, could be replaced by Time Horizon. If it were, you would then have a pretty good tool for determining where you are in your life stage analysis. Figure 3-4 does this and shows the asset allocations that might be best during each life stage.

Looking at Figure 3-4, think of the bottom axis as the time horizon in reverse or as the years of life remaining for the investor. The younger you are (the closer to the right side of the graph), the more heavily invested in stocks you should be. As the years pass and you enter the succeeding life stages, you will likely diversify away from stocks and more toward the less volatile bonds and cash. While this approach to asset allocation has its advantages, it often leaves open the question of how people decide with any conviction which life stage they are in, or simply where on the risk-return line they belong. Some discount brokerage firms have created questionnaires for clients to answer that question.

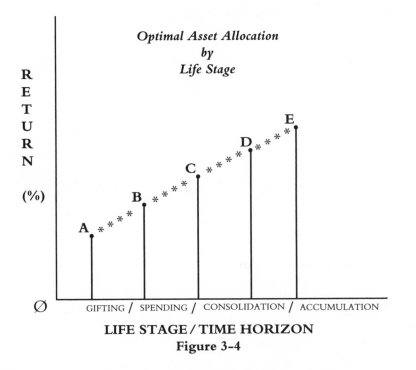

LIFE STAGE / TIME HORIZON
Figure 3-4

Below is Fidelity Investments' "Portfolio Allocation Worksheet," taken from their publication *Fidelity PortfolioMatch*.[SM] The questionnaire instructions suggest that you complete a different one for each particular goal you might have. In other words, complete one if you are saving for a house purchase, and complete another if you are also planning for your retirement.

For the sake of uniformity, we used Fidelity's five allocation suggestions as the basis for points A–E in Figures 3-3 and 3-4. These are not etched in stone, of course, but they do provide a well-reasoned point of departure for arriving at your optimal asset allocation. Check with the discount broker you choose to work with to see if they have similar questionnaires or advisory personnel who can assist you in the decision-making process.

Portfolio Allocation Worksheet

The questions below are designed to help you determine an asset allocation strategy appropriate for a particular goal. This worksheet takes into account your:

■ Time horizon

■ Risk tolerance

■ Financial condition

If you have a separate investment plan for each goal – such as retirement, a new home, or your children's education – complete this worksheet for each goal.

Point values vary according to the weight each factor should have in your investment decision. When you add up your total points, the result will suggest the mix of investments most suited for your goal. Use this suggested portfolio as a reference point in your personal decision to invest more conservatively or aggressively.

Choose the best answer for each question, and enter the corresponding point value in the spaces provided.

---

1   **The investable assets you have set aside or will be setting aside for your goal represent approximately what percentage of your total investment portfolio?**

(Your investment portfolio includes all your investments, excluding your primary residence. This percentage can help determine whether you should be conservative or aggressive right now.)

Less than 25% 8
Between 25% and 50%...7
Between 51% and 75%...3
More than 75% 2

POINTS ☐

Example: A family's entire investment portfolio includes $200,000 saved for retirement and a separate college savings plan of $50,000. In determining an asset allocation plan for their investments targeted for college, they calculate that their college savings plan represents 20% of their total portfolio ($50,000 divided by $250,000).

---

2   **Which one of the following describes your expected earnings over the next five years?**

Assume inflation will average 4% a year. If you expect your earnings to rise sharply, for example, you may want to be more aggressive with your money right now.

I expect my earnings increases will far outpace inflation 5
(due to promotions, new job, etc.)

I expect my earnings increases to stay ahead of inflation 3
I expect my earnings to keep pace with inflation 2
I expect my earnings to decrease 1
(retirement, part-time work, economically depressed industry, etc.)

POINTS ☐

3 Approximately what portion of your monthly take home income goes toward paying off debt (auto loans, credit cards, etc.) other than a home mortgage?

If the percentage is high, you may need more cash available for emergencies.

Less than 10% 8
Between 10% and 25%...6
Between 26% and 50%...3
More than 50% 1

POINTS

4 How many dependents do you have (including children or parents)?

The greater your family obligations, the more conservative you may need to be in investing.

None 4
One...3
Two to Three...2
More than Three 1

POINTS

5 Do you have emergency savings equal to at least three to six months' after-tax income?

Without such a cushion, you risk being forced to draw on long-term investments for short-term, unforeseen needs. If you don't have an emergency fund, a conservative investing approach might be more appropriate.

No 2
Yes, but less than six months of after-tax income 6
Yes, I have an adequate emergency fund....................................8

POINTS

6 Do you have a separate investment plan for other major expenses you expect to incur (college tuition, down payment on a home, renovations, etc.)?

Yes, I have a separate investment plan for these expenses 8
I do not expect to have any such expenses....................................6
I intend to withdraw a portion of this money for these expenses (note: please answer question 12 accordingly) 5
I have no separate investment plan for these expenses at this time 2

POINTS

Portfolio Allocation Worksheet

7 **Have you ever invested, or would you invest again, in individual bonds or bond mutual funds?**

No, and I would be uncomfortable with the risk if I did 1

No, but I would be comfortable with the risk if I did 9

Yes, but I was uncomfortable with the risk 2

Yes, and I felt comfortable with the risk 10

POINTS

8 **Have you ever invested, or would you invest again, in individual stocks or stock mutual funds?**

No, and I would be uncomfortable with the risk if I did 1

No, but I would be comfortable with the risk if I did 15

Yes, but I was uncomfortable with the risk 3

Yes, and I felt comfortable with the risk 16

POINTS

9 **Which one of the following statements describes your feelings toward choosing an investment?**

(Investing is a matter of balancing your risk tolerance with the desire to achieve specific goals.)

I would only select investments that have a low degree of risk associated with them (i.e., it is unlikely I will lose money) 2

I prefer a mix of investments with emphasis on those with a lower degree of risk, and a small portion in others that have a higher degree of risk but also higher return potential..................5

I prefer a balanced mix of investments – some that have a low degree of risk, others that have higher risk but also higher return potential 9

I prefer an aggressive mix of investments – emphasizing those that have a higher degree of risk and thus higher return potential, along with some lower-risk investments 12

I would only select investments that have a higher degree of risk and thus greater potential for high returns 16

POINTS

10 **If you could increase your chances of improving your returns by taking more risk, would you:**

Be willing to take a lot more risk with all your money 16

Be willing to take a lot more risk with some of your money..........12

Be willing to take a little more risk with all your money 10

Be willing to take a little more risk with some of your money 5

Be unlikely to take much more risk..2

POINTS

11 **In approximately how many years do you expect to need the money you're investing?**

Your investment time frame is very important in determining your strategy. The longer you have until you need money for a goal, the more aggressive you can afford to be.

Within 2 to 3 years 5

4 to 6 years 25

7 to 10 years 40

11 to 15 years 45

More than 15 years 50

POINTS ☐

12 **Do you expect to withdraw more than one-third of this money within 10 years?**

Note your answer to Question 6, regarding upcoming major expenses.

No, I don't 50

Yes, probably within 3 years 5

Yes, probably in 4 to 6 years.....................................30

Yes, probably in 7 to 10 years...................................50

POINTS ☐

POINTS ☐

SCORE: Add up total points for all 12 questions.

Remember, the asset allocation suggested by the worksheet point total is meant to offer an example of the type of allocation you might want to consider, based on the average person with a similar score. The final decision on an asset allocation model is yours, based on your individual situation, needs, goals, and risk tolerance, which may include factors or circumstances beyond the scope of the Worksheet. Furthermore, the example is based on your current assessment of these factors. If any of these factors should change, please review your investment strategy. At a minimum, you should review your allocation on an annual basis.

Now turn to the next page to match your total score with the portfolio that is appropriate for you.

Model Portfolios

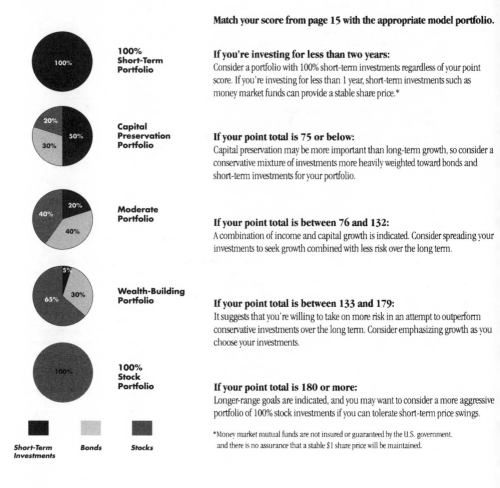

100% Short-Term Portfolio

Capital Preservation Portfolio

Moderate Portfolio

Wealth-Building Portfolio

100% Stock Portfolio

Short-Term Investments

Bonds

Stocks

Match your score from page 15 with the appropriate model portfolio.

If you're investing for less than two years:
Consider a portfolio with 100% short-term investments regardless of your point score. If you're investing for less than 1 year, short-term investments such as money market funds can provide a stable share price.*

If your point total is 75 or below:
Capital preservation may be more important than long-term growth, so consider a conservative mixture of investments more heavily weighted toward bonds and short-term investments for your portfolio.

If your point total is between 76 and 132:
A combination of income and capital growth is indicated. Consider spreading your investments to seek growth combined with less risk over the long term.

If your point total is between 133 and 179:
It suggests that you're willing to take on more risk in an attempt to outperform conservative investments over the long term. Consider emphasizing growth as you choose your investments.

If your point total is 180 or more:
Longer-range goals are indicated, and you may want to consider a more aggressive portfolio of 100% stock investments if you can tolerate short-term price swings.

*Money market mutual funds are not insured or guaranteed by the U.S. government. and there is no assurance that a stable $1 share price will be maintained.

Short-term investments are defined as investments with a maturity date of three years or less.

Provided by Fidelity Investments, Fidelity Distributors Corporation, Boston, MA 02109

KEEP IT SIMPLE

For those of you who cannot be bothered with questionnaires, scrutinizing graphs, or exploring asset allocation software, don't throw up your hands and put all of your money into a money market fund. Here are some simple guidelines you can follow in asset allocation:

■ For retirement planning, a conservative guideline is to take your age and subtract it from 100. The resulting number is the percent of your portfolio that should be invested in stocks. This is a favorite among financial planners because it is dynamic yet simple. It also ensures that after you have retired, presumably between the ages of sixty-five and seventy, you still have at least 20 to 30 percent of your portfolio in stocks as a hedge against future inflation diminishing your portfolio's purchasing power.

■ An even simpler strategy, and one decidedly more aggressive, is to invest 100 percent of your portfolio in stocks at all times, at least until the following time horizon emerges: Within four or five years of the stated goal, reduce the stock exposure by 20 percent each year. If the objective of the portfolio is "closed-ended," like home buying or college (all or most of the money is needed at that time), have the portfolio down to zero percent in stocks by the beginning of the last year before the terminal date is to arrive. If the portfolio objective is "open-ended" as in retirement (you do not need all the money at that time), bring the equity down to 20 percent by the year of retirement; then leave it there permanently, circumstances permitting.

■ Those of you who are totally uncomfortable with being invested 100 percent in stocks can try this allocation strategy, which is the ultimate in simplicity. Begin each year with the portfolio evenly divided, 50 percent in stocks and 50 percent in bonds/cash. At the end of the year, *rebalance* the portfolio back to the 50-50 ratio by selling and buying the appropriate combination of stocks, bonds, or cash. For those who feel compelled to tinker with things and perhaps dabble with *market timing*, use a 60-40 split. Put 60 percent in stocks when you are confident the stock market will rise and 40 percent in stocks if you think stocks will decline.

If you think such simple strategies are too elementary to be useful or successful, think again. A study reported in the *Wall Street Journal* showed that a fixed allocation of stocks, bonds, and cash outperformed the variable allocations accorded by an average of full-commission brokerage house strategists.[4] The fixed allocation used was: stocks 55 percent; bonds 35 percent; cash 10 percent. What this illustrates

[4]John R. Dorfman, "Allocation Robot Knows Mechanics of Investing," *Wall Street Journal*, November 3, 1995.

is that although asset allocation may be the most important part of the investment process, it doesn't need to be the most complicated part of the investment process to work successfully for you. Keep that fact in mind as we pursue the "less important" decisions described in succeeding chapters.

IN CONCLUSION

No matter what asset allocation strategy you decide to use, it will require of the investor two characteristics: *patience* and *fortitude*. You must have the *patience* to allow your portfolio to build over time without your being distracted by the hype of investment sales pitches. Since you've dispensed with the full-commission broker, those sales pitches should go away. Most important, you have to have the *fortitude* to hold to your strategy when the market plunges and things get scary. You will need even more fortitude to use those declines in the market, and they are relatively rare, as opportunities to add more money to stocks when most people are selling. If you can develop those characteristics of patience and fortitude, you will have an asset allocation program that will maximize your financial wealth over the years.

This chapter has been dedicated to the "do-it-yourself" aspects of arriving at an asset allocation plan for your portfolio(s). Because asset allocation is such an important part of your investment game plan, you should not hesitate to use the services of a money manager or financial planner to help you through the uncertainties of the process. Many will work with you, for a modest fee, to establish financial goals and an asset allocation strategy, even if you do not want to hire them to manage your assets. Chapter 7, Working with Fee-Only Professionals will offer some guidance in working with these advisers. The Resource Guide for this chapter will list various books and other tools you may find useful in formulating and implementing your financial goals.

RESOURCE GUIDE:
ASSET ALLOCATION

Newsletters

Most investment newsletters do not deal with asset allocation. Those that treat the subject are focused on other areas of investments, such as stocks or mutual funds. Below is a list of newsletters that give at least a passing glance at asset allocation. Refer to the page indicated in parentheses for more information on each newsletter

The Addison Report	(74)	Charles Cummings K.I.$.$.	(79)
Baxter	(76)	The Chartist	(79)
Cabot Market Letter	(78)	The Clean Yield	(80)

The Contrary Investor	(81)	Middle/Fixed Income Letter	(96)
Dow Theory Forecasts	(82)	Monday Morning Market Memo	(96)
Executive Wealth Advisory	(84)	Money Reporter	(97)
Fidelity Monitor	(183)	MPT Review	(97)
Finance Over 50	(84)	Mutual Fund Investing	(186)
Growth Stock Outlook	(87)	The Mutual Fund Letter	(186)
Industry Forecast	(89)	Mutual Fund Strategist	(186)
It's Your Money/The Jorgenson Report	(91)	Personal Finance	(100)
		The Peter Dag Investment Letter	(100)
Jacobs Report on Asset Protection Strategies	(92)	Rick Dupuis "Inside Money"	(103)
		Sentinel Investment Letter	(104)
Ken Gerbino's Smart Investing	(92)	Straight Talk on Your Money	(106)
Market Cycle Investing	(94)	The Wall Street Digest	(109)

Magazines and Periodicals

There are many magazines published today that deal with investing and general topics related to money. The following magazines provide a good balance between investment reporting and coverage of financial matters like budgeting, taxes, and financial planning, all of which are useful in the asset allocation process.

KIPLINGER'S PERSONAL FINANCE
Deals with savings, investments, managing your money, budgeting, and general interest items.
$19.95/yr.
Kiplinger Washington Editors Inc.
1729 H Street
Washington, DC 20006
800-544-0155

MONEY MAGAZINE
Personal finance topics: savings, spending, investments, mortgages, buyers' guides.
$35.95/yr.

Money Magazine
P.O. Box 60001
Tampa, FL 33660-0001
800-633-9970

WORTH MAGAZINE
Articles on investments and general business topics.
$14.97/10 issues
Capital Publishing Ltd. Partnership
575 Lexington Avenue
New York, NY 10022
800-777-1851

Books

There are only a few books published that address asset allocation head-on, and generally speaking, those are texts geared to investment professionals. There are, however, a number of books that deal with elements of asset allocation discussed in this chapter. If you select and read one or two (the third will begin to sound redundant), you'll come away with a good feel for how to proceed in assessing your own financial situation. Books are in hardcover unless otherwise noted.

THE A–Z OF WALL STREET: 2,500 TERMS FOR THE STREET SMART INVESTOR
Sandra S. Hildreth. Dearborn Financial, 1987.
$16.95 pbk. ISBN: 0-88462-711-X
Contains over 2,500 clearly written definitions useful to investors.

THE ABCS OF MANAGING YOUR MONEY
Jonathan D. Pond, Michael A. Dalton, and O'Neill Wyss. Irwin Professional, 1994.
$26.95 ISBN: 1-884383-00-9
Guide to personal financial planning. Topics cover investments, taxes, and estate planning, as well as providing for the major phases of one's life: retirement, education, death, divorce. Includes worksheets and checklists.

ASSET ALLOCATION
Roger C. Gibson.
Irwin Professional, 1995.
$50.00 ISBN: 1-55623-799-5
Written for professionals, this is still a book easily understood by individual investors. Nontechnical treatment of risk-return tradeoff and how to invest for varying time horizons.

THE BEARDSTOWN LADIES' STITCH-IN-TIME GUIDE TO GROWING YOUR NEST EGG
Hyperion, 1996.
$19.95 ISBN: 0-7868-6192-4
Down-home-style financial planning and budgeting advice. Recommends savings programs, wills, and some general counsel on investing.

BILL GRIFFETH'S 10 STEPS TO FINANCIAL PROSPERITY
Bill Griffeth. Irwin Professional, 1994.
$21.95 ISBN: 1-55738-575-0
Gives a ten-step program, including establishing goals, budgeting, mutual fund investing. Comes with software that allows user to track spending and expenses, savings schedule, and even write a will.

HOW TO BE YOUR OWN FINANCIAL PLANNER
Debra Wishik Englander. Prima, 1996.
$20.95 ISBN: 0-7615-0127-4
Covers budgeting and saving, credit, loans, investments, college planning, child care, taxes, estate and retirement planning. Light treatment of investing.

INVESTING FOR DUMMIES
Eric Tyson. IDG Books, 1996.
$19.99 ISBN: 1-56994-393-3
Thorough coverage of risk and return, stocks, bonds, mutual funds, real estate, small businesses, with a dose of financial planning thrown in.

THE ONLY INVESTMENT GUIDE YOU'LL EVER NEED
Andrew Tobias. Harcourt Brace, 1996.
$12.00 pbk. ISBN: 0-15-600337-6
Starts with basic commonsense goal setting and budgeting. Moves through brief description of every investment vehicle from Treasury bills to derivatives. Emphasizes setting goals and the best ways to achieve them.

PERSONAL FINANCE FOR DUMMIES

Eric Tyson. IDG Books, 1995.
$16.95 pbk. ISBN: 1-56884-150-7
Truly a book for the novice! Topics
include: spending and saving, debt,
taxes, mortgages; stocks, bonds, mutual funds, and other investments. Also
covers brokers, financial planners,
IRAs, college expenses, retirement
planning, and more.

PRICE WATERHOUSE PERSONAL FINANCIAL ADVISER

Irwin Professional, 1996.
$15.00 ISBN: 0-7863-0461-8
Relates the financial-planning function to different life events, like
marriage, divorce, disability, and retirement. Shows how to maximize financial benefits and minimize
taxation, often using real-life cases
from the accounting firm's files.

THE SIX CUPS, HOW TO MANAGE YOUR MONEY

Blankenship and Foster, 1992.
ISBN: 0-8403-8102-6
Written by practicing financial planners, this book explains the
relationship between your cash flow
and six most common uses for the
cash flow: consumption, insurance,
savings, education, investment, and retirement. Suggests methodology for
funding each of these. Includes various
worksheets. Not sold in bookstores.
To obtain a copy, contact:
Blankenship and Foster
Personal Financial Advisors

2775 Via de la Valle, Ste. 201
Del Mar, CA 92014
619-755-5166

SMART MONEY: HOW TO BE YOUR OWN FINANCIAL MANAGER

Ken Dolan and Daria Dolan.
Berkley Books, 1990.
$11.00 pbk. ISBN: 0-425-12179-8
The Dolans, financial experts on radio
and TV, share their knowledge on
topics such as portfolio planning, investments, insurance, choosing a financial adviser, credit, taxes, estate and
retirement planning, and more.

THE SMART MONEY FAMILY FINANCIAL PLANNER

Ken Dolan and Daria Dolan.
Berkley Books, 1992.
$10.95 pbk. ISBN: 0-425-13477-6
The Dolans return, sharing more information on investments, real estate,
college planning, insurance, taxes, retirement planning, among other topics. Has worksheets and information
to help you gain control of your finances.

THE WEALTHY BARBER

David Chilton. Prima, 1996.
$18.95 hardcover ISBN: 1-55958-096-8
$12.95 pbk. ISBN: 0-7615-0166-5
This financial planning book is written
as a story, so it is especially useful for
the novice investor. Topics include
insurance, taxes, investments, retirement planning, and more.

Asset Allocation Software

*If you are comfortable with computers, asset allocation software may be helpful to you in
quantifying risk and return. Some programs can also help you to create the portfolio asset*

mix that gives the best expected return. *This process is called* portfolio optimization, *referring to the creation of the set of portfolios that optimizes the risk-return relationship. As with any software, try to "test-drive" it before paying full price. Buy a demonstration copy ("demo disk") if one is available; some software companies give free demo disks away. Also before buying, ensure that your computer meets or exceeds the system requirements as specified by the software company.*

An asterisk (*) indicates that the product was mentioned in the 1995 Readers' Choice Awards, Technical Analysis of Stocks and Commodities *magazine (Bonus Issue 1996).* Contact:

Technical Analysis, Inc.
4757 California Avenue S.W.
Seattle, WA 98116-4499
Phone: 206-938-0570
Fax: 206-938-1307
http://www.traders.com/
mail@traders.com

ASSET ALLOCATOR*
System: DOS
$150
Allocates assets to minimize risk (standard deviation of rate of return). You can compare risk levels of different allocations. Different versions available. Update manually, from a spreadsheet, or on-line.
Portfolio Software
14 Lincoln Avenue
Quincy, MA 02170
617-328-8248

CRYSTAL BALL
Systems: WIN, MAC. Requires
  Excel or Lotus 1-2-3.
$295. Demo available.
Crystal Ball is a graphically oriented forecasting and risk analysis program for business, engineering, and science. It uses Monte Carlo analysis, a technique that is used when there are elements of uncertainty. It makes your spreadsheet analysis more reliable by showing you the probabilities of various outcomes.

Decisioneering, Inc.
2530 S. Parker Road, Ste. 220
Aurora, CO 80014
800-289-2550; 303-337-3531

FIDELITY RETIREMENT PLANNING
  THINKWARE
System: DOS
$15
Interactive program helps plan your retirement. Covers inflation, compounding, diversification, asset allocation, and more. Easy to install and use.
Fidelity Investments
82 Devonshire Street, R20A
Boston, MA 02190
800-544-0246

GOLDEN YEARS RETIREMENT RE-
  SOURCE MANAGER
System: WIN. Requires Lotus
1-2-3.
$500. Demo available.
Designed for financial planners to perform retirement planning. A menu-driven program that does not require knowledge of spreadsheets, but users may modify equations. All calculations and formulas are available for inspection. Prints out reports and summaries without numbering the pages; this allows the user to intersperse his/her own pages. Covers earned income and pensions, nonqualified savings and investments, qualified plans, personal

expenses, and Social Security benefits. Also covers life insurance, sale of residence, debt, and full income-tax calculations. Has over 35 report pages and four types of 3-D graphs. Very comprehensive program.

Money Tree Software
1753 Wooded Knolls Drive
Philomath, OR 97370
503-929-2140

PLAN AHEAD FOR YOUR FINANCIAL FUTURE
System: WIN. Requires CD-Rom.
$39.99

Clearly explains important retirement investment principles. Creates a customized report based on your situation. Tells how much one should save each month for retirement, what types of investment vehicles one should own, and the cost of maintaining a lifestyle after retirement. Has video interviews with financial experts, graphs, and interactive worksheets. Covers 401k, IRA, Keogh, etc. Discusses Social Security, building a home, and leaving money to heirs.

Dow Jones and Company, Inc.
P.O. Box 300
Princeton, NJ 08543
800-815-5100

PROSPER
System: WIN
$59.95

Helps you define your financial objectives and create a plan for achieving them. Create a personal balance sheet, decide between buying or renting a home, plan for college and retirement, or create your own goal. Also covers information concerning loans, income tax, estate tax, asset allocation, pension benefits, and more. Comes with a free trial membership to Reuters Money Network, an on-line service for investors that has research databases, alerts, quotes, and more.

Ernst and Young Prosper
P.O. Box 60337
King of Prussia, PA 19406
800-277-6773

QUICKEN FINANCIAL PLANNER
Systems: WIN; Quicken is optional. CD-Rom version available.
$50 ($40 for Quicken users)

Plan for a second home, college, retirement, etc. QFP suggests ways to reach your retirement goals and tells you how much you will need to retire. Financial columnist Jane Bryant Quinn gives practical advice within QFP. Has fifteen different reports and graphs. Covers over 4,400 mutual funds with analysis by Morningstar. Handles many major retirement plans including 410k, IRA, 403b, SEP, and Keogh. Handles hard-to-analyze investments, such as small businesses.

Quicken Investment Services, Inc.
(a subsidiary of Intuit Inc.)
P.O. Box 3014
Menlo Park, CA 94026
800-781-5999

RETIREMENT ANALYZER
Systems: WIN, MAC. Requires Excel.
$25

Covers estimated income required at retirement, your spending needs, sources of retirement income, and more. Analyzes mortality tables and Social Security data. Helps you figure out how much you need to save and how high a return you will need to reach retirement.

Baarns Publishing
11150 Sepulveda Blvd., Dept. D

Mission Hills, CA 91345
800-377-9235

**TIME-WEIGHTED INTERNAL RATE
OF RETURN**
Systems: WIN, MAC. Requires
Excel.
$30
Analyzes your investment and savings
plan. Compare three investment scenarios quickly and easily. Also handles
irregular dates and payments. Tells you
how well your investment is doing.
Baarns Publishing
11150 Sepulveda Blvd. Dept. D
Mission Hills, CA 91345
800-377-9235

WEALTHBUILDER
Systems: DOS, WIN, MAC
$50
Covers stocks, bonds, and mutual
funds. Performs financial planning,
portfolio management, and security
analysis. Enter your current income,
assets, and other information. Wealthbuilder will calculate how much you
need to save for a home, college, retirement, etc. Has a Nobel Prize–
winning asset allocation model. Filter

through a database of over 14,000
stocks, bonds, and mutual funds.
Comes with a free trial membership to
Reuters Money Network, an on-line
service for investors that has research
databases, alerts, quotes, and more.
Reality Technologies, Inc.
2200 Renaissance Boulevard
King of Prussia, PA 19406
800-346-2024; 610-277-7600

**WHAT'S BEST—THE SPREAD-
SHEET SOLVER**
Systems: DOS, WIN, MAC.
Requires Excel, Lotus 1-2-3,
Quattro Pro, or Symphony.
$149–$4,995. Demo available.
An add-in for spreadsheets that allows
you to solve complex problems. Uses
the power of linear, nonlinear, and
integer programming. Has in-depth
documentation including examples,
on-line help, and a tutorial. May be
used for portfolio asset allocation and
other financial planning issues.
Lindo Systems Inc.
1415 North Dayton Street
Chicago, IL 60622
800-441-2378; 312-871-2524

Portfolio Management Software

*No matter what asset allocation you decide upon, you will need a way to keep track accurately
and concisely of the securities in your portfolio. Those with only a few stocks or mutual
funds, all held by the same discount broker, may simply opt to rely on the monthly broker
statement for this information. Other investors, with many different assets or perhaps more
than one broker or custodian, may want to use software that categorizes the assets and
accounts for purchases and sales of securities, receipt of interest and dividends, and disburse-
ments of cash from the accounts. Several of the previously listed asset allocation programs
perform these functions, as well as others. The following are programs that specifically address
the portfolio accounting function.*

*An asterisk (*) indicates that the product was mentioned in the 1995 Readers' Choice
Awards sponsored by* Technical Analysis of Stocks and Commodities *magazine. (See
address page 50.)*

CAPTOOL
System: DOS
$149–$499

Covers stocks, bonds, and mutual funds. Supports all transactions and securities. Calculates return on investment (ROI) using the internal-rate-of-return method. Contains a stock evaluator that screens ratios such as price-to-earnings, price-to-book-value, etc. Has a bond evaluator that calculates yield-to-call, accrued interest, etc. Tracks your cost basis and helps you minimize taxes or maximize gains; also computes estimated taxes. Employs more than twenty-five reports. Update prices manually or on-line. Basic to professional versions available.

Techserve, Inc.
P.O. Box 9
Issaquah, WA 98027
800-826-8082

EASY ROR
System: DOS
$59. Demo $5.

Covers stocks, bonds, and mutual funds. Calculates performance. Provides internal rate of return as well as time-weighted rate of return on an investment. Monthly, quarterly, annual, and cumulative returns may be reported. Data may be exported to spreadsheets.

Hamilton Software, Inc.
6432 E. Mineral Place
Englewood, CO 80112
800-733-9607; 303-770-9607

THE EQUALIZER*
System: DOS
$59 plus on-line fees

Covers stocks, bonds, mutual funds, and options. Lets user enter portfolios and track them. Updates prices and information on holdings using Dow Jones News Retrieval and S&P Marketscope. Performs technical and fundamental analysis on stocks.

Charles Schwab and Company
101 Montgomery Street
Department S
San Francisco, CA 94104
800-334-4455; 415-627-7000

FIDELITY ON-LINE XPRESS*
System: DOS
$49.95

Covers stocks, bonds, mutual funds, and options. Allows user to access quotes and make trades in their Fidelity accounts. Accesses information available on Dow Jones News Retrieval and S&P Marketscope. Also lets customers access account information such as buys and sells, deposits and withdrawals, and capital gains reports.

Fidelity Investments
82 Devonshire Street, R20A
Boston, MA 02190
800-544-0246

FOLIOMAN PLUS
System: DOS
$129. Demo available.

Covers stocks, bonds, and mutual funds. Utilizes pull-down menus, scrollable multiwindows, and mouse support. Tracks an unlimited number of portfolios. Variety of reports include transaction register, summary of income, internal and total rate of return, asset allocation, and more. Has comprehensive information on bonds, including interest paid, yield, coupon rate, and automatic notification of payments coming due. Update manually or on-line.

E-sential Software
P.O. Box 41705
Los Angeles, CA 90041
213-257-2524

INVESTOR'S ACCOUNTANT
System: DOS
$395. Demo $5.
Covers stocks, bonds, and mutual funds. Easily organizes and evaluates an unlimited number of portfolios. Measures performance using internal rate of return and time-weighted rate of return. Analyzes securities with moving averages and other indicators. Has detailed reports including tax reports. Sets investment alerts. Update manually or on-line.
Hamilton Software, Inc.
6432 E. Mineral Place
Englewood, CO 80112
800-733-9607; 303-770-9607

THE INVESTOR'S EDGE
System: DOS
$49
Covers stocks, bonds, and mutual funds. Handles 200 accounts (396 investments per account). Has a general notepad and a notepad for each account. Screens and prints reports including asset allocation reports, net worth, and more. Computes internal rate of return. Also includes the following programs: loan amortization program, six special interest-rate programs, a bond program, and a stock graphing program. Menu-driven with on-screen help.
Edco Software Concepts
75 Van Tassel Lane
Orinda, CA 94563
510-254-7601

MANAGING YOUR MONEY*
Systems: DOS, Windows, MAC
$79.95
Covers stocks, bonds, futures, mutual funds, options, and real estate. Manages personal finances including bank accounts, assets, and bills. Tracks all investments with links to Fidelity's On-Line Xpress and Prodigy. Also performs asset allocation, and many other personal finance functions.
Meca Software
55 Walls Drive
Fairfield, CT 06430-5139
203-256-5000

MARKET MANAGER PLUS*
System: DOS
$299. Demo available.
Covers stocks, bonds, and mutual funds. Handles 256 accounts with 3,800 holdings per directory. Transactions include buy/sell, short sales, and receive and deliver. Adjusts for stock splits and dividend reinvestment. Has financial calendar to remember bond maturity, dividend due dates, etc. Categorize securities according to industry or user-defined classification. Experiment with hypothetical portfolios. Reports include transaction report, price alert report, gain/loss report, and more. Save reports in DIF format to incorporate into a word processor or spreadsheet. Update on-line.
Dow Jones and Company, Inc.
P.O. Box 300
Princeton, NJ 08543
800-815-5100; 609-520-4641

MONEY MAKER FOR WINDOWS
System: WIN
$99
Covers stocks, bonds, and mutual funds. Performs fundamental analysis, technical analysis, and portfolio management. Portfolio manager has twelve types of reports including average cost, ordinary income, and capital gains. Handles short sales and margin interest. The analysis program has price forecasting, a constant growth model, and a nonconstant growth

model. Performs bond and mutual fund analysis. Also has goal-planning analysis to help you plan for college and retirement. The charting program has many technical indicators and has a user-defined view range. Update manually or on-line.

Q-West Associates
P.O. Box 270699
San Diego, CA 92198
800-618-6618; 619-793-5813

NAIC PERSONAL RECORD KEEPER
System: DOS
$69. Demo $5.
Covers stocks, bonds, and mutual funds. Easy to use and menu-driven. Easily handles reinvestments, stock splits, stock dividends, and spin-offs. Has multiple-lot accounting. Income can be designated taxable or nontaxable; mutual fund distributions can be designated short-term or long-term. It excels in tracking dividend reinvestment plans (DRIPs). Has over twenty detailed reports that can be filtered by dates or from inception. Update manually or on-line. Has on-line help.

National Association of Investors
Corporation (NAIC)
P.O. Box 220
Royal Oak, MI 48068
810-583-6242

PERSONAL PORTFOLIO ANALYZER
System: DOS
$45
Covers stocks, bonds, and mutual funds. Menu-driven portfolio manager for individuals and small money managers. Maintains up to 255 securities in up to thirty-one portfolio files. Calculates market values, gains and losses, holding periods, betas, and relative strength. Calculates total return using a time-weighted return-on-investment

method and the expected yield. Has nine detailed reports and fifteen summary reports. Has on-line context-sensitive help. Update manually or on-line.

Charles L. Pack
25303 La Loma Drive
Los Altos Hills, CA 94022
415-949-0887

PFRIO
System: DOS
$79
Covers stocks, bonds, and mutual funds. Supports all transactions and security types. Calculates return on investment using the internal-rate-of-return method. Tracks your cost basis and helps you minimize taxes or maximize gains. Computes estimated taxes as well. Has over twenty reports. Update prices manually or on-line.

Techserve, Inc.
P.O. Box 9
Issaquah, WA 98027
800-826-8082

PORTFOLIO DATA MANAGER
System: DOS
$99.95
Covers stocks, bonds, and mutual funds. Allows record-keeping of specific tax-year files; monitors portfolio performance as a whole; has technical analysis including moving averages and relative strength; has special data fields for S&P ratings, P-E ratios, etc. Update manually.

Dynacomp, Inc.
The Dynacomp Office Building
178 Phillips Road
Webster, NY 14580
800-828-6772; 716-265-4040

PULSE PORTFOLIO MANAGEMENT
SYSTEM

System: DOS
$249. 60-day trial $49.
Covers stocks, bonds, and mutual funds. Handles up to seventy-five portfolios with an unlimited number of transactions. Tracks stocks, bonds, mutual funds, real estate, and more. Has over eighty calculations including accrued interest, annualized return, beta, yield-to-call, and total return. Reports include cost breakdown, valuation, performance, calendar reports, and more. Handles multicurrency portfolios, international date and numeric formats, etc. Update manually or on-line. Has pull-down menus and a help feature.
Equis International
3950 South 700 East, Ste. 100
Salt Lake City, UT 84107
800-882-3040; 801-265-8886

STOCK PORTFOLIO
Systems: WIN, MAC. Requires
  Excel.
$15
Covers stocks. Records routine trans-
actions in common and preferred stocks. Records buy/sell dates and prices, dividends, and commissions. Also handles partial sales, short sales, and long-term/short-term holding periods.
Baarns Publishing
11150 Sepulveda Blvd., Dept. D
Mission Hill, CA 91345
800-377-9235

TELESCAN PORTFOLIO MANAGER*
System: DOS
$395. Demo available.
Covers stocks, bonds, and mutual funds. Records trade dates, lots, cost basis, commissions, etc. Reports include asset allocation, tax summaries, and more. Has unlimited portfolios, easy price corrections, and alerts. Update manually or on-line.
Telescan, Inc.
10550 Richmond Avenue, Ste. 250
Houston, TX 77042
800-324-8246; 713-952-1060

Chapter 4

INVESTING IN STOCKS

s you know from the preceding chapter, stocks should be an important part of almost every portfolio. However, many investors neglect putting stocks in the portfolio because of the fear factor we spoke about in the introduction. Investors may be afraid of stock price volatility. They may be afraid of selecting the wrong stocks, stocks that go down in price rather than rising in value. The objective of this chapter is to allay those fears.

The issue of the stock market's volatility was discussed in Chapter 3. Figure 3-2 on page 32 outlined the long-term trend in stock prices: they rise in value. Over time, they rise dramatically in value, leaving all other asset groups in the dust. Is there some up-and-down price movement involved with stocks? Yes, there is. Despite that fact, the trend in stock prices is clearly to the upside, so why get all upset about some short-term gyrations in valuation? Several factors account for the upward bias to stock prices. First, if you stop and think about what it is you buy when you invest in a share of stock, you are buying a small piece of equity ownership in that company. Thus, the rise in share value over time reflects the growth in the overall economies in which the company does business, the growth of the industries in which the company operates, and the growth in the company's profitability. All these add to the company's intrinsic value, and therefore the stock's intrinsic value. Hence, as long as those elements of growth remain in place, there will be an upward bias to the valuations accorded that company and the thousands of other publicly traded companies.

Second, and perhaps more fundamentally, the wealth of investors themselves keeps growing. As it does, it means that there are more absolute dollars available for investment in stocks, even if the percentage of the income invested remains constant. These additional dollars enter the stock market looking for investment opportunities, and in the process they begin competing against other investors and their dollars for the same opportunities. The consequence is a bidding war between investors that results in rising stock prices. Prices decline when the reverse situation occurs, and sellers begin their own bidding war to see who can get out of the stock the most rapidly.

To reiterate this principle, stock prices do not rise and fall because of a company's book value, price-earnings ratio, dividend-payout ratio, or any other two-dimensional ratio or index. Prices rise when more money is flowing into the stock than flowing out of it. Prices decline when more money is exiting a stock than is getting into the stock. If you think about it, this is true of any commodity that trades in a nonmonopolistic environment: real estate, artwork, baseball cards, tulip bulbs . . . you get the picture. So don't be nervous about stock prices rising and falling in the short term. The long-term uptrend in values matches your long-term objectives, and that is the most important thing.

As for the fear of stock selection, that is a more complex issue but one that is easily remedied. There is a saying that goes, "A rising tide lifts all ships." The long-term uptrend in prices means that *most* (not all) stocks will appreciate in value with the overall trend of the general market. Nevertheless, this still leaves room for stocks that do decline in price over time or that trade in a narrow price range. In either case, these are the stocks you want to avoid. Instead of worrying about which stocks to pick, reorient your thinking about stock analysis to embrace the notion that you are identifying losers to avoid.

The purpose of the ratios, the indicators, all the number-crunching analyses and the databases that serve them up, is not so much for selection of good investments but rather the elimination of unworthy candidates from the thousands of stocks available for purchase. The average individual investor is going to create a stock portfolio comprised of three to twenty companies. The universe from which to choose consists of almost 4,000 *listed stocks* (stocks traded on the New York Stock Exchange or the American Stock Exchange) and over 5,000 *unlisted stocks* (stocks traded "over the counter" through NASDAQ). As such, it's no wonder that stock selection can seem a daunting task to most investors. Imagine sifting through 9,000 potential investment candidates in order to select three to twenty stocks for your portfolio. To make the task less daunting, think of the process as one of elimination rather than a process of selection. The real challenge, then, is to find a way to eliminate about 8,990 companies from consideration for inclusion in your portfolio. It's easier than you may think, and there are products and services that will assist you in doing this.

When the full-commission stockbroker calls you with a stock idea, what is really happening? Yes, we know he is calling to persuade you to make a transaction that will generate a commission for himself. Beyond that, he has selected, through some means, a stock to buy out of the 9,000 or so in the universe we described above. Generally this recommendation emanates from the brokerage firm's stock research department. So while the broker himself has not gone through the process of eliminating 8,999 stocks to arrive at this particular one, someone in the firm's research department has.

Research departments at the large full-commission brokerages are staffed with a small army of analysts and support personnel whose function is to be knowledgeable on a group of stocks and the industries in which they operate. These people consume millions of dollars and thousands of man-hours looking for ways to eliminate stocks from consideration so that they are left with a list of potential "buy" candidates. The analysts give the "buy" designation as corporate developments unfold for individual companies or as the price action of a particular stock presents a perceived buying opportunity. A bulletin is flashed to the retail stockbrokers alerting them to the buy recommendation, and the phone call to the brokers' clients follows.

For individual analysts, the process of elimination often begins with discarding companies that are not within their assigned industry or industries. For all but a few industries, this eliminates about 8,980 companies right there. Next analysts may limit the companies to those with a stock market *capitalization* (market price of stock multiplied by the number of shares outstanding) above some minimum level. The rationale there is that most of their clientele will want to invest in larger capitalization issues, because the higher volume of those shares traded makes buying and selling more expeditious. This whittles down another five companies, leaving fifteen companies to follow. They have successfully eliminated 8,985 companies from their universe.

If you queried any analyst or research department head, few if any would describe their function as the process of elimination to arrive at a stock recommendation. They would think of it as a selection process. Committees listen to analysts' investment recommendations before the stocks are included on a buy list, and I assure you that most of those committees are called Stock Selection Committees, not Stock Elimination Committees. Yet eliminating stocks is what they do. Later we'll return to the brokerage houses to discuss the "tricky triangle" that exists there. In the meantime, remember that many other professional investment firms also have research departments: investment advisory services, money managers, mutual fund companies, the larger trust departments, and the so-called "research boutiques." Their analysis is every bit as thorough as that of the brokers' research groups, and usually more objective and unbiased.

If this process of elimination works for the professionals, can't it work for you, the individual investor? Of course it can. You need only define your parameters, apply those to the 9,000-stock universe, work with those stocks that fall through the screen, and discard the rest. As an example, institutional investors like to use the Standard & Poor's 500 stock index (S&P 500) as a performance benchmark. This index is comprised of 500 of America's largest corporations. As with any index of stocks, some issues will rise in price over a certain time period, while the rest will decline or remain unchanged. In an effort to exceed the return on that index, institutional investors try to *eliminate* from their portfolios those stocks that will decline in price. Doing so almost guarantees a rate of return above the index.

However, finding the decliners is challenging in itself, but it is still easier than trying to figure which stocks will rise in value more than others. Let's look at some ways you can use to eliminate stocks from consideration for your portfolio.

INVESTMENT STYLES

Many investors, especially institutional investors, love to label themselves according to some investment methodology. The two most common styles are *value investing* and *growth investing*. *Value investing* looks at both the fundamentals of a company and the valuation that the market gives the company. The value investor is less concerned about sustained earnings growth coming from a company and more concerned if the valuation seems cheap. "Cheap" is often defined in terms of one or more measures related to income statement and balance sheet items such as:

■ Price-to-earnings ratio below the average for all stocks
■ Price-to-book-value ratio below 1.0
■ Current dividend yield above the average for all stocks

The rationale for this process is that the market will reassess valuations from time to time and adjust these low valuations upward. Eliminate the stocks not meeting these valuation criteria, and the anticipated result is better performance of those stocks relative to all others.

Growth investing largely ignores price, focusing instead on the prospects for future growth in earnings, dividends, book value, and profit margins. The logic in downplaying price is that growth stocks, by their nature, will always appear to be expensive relative to most other stocks. As long as the fundamental underpinnings of the company's growth are sound, the price will continue to rise in anticipation of future earnings. No matter which style you use, *value* or *growth*, by applying your criteria to the universe of stocks, you will be able to eliminate hundreds of stocks and zero in on the ones that meet your requirements.

Another contrast in investing styles is *large-capitalization stocks* as opposed to *small-capitalization stocks*. A glance back at Figure 3-1 (page 32) shows the difference in performance between the two groups. Small-cap stocks enjoy higher rates of return than the large-cap issues, but they are more volatile as well. Since we described the S&P 500 index as being a large-capitalization stock index, it's safe to regard all other stocks as being in the small-capitalization category. Large-capitalization issues are more easily tradeable and are better covered by the analytical community. Small-capitalization issues generally are covered by analysts from "boutique" research firms. By confining your stock search to those companies in the S&P 500, you have just eliminated 8,500 stocks. You still have your work cut out for you, but it is made easier by your having removed 95 percent of the stocks from consideration.

These are the most pronounced styles of investing, but there are many others based solely on one or two criteria: *high-yield stocks* versus *low-yield stocks*; *high-quality stocks* (however you want to define "high quality") versus *low-quality stocks*. Whether they realize it or not, most investors apply several criteria in eliminating stocks from consideration. For example, they may favor large-capitalization stocks, but since that only narrows it down to 500 companies, they need to use additional criteria in order to get to a workable number of stocks. So they decide to only use stocks that pay a dividend, which reduces the number down to 300 or so, and on and on it goes until the investor has a list with which they are comfortable.

As with asset allocation, there is no right or wrong style of investing. There is only the style that fits your personality, your objectives, and your comfort level. The difference in historic returns for large-capitalization stocks and small-capitalization stocks has been mentioned. Studies have been done that attempt to quantify the performance advantage of value investing over growth investing. The results are inconclusive because defining what stocks belong in which category varies according to the biases of those conducting the survey and according to the time frame in which the performance is measured. Suffice it to say that each style works well, although one will often produce better results than the other in short time intervals measured. Growth stocks will perform better than value stocks during some time periods, and value stocks outperform growth stocks during other intervals. To compensate for these anomalies, there are those who employ two or more styles of investing, using different methodologies to choose stocks for inclusion in their portfolio.

SECURITY ANALYSIS

Whether you have gone through the process of elimination yourself or have used another source for the elimination of stocks down to a workable number of investment candidates, you'll need to do some homework on the stocks that remain. A thorough treatment of security analysis is too copious to be included in this book. Refer to the books section of the Resource Guide at the end of this chapter for books that are devoted to security analysis. What we can do here is to highlight the type of material that professional stock analysts review and provide a cursory description of the analytical process. Stock analysts:

- Obtain data on the industry or industries in which the potential company operates; determine if the industry is growing, declining, or languishing; ascertain the company's position in the industry and what their share of the market is.
- Develop a familiarity with the company's specific products or services, how these are marketed and distributed, and how they are priced. Find out who their competition is.

■ Obtain annual reports or use other sources to review income statements and balance sheets for at least five years and preferably ten years.

■ Calculate the year-over-year growth rates for: a) sales; b) pretax earnings; c) net earnings; d) earnings per share (EPS); e) cash flow per share. Observe whether the trends in these are rising or falling. If growth is continuously declining, determine if a turnaround in growth is imminent; if not, eliminate the stock.

■ Calculate the following ratios: a) current ratio (current assets/current liabilities)—it should be greater than 2.0; b) total debt/shareholders' equity—a ratio above 0.5 indicates a highly leveraged capital structure; c) pretax earnings/sales—should be stable or rising, and compare this to their competitors' ratio; d) taxes/pretax earnings—tax rate should be stable, if rising or falling, find out why; e) return on equity (net earnings/shareholders' equity)—should be stable or rising, and generally greater than 10 percent; f) dividend payout (dividend per share/EPS)—preferably should be less than 0.5.

■ Apply valuation formula of your choice; for instance, discounted cash flow.

■ Eliminate those companies that are faltering in their industry position, have unsatisfactory financial strength, are not growing at a satisfactory rate, have declining pretax margins or return on equity, and are valued higher than fundamental factors suggest they should be.

■ Invest in those companies that have not been eliminated.

From this synopsis I omitted far more than I included, and I did that on purpose. I wanted to show that eliminating stocks (or selecting stocks) using your own security analysis is a substantial undertaking. Those who are competent in maneuvering through computer spreadsheets can reduce the effort involved considerably, at least after some investment of time setting up the worksheets. For those who perform the analysis "manually," it would not take long before the perceived benefit of analyzing stocks on your own would be overwhelmed by the process itself.

For those who find themselves in that predicament, do not despair, and *do not* go back to your full-commission broker because he gave you advice, told what to buy and sell, and when to do it. There are alternatives.

LET THE EXPERTS DO THE WORK

Unless you are receiving your investment ideas from your barber, chances are you are already using one or more services from some expert or group of experts. Even if you arrive at your own conclusions, you may be using a newsletter or data retrieval service that contributes to the decision-making process. In this section we want to introduce the notion that following the stock recommendations of investment advisory services, newsletters, on-line services, and other investment publications will generate a stock portfolio producing returns just as good as, if not better than, the returns on the brokers' recommendations or your own stock picks. We'll start by highlighting three investment publications, all with sizable circulation, and show how you can use them to make your stock investment decisions.

Analyst Watch, published twice monthly by Zacks Investment Research, Inc. (page 75), summarizes investment analysts' opinions on over 5,000 stocks. It shows the consensus of analysts' earnings per share estimates for the current business year and the next business year as well as the consensus opinions for buy-hold-sell. Other information on each stock includes some historic price, earnings, and other fundamental data. The consensus expectations for projected earnings growth are also presented. By itself all of this data would be useful to the investor in narrowing down stocks to a few names in which to invest. Stocks could be screened by dividend yields, buy recommendations, projected growth rates, to name a few factors. But Zacks has taken the analysis a step further.

Analyst Watch ranks all stocks that are covered by two or more analysts on a scale of 1 to 5. Stocks ranked 1 are expected to outperform the universe of all stocks, that is, have a higher rate of return than the return on the rest of the universe. The rankings are based on a proprietary model. They have been published by Zacks since 1979, and have been used by large institutional investors since then. The *Analyst Watch* publication was created several years ago, targeted at individual investors, as a condensed version of the larger institutional product. The 1 ranking is limited to the top 150 stocks, resulting in the "Zacks Recommended 150" list presented in each issue of the publication. While there are no sell recommendations from this list, names do come on and off the list; hence, a sell is implied when the ranking changes to 2 and below.

The performance of the Zacks Recommended 150 is impressive. For the sixteen-year period 1980–95, the returns on a portfolio consisting of equal-weighted holdings in the 1-ranked stocks exceeded the return on the S&P 500 index in all but one year. The cumulative *annualized* return for the "150" list was 36 percent. This happened to exceed the return on the S&P 500 (14.8 percent), but more important, here is an easy-to-use tool that eliminates about 850 stocks from consideration, and produces an attractive return on investment as well. Since most people will not have portfolios with 150 stocks in them, you need to do additional homework in order to reduce that number. Here is where using some of the publication's other data will be useful in culling out the buy candidates from the 150-stock universe. Probability theory dictates that even if you did nothing more than go through the list and randomly select every tenth stock, you should have a return on that fifteen-stock portfolio that approximates within a few percentage points the overall "150" return. Any way you choose your portfolio from the list, you have gone a long way toward realizing your financial goals simply by using a proven resource that helps to eliminate the fear and confusion of navigating through the stock selection process (or should we say, the elimination process).

———

Value Line Investment Survey is another advisory service (page 108). It scans a broad universe of stocks, currently numbering about 1,700 companies, and ranks them 1 through 5, referred to as its "Timeliness" rank. The premise of the service is simple: invest in stocks ranked 1 for Timeliness and sell them when they are downgraded to a 3, 4, or 5 ranking. The service updates these rankings weekly. Only 100 stocks are given the 1 ranking, so again, you receive the benefit of expert research from a large group of experienced analysts, who make the effort to eliminate 1,600 stocks from serious consideration. You obviously do not want to invest in all 100 stocks, but by applying other criteria of your choice, you will find the three to twenty stocks that meet your needs in building a portfolio.

How has the Value Line service performed? Out of twenty-one newsletters and services tracked for fifteen years ending December 31, 1995, *Hulbert Financial Digest* ranks Value Line second, with a 16.2 percent compounded annual return. Are you assured of achieving similar results if you use this as your primary analytical tool? Of course not. But again, you will have eliminated hundreds of stocks that did not perform as well as Value Line's stocks ranked 1.

The third product we'll examine is not a newsletter or service but an investment magazine, published monthly, called *Individual Investor* (page 71). Unlike most business magazines, *Individual Investor* is devoted solely to investment in common stocks and mutual funds. The magazine's orientation is toward smaller stocks that are growing faster than companies like, let's say, those in the S&P 500 index. For investors willing to take on a little more volatility in their portfolios, *Individual Investor* each January publishes a list of stocks dubbed "The Magic 25," an inventory of twenty-five rapidly growing companies that have been screened and researched by the magazine's analysts. It is almost a ready-made portfolio for investors who want to do minimal research and effort in eliminating 8,975 stocks to arrive at this grouping. The unique part of The Magic 25 is that the list is created and is not changed for twelve months, no matter what is happening to the market or the twenty-five stocks in the interim. So it is definitely a "buy and hold" philosophy at work here, even if the holding period is only twelve months.

The rate of return for the four years that The Magic 25 has been published is as impressive as that of the other two products mentioned before. The annualized rate of return for The Magic 25, assuming an equal dollar investment in each name on the list, has been about 30 percent. In contrast, the S&P 500 annualized return has approximated 16 percent during the same interval.

USING INVESTMENT NEWSLETTERS

A valuable resource not to be overlooked are the many investment newsletters now being published. The estimated number of newsletters exceeds 500, and is continuously growing due to the ease of entering the newsletter business. We have already looked at one, the *Value Line Investment Survey,* which is considered a newsletter by most but, at 140-plus pages per weekly issue, is far more comprehensive than any other letter you'll find. Most investment newsletters are between four and sixteen pages in length. Despite their succinctness, many letters cram each issue with general commentary on the economy and the stock and bond markets. They also review one or more stocks and may prescribe an asset allocation or weightings of stocks, bonds, and cash. Most letters offer stock recommendations in which the reader may invest some or all of his own portfolio.

As when you stare at a large universe of stocks and wonder which you should buy, you could ogle the large universe of newsletters and ponder, "Which ones are any good?" Well, there's happy news. The *Hulbert Financial Digest* newsletter (HFD) (page 88) has tracked the performance of investment newsletters for more than fifteen years. More specifically, HFD has evaluated twenty-one letters over the fifteen-year time horizon, fifty-six letters over a ten-year period, and one hundred letters during the last five years. The end product is a compilation of the annualized rates of return for hundreds of investment newsletters.

Once again, the elimination process can begin with your discarding letters that are not rated in HFD or that have been rated for fewer than five years. You can then consider following those letters that have significant returns during the five-year and ten-year intervals, and possibly even use the fifteen-year interval. Those letters that make a respectable showing in each time interval have the best chance of producing above-average results for you in the future. Having identified the most viable newsletter candidates, contact each for a sample copy. Study the issue and whatever promotional material accompanies it. If the philosophy of the letter and the types of investments it recommends are compatible with your tastes, make the move and subscribe. Features of certain letters that you may find helpful are a model portfolio and a telephone "hotline" that apprises subscribers of portfolio changes on a timely basis.

To assist you in identifying the newsletters rated by Hulbert, Table 4-1 (page 66) gives the performance rankings of those letters that HFD has rated over the fifteen-year period and their respective rates of return. Also, in the Resource Guide at the end of this chapter are listed many newsletters, including many that are not rated by HFD. Those that have been rated by HFD are signified by "HR" following pricing information. Since the following tabulation will be outdated when you read this, it is strongly recommended that you contact the *Hulbert Financial Digest* for an updated list of letters and their performance.

BEATING THE DOW JONES INDUSTRIAL AVERAGE

For those who want to use their own "hands-on" technique, I will profile one easy-to-use methodology. The process is outlined in detail in the book *Beating the Dow* (page 112). It starts by using only the thirty stocks in the Dow Jones Industrial

Average (DJIA). This technique looks good already, because with no effort at all you've eliminated 8,970 stocks from the universe. On the first trading day of the year, invest equal dollar amounts in each of the ten stocks in the DJIA that have the highest dividend yields. Then, do nothing else. On the first trading day of the following year, determine the ten highest-yield stocks at that point in time, and rebalance the portfolio accordingly. Although this procedure seems ridiculously simple, it has exceeded the return on the DJIA about 80 percent of the time over the last twenty years.

TABLE 4-1
HULBERT FINANCIAL DIGEST NEWSLETTER PERFORMANCE

Newsletter	Rate of Return*
The Prudent Speculator	16.6%
The Value Line Investment Survey	16.2%
The Chartist	15.6%
The Zweig Forecast	15.0%
No Load Fund-X	11.7%
Market Logic	11.4%
Value Line OTC Special Situations Service	10.8%
Fabians' Investment Resource	10.7%
Growth Stock Outlook	10.7%
Dow Theory Forecasts	10.6%
The Outlook	10.4%
The Cabot Market Letter	10.2%
Growth Fund Guide	8.7%
Harry Browne's Special Reports	7.3%
Kinsman's Stock Pattern Recognition Service	7.2%
The International Harry Schultz Letter	4.4%
The Ruff Times	4.4%
United & Babson Investment Report	3.9%
The Dines Letter	2.5%
The Professional Tape Reader	0.3%
The Granville Market Letter	−27.7%

*Annualized Rate of Return for period 1/1/81 through 12/31/95
Source: *Hulbert Financial Digest*, Alexandria, Virginia

In leaving this section, we want to recap that there are numerous products out there that can be used as your screening tool in coming up with a list of "buy" candidates for your portfolio. Each is available at reasonable cost to you, and each has been shown to produce competitive returns. No doubt there are other services available that will generate profitable investment ideas. By no means are we recommending any particular newsletter, publication, or other service. Furthermore, as the often-seen disclaimer states, "Past performance does not guarantee future results." Most important, you should *never* invest in a company without having done some homework on it, no matter whose recommended list it appears on. To some extent, you should follow the analytical outline on pages 61 and 62.

Hopefully, these few examples have convinced you that you can create a portfolio of stocks without having to rely on a broker's advice. There is no need to be apprehensive and fearful about employing any one of these, or similar, methodologies. Remember, these services, and dozens more, publish their results for all the world to see. Is your broker's track record published anywhere?

THE TRICKY TRIANGLE

This leads us to discuss the research that is published by the brokerage houses. As a stock analyst myself for eight years, I had the opportunity to work with and utilize the expertise of many brokerage analysts in a variety of industries. I have the utmost admiration and respect for their perseverance, creativity, and proficiency in their pursuit of the analytical process. However, the research departments in which they function are not profit centers. The research department's output is used by two other departments that *are* profit centers: the sales department (which is actually two departments—retail and institutional) and the underwriting department (which brings stock and bond offerings to the market). These three departments form the tricky triangle.

In a perfect world, the research analysts would perform unbiased research, draw their conclusions, and convey those to the other two departments without hesitation. In other words, they'd call 'em as they see 'em. But here's where the triangle turns tricky. When a company is faltering and does not present an attractive investment opportunity, the analyst should advise clients, through the sales force, to sell. In the real world, that usually does not happen.

A sell recommendation from a brokerage analyst guarantees that the firm's underwriting department will not even have a chance to compete for the spurned company's underwriting business. That would greatly displease the underwriting department because it is denied access to very lucrative fees. The sales department is also unhappy because it is denied the opportunity to make big commissions (the payout to brokers on new issues is much greater than ordinary trades of similar size). Consequently, you will see very few sell recommendations from brokerage analysts. When the analyst becomes bearish enough, he simply stops writing about the company in question. There was a well-publicized case several years ago in which an analyst was fired from a brokerage firm, at the insistence of the underwriting client, after the analyst predicted that the client's Atlantic City casino would experience financial difficulty. The analyst proved to be correct, and he subsequently won a sizable settlement in arbitration.[5]

All this calls into question the objectivity of brokerage research in general. As

[5]E. S. Browning, "Please Don't Talk to the Bearish Analyst," *Wall Street Journal*, May 2, 1995.

another example, you will never see brokerage firm strategists turn decidedly negative on the stock market. Instead they move back and forth within a stock allocation range between 40 and 70 percent. Why would a strategist want to reduce the stock weighting down to 10 or 20 percent, even if he was convinced the market was going down? If the clients were persuaded to reduce stock exposure significantly, after the initial rebalancing of portfolios, there would be no trades that create the commissions that generate the profits that make the brokers as wealthy as they are.

In contrast, none of the services we profiled earlier has anyone to answer to other than the investors who use their products. They have only one mission: to provide investment ideas that will make you money. Their results have been quantified, and if they falter in their mission, their revenue will suffer. Remember this if you have reservations about using the ideas contained in a newsletter, magazine, or other advisory service that has a record of success. There are those who will turn up their noses at the notion of using an investment newsletter or comparable product as the primary source of investment ideas. But if you think about it, there is no difference between what function is performed by these analysts, and the function performed by the analysts at brokerage firms, money managers, or trust departments. The main difference is in some investors' perception of their analysis as being less credible than that of a broker's analyst. In truth, perception is rarely in sync with reality.

DIVIDEND REINVESTMENT PLANS

For those investors who want to minimize brokerage commissions from either full-commission brokers *or* discount brokers, the dividend reinvestment plan (DRP, or DRIP) is the way to go. The DRIP allows shareholders of companies that have DRIPs to purchase additional shares with the cash that would otherwise be paid as cash dividends. Once the investor has at least one share of that company's stock, he can arrange to have a DRIP account established. Some DRIPs allow for a shareholder to make supplemental cash deposits to purchase even more shares over and above what the dividend payment would allow. Purchases of shares are then transacted without brokerage commissions, although there is often a small transactional charge to cover the costs of administering the account.

Almost nine hundred companies have DRIPs established. Again, most of these require that the investor already own the company's stock before they will open a DRIP for that investor. However, there are about ninety companies who will transact the initial share purchase through a DRIP or some other direct share-purchase plan. The latter companies are often referred to as "no-load stocks," a takeoff on "no-load mutual funds," funds that do not charge a sales commission for investing in them. The Resource Guide at the end of this chapter contains several books and newsletters dedicated to DRIPs. *Buying Stocks Without a Broker* and *No Load Stocks* are both written by Charles B. Carlson. In addition to being the editor of *Dow Theory Forecasts* newsletter, Mr. Carlson is also the editor of *DRIP Investor* newsletter. Both this publication and a competing letter, *The Moneypaper,* discuss in more detail how to establish DRIPs and what the mechanics of the plans are, and they also give an up-to-date list of the companies that offer DRIPs. For your information, Appendix A has a listing of the companies that offered DRIPs at this writing. You will still need to contact one of the publications mentioned above to learn how to reach these companies.

INVESTMENT CLUBS

It is a well-documented phenomenon of human behavior that when people attempt to do some activity with others with similar interests, they are more apt to pursue conscientiously the activity in question and to do it with more enjoyment and success. Whether it is an exercise class, a book club, or a sewing circle, the group dynamic motivates its members to participate and contribute. So it is with investment clubs.

Investment clubs are simply a group of investors who meet at regular intervals, contribute an equal amount of money into the club's pool, and then invest the money in a portfolio of stocks and/or mutual funds. Some clubs may invest in bonds as well, but stocks and mutual funds seem to be the vehicles of choice for most clubs. The members give the club a name, set up an account with a broker (make that a discount broker), establish some ground rules for selecting stocks (or eliminating stocks, as the case may be), and then at each meeting they discuss their current holdings, as well as whether to make changes in the portfolio. Each member may be assigned an industry to monitor and from which to draw stock recommendations. Periodically, each member will present a stock idea to the group, which then votes to decide whether or not to include the investment in their portfolio. Sell decisions occur similarly, although because new cash is continually flowing into the cash pool, stocks are usually bought and held. Sales typically occur when the company's business prospects deteriorate.

In the Resource Guide for this chapter you will find three books that deal with investment clubs. *The Investment Club Book* and *Investment Clubs* deal with the how-to and what-for of forming an investment club. *The Beardstown Ladies' Common-Sense Investment Guide* puts a human face on the investment club topic by profiling the members of an investment club in Illinois and the success they have achieved. For more information on establishing and running a club, contact the *National Association of Investors Corporation* (NAIC) (pages 97–98).

Whether you decide to study and monitor a favored newsletter's stock recommendations, or you choose to gather with friends in an investment club, creating your own stock portfolio is fun. It need not be a laborious, time-consuming process that is a source of fear and trepidation. Spend a little time getting to know several of the many resources listed in the Resource Guide that follows. Subscribe to at least one of the daily business newspapers and at least one of the general interest investment periodicals. These will keep you current on economic and business issues of the day, as well as the tone of the stock market. They may also provide you with some investment ideas.

As we suggested earlier, samples of some of the newsletters that may be of interest to you. In the spirit of our "keep it simple, sweetheart" philosophy, you may want to subscribe to only one newsletter at first, trying out some of its investment recommendations. There is no rule, however, that says you cannot take ideas from more than one publication once you are comfortable with them. With ideas in hand, go ahead and structure your portfolio, buying those stocks through the discount broker of your choice. As you do, know that you are well on your way to building your wealth and achieving your financial goals.

RESOURCE GUIDE-
INVESTING IN STOCKS

Magazines and Periodicals

Included in this section are magazines, newspapers, chart services, and miscellaneous research products to which investors can subscribe.

BARRON'S NATIONAL BUSINESS AND FINANCIAL WEEKLY
In addition to weekly tables of quotes, this weekly newspaper has sections on technical analysis indicators, mutual funds, interviews, and articles on investment topics.
$129/yr.
Dow Jones & Company, Inc.
P.O. Box 7014
Chicopee, MA 01021-9901
800-328-6800

CHARTCRAFT, INC.
Covers stocks, mutual funds, asset allocation. Technical analysis. Charting service, includes fifty technical indicators. Covers stocks plus eighty-eight industry groups, and indices. Has hotline.
$100/yr. Quarterly
Chartcraft, Inc.
30 Church Street
P.O. Box 2046

New Rochelle, NY 10801
914-632-0422

CHARTCRAFT MONTHLY P&F CHARTBOOK ON NYSE/ASE/OTC POINT AND FIGURE CHARTBOOK
Covers stocks. Technical analysis. Stock charts with technical indicators included.
$104/yr. Monthly/Quarterly
Chartcraft, Inc.
30 Church St.
P.O. Box 2046
New Rochelle, NY 10801
914-632-0422

CHARTCRAFT TECHNICAL INDICATOR REVIEW
Covers stocks. Technical and fundamental analysis. Gives fundamental and technical analysis of all Dow stocks. Lists each stock as bullish or bearish.
$90/yr. Biweekly

Chartcraft, Inc.
30 Church Street
P.O. Box 2046
New Rochelle, NY 10801
914-632-0422

CHARTCRAFT WEEKLY BREAKOUT SERVICE

Covers stocks. Technical analysis. Has P&F charts of all new breakout stocks on the NYSE. Includes moving averages, RSI, P-E, and yield. Also available for AMEX and NASDAQ stocks.
$168/yr. Weekly
Chartcraft, Inc.
30 Church Street
P.O. Box 2046
New Rochelle, NY 10801
914-632-0422

CHARTCRAFT WEEKLY SERVICE

Covers stocks. Fundamental analysis. Includes technical analysis of charts and graphs from listed and OTC stocks.
$224/yr. Weekly
Chartcraft, Inc.
30 Church Street
P.O. Box 2046
New Rochelle, NY 10801
914-632-0422

DAILY GRAPHS

Chart service covering stocks. Technical and fundamental analysis. Each chart includes forty-one fundamental and twenty-six technical analyses.

	NYSE	AMEX/OTC
Weekly	$429/yr.	$719/yr.
Biweekly	$395/yr.	$549/yr.
Monthly	$203/yr.	$345/yr.

William O'Neil and Co. Inc.
Box 24933
Los Angeles, CA 90024-0933
213-820-2583

HANDBOOK OF COMMON STOCKS
HANDBOOK OF NASDAQ STOCKS

Offers summary reports on NYSE and AMEX stocks (*Common Stocks* book) and over-the-counter stocks (*NASDAQ Stocks* book). Company profiles, financial statistics, historic price performance.

Common Stocks   **$235/yr.**
NASDAQ Stocks   **$175/yr.**
Quarterly
Moody's Financial Information Services
99 Church Street
New York, NY 10007
212-553-0435

INDIVIDUAL INVESTOR

Covers companies for potential investment, focusing primarily on small-growth stocks. Features include an annual list of stocks ("The Magic 25"), fastest-growing companies, initial public offerings, and mutual funds.
$22.95/yr. Monthly
Individual Investor Subscription Fulfillment
P.O. Box 681
Mt. Morris, IL 61054-0681
800-383-5901

INVESTOR'S BUSINESS DAILY

Covers all foreign and domestic markets, including quote tables with proprietary analytical data. Articles on companies, general business topics, technical analysis, tax issues, and mutual funds.
$179/yr. Daily newspaper
Investor's Business Daily
12655 Beatrice Street
Los Angeles, CA 90066
800-831-2525

MANSFIELD STOCK CHART SERVICE

Chart service. Technical analysis. NYSE, AMEX, and NASDAQ charts updated every Friday and mailed.

	Weekly	Biweekly	Monthly
1 exchange	$688	$422	$217
2 exchanges	$1,208	$770	$398
3 exchanges	$1,706	$1,081	$559

Mansfield Investments
2173 Kennedy Blvd.
Jersey City, NJ 07306
201-795-0629

MARKET CHARTS
Covers stocks. Technical analysis. Chart service, P&F charts including short- and long-term indicators.

Twice monthly	$550
Monthly	$335
1 point single issue	$ 35
3 point single issue	$ 65

Market Charts, Inc.
20 Exchange Place, 13th Floor
New York, NY 10005
800-431-6082

NELSON'S EARNINGS OUTLOOK
A compendium of consensus earnings estimates and buy-hold-sell recommendations on over 3,000 stocks, derived from hundreds of securities analysts around the country.
$240/yr. Monthly
Nelson Publications
One Gateway Plaza
Port Chester, NY 10573
800-333-6357

RED BOOK OF 5-TREND SECURITY CHARTS
Covers stocks. Technical analysis. Chart service covering 1,100 stocks.
$124/yr. Monthly
Securities Research Co.
101 Prescott Street
Wellesley Hills, MA 02181
617-235-0900

SMART MONEY
Magazine profiles companies as potential investments. Has a model stock portfolio. Treats tax issues. Special features, including an annual rating of discount brokers.
$15/yr. Monthly
Hearst Corporation/Dow Jones
1790 Broadway
New York, NY 10019
800-444-4204

SRC (SECURITIES RESEARCH CO.) BLUE BOOK OF 5-TREND CYCLIC GRAPH
Covers stocks. Technical analysis. Chart service covers 1,108 listed stocks. Also available on an individual-issue basis.
$104/yr. Quarterly
Babson-United Investment Advisors, Inc.
101 Prescott Street
Wellesley Hills, MA 02181
617-235-0900

SRC (SECURITIES RESEARCH CO.) ORANGE BOOK OF 1,012 ACTIVE OTC STOCKS
Covers stocks. Technical analysis. Chart service covers 1,012 OTC stocks. Also available on an individual-issue basis.
$114/yr. Quarterly
Babson-United Investment Advisors, Inc.
101 Prescott Street
Wellesley Hills, MA 02181
617-235-0900

SRC (SECURITIES RESEARCH CO.) RED BOOK OF 1,108 SECURITY CHARTS
Covers stocks. Technical analysis. Chart service covers 1,108 listed

stocks with technical analysis. Also available on an individual-issue basis.
$124/yr. Quarterly
Babson-United Investment Advisors, Inc.
101 Prescott Street
Wellesley Hills, MA 02181
617-235-0900

TECHNICAL TRENDS—THE INDICATOR ACCURACY SERVICE

Covers stocks. Technical analysis. Chart service, includes market commentary.
$147/yr. Weekly
Technical Trends
P.O. Box 7115
Jupiter, FL 33468
800-736-0229; 203-762-0299

TRENDLINE CHART GUIDE

Covers mutual funds and stocks. Technical analysis. Chart service covers over 4,400 listed and OTC stocks for preceding twelve months.
$155/yr. Monthly
Standard & Poor's
25 Broadway
New York, NY 10004
800-221-5277; 212-208-8792

TRENDLINE CURRENT MARKET PROSPECTIVES

Covers stocks. Technical analysis. Chart service includes weekly price volume charts with four-year history for 1,400 stocks.
$195/yr. Monthly
Standard & Poor's
25 Broadway
New York, NY 10004
800-777-4858; 212-208-8768

TRENDLINE DAILY ACTION STOCK CHARTS

Covers stocks. Technical analysis.

Chart service, twelve-month history on 728 listed stocks. Includes most actively traded options.
$520/yr. Weekly
Standard & Poor's
25 Broadway
New York, NY 10004
800-777-4858; 212-208-8768

TRENDLINE OTC CHART MANUAL

Covers stocks. Technical analysis. Chart service, four-year price volume history on over 800 actively traded OTC stocks.
$520/yr. Weekly
Standard & Poor's
25 Broadway
New York, NY 10004
800-777-4858; 212-208-8768

WALL STREET JOURNAL

Covers all foreign and domestic markets: stocks, bonds, commodities, mutual funds. Broad news coverage of business and political people and events. Complete quotations.
$164/yr. Business daily newspaper.
Dow Jones & Company, Inc.
200 Burnett Road
Chicopee, MA 01020
800-841-8000

WEEKLY STOCK CHARTS—CANADIAN AND U.S. INDUSTRIAL COMPANIES

Covers stocks. Chart service, price, and volume of 1,000 Canadian and U.S. industrial companies.
$25.60 (Canadian)/yr. Annual
Independent Survey Co.
P.O. Box 6000
Vancouver, BC, V6B-4B9, Canada
604-731-5777

WEEKLY STOCK CHARTS—CANA-DIAN RESOURCE COMPANIES
Covers stocks. Chart service, price, and volume of 1,200 Canadian mining and oil stocks.
$25.60 (Canadian)/yr. Annual

Independent Survey Co.
P.O. Box 6000
Vancouver, BC, V6B-4B9, Canada
604-731-5777

Newsletters

The following listing contains newsletters that cover primarily stocks. However, many treat other topics as well, including asset allocation, bonds, mutual funds, commodities, and derivatives. The **HR** *designation next to the subscription price means the letter is ranked by the* Hulbert Financial Digest *newsletter.*

AAII JOURNAL
Covers stocks, bonds, and mutual funds. Includes information on investment theory with practical demonstrations. Has interviews with investment professionals. Includes access to real-time quotes on stocks, options, and mutual funds. Financial planning, stock screening, and insurance products are also included in the journal.
$45/yr. (free to members of AAII)
10 times a year
American Association of Individual Investors
625 N. Michigan Avenue
Chicago, IL 60611-3110
312-280-0170

THE ACKER LETTER
Covers stocks (NYSE, AMEX, OTC) with minimal analyst coverage. Directed towards middle-income investors.
$95/yr.
2718 E. 63rd Street
Brooklyn, NY 11234
718-531-8981

THE ADDISON REPORT
Fundamental and technical analysis. Covers stocks, bonds, and mutual funds (stock and bond). Has hotline.

Contains market overviews and mutual fund switch advice. Thirty to forty stock recommendations per issue. Utilizes conservative and aggressive model portfolios. Has special quarterly reports on the technical condition of the Dow and various stock groups.
$250/yr. Every 3 weeks—HR
P.O. Box 402
Franklin, MA 02038
508-528-8678

ADRIAN DAY'S INVESTMENT ANALYST
Fundamental analysis. Covers stocks, bonds, and mutual funds (stock and bond). Has hotline. Mr. Day buys and sells short investments spanning the globe. Contains model portfolios.
$109/yr. Monthly—HR
824 E. Baltimore Street
Baltimore, MD 21202
410-234-0691

AGBIOTECH STOCK LETTER
Fundamental analysis. Covers biotech stocks. Focuses mainly on young biotech stocks without products on the market. Editor Jim McCamant follows a long-term strategy, and usually stays fully invested.

$165/yr. Monthly—HR
P.O. Box 40460
Berkeley, CA 94704
510-843-1842

AIC INVESTMENT BULLETIN

Covers all investments including stocks, bonds, precious metals, financial markets, and business conditions. Has fundamental analysis and technical analysis (stock charts). Gives analysis of industries and specific stocks.
$60/yr. Semimonthly
AIC Investment Management
440 South Street
Pittsfield, MA 01201
413-499-1111

ANALYST WATCH

Fundamental analysis. Covers stocks. Lists earnings-estimate consensus, brokerage recommendations, and other quantitative analysis on over 5,000 stocks. Also has a model portfolio consisting of 150 stocks, picked on the basis of estimate revisions, eps (earnings per share) surprises, valuation, and economic sector considerations. Contains in-depth analysis on additions to recommended stocks. Has a daily hotline.
$295/yr. Weekly—HR
Zacks Investment Research
155 N. Wacker Drive
Chicago, IL 60606
800-399-6659

ARGUS VIEWPOINT

Fundamental analysis. Covers stocks. Explains Argus's investment policy and its impact from macroeconomic conditions. Includes stock and bond investment strategies and a recommended stock list.
$390/yr. Monthly—HR
Argus Research Company

17 Battery Place
New York, NY 10004
212-425-7500

THE ASTRO-INVESTOR

Covers stocks. Gives daily market forecasts and stock selections. Includes general investment news and book reviews.
$45/yr. Monthly
Mull Publications
P.O. Box 11133
Indianapolis, IN 46201-0133

THE ASTUTE ADVISORY

Fundamental analysis. Includes stocks. Identifies selected stocks that are suitable for long-term holds.
$95/yr. 9 issues/yr.
Astute Publishing
P.O. Box 291
Draper, UT 84020
801-272-2113

THE ASTUTE INVESTOR

Covers stocks. Includes a proprietary value stock list, discusses investment philosophies, and reviews other writings. Includes a reference list with addresses and phone numbers of all companies mentioned.
$30/yr. Monthly
135 Beachwood Lane
Kingston, TN 37763
615-376-2732

ASUI NEWSLETTER

Fundamental analysis. Covers utility stocks. Reports on stock market statistics that are directly relevant to gas and electric stocks. Analyzes government legislation and regulatory agency activities that affect utilities. Summarizes news relevant to the industry.
$190/yr. Quarterly

American Society of Utility Investors (ASUI)
P.O. Box 342
New Cumberland, PA 17070
717-774-8434

BANK STOCK ANALYSIS
Fundamental and quantitative analysis. Includes bank stocks. Includes historical earnings, earnings growth rate, nonperforming loans, P-E and price-to-book-value ratios, return on assets, and return on equity. Discusses risk and rewards of investing in bank stocks.
Free with subscription to *Growth Stock Outlook*. **Semiannual.**
P.O. Box 15381
Chevy Chase, MD 20825
301-654-5205

THE BARTLET LETTERS
Fundamental and quantitative analysis. Includes stocks. A weekly advisory on growth stocks including statistics. Has a model portfolio of ten stocks.
$475/yr. Weekly
P.O. Box 465
Aurora, IL 60507
312-896-3143

BAXTER
Fundamental analysis. Covers stocks, treasuries. Monitors business, economic developments, and monetary conditions (domestic and foreign). Gives stock recommendations with follow-up, and analysis of treasury securities.
$195/yr. Biweekly
Baxter World Economic Service
1030 E. Putnam Avenue
Greenwich, CT 06830
203-637-4559

THE BENCH INVESTMENT LETTER
Fundamental and technical analysis. Includes growth and income stocks, bonds, mutual funds. Includes economic forecasts and makes recommendations based on those forecasts. Has a list of recommended securities and a follow-up on recommendations.
$120/yr. Monthly
Bench Corp.
222 Bridge Plaza South
Fort Lee, NJ 07024
201-585-2333

BI RESEARCH
Fundamental analysis. Covers stocks. BI Research closely examines one stock per issue. Most recommendations are of unknown firms with high growth rates, or they are undervalued. Holds stocks for the long term. Updates each previous recommendation. Does not have a model portfolio.
$90/yr. Every 6 weeks—HR
P.O. Box 133
Redding, CT 06875
203-270-9244

THE BLUE BOOK OF CBS (CANADIAN BUSINESS SERVICE) STOCK REPORTS
Covers stocks. Fundamental and technical analysis. In-depth coverage and financial analysis of Canadian stocks.
$245/yr. Biweekly
Canadian Business Service (CBS)
Marpep Publishing Limited
133 Richmond Street West
Suite 700
Toronto, ON M5H-3M8, Canada
416-869-1177

BLUE CHIP BAROMETER
Covers stocks. Technical analysis. Gives econometric model covering stock market timing. Forecasts the

Dow Industrial Average and twenty-six other industries for the coming six months.
$195/yr. Twice monthly
P.O. Box 42023
Philadelphia, PA 19101

THE BLUE CHIP INVESTOR

Fundamental analysis. Covers stocks. Has hotline. Mr. Check invests in blue-chip stocks. His growth model portfolio screens for growing earnings, industry dominance, and a high Standard & Poor's rating. The contrarian model portfolio searches for out-of-favor stocks that are financially strong.
$179/yr. Monthly—HR
575 Anton Boulevard, Ste. 570
Costa Mesa, CA 92626
714-641-3579

BLUE CHIP STOCKS

Covers stocks. Fundamental analysis. Makes blue-chip stock recommendations based on earnings and dividends.
$45/yr. Annual
4016 S. Michigan Street
South Bend, IN 46614-3823
800-553-5866; 219-291-3823

BOB BLACK'S TAKING STOCK

Covers stocks. Fundamental analysis. Gives research on what it considers to be stocks that are undervalued or selling at distressed levels. Has model portfolio.
$95/yr. Twice monthly
Taking Stock Inc.
1400 Temple Building
Rochester, NY 14604
716-232-4268

BOB BRINKER'S MARKETIMER

Covers mutual funds, stocks, bonds, and commodities. Technical and fundamental analysis. Makes recommen-

dations for no-load mutual funds and has model portfolios. Includes analysis of Fed's monetary policy and the business cycle.
$185/yr. Monthly—HR
Robert J. Brinker Investment
   Advisory Services Ltd.
P.O. Box 321580
Coco Beach, FL 37932
800-700-1030; 407-784-5003

BOB CZESCHIN'S WORLD INVESTOR

Fundamental analysis. Covers stocks, bonds, and mutual funds (stock and bond). Has hotline. Mr. Czeschin invests in companies all over the globe. Has an income model portfolio, a growth portfolio, and the "Jaguar" portfolio.
$99/yr. Monthly
824 E. Baltimore Street
Baltimore, MD 21202
410-234-0691

BOB NUROCK'S ADVISORY

Fundamental and technical analysis. Covers stocks, bonds, mutual funds, and gold. Comments on and provides insight into the economy and interest rates. Has specific buy-sell ideas on stocks, mutual funds, bonds, and gold. Includes technical analysis. Sample available for $5.00.
$247/yr. Monthly—HR
P.O. Box 460
Santa Fe, NM 87504
800-227-8883; 505-820-2737

THE BOWSER DIRECTORY OF SMALL STOCKS

Covers stocks. Fundamental analysis. Includes fourteen fields of information on over 700 low-priced stocks, listed and OTC. Information is current and gives price movement.

$89/yr. Monthly
P.O. Box 6278
Newport News, VA 23606
804-877-5979

THE BOWSER REPORT
Covers stocks. Fundamental analysis.
Analyzes stocks that sell for less than
$3.00 per share. Spotlights one com-
pany every month. Makes specific rec-
ommendations.
$39/yr. Monthly—HR
P.O. Box 6278
Newport News, VA 23606
804-877-5979

BRAUN'S SYSTEM NETWORK
Covers stocks, options, bonds, and futures.
$295/yr. Weekly
Braun's Systems
317 Wynt Field Drive
Lewisville, NC 27023
919-945-9110

BSMA: BILL STATON'S MONEY ADVISORY
Covers stocks, bonds, and mutual
funds. Fundamental analysis. This is a
general financial newsletter covering
investing and taxation. Does not provide any regular recommendations.
$89/yr. 3 times monthly
2113 E. 5th Street
Charlotte, NC 28203
800-216-1818; 704-335-0276

THE BULLION ADVISORY
Covers precious metals. Technical and
fundamental analysis. Makes recommendations on precious-metal purchases. Lists resources for
precious-metal investors.
$36/yr. Monthly
Money Power
4257 46th Avenue North, #207

P.O. Box 22586
Minneapolis, MN 55422
612-537-8096

THE CABOT MARKET LETTER
Covers stocks. Fundamental and technical analysis. Makes specific stock
recommendations and follows growth
stocks.
$270/yr. Bimonthly—HR
P.O. Box 3067
Salem, MA 01970
800-777-2658

CALIFORNIA TECHNOLOGY STOCK LETTER
Fundamental analysis and technical
analysis. Covers stocks and market
timing. Has hotline. Focuses on technology stocks. They examine a company's product line, financial
statements, etc. But they use technical
analysis for market timing. Has model
portfolio.
$295/yr. Biweekly—HR
P.O. Box 308
Half Moon Bay, CA 94019
415-726-8495

CAMBRIDGE FINANCIAL MANAGER
Covers stocks, bonds, and mutual
funds. Fundamental and technical
analysis. Specializes in futures market,
especially stock indices and foreign
currencies. Gives advice on stock,
bond, and mutual fund investments.
Has hotline.
$349/yr. Monthly
Cambridge Commodities Corp.
55 Cambridge River Front, #2
Cambridge, MA 02142
617-621-8500

CANADIAN HIGH-GROWTH INVEST-MENT LETTER
Covers Canadian stocks. Fundamental

analysis. Gives advice on technology and other high-growth stocks listed on the Toronto Stock Exchange.
$245/yr. Monthly
12 Sheppard Street, Ste. 422
Toronto, ON M5H-3A1, Canada
416-364-4949

CANADIAN MARKET CONFIDENTIAL

Covers Canadian stocks. Fundamental and technical analysis. Gives investment advice on Canadian stocks.
$79/yr. Monthly
Phoenix Communications Group, Ltd.
P.O. Box 670
Colorado Springs, CO 80901-0670
719-576-9200

CAPITAL GROWTH LETTER

Covers bonds and stocks. Technical analysis. Has technical analysis with commentary on stocks and the stock market, bonds, international markets, and commodities. Has hotline updated twice weekly.
$225/yr. Monthly
Bollinger Capital Management
P.O. Box 3358
Manhattan Beach, CA 90266
310-798-8855

CAROL MULL'S MARKET FORECASTER

Covers stocks. Fundamental and technical analysis. Uses the author's fundamental research, combined with technical analysis, to forecast market trends. Includes individual stocks, industries, and the market as a whole.
$45/yr. Monthly
Mull Publications
P.O. Box 11133
Indianapolis, IN 46201-0133
317-357-6855

CASH RICH COMPANIES

Covers stocks. Quantitative and fundamental analysis. Gives insight into the forty most widely traded stocks cash positions (net quick cash).
$24/yr. Monthly
135 Beechwood Lane
Kingston, TN 37763
615-376-2732

CHARLES CUMMINGS K.I.$.$.

Covers stocks, bonds, asset allocation. Fundamental analysis. Editor Charles Cummings is a private investor. Uses a portfolio model. Includes guest columns.
$144/yr. 13 times/yr.
R.R. 6
Guelph, ON N1H-6J3, Canada

THE CHARTIST

Technical analysis. Covers stocks and market timing. Has hotline. Uses technical analysis to time the market and choose stocks. Has proprietary indicators. Buys stocks with high relative strength. The Actual Cash Account model portfolio actually tracks a real-world portfolio owned by the Sullivan family. It is for long-term investors. The Trader's Portfolio is for the short to intermediate term. Includes the views of leading investment advisers.
$150/yr. Every 3 weeks—HR
P.O. Box 758
Seal Beach, CA 90740
310-596-2385

THE CHEAP INVESTOR

Covers stocks. Fundamental analysis. Focuses on stocks under $5.00. Contains buy recommendations, with follow-up.
$87/yr. Monthly
Mathews and Associates, Inc.

2549 W. Golf Road
Hoffman Estates, IL 60194
708-830-5666

THE CLEAN YIELD
Covers stocks and asset allocation.
Fundamental and technical analysis.
Gives specific buy and sell recommen-
dations on socially responsible compa-
nies.
$95/yr. Monthly—HR
Clean Yield Publications
P.O. Box 1880
Greensboro Bend, VT 05842
802-533-7178

COLLEGE OF COMMON SENSE
  BULLETIN
Covers stocks and bonds. Fundamen-
tal analysis. Makes specific stock and
bond purchase recommendations and
economic forecasts.
$48/yr. Monthly
Steve Garrett and Associates
P.O. Box 66115
Arcadia, CA 91066
818-355-7666

THE COMPLETE STRATEGIST
Covers mutual funds, stocks, and derivatives. Fundamental and technical
analysis. Has model portfolio with buy
and sell targets, predicts market direction.
$50/yr. Monthly
Wall Street On-Line Publishing
P.O. Box 6
Riverdale, NY 10471
212-884-5408

COMPUTERIZED INVESTING
Covers investment software. Gives reviews and news of new and upcoming
investment software.
$60/yr. ($30 for AAII members)
  Every 2 months

American Association of Individ-
  ual Investors (AAII)
625 N. Michigan Avenue
Chicago, IL 60611-3110
312-280-0170

THE CONCORDIA LETTER
Covers stocks. Fundamental and technical analysis. Makes specific recommendations. Has stock market hotline.
$140/yr. Biweekly
656 Harbor Road
Southport, CT 06490
203-227-0856

CONSENSUS OF INSIDERS
Covers stocks. Fundamental and technical analysis. Makes stock recommendations based on insiders and
specialists and discusses institutional
impact on the market.
$72/yr. Quarterly
P.O. Box 24349
Ft. Lauderdale, FL 33307-4349
305-772-7186

CONSERVATIVE SPECULATOR
Covers stocks. Fundamental and technical analysis. Gives in-depth review
of small-cap companies. Includes
model portfolio.
$198/yr. Monthly
Guidera Publishing Corporation
3 Myrtle Bank Road
Hilton Head, SC 29926
803-681-3399

THE CONTRARIAN'S VIEW
Fundamental analysis. Covers stocks.
Follows a strategy of placing limit orders placed below market. Cash positions are a reflection of the number of
limit orders that have been filled. Has
both conservative and aggressive portfolios.
$39/yr. 11 times/yr.—HR

132 Moreland Street
Worcester, MA 01609
508-757-2881

THE CONTRARY INVESTOR

Covers stocks, bonds, and asset allocation. Fundamental analysis. Recommends specific stocks based upon a
contrarian speculative strategy.
$95/yr. Biweekly
Fraser Management Associates,
  Inc.
P.O. Box 494
309 S. Willard Street
Burlington, VT 05402
802-658-0322

CURRENT YIELD

Covers bonds and asset allocation.
Fundamental analysis. Makes recommendations on bond purchases as well
as asset allocation. Includes bond
funds.
$80/yr. Monthly
Ostrander Asset Management
711 N.E. Windrose Court, Ste. A
Kansas City, MO 64155
816-468-7521

CYCLES RESEARCH

Covers bonds, stocks, and commodities. Technical analysis. Makes recommendations on stock market cycles.
Hotline available to subscribers and
nonsubscribers for an additional fee.
$200/yr. Monthly
Advertising and Marketing Strate-
  gies
1314 Alps Drive
McLean, VA 22102
703-448-3358

CYCLE WATCH

Covers stocks, bonds, options, commodities. Technical analysis. Includes
charts with commentary, identifies

market tops and bottoms. Has a hotline for an additional fee.
$179/yr. Monthly
6987 N. Oracle Road
Tucson, AZ 85704
800-677-0120

THE DAILY STOCKWATCH

Covers Canadian stocks. Fundamental
analysis. Includes reports published by
companies listed on the Vancouver
Stock Exchange, review of annual and
semiannual reports, shareholder control changes, etc.
$395/yr. Daily, weekly, monthly.
Canjex Publishing, Ltd.
700 W. Georgia Street
Box 10371, Pacific Centre
Vancouver, BC V7Y-1J6, Canada
604-687-1500

DESSAUER'S JOURNAL OF FINAN-
CIAL MARKETS

Covers stocks. Fundamental analysis.
Provides analysis and advice on world
financial markets and their relation to
the U.S. stock market.
$195/yr. Twice monthly
P.O. Box 1718
Orleans, MA 02653
(800) 272-7550; 508-255-1651

DICK DAVIS DIGEST

Fundamental and technical analysis.
Covers stocks and mutual funds (stock
and bond). This newsletter looks at
over 400 newsletters and creates a
twelve-page digest. Gives the stock
market predictions and recommendations of many newsletter writers.
$165/yr. Biweekly
P.O. Box 350630
Ft. Lauderdale, FL 33335-0630
800-654-1514, x.1325

THE DINES LETTER
Covers stocks and precious metals. Technical analysis. Makes specific buy and sell recommendations on precious metals; includes information on metals markets as well as portfolio strategies. Fax service available for an additional fee.
$195/yr. Twice monthly—HR
James Dines
P.O. Box 22
Belvedere, CA 94920
800-84-LUCKY

DOW THEORY FORECASTS
Fundamental and technical analysis. Covers stocks and market timing. Uses Dow theory to time the market, but mainly uses fundamental analysis to choose stocks. Has conservative and aggressive model portfolios.
$233/yr. Weekly—HR
7412 Calumet Avenue
Hammond, IN 46324
219-931-6480

DOW THEORY LETTERS
Covers stocks, mutual funds, and precious metals. Technical analysis. Focuses primarily on investment trends, includes some general investment recommendations.
$250/yr. Biweekly—HR
P.O. Box 1759
La Jolla, CA 92038
619-454-0481

DOWBEATERS
Covers stocks. Fundamental analysis. Includes overlooked and emerging growth stocks, makes specific stock recommendations.
$100/yr. Monthly
Peter DeAngelis, CFA
P.O. Box 284

Ionia, NJ 07845
201-543-4860

DRIP INVESTOR
Fundamental and some technical analysis. Covers stocks (DRIPs). This letter covers dividend reinvestment plans (DRIPs) exclusively. Tells you which firms are starting DRIPs, what changes are being made to existing DRIP programs, and discusses investment strategies. It even covers overseas DRIP programs. Has model portfolios.
$79/yr. Monthly
7412 Calumet Avenue
Hammond, IN 46324
219-931-6480

THE DYNAMIC INVESTOR
Covers stocks. Fundamental and technical analysis. Makes specific buy and sell recommendations on small-cap and -growth stocks.
$158/yr. Monthly—HR
8010 S. Highway 101
Ukiah, CA 95482
800-743-6960

THE ECONOMY AT A GLANCE
Covers economics. Fundamental analysis. Includes graphs of economic trends with commentary. Also has calendar of economic data release dates.
$160/yr. Monthly
Argus Research Corporation
17 Battery Place
New York, NY 10004
212-425-7500

THE EHRENKRANTZ REPORT
Covers stocks. Fundamental analysis. Highlights a specific stock each month. Has model portfolio.
$120/yr. Monthly
635 Madison Avenue

New York, NY 10022
800-867-8600; 212-407-0575

ELECTRIC UTILITY RANKINGS
Covers utility stocks. Fundamental analysis. Selects five or six specific utility stocks to review and makes buy, sell, or hold recommendations. Includes a subscription to *Electric Utility Spotlight*.
$225/yr. Monthly
Argus Research Corporation
17 Battery Place
New York, NY 10004
212-425-7500

ELECTRIC UTILITY SPOTLIGHT
Covers utility stocks. Fundamental analysis. A general overview of the electric utilities industry. Includes a subscription to *Electric Utility Rankings*.
$225/yr. Monthly
Argus Research Corporation
17 Battery Place
New York, NY 10004
212-425-7500

THE ELLIOTT WAVE THEORIST
Technical analysis. Covers market timing for stocks and bonds. Has hotline. Mr. Prechter uses the Elliott wave theory to time the markets. He does not give specific recommendations.
$233/yr. Monthly—HR
P.O. Box 1618
Gainesville, GA 30503
800-336-1618; 770-536-0309

EMERGING AND SPECIAL SITUATIONS
Covers stocks. Fundamental analysis. S&P analysts point out lesser-known small stocks and new issues before they go public.
$259/yr. Monthly—HR

Standard & Poor's
25 Broadway
New York, NY 10004
800-777-4858; 212-208-8768

EMERGING PROFIT NEWSLETTER
Covers stocks. Fundamental analysis. Specializes in high-tech companies' stock. Makes specific recommendations and includes model portfolio.
$120/yr. Monthly
26127 Edgemont Drive
Highland, CA 92346

ENVIRONMENTAL INVESTING NEWS
Covers stocks. Fundamental analysis. Focuses on environmental industry, including news and new regulations. Highlights several companies each issue.
$108/yr. Monthly
Robert Mitchell Associates
2 Cannon Street
Newton, MA 02161-9923
617-244-7819

EQUITIES SPECIAL SITUATIONS
Fundamental analysis. Covers OTC stocks. Includes a special-situation buy recommendation on a monthly basis. Portfolio consists of previous buy and hold recommendations.
$175/yr. Monthly—HR
P.O. Box 1708
Riverton, NJ 08077
800-237-8400, x.61

EXECUTIVE STOCK REPORT
Covers stocks. Fundamental analysis. Includes performance and financial data on 7,000 publicly held companies.
$236/yr. Monthly
$182/yr. Quarterly
Media General Financial Services

301 E. Grace Street
Richmond, VA 23219
800-446-7922

EXECUTIVE WEALTH ADVISORY
Covers stocks, bonds, and mutual
funds. Fundamental and technical
analysis. An all-encompassing guide to
personal investment management.
$72/yr. Twice monthly
National Institute of Business
   Management, Inc.
1328 Broadway
New York, NY 10001
800-543-2054; 212-971-3300

THE FED TRACKER
Covers stocks, bonds, and futures.
Fundamental analysis. Overview of
economy and its effect on financial
markets. Makes specific recommendations.
$96/yr. Monthly
Seraphim Press
4805 Courageous Lane
Carlsbad, CA 92008
619-720-0107

FINANCE OVER 50
Covers stocks, bonds, and mutual
funds. Fundamental analysis. Gives
conservative investment, tax, and real
estate advice. Aimed at older investors
who want less risk.
$79/yr. Monthly
The Ron Jackson Company
661 Calmar Avenue, Ste. 1002
Oakland, CA 94610

FINANCIAL WORLD
Covers stocks, mutual funds, and business news. Fundamental analysis. In
every issue stocks and mutual funds
are given a letter grade. Does not have
a specific portfolio. Also includes general business news, and interviews.

$37.50/yr. Biweekly—HR
P.O. Box 10750
Des Moines, IA 50340
800-666-6639

**FORBES SPECIAL SITUATION SUR-
VEY**
Covers stocks. Fundamental analysis.
Gives advice on speculative investments, makes specific recommendations.
$495/yr. Monthly
**Forbes Investors Advisory Insti-
   tute, Inc.**
60 Fifth Avenue
New York, NY 10011
212-620-2210

FORD VALUE REPORT
Fundamental analysis. Covers stocks.
The "Ford Value Report" provides
data for 2,680 stocks. Has two proprietary tools: the price/value ratio and
the earnings trend. Also covers foreign
markets. Does not have a model portfolio, but it does have a section called
"Selected Stocks."
$120/yr. Monthly—HR
Ford Investor Services
11722 Sorrento Valley Road, Ste. I
San Diego, CA 92121
619-755-1327

FORECASTS & STRATEGIES
Covers stocks, bonds, and mutual
funds. Fundamental analysis. Gives advice on low-risk, capital preservation
strategies. Makes specific recommendations.
$139/yr. Monthly
Phillips Publishing, Inc.
7811 Montrose Road
Potomac, MD 20854
301-340-2100

FOREIGN MARKETS ADVISORY
Fundamental analysis. Covers foreign stocks. Follows stock markets and economies for forty countries. Has a listing of foreign stocks traded in the U.S. and a model portfolio.
$225/yr. Monthly—HR
Muller Associates, Inc.
Box 75
Fairfax Station, VA 22039
703-425-5961

FRANKLIN'S INSIGHT
Covers stocks, bonds, and mutual funds. Fundamental analysis. Gives investment advice for investing in socially responsible companies. Has model portfolio.
$195/yr. Monthly
Franklin Research & Development
711 Atlantic Avenue
Boston, MA 02111
617-423-6655

THE FRASER OPINION LETTER
Covers economics and business. Fundamental analysis. Gives commentary on economic and business trends.
$70/yr. Biweekly
Fraser Management Associates, Inc.
309 S. Willard Street
Burlington, VT 05402
802-658-0322

F.X.C. INVESTORS CORP.
Fundamental analysis. Covers stocks. Mr. Curzio discusses the background of companies, their financial position, and other data (including S&P rank and Value Line rank) along with his recommendations. Does not have a model portfolio.
$190/yr. Biweekly—HR
62-19 Cooper Avenue

Glendale, NY 11385
800-FXC-0992; 718-417-1330

THE GARSIDE FORECAST
Technical analysis. Covers stocks, bonds, and market timing. Has hotline. Mr. Garside relies heavily on proprietary indicators to time markets. Part of his technique involves contra-trend signals.
$125/yr. Biweekly—HR
5200 Irvine Boulevard, #370
Irvine, CA 92720
714-259-1670

GLOBAL BUSINESS CONDITIONS
Covers economic conditions. Fundamental analysis. Has charts and commentary of world economic conditions, including GDP, currency, and stock market information.
$95/yr. Monthly
802 Main Street
P.O. Box 849
Cedar Falls, IA 50613
319-268-0441

GLOBAL MARKET PERSPECTIVE
Covers stocks, bonds, commodities, and currencies. Technical analysis. Includes charts and commentary on over twenty global equity markets.
$599/yr. Monthly
Elliot Wave International
P.O. Box 1618-B
Gainesville, GA 30503
800-472-9283; 404-534-6680

THE GLOBAL MARKET STRATEGIST
Covers stocks, bonds, commodities. Gives technical analysis of financial markets using Elliot wave analysis.
$297/yr. Monthly
Supercycle Research, Inc.
P.O. Box 5309-H

Gainesville, GA 30504
800-633-1332; 404-967-1332

GLOBAL RESEARCH
Covers stocks. Fundamental analysis.
A catalog of over 50,000 reports each
year on companies worldwide.
$95/yr. 10 times yearly
Nelson Publications
1 Gateway Plaza
Port Chester, NY 10573
800-333-6357

**GOERLICH/VAN BRUNT NEWSLET-
TER**
Covers stocks. Technical analysis.
Covers stock market timing, and in-
cludes bullish list of 50–75 stocks.
$160/yr. Bimonthly
604 S. Washington Square,
Ste. 2715
Philadelphia, PA 19106
215-923-8870

**GOING PUBLIC: THE IPO RE-
PORTER**
Reports on initial public offerings
(IPOs) of common stock. Lists offerings that are coming to market and reviews stocks that have recently been
issued.
$950/yr. Weekly
IDD Enterprises
2 World Trade Center
New York, NY 10048
212-432-0045

GOLD AND GOLD STOCKS
Covers stocks. Fundamental analysis.
Gives advice on investing in junior
gold-mining stocks. Makes specific
recommendations with model portfo-
lio.
$99/yr. Approx. weekly
Taylor Hard Money Advisors, Inc.
P.O. Box 770871

Woodside, NY 11377
718-457-1426

GOLD MINING STOCK REPORT
Covers stocks. Fundamental analysis.
Gives analysis with specific recom-
mendations on penny gold stocks
traded on the Vancouver exchange.
$119/yr. Monthly
Target, Inc.
Box 1217
Lafayette, CA 94549-1217
510-283-4848

GOLD NEWS
Covers gold. Fundamental and technical analysis. Includes current gold
price trends and research items. Has a
gold price chart.
$25/yr. Bimonthly
Gold Institute
1112 16th Street N.W., Ste. 240
Washington, DC 20036
202-835-0185

GOLD NEWSLETTER
Covers gold. Fundamental analysis.
Gives commentary on the general
economy and how it relates to gold
prices.
$95/yr. Monthly
Jefferson Financial, Inc.
2400 Jefferson Highway, Ste. 600
Jefferson, LA 70121
800-877-8847; 504-837-3033

GOLD STOCKS ADVISORY
Covers stocks. Fundamental analysis.
Gives commentary on financial, eco-
nomic, and other news related to gold-
mining shares.
$96/yr. Monthly
Box 1437
Burnsville, MN 55337

GOLF INSIGHT AND INVESTING

Covers golf stocks. Fundamental and technical analysis. Includes news briefs, emerging company updates, golf market trends, and market perspectives of the twenty-four-company golf stock market.
$99/yr. Monthly
LSI Publishing
P.O. Box 151438
San Diego, CA 92175
800-494-6539

GOOD MONEY

Covers stocks, bonds, and mutual funds. Fundamental analysis. Lists socially responsible mutual funds, gives performance and social analysis of each fund.
$75/yr. Bimonthly
Good Money Publications
P.O. Box 363
Worcester, VT 05682
800-535-3551

GRANT'S INTEREST RATE OBSERVER

Covers stocks, bonds, and mutual funds. Fundamental analysis. Includes analysis of the credit market and interest rate movements, as well as other economic issues.
$450/yr. Every other Friday.
233 Broadway
New York, NY 10279
212-608-7994

THE GRANVILLE MARKET LETTER

Technical analysis. Covers stocks and market timing. Has hotline. Gives commentary on the market and various indicators. During bearish times, Mr. Granville lists stocks called "crash proof stocks." Has recommendations including short sale recommendations.
$250/yr. 46 times/yr.—HR

P.O. Drawer 413006
Kansas City, MO 64141
816-474-5353

GROWTH STOCK OUTLOOK

Fundamental analysis. Covers stocks. Has hotline. Mr. Allmon believes that no one can time the market. He seeks undervalued stocks to be held for years. Contains model portfolio. Sends out quarterly reports that cover junior growth stocks, new issues, utility stocks, and bank stocks.
$195/yr. Biweekly—HR
P.O. Box 15381
Chevy Chase, MD 20825
800-742-5476; 301-654-5205

GUARDIAN RESEARCH REPORT

Covers stocks. Fundamental analysis. Gives commentary on the stock market. Includes two model portfolios.
$180/yr. Monthly
Guardian Financial Corporation
2207 Third Street
Livermore, CA 94550
510-443-7010

HARRY BROWNE'S SPECIAL REPORTS

Covers stocks, bonds, mutual funds, options, and futures/commodities. Fundamental and technical analysis. Includes model portfolio and recommendations for a conservative strategy and another for an aggressive strategy.
$225/yr. 8–10 times/yr.—HR
P.O. Box 5586
Austin, TX 78763
800-531-5142; 512-453-7313

HEIM INVESTMENT LETTER

Covers stocks, options, futures/commodities. Fundamental and technical analysis. Includes studies on all national and international issues affecting financial markets.

$150/yr. Biweekly
Heim Investment Services, Inc.
P.O. Box 19435
Portland, OR 97219
503-228-9553

THE HULBERT FINANCIAL DIGEST

Fundamental and technical analysis. Covers stocks, bonds, and mutual funds (stock and bond). This newsletter ranks and analyzes other newsletters and is the unofficial watchdog of the newsletter industry. Has profiles of top performers, stock and mutual fund recommendations from newsletter writers, the consensus opinion of market timers, and more.

$135/yr. Monthly
316 Commerce Street
Alexandria, VA 22314
703-683-5905

THE HUME MONEYLETTER

Covers stocks, bonds, mutual funds. Fundamental analysis. Includes several authors, each of whom makes specific recommendations. Updates previous recommendations.

$95/yr. Bimonthly
Hume Publishing, Inc.
835 Franklin Court
Marietta, GA 30067
800-222-4863; 404-426-1920

HUSSMAN ECONOMETRICS

Fundamental analysis. Covers stocks, bonds, mutual funds (stock and bond), and market timing. Has hotline. Dr. Hussman has developed a tool called "conditional excess yield." This is the yield of a security above what it should be in an efficient market. Dr. Hussman's method is to buy securities with excessive yields and to sell when

yields are not excessive. He also uses other fundamental data as well. This yield-based method is also used in his market timing. Has model portfolios.

$195/yr. Monthly—HR
P.O. Box 3199
Farmington Hills, MI 48333
800-487-7626; 810-553-8383

INCOME STOCKS

Covers stocks. Fundamental analysis. Makes recommendations on stocks that have high dividend yields.

$45/yr. Annual
4016 S. Michigan Street
South Bend, IN 46614-3823
800-553-5866

INDEPENDENT INVESTOR DIGEST

Covers stocks. Surveys newsletters that have the best performance, according to *Hulbert Financial Digest,* and screens their recommendations down to a workable list from which investors can select.

$249/yr. Weekly
Independent Investor Digest
P.O. Box 270487
West Hartford, CT 06127-0487
800-491-7119; 860-313-0242

INDIVIDUAL INVESTOR SPECIAL SITUATIONS REPORT

Covers stocks. Fundamental analysis. Every month *Individual Investor* picks one stock to recommend and do an in-depth report on.

$150/yr. Monthly—HR
Financial Data Systems, Inc.
38 E. 29th Street, 4th Floor
New York, NY 10016
800-321-5200; 212-689-2777

INDUSTRISCOPE

Covers stocks and bonds. Includes fi-

nancial data on 7,000 companies listed by industry.
$324/yr. Monthly
Media General Financial Services
P.O. Box 85333
Richmond, VA 23293
800-446-7922; 804-649-6587

INDUSTRY FORECAST
Covers economy. Fundamental analysis. Updates current economic conditions and makes economic forecasts.
$250/yr. Monthly
The Jerome Levy Economic Forecasts
P.O. Box 26
Chappaqua, NY 10514
914-238-8470

INSIDER ALERT
Covers stocks. Fundamental analysis. Reports on how political events affect the financial markets.
$87/yr. Monthly
Soundview Publications
1350 Center Drive, #100
Dunwoody, GA 30338
800-728-2288; 404-668-0432

INSIDER REPORT
Covers stocks. Fundamental analysis. Reports insider trading activity of corporate officers, including name, title, price per share, and number of shares.
$199/yr. Monthly
P.O. Box 84903
Phoenix, AZ 85071
800-528-0559; 602-252-4477

THE INSIDERS
Fundamental analysis. Covers stocks. Has hotline. Provides information on insider trading activity. Ranks groups according to insider trading; has ratings on many stocks; has market indi-

cators based on insider trading. Has model portfolio.
$100/yr. Biweekly—HR
The Institute for Econometric Research
2200 S.W. 10th Street
Deerfield Beach, FL 33442
800-442-9000

INSIGHTFUL INVESTOR
Covers stocks and bonds. Technical and fundamental analysis. Gives editor's analysis on stocks and bonds.
$59/yr. Monthly
Agora, Inc.
824 E. Baltimore Street
Baltimore, MD 21202-4799
800-433-1528; 401-234-0515

INSTITUTIONAL PORTFOLIO GUIDE
Covers U.S. and Canadian stocks and mutual funds. Fundamental analysis. Lists positions held by large investment management companies in the U.S. and Canada.
$695/yr. Quarterly
Vickers Stock Research Corp.
226 New York Avenue
Huntington, NY 11743
516-423-7710

INTELLIGENCE REPORT
Covers mutual funds and stocks. Fundamental analysis. Gives investment advice with specific recommendations and model portfolio.
$99.95/yr. Monthly
Phillips Business Information, Inc.
1201 Steven Locks Road
Potomac, MD 20854-3394
800-677-5005

INTERINVEST REVIEW AND OUTLOOK
Covers stocks. Fundamental analysis.

Reviews global financial markets and related political issues.
$125/yr. Monthly
Interinvest Corporation
294 Washington Street, Ste. 754
Boston, MA 02108
617-423-1166

The International Harry Schultz Letter

Covers stocks. Fundamental analysis. Approaches investing from a global perspective. Includes commentary on investing, politics, and other assorted subjects. Gives specific and general recommendations.
$275/yr. Monthly—HR
P.O. Box 622
FERC
CH-1001, Lausanne
Switzerland
32-16-533684

Investech Market Analyst

Fundamental and technical analysis. Covers stocks, bonds, and market timing. Has hotline. James Stack has done extensive work to make technical analysis more of a science than an art. He blends monetary analysis of the Federal Reserve with technical analysis of the stock market. Has one of the largest private databanks of financial information in America. Avoids undue risk. Has model portfolio. Also includes InvesTech Mutual Fund Advisor, which covers stock and bond funds.
$160/yr. Every 3 weeks—HR
2472 Birch Glen
Whitefish, MT 59937
800-955-8500; 406-862-7777

Investing with Barry Ziskin

Fundamental and technical analysis. Covers stocks and market timing. Mr.

Ziskin is a global investor. Has a global model portfolio.
$129/yr. Monthly—HR
824 E. Baltimore Street
Baltimore, MD 21202
410-234-0691

Investment Guide

Covers stocks. Fundamental analysis. Gives stock market analysis and trading strategies.
$49/yr. Monthly
American Investment Services, Inc.
Division Street
Great Barrington, MA 01230
413-528-1216

Investment Horizons

Fundamental analysis. Covers stocks. Dr. Perritt highlights a handful of small-cap stocks in each issue. Each highlight includes fundamental information such as revenues, earnings, beta, etc. Also lists all of the stocks that are currently recommended.
$250/yr. Biweekly—HR
680 N. Lake Shore Drive
2038 Tower Offices
Chicago, IL 60611
800-326-6941

Investment Quality Trends

Fundamental and technical analysis. Covers stocks and market timing. Geraldine Weiss believes that an investor is buying a stream of dividend payments, so one should buy stocks that have high dividends. She examines about 350 blue chip stocks and ranks them. Has model portfolio.
$275/yr. Biweekly—HR
7440 Girard Avenue, Ste. 4
La Jolla, CA 92037
619-459-3818

INVESTMENT REPORTER

Covers stocks. Fundamental analysis. Gives analysis of Canadian stocks, includes specific stock recommendations. Has hotline for an additional fee.
$275/yr. Weekly—HR
MPL Communications, Inc.
133 Richmond Street West, Ste. 700
Toronto, ON M5H-3M8, Canada
416-869-1177

INVESTOR FORECASTS

Covers stocks, bonds, mutual funds, commodities. Technical and fundamental analysis. Gives timing on stock, bond, mutual fund, and commodity purchases. Highlights undervalued stocks.
$195/yr. Every 3 weeks
Asset Management Research Corp.
P.O. Box 352016
4440 N. Oceanshore Boulevard
Palm Coast, FL 32135
904-446-0823

INVESTOR'S DIGEST

Fundamental and technical analysis. Covers stocks and market timing. Has hotline. Gives the stock market predictions and recommendations of many newsletter writers.
$100/yr. Monthly
The Institute for Econometric Research
2200 S.W. 10th Street
Deerfield Beach, FL 33442
800-442-9000; 305-421-1000

INVESTOR'S FAX WEEKLY

Covers stocks. Fundamental analysis. Uses a computer screening model to pick stocks, based on earnings, new

highs, shares outstanding, institutional ownership, and market movement.
$150/yr. Weekly
12335 Santa Monica Boulevard, Ste. 128
Los Angeles, CA 90025
900-535-9800; 213-479-0645 x.627

INVESTORS INTELLIGENCE

Fundamental and technical analysis. Covers stocks, bonds, mutual funds (stock and bond), and market timing. Has hotline. One of the oldest newsletters in existence. Is most famous for its sentiment indicator, which measures how bullish or bearish various newsletter writers are. Searches for investments that have been unpopular for a long time and are becoming popular. Uses point and figure charts and relative strength. Also prints the views of other newsletters. Has model portfolios, including Fidelity mutual fund portfolios.
$184/yr. Biweekly—HR
P.O. Box 2046
30 Church Street
New Rochelle, NY 10801
914-632-0422

IRA STOCKS

Covers stocks. Fundamental analysis. Selects stocks with strong earnings and a good dividend history that the author feels would be suitable for an IRA investment.
$45/yr. Annual
4016 S. Michigan Street
South Bend, IN 46614-3823
800-553-5866; 219-291-3823

IT'S YOUR MONEY/THE JORGENSEN REPORT

Covers stocks, bonds, and mutual funds. Fundamental analysis. A general

financial planning information newsletter.
$45/yr. Annual
Jorgensen & Associates, Inc.
810 Idyllberry Road
San Rafael, CA 94903
800-359-6267; 415-472-6265

J&J'S UNDERVALUED GROWTH STOCKS LETTER
Covers stocks. Fundamental analysis. Needs IBM-compatible PC for electronic delivery. Makes specific recommendations and has a model portfolio based on a value/growth model.
$135/yr. Weekly
J&J Market Letters
1112 Bering Drive, Ste. 65
Houston, TX 77057
800-992-6123

JACOBS REPORT ON ASSET PROTECTION STRATEGIES
Covers stocks, bonds, mutual funds, and general investment planning. Fundamental analysis. An easy-to-understand newsletter directed at the novice with advice on estate and retirement planning.
$145/yr. Monthly
Research Press, Inc.
4500 W. 72nd Terrace
P.O. Box 8137
Prairie Village, KS 66208-2824
913-362-9667

JAY TAYLOR'S GOLD AND GOLD STOCKS
Covers gold stocks. Fundamental and technical analysis. Gives coverage of the gold industry as a whole, including special situations. Has model portfolio.
$89/yr. Monthly
Taylor Hard Money Advisors, Inc.
P.O. Box 1065

Jackson Heights, NY 11372
718-457-1426 (weekly hotline)

JOHN BOLLINGER'S CAPITAL GROWTH LETTER
Covers stocks, bonds, gold, and asset allocation. Technical and fundamental analysis. Makes specific investment recommendations based on Bollinger Band analysis. Has a hotline updated weekly, and daily Bollinger Band numbers.
$169/yr. Monthly
P.O. Box 3358
Manhattan Beach, CA 90266
800-888-8400; 213-545-0610

JOURNAL PHONE
Covers economic and company news as well as stock quotes. 24-hour hotline covering all news items is updated continuously. The 800 number requires a credit card for access, while 900 calls are billed to the telephone used. To receive more information before using, call 800-345-NEWS.
$.75 per minute.
Dow Jones Information Services
World Financial Center
200 Liberty Street
ew York, NY 10281
800-800-4WSJ; 900-JOURNAL

KEN GERBINO'S SMART INVESTING
Covers stocks, bonds, mutual funds, and asset allocation. Fundamental analysis. Directed toward novice investors. Gives economic analysis and investment strategy.
$139/yr. Monthly
Phillips Publishing, Inc.
7811 Montrose Road
Potomac, MD 20854
800-777-5005; 301-424-3700

KENNETH J. GERBINO INVESTMENT LETTER

Covers stocks and commodities. Fundamental analysis. Focuses on gold and gold stocks. Includes stock market strategy with editorial and analysis.
$78/yr. Monthly
Ken Gerbino and Co.
9595 Wilshire Boulevard
Ste. 200
Beverly Hills, CA 90212
213-550-6304

THE KIPLINGER WASHINGTON LETTER

Covers stocks, bonds, and mutual funds. Fundamental analysis. Includes business and economic news and forecasts. In publication for over seventy years.
$63/yr. Weekly
1729 H Street N.W.
Washington, DC 20077-2733
800-544-0155; 202-887-6400

KIRKPATRICK'S MARKET STRATEGIST

Covers stocks. Fundamental and technical analysis. A weekly fax of recommended stocks generated from a computer database. Includes a monthly newsletter with market commentary.
$495/yr. Weekly
Kirkpatrick & Co.
Box 1066
Exeter, NH 03833-1066
603-772-5551

THE KON-LIN LETTER

Covers stocks. Fundamental and technical analysis. Features a list of thirty to thirty-five stocks under $10 that editor feels have strong growth potential. Makes suggestions on market timing based on technical analysis.
$95/yr. Monthly
Kon-Lin Research and Analysis Corporation
5 Water Road
Rocky Point, NY 11778
516-744-8536

LA LOGGIA'S SPECIAL SITUATION REPORT AND STOCK MARKET FORECAST

Covers stocks and bonds. Fundamental analysis. Gives market analysis and economic outlook. Picks short-sell and takeover candidates.
$230/yr. Every 3 weeks—HR
P.O. Box 167
Rochester, NY 14601
800-836-4330

THE LANCZ LETTER

Covers stocks. Fundamental analysis. Gives market commentary, includes a number of model portfolios with different objectives.
$250/yr. Monthly
Alan B. Lancz and Associates, Inc.
3930 Sunforest Court, #110
Toledo, OH 43623
419-474-6733

LONG-TERM VALUES

Covers stocks. Technical analysis. Fifteen-year graphs on over 4,000 stocks. Also includes earnings, sales, and beta information.
$227/yr. Every 6 weeks
Daily Graphs
William O'Neil & Co.
P.O. Box 24933
Los Angeles, CA 90024-0933
310-448-6843

LOUIS RUKEYSER'S WALL STREET

Covers stocks, bonds, mutual funds. Fundamental analysis. Compilation of

recommendations and forecasts from different analysts.
$39/yr. Monthly
1101 King Street, Ste. 400
Alexandria, VA 22314
800-892-9702

THE LOW-PRICED STOCK SURVEY
Covers stocks. Fundamental analysis. Makes specific recommendations for stocks priced under $15 from a broad range of industries.
$96/yr. Biweekly
Dow Theory Forecasts, Inc.
7412 Calumet Avenue
Hammond, IN 46324-2692
219-931-6480

LOW-PRICED STOCKS
Covers stocks. Fundamental analysis. Makes specific recommendations for low-priced stocks with strong earnings and dividends records.
$45/yr. Annual
4016 S. Michigan Street
South Bend, IN 46614-3823
800-553-5866

LYNCH INTERNATIONAL INVESTMENT SURVEY
Covers stocks and bonds. Fundamental analysis. Has a model portfolio and makes specific recommendations.
$175/yr. Weekly
Lynch-Bowes, Inc.
301 Main Street, Ste. 206
Port Washington, NY 11050-2705
516-883-7094

MARGO'S MARKET MONITOR
Covers stocks and mutual funds. Fundamental and technical analysis. Includes charts and three model portfolios for long-term investors.
$125/yr. Twice monthly—HR

Margo Parrish/Minuteman Publishing Co.
P.O. Box 642
Lexington, MA 02173
617-861-0302

MARKET ACTION
Covers stocks, mutual funds, futures, and options. Technical and fundamental analysis. Has techniques for low-risk trading strategies based upon market timing.
$69/yr. Biweekly
New Era Trading Company
6205 S. Mirror Lake Drive
Sebastian, FL 32958

MARKET BEAT
Covers stocks. Technical analysis. Has a proprietary trading signal that it claims has outperformed the Dow. Predicts market highs and lows. Includes hotline.
$150/yr. Monthly
Market Beat, Inc.
1436 Granada
Ann Arbor, MI 48103
313-426-2146

MARKET CYCLE INVESTING
Covers stocks, bonds, and mutual funds. Fundamental analysis. Editor gives his opinion of financial trends and market cycles.
$140/yr. 17 times per year
Andrews Publications
995 Oak Park Drive
Morgan Hill, CA 95037
408-778-2925

MARKET LOGIC
Fundamental and technical analysis. Covers stocks and market timing. Has hotline. Looks at monetary policy, fundamentals, technical trends, and sentiment to forecast the market. Em-

ploys a long-term approach; some stocks are held for years. Contains model portfolios.
$200/yr. Biweekly—HR
The Institute for Econometric Research
2200 S.W. 10th St.
Deerfield Beach, FL 33442
800-442-9000

MARKET MANIA
Covers stocks. Fundamental analysis. Follows growth and value stocks under $20. Also includes insider buying and other special situations. Has hotline.
$119/yr. Monthly
Market Mania, Inc.
P.O. Box 1234
Pacifica, CA 94044
415-952-8853

MARKET MOMENTUM
Covers mutual funds and stocks. Tries to determine markets' direction using technical analysis. Makes specific buy and sell recommendations. Includes hotline for an additional charge.
$175/yr. Monthly
Thomas D. Kienlen Corp.
P.O. Box 2245
Jasper, OR 97438
800-999-3303

MARKET MONTH
Covers stocks. Fundamental analysis. Provides current market information in order to present new opportunities to individual investors. Makes specific buy, sell, and portfolio recommendations.
$53/yr. Monthly
Standard & Poor's
25 Broadway
New York, NY 10004
212-208-8000

MARKET TREND ANALYSIS
Covers stocks. Technical analysis. Has a weekly market trend analysis and special report.
$260/yr. Weekly
631 U.S. Highway 1
North Palm Beach, FL 33408
800-345-0186

MARKET-SCAN REPORT
Covers stocks. Fundamental and technical analysis. Screens a universe of over 6,500 stocks to find top performers and then features reports on the stock.
$69/yr. Monthly
Hamilton Asset Management
303 Congress St.
Boston, MA 02210
800-237-8400 x.722

THE MARKETARIAN LETTER
Covers stocks, mutual funds, commodities. Technical and fundamental analysis. Includes specific stock recommendations and industry analysis. Has model portfolio and hotline for an additional fee.
$225/yr. Every 3 Weeks—HR
Marketarian, Inc.
P.O. Box 1283
Grand Island, NE 68802-1283
800-658-4325; 308-381-2121

MARPLES BUSINESS NEWSLETTER
Covers stocks and bonds. Fundamental analysis. Focuses on economy of the Pacific Northwest. Includes company profiles.
$72/yr. Every other Wednesday
117 W. Mercer St.
Seattle, WA 98119-3960
206-622-0155

MASTER INDICATOR OF THE STOCK MARKET

Covers stocks. Technical analysis. Uses technical analysis to determine leading industries and stocks.
$79/yr. Every 3 weeks
P.O. Box 3024
West Palm Beach, FL 33402
407-793-8316

MCALVANY INTELLIGENCE ADVISOR

Covers stocks, options, commodities. Fundamental and technical analysis. Economic review of economic and political trends that impact the precious-metal markets.
$95/yr. Monthly
Research Publications
P.O. Box 84904
Phoenix, AZ 85071
800-528-0559 in Colorado

MEDICAL TECHNOLOGY STOCK LETTER

Fundamental analysis. Covers stocks and market timing. Has hotline. Discusses medical technology and gives recommendations. Many of the companies are young and have volatile stock prices, so editor buys and holds on. Has model portfolios.
$320/yr. Biweekly—HR
P.O. Box 40460
Berkeley, CA 94704
510-843-1857

MIDDLE/FIXED INCOME LETTER

Covers stocks, bonds, mutual funds. Fundamental analysis. Designed to educate beginning investors on various financial instruments.
$45/yr. Monthly
MASTCA Publishing Corp.
P.O. Box 55
Loch Sheldrake, NY 12759
914-794-5792

MOMENTUM

Covers stocks, mutual funds, market timing, and convertible bonds. Fundamental analysis. Has stock and mutual fund analysis by industry and includes specific buy and sell recommendations. Has six model portfolios.
$88/yr. Monthly
7516 Castlebar Road
P.O. Box 470146
Charlotte, NC 28226
704-365-4070

MONDAY MORNING MARKET MEMO

Covers stocks, bonds, and asset allocation. Fundamental and technical analysis. Recap of market as well as predictions for intermediate term. Makes stock recommendations.
$200/yr. Weekly
Ehrenkrantz King Nussbaum, Inc.
635 Madison Ave.
New York, NY 10022
212-407-0576

MONETARY AND ECONOMIC REVIEW

Covers options, stocks, commodities/futures, and precious metals. Fundamental analysis. Domestic and international economic and political review. Includes educational segments and a book review.
$150/yr. Monthly
FAMC, Inc.
3500 JFK Parkway
United Bank Building
Fort Collins, CO 80525
800-325-0919

MONEYLINE

Covers stocks, bonds, and mutual funds. Telephone service providing stock quotes, CD rates, and interest rates.

$0.95/minute; continuously up-
dated
USA Today
1000 Wilson Blvd.
Arlington, CA 22229
800-USA-0001; 900-555-5555

THE MONEYPAPER

Covers bonds and stocks. Fundamental analysis. Has market outlook and
makes specific recommendations. Includes model portfolio.
$72/yr. Monthly
Temper of the Times Communi-
   cations, Inc.
1010 Mamaroneck Avenue
Mamaroneck, NY 10543
914-381-5400

MONEY REPORTER

Covers Canadian stocks. Fundamental
analysis. Provides general investment
and financial information.
$197/yr. Biweekly
MPL Communications
133 Richmond Street West, Ste.
700
Toronto, ON M5H-3M8, Canada
416-869-1177

MORNINGSTAR INTERNATIONAL
   STOCKS

Fundamental analysis. Covers stocks.
Previously *Morningstar ADR's*. Covers
700 foreign stocks that trade in the
United States. Each ADR page contains a business summary, sales segments, interim results, and balance
sheet information. Also has graphs, annual data for the past ten years,
growth rates, and valuation ratios. It
even tells you which mutual funds
have the largest positions in a particular ADR. All information is translated
into U.S. dollars. Has written analyst
evaluations.

$295/yr. Biweekly
Morningstar
225 W. Wacker Drive
Chicago, IL 60606
800-876-5005; 312-696-6000

MOTION PICTURE INVESTOR

Covers stocks. Fundamental analysis.
Gives analysis of motion-picture
stocks and reports industry news.
$550/yr. Monthly
Paul Kagan Associates, Inc.
126 Clock Tower Place
Carmel, CA 93923-8734
408-624-1536

MPT REVIEW

Fundamental analysis. Covers stocks.
Has hotline. Louis Navellier stays fully
invested; he does, however, change
his stock picks depending upon market conditions. He favors stocks that
have done well with the least amount
of volatility. Has many model portfolios that differ in dollar amounts and
range from conservative to aggressive.
$225/yr. Monthly
P.O. Box 10012
Incline Village, NV 89450
800-454-1395; 702-831-1396

MYERS FINANCE REVIEW

Covers stocks and precious metals.
Fundamental analysis. Gives overview
of world economy and makes recom-
mendations based on observations.
$149/yr. Monthly
Myers Finance and Energy
P.O. Box 3082
Spokane, WA 99220
509-534-7132

NATIONAL ASSOCIATION OF IN-
   VESTORS CORPORATION'S IN-
   VESTOR ADVISORY SERVICE

Covers stocks. Fundamental analysis.

Selects three stocks for purchase recommendations, gives detailed information on selected stocks.

$108/yr. Monthly
National Association of Investors Corp.
1515 E. Eleven Mile Road
Royal Oak, MI 48067
313-543-0612

NEW ISSUES

Fundamental analysis. Covers stocks. Has hotline. Provides information on initial public offerings including recommendations and a calendar of upcoming offerings.

$200/yr. Monthly—HR
The Institute for Econometric Research
2200 S.W. 10th Street
Deerfield Beach, FL 33442
800-442-9000

NEW ISSUES OUTLOOK

Fundamental analysis. Covers stocks. General commentary about new issues market, plus description of companies coming to market with offerings. Includes financial summary.

$435/yr. 35 issues
National Corporate Sciences, Inc.
50 Main Street
White Plains, NY 10606
800-477-3331; 914-421-1500

THE NEY STOCK AND FUND REPORT

Fundamental and technical analysis. Covers stocks, mutual funds, and market timing. Has hotline. Mr. Ney has a unique method of choosing stocks: He watches what the specialists on the stock exchanges are doing. A specialist is a person that is assigned to buy and sell a particular stock and provide liquidity for that stock; a specialist, in a sense, controls or influences the price of the stock he/she is assigned. Mr. Ney buys when the specialists are accumulating and sells when they are distributing. Has model portfolios.

$195/yr. Monthly—HR
P.O. Box 92223
Pasadena, CA 91109
800-444-2044; 818-441-2222

NIELSEN'S INTERNATIONAL INVESTMENT LETTER

Covers stocks, bonds, commodities, asset allocation. Fundamental analysis. General investment newsletter. Makes specific buy and sell recommendations.

Free to clients. Frequency varies.
P.O. Box 7532
Olympia, WA 98507

THE OBERWEIS REPORT

Fundamental analysis. Covers stocks. Has commentary on the market, the economy, and individual stocks. Covers smaller, more speculative companies that are growing rapidly. The model portfolio is for the investor that accepts high volatility in return for potentially superior performance.

$119/yr. Monthly—HR
One Constitution Drive
Aurora, IL 60506
800-323-6166

O.I.L.: OIL INCOME LETTER

Covers stocks and mutual funds. Fundamental analysis. Gives analysis of current events in the oil industry, and advises on oil and gas funds as investments and tax shelters.

$145/yr. Monthly
Securities Investigations, Inc.
Mill Hill Road
P.O. Box 888

Woodstock, NY 12498
914-679-2300

ON THE WIRES

Covers business news. Recap of prior news highlights.
Free monthly
Dow Jones News Services
Dow Jones and Company, Inc.
P.O. Box 300
Princeton, NJ 08543-0300
800-223-2274

OTC GROWTH STOCK WATCH

Focuses on small companies with sales of under $100 million annually. Criteria for stock selection also includes a minimum 2-to-1 current ratio, minimal long-term debt, and rapid earnings growth for previous two years. Includes hotline.
$299/yr. Monthly
OTC Research Corp.
1040 Great Plain Ave.
Needham, MA 02192
617-327-8420

OTC INSIGHT

Fundamental and technical analysis. Covers stocks. Has hotline. Has a very quantitative approach to choosing over-the-counter (OTC) stocks. Though technical analysis is used, the newsletter is fully invested at all times. But as market conditions change, the average beta (volatility) of a model portfolio will be adjusted. This newsletter takes substantially more risk than the market. Has many model portfolios.
$295/yr. Monthly—HR
P.O. Box 5759
1656 N. California Boulevard
Ste. 300
Walnut Creek, CA 94596
800-955-9566; 510-274-5000

THE OUTLOOK

Fundamental analysis. Covers stocks, bonds, and mutual funds (stock and bond). Provides commentary on the economy, the markets, and has model portfolios.
$298/yr. Weekly—HR
Standard & Poor's
25 Broadway
New York, NY 10004
800-852-1641

OUTSTANDING INVESTOR DIGEST

Covers stocks. Fundamental analysis. Includes monthly interviews with money managers and gives their investment philosophies.
$495/yr. Monthly
Portfolio Reports
14 E. 4th Street, Ste. 501
New York, NY 10012
212-777-3330

OVERPRICED STOCK SERVICE

Covers stocks. Fundamental analysis. Gives short-selling opportunities, has hotline updated twice weekly.
$495/yr. Monthly
P.O. Box 308
Half Moon Bay, CA 94019
415-762-8495

THE PAD SYSTEM REPORT

Fundamental analysis. Covers stocks, mutual funds, and market timing. Has hotline. The PAD system has a long-term approach and may hold stocks for years, but it also raises cash when stocks are too high. Has model portfolios.
$195/yr. Monthly—HR
P.O. Box 43285
Cincinnati, OH 45243
513-529-2863

PEARSON INVESTMENT LETTER
Covers stocks. Fundamental analysis.
Analyzes current economic conditions
and makes specific stock recommendations.
$150/yr. Monthly
1628 White Arrow
Dover, FL 33527
813-659-2560

THE PENNY STOCK ANALYST
Covers stocks. Fundamental analysis.
Gives specific recommendations on
penny stocks.
$45/yr. Monthly
P.O. Box 333
Woodstock, MD 21163-0333

PERSONAL FINANCE
Covers stocks, bonds, and mutual
funds. Fundamental analysis. Includes
a model portfolio and an investment
strategy; also discusses other financial
issues of interest.
$59/yr. Bimonthly—HR
KCI Communications, Inc.
1101 King Street, Ste. 400
Alexandria, VA 22314
800-832-2330

THE PETER DAG PORTFOLIO
   STRATEGY AND MANAGEMENT
Fundamental and technical analysis.
Covers stocks, bonds, mutual funds
(stock and bond), and market timing.
Has mutual fund model portfolios
(Vanguard, Fidelity) and a stock
model portfolio. Also gives asset allo-
cation recommendations.
$195/yr. Biweekly—HR
Peter Dag and Associates, Inc.
65 Lake Front Drive
Akron, OH 44319
800-833-2782; 216-644-2782

THE PETER DAG INVESTMENT
   LETTER
Covers stocks, bonds, mutual funds,
and asset allocation. Fundamental
analysis. Helps readers develop an investment strategy, also makes market
forecasts.
$250/yr. 29 times/yr.
Peter Dag and Associates, Inc.
65 Lake Front Drive
Akron, OH 44319
800-833-2782; 216-644-2782

PETROLEUM OUTLOOK
Covers stocks. Fundamental and technical analysis. Analyzes developments
in the petroleum, oil, and oil services
industries.
$520/yr. Monthly
5 Edgewood Avenue
Greenwich, CT 06830
203-869-2585

THE PHILADELPHIA ADVISOR
Covers stocks, options, and commodities. Technical analysis. Makes recommendations based on technical
analysis, has hotline.
$595/yr. Bimonthly
P.O. Box 1369
Woodstock, GA 30188
404-591-7030

PLAIN TALK INVESTOR
Covers stocks. Fundamental and technical analysis. Has a model portfolio,
which it follows up with news and
selling points.
$115/yr. Every 3 weeks
Plain Talk Investor, Inc.
1500 Skokie Boulevard, Ste. 203
Northbrook, IL 60062
708-564-1955

PORTFOLIO REPORTS
Covers stocks. Fundamental analysis.

Includes stock purchases by seasoned money managers. Lists ten most-purchased stocks.
$575/yr. Monthly
Outstanding Investor Digest, Inc.
14 E. 4th Street
New York, NY 10012
212-777-3330

PORTFOLIO SELECTOR

Covers stocks. Fundamental analysis. Makes specific stock recommendations for each major investment objective. Includes commentary on recommended stocks.
$390/yr. Monthly
Argus Research Corporation
17 Battery Place
New York, NY 10004
212-425-7500

PORTFOLIOS INVESTMENT ADVISORY

Covers stocks. Fundamental analysis. General investment newsletter.
$150/yr. Monthly
Box 997
Lynchburg, VA 24505-0997
804-384-3261

POWER AND VELOCITY RATINGS

Covers stocks. Technical analysis. Charting service covering about 700 stocks, has relative strength rankings.
$260/yr. Weekly
631 U.S. Highway 1
North Palm Beach, FL 33408
800-345-0816

PQ WALL FORECASTS, INC.

Covers stocks. Fundamental analysis. Makes specific stock recommendations. Includes editor's market commentary and timing theories. Hotline available for an additional fee.
$198/yr. Monthly—HR

P.Q. Wall
P.O. Box 15558
New Orleans, LA 70175
800-259-0088

THE PROFESSIONAL TAPE READER

Technical analysis. Covers stocks, mutual funds, and market timing. Has hotline. Stan Weinstein has dozens of indicators that make up his "weight of the evidence" method of timing the market. He first looks at whether we are in a bull or bear market; he then analyzes which sectors are attractive and unattractive; then he chooses individual stocks and mutual funds.
$295/yr. Biweekly—HR
P.O. Box 2407
Hollywood, FL 33022
800-868-7857

PROFESSIONAL TIMING SERVICE

Fundamental and technical analysis. Covers stocks, bonds, mutual funds (stock and bond), and market timing. Has hotline. Mr. Hesler uses a trading system called the "supply/demand formula" that he claims was developed in the 1930s and has been used ever since then. He uses the supply/demand formula to time the market. For mutual fund trades he uses a system called "Dynamo." It is designed for low-risk mutual fund trading. Dynamo is based on how money flows into the stock market. He also has a model to time the bond market. Has model portfolios, including one that uses the Rydex family of funds (one Rydex fund shorts the stock market, and another Rydex fund shorts the bond market).
$185/yr. Monthly—HR
Curtis Hesler
P.O. Box 7483

Missoula, MT 59807
406-543-4131

THE PRIMARY TREND

Covers stocks, bonds, and mutual
funds. Fundamental analysis. Gives editor's comments on the market with
specific stock recommendations.
$180/yr. Every 3 weeks
Arnold Investment Counsel, Inc.
First Financial Center
700 N. Water Street
Milwaukee, WI 53202
800-443-6544; 414-271-2726

PRING MARKET REVIEW

Covers stocks, options, and mutual
funds. Technical analysis. Makes market timing recommendations based on
technical analysis.
$395/yr. Monthly
International Institute for Eco-
    nomic Research
P.O. Box 329
Washington Depot, CT 06794
800-221-7514; 203-868-7772

THE PRUDENT SPECULATOR

Fundamental and technical analysis.
Covers stocks and market timing. Al
Frank's personal portfolio is listed in
his letter as well as other recommended stocks. Uses value investing
for stock selection with technical analysis for market timing.
$175/yr. Monthly—HR
P.O. Box 1767
Santa Monica, CA 90406
310-587-2410

RATIONAL INVESTMENT OUTLOOK

Covers stocks and mutual funds.
Technical analysis. Uses a proprietary
method to forecast market and make
specific stock and mutual fund recom-

mendations. Includes advice on in-
vestment strategies.
$139/yr. Monthly
Vilner Enterprises, Inc.
Bowling Green Station
P.O. Box 1605
New York, NY 10274-1132

REIT WATCH

Covers REITs. Fundamental analysis.
Reviews industry performance, activities, comparative return, and general
industry news.
$145/yr. Quarterly
National Association of Real Es-
    tate Investment Trusts, Inc.
1129 20th Street N.W., Ste. 705
Washington, DC 20036
202-785-8717

RETIREMENT LETTER

Covers stocks and mutual funds. Fundamental analysis. Editor gives economic and market outlook, and
provides analysis of eighty-three mutual funds. Has two model portfolios.
$49/yr. Monthly
Phillips Publishing, Inc.
7811 Montrose Road
Potomac, MD 20854
800-722-9000

RICHARD E. BAND'S PROFITABLE INVESTING

Covers stocks, bonds, and cash. Fundamental analysis. Takes a broader
perspective than most investment
newsletters. Has a "Total Return
Portfolio," which includes stocks,
bonds, and cash. More conservative
than most investment letters. Has a
telephone hotline.
$99/yr. Monthly—HR
Phillips Publishing, Inc.
7811 Montrose Rd.

Potomac, MD 20854
301-424-3700

RICHARD RUSSELL'S DOW THEORY LETTERS
Covers stocks, mutual funds, and commodities. Fundamental and technical analysis. Gives information on the stock and bond markets, makes general recommendations.
$49.91/yr. Biweekly
P.O. Box 1759
La Jolla, CA 92038
619-454-0481

RICHARD YOUNG'S INTELLIGENCE REPORT
Covers stocks. Fundamental analysis. Explains how to build wealth without building principal, includes three model portfolios and specific recommendations.
$99.95/yr. Monthly
Phillips Publishing, Inc.
7811 Montrose Rd.
Potomac, MD 20854
800-777-5005; 301-340-2100

THE RICHLAND REPORT
Covers stocks, mutual funds, and market timing. Technical and fundamental analysis. General overview of the market including analysis of the McClellan Oscillator.
$197/yr. Biweekly
P.O. Box 222
La Jolla, California 92038
619-459-2611

RICK DUPUIS "INSIDE MONEY" NEWSLETTER
Covers all investments. Fundamental analysis. Useful investment ideas from Rick Dupuis, the host of *Inside Money* on PBS.
Free

2061 Boca Raton Boulevard.
Suite 103
Boca Raton, FL 33431
800-749-6785

RISK FACTOR METHOD OF INVESTING
Covers stocks. Technical and fundamental analysis. Has charts and editor's commentary on the market. Has model portfolio.
$100/yr. Monthly
Invest/O
65575 Sisemore Road
P.O. Box 5996
Bend, OR 97708-5996
503-389-3676

THE RISK REPORT
Covers stocks, bonds, and mutual funds. Technical analysis. Investment newsletter directed toward the beginner. Also has a fax and on-line service for an additional fee.
$199/yr. Every 3 weeks
3479 N. High Street
Columbus, OH 43214
800-466-RISK

THE ROESCH MARKET MEMO
Covers stocks and asset allocation. Technical and fundamental analysis. Reviews effect of economics and politics on the financial markets, makes specific recommendations. Has model portfolio.
$42/yr. Monthly
P.O. Box 4242
Shawnee Mission, KS 66204
913-381-0857

THE RON PAUL SURVIVAL REPORT
Covers stocks, bonds, and mutual funds. Fundamental analysis. Makes specific recommendations for conservative investments.

$99/yr. Monthly
Ron Paul & Associates
18333 Egret Bay, Ste. 265
Houston, TX 77058
713-333-4888

THE RUFF TIMES
Covers stocks, bonds, and mutual
funds. Fundamental analysis. Makes
investment recommendations based on
long-term market trends.
$89/yr. Every 3 weeks—HR
757 South Main
Springville, UT 84663
801-489-0222

**THE RUTA FINANCIAL NEWSLET-
TER**
Covers stocks. Fundamental analysis.
Editor gives reports on all kinds of dif-
ferent stocks. Has hotline.
$90/yr. Monthly
P.O. Box 952
Bronxville, NY 10708
800-832-1891; 914-779-1983

SAFE MONEY REPORT
Covers stocks, bonds, and mutual
funds. Fundamental analysis. Includes
articles relating to government bonds,
interest rates, and more.
$145/yr. Monthly
Weiss Research, Inc.
2200 N. Florida Mango Road
West Palm Beach, FL 33409
800-289-9222; 407-684-8100

SAN DIEGO STOCK REPORT
Covers stocks. Fundamental and technical analysis. Provides coverage analysis of the 110 publicly traded
companies headquartered in San Diego.
$99/yr. Monthly
LSI Publishing
P.O. Box 151438

San Diego, CA 92175
800-494-6539

SARCOH REPORT
Covers general investments. Fundamental and technical analysis. Advises
readers on conservative investments,
makes specific recommendations. Has
hotline.
$165/yr. 20–24 issues/yr.
Sarcoh Report, Inc.
48 Park Terrace
Spring Valley, NY 10977
914-354-0030

SCIENTIFIC INVESTMENTS
Covers stocks. Fundamental analysis.
Reports on emerging tech stocks with
high growth potential.
$49/yr. Monthly—HR
Predictions Agora, Inc.
824 E. Baltimore Street
Baltimore, MD 21202-4799
410-234-0691

SELECT INFORMATION EXCHANGE
Not a newsletter but a service for obtaining trial issues of investment newsletters. Dozens of top newsletters from
which to choose.
244 E. 54th Street
New York, NY 10019
800-743-9346; 212-247-7123

SENTINEL INVESTMENT LETTER
Covers stocks, bonds, mutual funds.
Fundamental analysis. Reports on
events that affect the markets. Discusses buying and selling opportunities.
$150/yr. Monthly
Hanover Investment Management
    Corp.
P.O. Box 189
52 S. Main Street

New Hope, PA 18938
215-862-5454

SHELBURNE SECURITIES FORE-
CAST
Covers stocks. Fundamental analysis.
Reports on utility stocks.
$49/yr. Twice monthly
P.O. Box 5566
Arlington, CA 22205
703-532-4416

SHORTEX
Covers stocks. Fundamental and technical analysis. Makes recommendations
for short sales, includes cover- and
stop-loss price.
$249/yr. Biweekly
6669 Security Boulevard, #201
Dept. S
Baltimore, MD 21207-4024
800-877-6555

SMART MONEY
Covers stocks. Fundamental analysis.
Reports on little-known companies
that have good investment potential.
$98/yr. Monthly
The Hirsch Organization
6 Deer Trail
Old Tappan, NJ 07675
201-664-3400

SOUND ADVICE
Covers stocks and commodities. Fundamental and technical analysis. Includes features such as: Business Cycle
Signals, The Stock Market Risk Indicator, Precious Metals, and Portfolio
Update.
$150/yr. Monthly—HR
370 Diablo Road, Ste. 201
Danville, CA 94526
800-423-8423

SOUTHEAST BUSINESS ALERT
Covers stocks and bonds. Fundamental analysis. Features business based in
the Southeast, gives charts, insider
trading activity, and business summary.
$198/yr. Monthly
Word Merchants, Inc.
2000 Riveredge Parkway
Atlanta, GA 30328
404-984-0151

SPECIAL INVESTMENT SITUATIONS
Covers stocks. Fundamental analysis.
Focuses on speculative stock opportunities, includes a description of the
company, financial data, and the reason for the recommendation.
$160/yr. Monthly
P.O. Box 4254
Chattanooga, TN 37405
615-886-1628

SPECIAL SITUATION
Covers stocks. Fundamental analysis.
Makes a specific recommendation in
every other issue. Updates quantitative
data on previous recommendations.
$390/yr. Monthly
Argus Research Corporation
17 Battery Place
New York, NY 10004
212-425-7500

SPECIAL SITUATION NEWSLETTER
Covers stocks. Fundamental analysis.
Profiles and analyzes selected companies, and recommends investment
strategies.
$100/yr. Monthly
150 Nassau Street, Room 1926
New York, NY 10038
212-908-4168

SPECIAL SITUATION REPORT
Covers stocks. Fundamental and tech-

nical analysis. Gives commentary on what to look for in a takeover target, and makes other recommendations based on insider transactions.
$230/yr. Every 3 weeks
P.O. Box 167
Rochester, NY 14601
716-232-1240

SPECIAL SITUATION REPORT
Covers stocks. Fundamental analysis. Features small-cap stocks. Includes research reports with specific buy and sell recommendations.
$195/yr. Monthly
Individual Investor
P.O. Box 2484
Secaucus, NJ 07094-2484
800-995-1695

THE SPECULATOR
Covers stocks. Fundamental and technical analysis. Specializes in low-priced stock-buying opportunities, makes specific stock recommendations.
$175/yr. Every 3 weeks
Growth in Funds, Inc.
77 South Palm Avenue
Sarasota, FL 34236
813-954-0330

THE SPRINGFIELD REPORT
Covers stocks. Technical and fundamental analysis. Includes market and economic commentary, and specific stock recommendations.
$95/yr. Monthly
1131 West B Street, Ste. 4
Ontario, CA 91762
909-984-7423

STANDARD & POOR'S THE EDGE
Covers stocks. Fundamental analysis. Has a model portfolio based on recommendations from 2,500 securities

brokerage analysts combined with S&P selection strategies.
$360/yr. Twice monthly
Standard & Poor's
25 Broadway
New York, NY 10004
800-777-4858; 212-208-8768

STANDARD & POOR'S TRENDLINE CHART GUIDE
Covers stocks. Fundamental and technical analysis. Includes data, charts, and analysis on over 4,400 listed and OTC stocks.
$108/yr. Monthly
Standard & Poor's
25 Broadway
New York, NY 10004
800-777-4858

THE STOCK OF THE MONTH CLUB
Covers stocks. Fundamental and technical analysis. Profiles a top performing stock monthly, selected from a universe of 6,500 stocks.
$119/yr. Monthly
8 Park Plaza
Suite 417
Boston, MA 02117
800-237-8400 x.722

STOCKMARKET CYCLES
Covers stocks and mutual funds. Technical analysis. Has two model portfolios: one made up of Fidelity sector funds, and the other of stocks. Has a telephone hotline.
$198/yr. Every 3 weeks—HR
P.O. Box 6873
Santa Rosa, CA 95406
707-579-8444

STRAIGHT TALK ON YOUR MONEY
Covers general finance. Fundamental analysis. Gives advice on individual financial planning.

$39.50/yr. Monthly
7811 Montrose Road
Potomac, MD 20854
800-777-5005

STRATEGIC INVESTMENTS
Covers stocks. Fundamental analysis.
Focuses on bearishness about the U.S.
economy and stock market. Includes
three very aggressive portfolios and
one very conservative portfolio. Has a
hotline for an additional cost.
$59/yr. Monthly—HR
824 E. Baltimore Street
Baltimore, MD 21202
410-234-0691

STRENGTH INDICATOR REPORT
Covers stocks. Fundamental and technical analysis. Uses a proprietary technique that graphically shows readers
institutional investor accumulation
patterns in growth stocks.
$125/yr. Monthly
LSI Publishing
P.O. Box 151438
San Diego, CA 92175
800-494-6539

SYSTEMS AND FORECASTS
Technical analysis. Covers stocks,
bonds, mutual funds (stock and bond),
and market timing. Gerald Appel's approach to technical analysis is more
statistical than that of other technicians. He is a short-term trader who
keeps portfolio risk low. His model
portfolios can be quite active, generating several signals per year.
$225/yr. Biweekly—HR
150 Great Neck Road, Ste. 301
Great Neck, NY 11021
800-829-6224; 516-829-6444

TECHNICAL ALERT LETTER
Covers general finance. Technical and

fundamental analysis. Gives general
commentary on the market and general investment advice, includes two
model portfolios.
$75/yr. Monthly
P.O. Box 893
Floral City, FL 32636
904-726-1339

**TECHNICAL TRENDS—THE INDI-
CATOR ACCURACY SERVICE**
Covers stocks. Technical analysis.
Chart service, includes market com-
mentary.
$147/yr. Weekly
Technical Trends
P.O. Box 7115
Jupiter, FL 33468
800-736-0229; 203-762-0229

TIMER DIGEST
Fundamental and technical analysis.
Covers stocks, bonds, mutual funds,
and market timing. Has hotline. Mr.
Schmidt monitors dozens of market
timers and rates their timing performance. He also constructs timing indicators out of the predictions of the top
ten timers, and he has his own proprietary timing indicator. Also has model
portfolios.
$225/yr. Every 3 weeks—HR
P.O. Box 1688
Greenwich, CT 06836
800-356-2527

THE TURNAROUND LETTER
Focuses on bankrupt and financially
distressed companies with low-priced
stocks. Recommends out-of-favor
companies in turnaround situations.
$195/yr. Monthly—HR
New Generations, Inc.
225 Friend Street, Ste. 801
Boston, MA 02114
617-573-9550

TUXWORTHY STOCK ADVISORY
Covers stocks. Fundamental and technical analysis. Gives market commentary and includes proprietary "market direction indicator." Has model portfolio.
$180/yr. Monthly
P.O. Box 33794
Decatur, GA 30033-0794
404-325-8348

U.S. INVESTMENT REPORT
Covers stocks. Fundamental analysis. Includes two model portfolios based on aggressive and conservative models. Makes specific buy and sell recommendations with price targets.
$228/yr. Biweekly—HR
25 Fifth Avenue, #4-C
New York, NY 10003
212-995-2963

UNITED & BABSON INVESTMENT REPORT
Fundamental analysis. Covers stocks, bonds, and mutual funds (stock and bond). Has concise coverage of Washington developments, key business barometers, and other factors affecting the market. Gives guidance on personal and estate planning. Has model portfolios. Also publishes the views of other newsletter writers.
$268/yr. Monthly—HR
Babson-United Building
101 Prescott Street
Wellesley Hills, MA 02181
617-235-0900

VALUE INVESTING LETTERS
Covers stocks. Fundamental analysis. Gives market commentary and stock-picking strategy. Makes specific stock recommendations.
$55/yr. 8 times/yr.
41 Sutter Street, #1355

San Francisco, CA 94104
415-776-5622

VALUE LINE CONVERTIBLES
Covers bonds and stocks. Fundamental analysis. Gives strategies on building a portfolio of convertibles and managing risk.
$475/yr. Weekly—HR
Value Line, Inc.
711 Third Avenue
New York, NY 10017
800-633-2252; 212-687-3965

VALUE LINE INVESTMENT SURVEY
Fundamental and technical analysis. Covers stocks. Value Line ranks 1,700 stocks into five groups based on their potential over the next twelve months. Each weekly update also analyzes 130 stocks grouped by industry; these full-page reports include a long-term stock chart, financial statement information, institutional ownership, and projections from Value Line. Value Line has one of the largest independent staff of stock analysts in the world, and their investment survey is very comprehensive. Has model portfolios.
$525/yr. Weekly—HR
Value Line, Inc.
P.O. Box 3988
New York, NY 10008
800-833-0046

VANCOUVER STOCKWATCH
Covers Canadian stocks. Fundamental analysis. An informational newsletter covering every stock on the Vancouver exchange.
$395/yr. Weekly
Canjex Publishing, Ltd.
700 W. Georgia Street
Box 10371
Pacific Centre

Vancouver, BC V7Y-136, Canada
800-267-7400

THE VENTURE CAPITAL PORTFO-LIO

Covers stocks. Technical analysis. Analyzes stocks of companies that have been financed by professional venture capitalists. Has model portfolio and hotline available at an additional charge.
$195/yr. Monthly
Zin Investment Services
7 Switchbud Place, #192-312
The Woodlands, TX 77380
713-363-1000

VENTURE RETURNS

Covers stocks, bonds, and options. Fundamental analysis. Gives economic and market commentary. Makes specific recommendations.
$75/yr. Twice monthly
1855 N.W. Tyler Avenue
Corvallis, OR 97330
503-758-4706

VICKERS WEEKLY INSIDER REPORT

Covers stocks. Fundamental analysis. Covers and analyzes insider transactions on listed and OTC stocks.
$97/yr. Weekly—HR
Vickers Stock Research Corp.
226 New York Avenue
Huntington, NY 11743
800-645-5043; 516-423-7710

THE VOLUME REVERSAL SURVEY

Covers stocks and options. Technical analysis. Makes specific buy and sell recommendations based on volume analysis.
$360/yr. Every 3 weeks
Almarco Trading Corp.
P.O. Box 1451

Sedonia, AZ 86336
800-554-5551

VOMUND INVESTMENT SERVICES FAX ADVISORY

Covers mutual funds and stocks. Fundamental and technical analysis. Uses AIQ TradingExpert software to analyze market timing, industry timing, and stock selection.
Stock Alert: $298/yr. Weekly
Fund Alert: $238/yr. Weekly
Vomund Investment Services
P.O. Box 6253
Incline Village, NV 89450
702-831-1544

WALL STREET BARGAINS

Covers mutual funds and stocks. Fundamental analysis. Covers low-priced stocks and mutual funds between $5 and $25.
$39/yr. Monthly
KCI Communications, Inc.
1101 King Street, Ste. 400
Alexandria, VA 22314
800-832-2330

THE WALL STREET DIGEST

Covers stocks and bonds. Fundamental analysis. Compiles investment advice from leading investment advisers.
$150/yr. Monthly—HR
1 Sarasota Tower, #602
2 N. Tamiami Trail
Sarasota, FL 34236
813-954-5500

THE WALL STREET GENERALIST

Covers mutual funds and stocks. Fundamental and technical analysis. Devises long-term investment strategies based on computer-generated models.
$160/yr. Every 3 weeks
800 Sarasota Quay

Sarasota, FL 34236
813-366-5645

**WASHINGTON INTERNATIONAL
   BUSINESS REPORT**
Covers general investments. Fundamental analysis. Reports on major
government developments impacting
international commerce.
$288/yr. Monthly
IBC, Inc.
818 Connecticut Avenue N.W.
Ste. 1200
Washington, DC 20006
202-872-8181

**WATER INVESTMENT NEWSLET-
   TER**
Covers stocks. Fundamental analysis.
Provides data and news of companies
in the water industry. Has model
portfolio.
$140/yr. Monthly
U.S. Water News, Inc.
230 Main Street
Halstead, KS 67056
800-251-0046

WELLINGTON LETTER
Covers stocks, bonds, mutual funds,
and commodities. Fundamental analysis. Analysis of financial markets and
the economy; makes specific stock
recommendations.
$45/yr. Monthly
Wellington Financial Corp.
733 Bishop Street, Ste. 1800
Honolulu, HI 96813
800-992-9989; 808-524-8063

**WORLD INVESTMENT STRATEGIC
   EDGE**
Covers bonds, stock, and commodities. Fundamental analysis. Includes
market commentary and makes specific recommendations for stock,

bond, currency, and commodity in-
vestments.
$395/yr. 20 times/yr.
Pinnacle Capital Management
P.O. Box 135
Cooper Station
New York, NY 10276-0135
212-254-6613

WORLDWIDE INVESTMENT NEWS
Covers stocks, bonds, and mutual
funds. Fundamental analysis. Gives advice on international investment opportunities and an international
resources directory.
$90/yr. Monthly
Offshore Banking News Service
301 Plymouth Drive N.E.
Dalton, GA 30721-9983
770-259-6035

THE ZWEIG FORECAST
Covers stocks and market timing.
Technical analysis. Martin Zweig's
main concern is never to get badly
hurt. His goal is to capture most of
the profits of a bull market while
avoiding the large declines of a bear
market. He uses thirty-six technical
indicators combined with a monetary
model of twenty-two interest-rate and
Fed indicators. He uses stock-index
futures and options to quickly change
exposure, so some investors will not
be able to follow his recommendations
precisely. Has model portfolio. Has
hotline.
$265/yr. Every 3 weeks
P.O. Box 360
Bellmore, NY 11710
516-223-3800

**THE ZWEIG PERFORMANCE RAT-
   INGS REPORT**
Covers stocks. Fundamental analysis.
Gives numerical rankings (1 through

9) to 3,400 stocks for expected price performance over the next six months. $265/yr. Every 3 weeks—HR

P.O. Box 360
Bellmore, NY 11710
516-223-3800

Books—General Reference

The following three books are singled out because of their exhaustive information content. These were used in gathering some of the information for this book. They cover many investment topics other than stocks.

BARRON'S FINANCE AND INVESTMENT HANDBOOK

John Downes and Jordan Elliott Goodman. Barron's Educational Series, 1995.
$35.00 ISBN: 0-8120-6465-8
Reference book. 1,234 pages of reference information. Defines over 5,000 terms, has a directory of 4,000 major corporations, and has complete lists of brokerage firms. Also lists mutual fund firms, investment newsletters, and investment magazines. Discusses how to read an annual report, how to read the financial pages, and much more. Has historical data on various indexes.

THE INDIVIDUAL INVESTOR'S GUIDE TO COMPUTERIZED INVESTING

American Association of Individual Investors, 1995.
$24.95 pbk. ISBN: 0-942641-57-4
A comprehensive reference book that describes hundreds of software titles and information services related to investing.

THE INVESTOR'S INFORMATION SOURCEBOOK

Spencer McGowan. New York Institute of Finance, 1995.
$21.95 pbk. ISBN: 0-13-125162-7
Reference book. A well-organized catalog of possibly every product and service related to investments: books, newsletters, software, quote services, charts, periodicals, and research publications.

Books—General Stock Investing

AL FRANK'S NEW PRUDENT SPECULATOR

Al Frank. Irwin Professional, 1996.
$24.95 ISBN: 1-55738-873-3
The editor of *The Prudent Speculator* newsletter expounds on the investment philosophy and methodology that has earned his newsletter one of the highest performance rankings over the last fifteen years.

THE BEARDSTOWN LADIES' COMMON-SENSE INVESTMENT GUIDE

Hyperion, 1994.
$19.95 hc ISBN: 0-7868-6043-X
$10.95 pbk. ISBN: 0-7868-8120-8
Members of a Midwestern investment club discuss how their club functions; reveals their analytical methodology and the results. The members' favorite recipes are thrown in for good measure.

BEATING THE DOW
Michael O'Higgins. Harper-
   Collins, 1992.
$12.00 pbk. ISBN: 0-06-098404-X
Michael O'Higgins offers one of the
simplest methods for choosing stocks:
Only pick stocks that are part of the
Dow Jones Industrial Average. And
within those thirty Dow stocks choose
only one, five, or ten depending upon
your risk tolerance.

BEATING THE STREET
Peter Lynch. Simon & Schuster,
   1994.
$23.00 hc ISBN: 0-671-75915-9
$12.50 pbk. ISBN: 0-671-89163-4
Peter Lynch gives insights into how
he chooses stocks. He illustrates his
techniques by writing about his stock
picks from the 1992 Barron's Round-
table. He uses fundamental analysis
and common sense. And he describes
what happened to these stocks during
the next few months. He also discusses
his years as the manager of Fidelity
Magellan Fund and how to invest in
mutual funds.

**BUYING STOCKS WITHOUT A BRO-
   KER**
Charles B. Carlson. McGraw-Hill,
   1996.
$17.95 pbk. ISBN: 0-07-011501-X
Charles Carlson, editor of *DRIP Investor*, shows you how to invest using
dividend reinvestment plans (DRIPs).
These plans allow you to purchase
stocks directly from the company and
avoid paying a commission to a broker. Has a directory listing nearly
1,000 DRIPs; has a rating of every
DRIP; gives corporate profiles and
performance ratings; and has model
portfolios.

**CYBER-INVESTING: CRACKING
   WALL STREET WITH YOUR PER-
   SONAL COMPUTER**
David Brown and Kassandra
   Bentley. John Wiley & Sons,
   1995.
$49.95 hc ISBN: 0-471-11925-3
$24.95 pbk. ISBN: 0-471-11926-1
Kassandra Bentley and David Brown
(CEO of Telescan, Inc., an on-line
services firm) show you how to pick
stocks with your computer. They believe that 20 percent gains annually are
possible. The book includes a trial
subscription to Telescan's investment
service. Also includes software demos
and information from other firms.
Their approach combines fundamental
and technical analysis to choose stocks.

**THE DIVIDEND CONNECTION: HOW
   DIVIDENDS CREATE VALUE IN
   THE STOCK MARKET**
Geraldine Weiss and Gregory
   Weiss. Dearborn Financial,
   1995.
$24.95 ISBN: 0-7931-1022-X
Explores dividend yield theory and
how to use it in stock selection. Discusses when to sell as well as when to
buy. Relates to different objectives:
short-term, long-term, and current income requirements.

**DIVIDENDS DON'T LIE: FINDING
   VALUE IN BLUE-CHIP STOCK**
Geraldine Weiss and Janet Lowe.
   Dearborn Financial, 1989.
$23.95 hc ISBN: 0-88462-115-4
$12.95 pbk. ISBN: 0-7931-0023-2
Weiss, the editor of *Investment Quality
Trends*, shares her method of picking
stocks. She shows how to choose high-
quality blue chips and when to sell
them. Her approach relies heavily on
examining dividends. Topics include

why dividends are fundamental, identifying quality, bargains coming in cycles, undervalued stocks, the overvalued stage, and utility stocks. She also discusses planning a portfolio and investing in different market environments.

DIVINING THE DOW
Richard J. Maturi. Irwin Professional, 1993.
$24.95 ISBN: 1-55738-475-4
Profiles 100 theories, strategies, indicators, and predictors of stock price movements. If you're an investor in search of an investment philosophy, you'll find it here.

THE FRUGAL INVESTOR
Scott Spiering. AMACOM, 1995.
$21.95 hc ISBN: 0-8144-0270-4
Most people overlook the costs of investing. This book shows why cost should be a priority in creating a portfolio. Author shows how to build a low-risk, high-return portfolio by watching costs closely and by focusing on the long term. He covers dividend reinvestment programs, fixed-income investing, international investing, and indexing strategies. He also covers asset allocation and how to adjust the assets in the future.

THE GUIDE TO UNDERSTANDING FINANCIAL STATEMENTS
S. B. Costales and Geza Szurovy. McGraw-Hill, 1994.
$12.95 pbk. ISBN: 0-07-013197-X
This book is a helpful guide for those with no accounting background. Covers the balance sheet, income statement, and statement of cash flows. Also explains important ratios and how to analyze financial statements. Includes case studies.

THE HANDBOOK OF TECHNICAL ANALYSIS
Darrell R. Jobman, Editor. Probus, 1995.
$55.00 ISBN: 1-55738-597-1
This reference book covers virtually every major technical approach, and it has contributions from some of the top technicians. Each chapter is a self-contained unit.

THE HOMETOWN INVESTOR
Richard J. Maturi. McGraw-Hill, 1996.
$22.95 ISBN: 0-07-040944-7
Describes where and how to look for investment opportunities where you live. Deals not only with stocks of companies in your area but also municipal bonds, mutual funds, and even franchises.

HOW TO MAKE MONEY IN STOCKS
William J. O'Neil. McGraw-Hill, 1995.
$22.95 hc ISBN: 0-07-048059-1
$10.95 pbk. ISBN: 0-07-048017-6
William O'Neil, the founder of *Investor's Business Daily* and his own investment firm, shows readers a simple method to pick stocks. His C-A-N S-L-I-M system helps maximize profits while minimizing risk. His guidelines are based on looking at some of the best-performing stocks from the last few decades. He also discusses how to find a broker, keep efficient records, and the importance of diversification.

HOW TO PROFIT FROM READING ANNUAL REPORTS
Richard B. Loth. Dearborn Financial, 1993.
$19.95 pbk. ISBN: 0-79310-240-5
This book is aimed at investors eager

to learn about annual reports. It covers a wide range of topics from the auditors' report right down to some common footnotes. He shows how to read and analyze a balance sheet, income statement, and statement of cash flows.

How to Read a Financial Report

John A. Tracy. John Wiley & Sons, 1994.
$14.95 pbk. ISBN: 0-471-59391-5
Covers the balance sheet, income statement, and statement of cash flows as do many other authors; but he goes one step beyond and shows how the three statements relate to each other. His diagrams show how a number from the income statement goes into the balance sheet, which in turn shows up in the statement of cash flows.

The Hulbert Guide to Financial Newsletters

Mark Hulbert. New York Institute of Finance/Simon & Schuster, 1993.
$27.95 pbk. ISBN: 0-7931-0619-2
Mark Hulbert, editor of *The Hulbert Financial Digest,* ranks and discusses over 100 newsletters. He explains the methodologies used in his calculations for his newsletter. He discusses the factors involved in choosing a newsletter. Particularly useful is a discussion of risk and risk-adjusted performance.

The Intelligent Investor

Benjamin Graham. HarperCollins, 1973, 1986.
$30.00 ISBN: 0-06-015547-7
Ben Graham, one of the pioneers of value investing, offers his philosophy of investing. He focuses on the principles of long-term investing in this book rather than on an investment method. Also discusses the stock market in historical terms.

The Investment Club Book

John F. Wasik. Warner Books, 1995.
$11.99 pbk. ISBN: 0-446-67147-9
How to establish an investment club and the basics of analyzing and selecting stocks and mutual funds.

Investment Clubs

Kathryn Shaw. Dearborn Financial, 1995.
$14.95 pbk. ISBN: 0-7931-1345-8
Unlike the book above, this one deals strictly with the mechanics of starting a club and running it in a businesslike manner. Discusses finding the right members, legal requirements, creating a simple accounting system, and more.

Investor's Guide to the Net

Paul B. Farrell. John Wiley & Sons, 1996.
$24.95 ISBN: 0-471-14444-4
A thorough guidebook through the many investment resources accessible through the Internet: brokers, news services, databases, research reports, government data, newsletters, and investment clubs. In addition to services dealing with stocks, it also profiles services for bonds, mutual funds, futures, and options.

The Irwin Guide to Using the Wall Street Journal

Michael B. Lehman. Irwin Professional, 1996.
$29.95 ISBN: 0-7863-0483-9
Provides definitions of financial terms and discusses economic issues that will enhance reader's use of the *Journal.*

IT'S WHEN YOU SELL THAT COUNTS
Donald L. Cassidy. Irwin Professional, 1994.
$19.95 pbk. ISBN: 1-55738-594-7
Delves into the technical and psychological aspects of selling strategies. Treats an important topic that most investment books never address.

LEARN TO EARN
Peter Lynch and John Rothchild. Fireside, 1995.
$13.00 pbk. ISBN: 0-684-81163-4
Philosophic overview of capitalism and a broad-brush primer of investment principles. Describes the various life stages of a company and deals with management's role in the process more than most other investment books do.

MAIN STREET BEATS WALL STREET
Richard J. Maturi. Irwin Professional, 1995.
$22.95 ISBN: 1-55738-804-0
Interested in learning about investment clubs? Richard Maturi explains why investment clubs are so successful, covering such strategies as dollar-cost averaging and diversification. He also shows how you can start your own club.

MANAGING INVESTMENT PORTFOLIOS: A DYNAMIC PROCESS
John L. Maginn and Donald L. Tuttle. Warren, Gorham, and Lamont, 1990.
$50.00 ISBN: 0-7913-0322-5
Comprehensive textbook covering many investment topics from contributing investment professionals. Areas include fundamentals of portfolio management, determining investment objectives and constraints, asset allocation, portfolio construction, and more.

THE MOTLEY FOOL INVESTMENT GUIDE
David Gardner and Tom Gardner. Simon & Schuster, 1996.
$24.00 ISBN: 0-684-81594-X
Humorous investment advice from the founders of an on-line investment club. Suggests simple market strategies that have beaten the market averages over time.

NO-LOAD STOCKS
Charles B. Carlson. McGraw-Hill, 1995.
$14.95 pbk. ISBN: 0-07-011187-1
Charles Carlson, editor of *DRIP Investor,* shows you how to invest using dividend reinvestment plans (DRIPs). These plans allow you to purchase stocks directly from the company and avoid paying a commission to a broker. Has model portfolios, investment strategies, and a directory of DRIPs. The directory gives corporate profiles, performance ratings, plan specifics, and investment advice.

101 INVESTMENT DECISION TOOLS: BAROMETERS, INSTRUMENTS AND KEYS (WHERE TO FIND THEM AND HOW THEY'RE USED)
Jae K. Shim, Joel G. Siegel, and Jonathan Lansner. International, 1994.
$19.95 ISBN: 0-94-264144-2
Concisely covers stock indexes, bond indexes, and commodity indexes. Also covers economic indicators, interest rates, and more. They explain what the indicators measure, who compiles

them, where to find them, and how to use them.

ONE UP ON WALL STREET
Peter Lynch. Simon & Schuster, 1989.
$19.95 hc ISBN: 0-318-41474-0
$12.95 pbk. ISBN: 0-14-012792-5
Peter Lynch, former manager of the Fidelity Magellan Fund, shows readers how to pick stocks. He emphasizes holding a stock for fundamental reasons and to ignore the daily fluctuations. He discusses who should be involved in the stock market and why the small investor can outperform the pros.

THE ON-LINE INVESTOR
Ted Allrich. St. Martin's Press, 1995.
$22.95 ISBN: 0-312-13576-9
Shows you how to invest in small-cap stocks using your computer. Topics include: buying a computer, selecting an on-line service, developing your own portfolio, and analyzing small-cap stocks and mutual funds.

QUALITY OF EARNINGS
Thornton L. O'Glove. The Free Press (A division of Macmillan, Inc.), 1987.
$29.95 ISBN: 0-02-922630-9
This book assumes that the reader has some knowledge of accounting. His main point is that a company can manipulate the earnings it reports, so investors should not take earnings reports at face value. One of the most interesting chapters deals with accounts receivable and inventory analysis; using this tool can help you find the stocks that are ready to crash and those that are ready to go up. Other topics include nonoperating and non-recurring income, shareholder report-

ing versus tax reporting, and restructuring.

SAFE INVESTING
John Slatter. New York Institute of Finance/Simon & Schuster, 1991.
$14.95 pbk. ISBN: 0-13-786195-8
Looks at twenty investment strategies with emphasis on secure industries: utilities, oil companies, banks. Also covers convertible securities, tax-free bonds, and annuities.

SECURITY ANALYSIS
Sidney Cottle, Roger Murray, and Frank Block. McGraw-Hill, 1988.
$59.95 ISBN: 0-070-132356
This is the updated version of Graham and Dodd's classic *Security Analysis*. This book is considered the bible of fundamental analysis. This very comprehensive book shows investors how to analyze stocks and bonds. The focus is on figuring out what a company is worth by using publicly available financial statements. The goal is to make stock selection more a science than an art.

STAN WEINSTEIN'S SECRETS FOR PROFITING IN BULL AND BEAR MARKETS
Stan Weinstein. Irwin Professional, 1988.
$19.00 pbk. ISBN: 1-55623-683-2
Stan Weinstein, editor of *The Professional Tape Reader*, shows you how to time the market, choose good sectors, and choose winning stocks using technical analysis. The book is very useful for the novice interested in technical analysis. Also discusses mutual funds.

STANDARD AND POOR'S 500 GUIDE

STANDARD AND POOR'S MIDCAP 400 GUIDE

STANDARD AND POOR'S SMALL CAP 600 GUIDE

McGraw-Hill, updated annually. $24.95 pbk.

Reference book. Contains the S&P stock sheets for the companies in each index. Each report contains company description and historical operating and financial data. Good source to begin narrowing down the stocks in which you will want to invest.

STARTING AND RUNNING A PROFITABLE INVESTMENT CLUB

Thomas E. O'Hara and Kenneth S. Janke, Sr.

Time Business–Random House, 1996.

$23.00 ISBN: 0-8129-2686-2

The authors are both officers of the National Association of Investment Clubs. This book gives a thorough treatment of starting and operating an investment club. Takes the reader through the research process, using NAIC's investment selection criteria. Includes different resources available from NAIC. Also deals with funding members, accounting for and reporting taxable income, and working with a broker (surely a discount broker).

THE STOCK MARKET

Richard J. Teweles, Edward S. Bradley, and Ted M. Teweles.

John Wiley & Sons, 1992.

$24.95 ISBN: 0-472-54019-6

Extensive descriptions of how the stock market functions. Explains order execution, trade settlement, stock options, trading strategies, and some light treatment of different investment theories.

STOCK MARKET LOGIC

Norman Fosback. Dearborn Financial, 1995.

$30.00 pbk. ISBN: 0-79310-148-4

Norman Fosback, editor of *Stock Market Logic,* covers technical analysis, econometrics, stock selection theories, portfolio management, and more in this classic investment book.

STOCKS, BONDS, BILLS AND INFLATION YEARBOOK

Ibbotson Associates, annual edition.

$95.00

Contact 1-800-758-3557

Provides a multitude of historic investment data, including annual returns since 1926 for various stock indices, different types of bonds, and inflation measures. Data are presented in tabular format as well as in numerous charts.

STOCKS FOR THE LONG RUN

Jeremy J. Siegel. Irwin Professional, 1994.

$27.50 ISBN: 1-55623-804-5

Shows historical performance of the U.S. markets since 1802. Analyzes the interaction between the capital markets with economic and political events such as war, taxation, and inflation. Relates these to how an investor can benefit from future occurrence of such events, concluding with the principle that the stock market is the place to invest.

STYLE INVESTING

Richard Bernstein. John Wiley & sons, 1995.

$60.00 ISBN: 0-471-03570-X

For investors who have an identity crisis, this book will help. Looks at the characteristics and tradeoffs of different investment styles: growth versus value, high quality versus low quality, high beta versus low beta, large cap versus small cap, and others.

TAKING CONTROL OF YOUR FINANCIAL FUTURE
Thomas E. O'Hara and Helen J. McLane. Irwin Professional, 1994.
$25.00 ISBN: 0-7863-0139-2
Covers stocks and mutual funds. Offers stock-picking techniques used by National Association of Investors Corporation. How to measure a company's growth potential and identify its risks.

TECHNICAL ANALYSIS EXPLAINED
Martin J. Pring. McGraw-Hill, 1991.
$49.95 ISBN: 0-07-051042-3
Respected technician and editor of *Pring Market Review* provides readers with a comprehensive book on technical analysis. The focus is on stocks, but the methods apply to other markets as well. This is not a book that teaches a method for making money; it is a book that teaches principles of technical analysis and shows how complex it can be.

TECHNICAL ANALYSIS OF STOCK TRENDS
Robert Edwards and John Magee. New York Institute of Finance, 1992.
$69.95 ISBN: 0-13-904343-8
Considered the definitive work on technical analysis. Covers Dow theory, reversal patterns, consolidation patterns, trendlines, how to select stocks and much more.

VALUE INVESTING TODAY
Charles Brandes. Irwin Professional, 1989.
$32.50 ISBN: 1-55623-178-4
The author shows readers how to invest for the long term. He discusses the advantages of value investing, how to choose stocks, and when to sell. Other topics include risk, diversification, and applying the approach to overseas investing.

WALL STREET GURUS: HOW YOU CAN PROFIT FROM INVESTMENT NEWSLETTERS
Peter Brimelow. Random House, 1986.
$19.95 ISBN: 0-394-54202-9
Discusses the many different types of newsletters and how to use them in investment decision-making. Makes use of data from *Hulbert Financial Digest*.

THE WAY TO INVEST
Ginita Wall. Henry Holt, 1995.
$10.95 pbk. ISBN: 0-8050-3493-5
Provides a simple, straightforward approach to achieving financial objectives through mutual fund investing.

WINNING ON WALL STREET
Martin E. Zweig. Warner Books, 1994.
$12.99 pbk. ISBN: 0-446-670-146
Martin Zweig, publisher of *The Zweig Forecast,* provides readers with a method for picking stocks and timing the stock market. He lets winners ride and cuts losses short. He uses market timing to avoid bear markets and to enter bull markets. His approach will

not pinpoint the top or bottom or a market, but it will keep you invested during the profitable middle portion of the trend. He is averse to undue risk.

Software

The following software packages are most useful in stock investing, providing research data, technical analysis, and data retrieval and screening capabilities.

An asterisk (*) indicates that the product was mentioned in the 1995 Readers' Choice Awards (Bonus Issue 1996) Technical Analysis of STOCKS & COMMODITIES™ *magazine. Contact:*

Technical Analysis, Inc.
4757 California Avenue S.W.
Seattle, WA 98116-4499
Phone: 206-938-0570
Fax: 206-938-1307
http://www.traders.com/
mail@traders.com

AAII FUNDAMENTAL DISK
Systems: DOS, WIN, MAC. Requires spreadsheet program compatible with Lotus 1-2-3.
$20.
Covers stocks. Fundamental analysis. Spreadsheet templates for analyzing financial statements. Calculates ratios; allows common-size income statements and balance sheets. Contains many valuation models and ratios such as dividend discount model, Graham earnings multiplier, price-to-sales ratio, and more.
American Association of Individual Investors
625 N. Michigan Avenue,
Ste. 1900
Chicago, IL 60611
312-280-0170

AB-DATA DISK
Systems: Any spreadsheet.
$50

Covers stocks. Fundamental analysis. Provides information on company quarterly and annual reports. Compatible with many spreadsheets for easy use of data.
AB-Data, Inc.
194 Rock Road
Glen Rock, NJ 07452
201-612-0870

AIQ MARKETEXPERT*
System: DOS. Math coprocessor recommended.
$249. Trial $44.
Covers stock indexes. Technical analysis, expert system. Has dozens of technical indicators and several hundred expert rules that are combined to generate market signals. You may chart the indicators to confirm the signals and increase your confidence in them. The indicators and expert rules that generate a particular signal may be displayed. You may change parameters of the indicators. Update manually or on-line. MarketExpert is incorporated in AIQ's StockExpert and TradingExpert
AIQ Inc.
916 Southwood Boulevard
P.O. Drawer 7530
Incline Village, NV 89450
800-332-2999

AIQ STOCKEXPERT*
System: DOS. Math coprocessor
   recommended.
$498. Trial $44.
Covers stocks. Technical analysis,
expert system. Uses AIQ's market
timing system found in MarketExpert.
Employs multiple technical indicators
and expert rules to tell you what
stocks to buy and sell. You may
change parameters for indicators. Has
portfolio manager and system reports.
Update manually or on-line.
AIQ Inc.
916 Southwood Boulevard.
P.O. Drawer 7530
Incline Village, NV 89450
800-332-2999

AIQ TRADINGEXPERT*
System: WIN. Math coprocessor
   recommended.
$996. Trial $88.
Covers stocks and mutual funds.
Technical analysis, expert system. Uses
AIQ's market timing system found in
MarketExpert. It also analyzes market
sectors and tells you what stocks to
buy and sell. Can also rank stocks according to fundamental factors. You
may change parameters of indicators.
Has portfolio manager and system reports. Update manually or on-line.
AIQ Inc.
916 Southwood Boulevard
P.O. Drawer 7530
Incline Village, NV 89450
800-332-2999

BEHOLD*
System: MAC
$995
Covers stocks, bonds, futures, and
mutual funds. Technical analysis program with back-testing capabilities for
optimization of trading strategies. Real-

time data are supported with a link to
Ticker Watcher.
Jerome Technology
P.O. Box 403
Raritan, NJ 08869
908-369-7503

BRAINMAKER*
Systems: DOS, WIN, MAC
$195 and up
Neural network. User can design,
build, test, and run a neural network.
Recognizes patterns and makes predictions. Has tutorials, examples, and
is usable by novices. Can be used in
the financial markets.
California Scientific Software
10024 Newton Road
Nevada City, CA 95959
800-284-8112; 916-478-9040

CANDLEPOWER*
System: DOS
$395
Covers stocks, options, and futures.
Technical analysis package performs
Japanese candlestick charting, equi-
volume charting, and standard bar
charting. Combines candlestick chart-
ing with equivolume charting.
N. North Systems
4443 Nalani Court S.E.
Salem, OR 97302
503-364-3829

CANDLESTICK FORECASTER*
System: DOS
$249 ($800 for advanced version).
   Demo available.
Covers stocks, bonds, and mutual
funds. Technical analysis, expert system, neural network. A candlestick
charting program that interprets over
700 complex patterns. Monitors technical indicators and candlestick patterns. Also gives detailed information

on candlestick patterns. Gives buy/sell signals. Has tutorial and on-line help. Update on-line.

International Pacific Trading Company
1010 Calle Cordillera, #101
San Clemente, CA 92673
800-444-9993; 714-498-4009

CHARTPRO
Systems: DOS, WIN
$54
Covers stocks. Technical analysis. Menu-driven charting software with high-resolution graphics. Includes indicators such as RSI, Fibonacci lines, line oscillators, moving averages, MACD CCI, stochastics, and much more.

Ret-Tech Software, Inc.
151 Deer Lane
Barrington, IL 60010
708-382-3903

COMMON STOCK SELECTOR
Systems: DOS, WIN
$59
Covers stocks. Fundamental analysis. Shows earnings growth rates, price-earnings ratio ranges, projected high/low prices per share, and compounded returns. Compares stock performance with Dow Jones Industrial Average and Standard & Poor's 500.

Village Software
186 Lincoln Street
Boston, MA 02111
800-724-9332

COMPU/CHART EGA
System: DOS
$239
Covers stocks, mutual funds, commodities. Technical analysis. Charting and technical analysis software with high-resolution graphics. Can display nine different markets per screen. Has point and figure charting, and many other indicators.

New Tek Industries
P.O. Box 46116
Los Angeles, CA 90046
213-874-6669

DIVIDEND REINVESTMENT PLAN STOCKS
System: DOS
$40
Covers stocks. Database including stocks with dividend reinvestment plans. Has investing guidelines in text format.

Heizer Software
P.O. Box 232019
Pleasant Hill, CA 94523
800-888-7667; 510-943-7667

DOLLARLINK*
System: DOS
$1,300 or lease for $100/month
Covers stocks, futures, mutual funds, and options. Uses Signal or BMI data. Tracks up to 1,000 symbols. Has charting capabilities with technical analysis. Allows user to define own indexes.

Dollarlink Software
1407 Douglass Street
San Francisco, CA 94131
415-641-0721

DRPDISK
System: DOS
$36
Covers stocks. Gives a listing of companies with dividend reinvestment programs. Includes some details about each company's program.

DRPSoft
P.O. Box 169
Oxford, MA 01540
508-987-1962

ENSIGN 6
System: DOS
$1,295
Covers stocks, bonds, mutual funds, futures, and options. Charting software for BMI data feed. Performs technical analysis, including stochastics, moving averages, relative strength (RSI), Fibonacci time and price, and many more.
Ensign Software
2641 Shannon Court
Idaho Falls, ID 83404
800-255-7374; 208-524-0755

EPOCH PRO*
System: DOS
$995
Covers stocks, bonds, and futures. Generates mechanical buy and sell signals based on short-term cycles. Provides specific stop-loss values. Trading record can be back-tested.
Mesa Software
P.O. Box 1801
Goleta, CA 93116
800-633-6372; 805-969-6478

FIBINODES*
System: DOS
$595
Covers stocks, bonds, mutual funds, futures, indexes, and options. Performs Fibonacci retracement on all securities, specifically designed for intraday and position trading when stop losses needed. Calculates the two major nodes or up to fifty-eight combined nodes per market swing and recalculates within ten seconds of a new high.
Coast Investment Software
358 Avenida Milano
Sarasota, FL 34242-1517
813-346-3801

FINANCIAL STATEMENT ANALYZER
System: DOS
$89
Covers stocks. Fundamental analysis. Has over seventy-nine financial and business ratios. User may create ratios as well. Calculates solvency, efficiency, profitability, and liquidity. Has standard formats built in to save time. Performs horizontal, vertical, and common-size analysis. Has reports and pie charts. User may add notes. Update manually.
E-Sential Software Corp.
1126 South 70th Street, Ste. 422A
West Allis, WI 53214
414-475-3450

FIN VAL/FINSTOCK
System: DOS
$495. Demo $20.
Covers stocks. Fundamental analysis. Predicts earnings, cash flows, and stock price. Has reports and graphs showing past and expected financial ratios and numbers. The discounted cash flow model has 150 values using six methods (P-E ratio, book value, cash flow to perpetuity, Graham, EBIT multiples). Has executive summaries, common-size reports, and more. Enter data manually or from an on-line service. Also includes FINSTOCK, another analysis program.
PC Solutions, Inc.
104-40 Queens Boulevard
Forest Hills, NY 11375
718-275-7930

GANNTRADER 2.0*
System: DOS
$1,295
Covers stocks, bonds, futures, mutual funds, and options. Plots price charts

with angles; angles from highs, lows, 360-degree angles, squares, and planets. Analyzes up to 5 Gann squares. Calculates MOF, CE average, aspects, plot planets, average support and resistance, square of 9, hexagon chart positions.
Gannsoft Publishing Co.
11670 Riverbend Drive
Leavenworth, WA 98826-9353
509-548-5990

GENESIS FINANCIAL DATA SERVICES*
Systems: DOS, WIN
Call for price.
Covers stocks, mutual funds, futures, and options. Historical data compatible with Metastock, CompuTrac, AIQ, and CSI.
Genesis Data Service
P.O. Box 49578
Colorado Springs, CO 80949
800-808-DATA; 716-260-6111

INVESTOGRAPH PLUS FOR WINDOWS*
System: WIN
$795. Demo available.
Covers stocks, bonds, mutual funds. Technical analysis. Includes the standard indicators and graphics tools, as well as indicators and tools not available in other programs. Has a "well-designed, easy-to-operate user's interface." Has a systems tester and allows you to create your own systems. Highlights trading opportunities on a chart that meets your conditions. Saves time by screening a price database. Has a natural language that makes it easier to create custom indicators, filters, and trading systems. Designed for minimal hand and mouse movement to improve efficiency. Has

trading simulation feature and on-line help. Update on-line.
Liberty Research Corporation
Building 2, Ste. 304
1250 Capital of Texas Highway
Austin, TX 78746
800-827-0090; 512-329-2762

THE INVESTOR
Systems: DOS, WIN
$129
Covers stocks. Technical analysis. Charting software that tracks individual securities. Assists user in making buy/sell decision based on information from forty different indicators.
Village Software
186 Lincoln Street
Boston, MA 02111
800-724-9332

KLATU SOFTWARE
System: WIN
$595
Covers Stocks and mutual funds. Downloading software. Automatically dials and downloads batch files from data providers. Allows user to set download times for off-peak hours. Also transports data between programs.
Nirvana Systems, Inc.
3415 Greystone Drive
Suite 205
Austin, TX 78731
512-345-2545

LIVEWIRE
System: DOS
$595. $295 for Personal Investor version. 45-day trial $45.
Covers stocks, bonds, and mutual funds. Technical analysis, portfolio management. Has dozens of indicators and price-volume alarms. View two securities with different time periods

simultaneously. Have up to seven live charts at once. Create your own stock groups and create stock screens. The portfolio manager calculates rate of return, has "what if" capability, and uses tax lot accounting. Update on-line.
Cablesoft, Inc.
530 W. Ojai Avenue, Ste. 109
Ojai, CA 93023
805-646-0094

MARKET ANALYZER PLUS*
Systems: DOS, MAC
$149 for Dow Jones News
   Retrieval subscribers. Demo
   available.
Covers stocks, bonds, and mutual funds. Technical analysis. A complement to the on-line service Dow Jones News Retrieval. Create custom formulas, use the extensive library of indicators and formulas, and access historical and current quotes. Automates routine tasks such as updating data and reporting results.
Dow Jones & Company, Inc.
P.O. Box 300
Princeton, NJ 08543
800-815-5100; 609-520-4641

MARKETMAKER FOR WINDOWS
Systems: DOS, WIN
$29
Covers stocks. Fundamental analysis. User enters data from financial reports. Two periods of data are minimum. Program will project future earnings and share price. Calculates the stability of sales, debt ratio, etc. Also has a report section, story section, and graphs. Has "what if" analysis also.
International Software Systems
1832 Dauphin Street
Mobile, AL 36606
205-478-8637

MARKET MASTER*
System: DOS
$195–$1,195. Trial $59.
Covers stocks, bonds, and mutual funds. Technical analysis, expert system. Creates leading indicators to forecast the direction and magnitude of a price movement. Uses quantitative pattern analysis; also automatically detects errors and learns from its mistakes. Update on-line.
RMC
P.O. Box 60842
Sunnyvale, CA 94088
408-773-8715

MASTER CHARTIST
System: DOS
$295
Covers stocks, bonds, and mutual funds. Technical analysis. Charting software with multiple windows for charts and quotes. Includes more than fifty technical indicators. Supports data from a variety of vendors.
Robert-Slade, Inc.
750 N. Freedom Boulevard
Ste. 301-B
Provo, UT 84601
800-433-4276 x.250

MEGATECH CHART SYSTEM*
System: DOS
$175
Covers stocks, bonds, futures, mutual funds, and options. Charting software; performs moving averages, point and figure, candle charts, stochastics, Arms index, McClellan oscillator, trend lines, fans, angles, parallel lines, money flow, open interest, spreads, multiple tissue overlay, MACD, CCI, relative strength, oscillators, DMI, parabolic time/price, and more. Allows user to

program up to thirty different call screens with sixteen stocks each.

Ret-Tech Software
151 Deer Lane
Barrington, IL 60010
708-382-3903

MESA FOR WINDOWS
System: WIN. Math coprocessor recommended.
$350. Demo available.
Covers stocks and bonds. Predicts short-term market cycles based on maximum entropy techniques (the technique used in seismic exploration and in missile defense systems). The main cycle is plotted as a time graph on a bar chart, and the measured cycles are shown as a spectrograph. Has a proprietary band pass indicator.

Mesa
P.O. Box 1801
Goleta, CA 93116
800-633-6372; 805-969-6478; 805-969-1358

METASTOCK*
System: DOS
$349. Demo available.
Covers stocks, bonds, and mutual funds. Technical analysis. One of the premier technical analysis programs. Has over seventy-five technical indicators and dozens of built-in functions. User may create custom indicators and formulas. Displays fifty charts simultaneously for easier comparison. Has eight charting methods, including bar, Japanese candlesticks, and point and figure. Has stock screening and a systems tester. On-line help available. Update on-line.

Equis International, Inc.
3950 S. 700 East, Ste. 100

Salt Lake City, UT 84107
800-882-3040; 801-265-8886

METASTOCK FOR WINDOWS*
System: WIN
$349. Demo available.
Covers stocks, bonds, and mutual funds. Technical analysis. The Windows version of MetaStock. Has over eighty technical indicators and over 160 built-in formula functions. Create custom indicators and formulas as well. Displays up to 7,000 days at once. Has a true object-oriented interface, where all commands are built into the subject for easy access. Utilizes "sticky text" for notes. Has stock screening and a systems tester. Contains a tutorial and on-line help. Update on-line.

Equis International, Inc.
3950 S. 700 East, Ste. 100
Salt Lake City, UT 84107
(800) 882-3040; (801) 265-8886

METASTOCK RT*
System: DOS
$495. Demo available.
Covers stocks, bonds, and mutual funds. Technical analysis. Version of MetaStock for use with a live, real-time data feed. Includes all the features as MetaStock plus capabilities for using tick charts, one-, two-, and five-minute bars. User may create custom indicators and formulas. Displays fifty charts simultaneously for easier comparison. Has eight charting methods, including bar, Japanese candlesticks, and point and figure. Has stock screening and a systems tester. On-line help available.

Equis International, Inc.
3950 S. 700 East, Ste. 100

Salt Lake City, UT 84107
800-882-3040; 801-265-8886

MIRAT
System: DOS
$250. Demo $25.
Covers indexes. Technical analysis.
Very simple stock-market timing system. Based on the theory that peaks
and troughs in the number of new
lows define the market cycle. Requires only four data items daily. Update manually or on-line.
Tools for Timing
11345 Highway 7, #499
Minnetonka, MN 55305
800-325-1344; 612-939-0076

NAVA PATTERNS*
System: DOS
$495
Covers stocks, options, and futures.
Technical analysis, devises trading patterns based on statistical patterns. User
can project a performance chart for
the following thirty days.
Nava Development Corporation
251-A Portage Road
Lewiston, NY 14092-1710
716-754-9254

NAVIGATOR*
System: DOS
$195
Covers stocks, mutual funds, options,
and futures. Data editing. Allows user
to convert files from CSI, Compu
Trac, MetaStock, ASCII, and Lotus
1-2-3.
Genesis Financial Data Services
411 Woodman Court
Colorado Springs, CO 80919
800-808-3282; 719-260-6111

NEURALYST FOR EXCEL*
Systems: DOS, WIN

$195
Covers stocks, bonds, futures, mutual
funds, indexes, and options. Neural
network. Analyzes any numeric data
series and identifies historic patterns
and relationships, which it uses to
make future predictions. Professional
version available.
Epic Systems Corp.
P.O. Box 277
Sierra Madre, CA 91025-0277
818-355-2988

N-TRAIN*
Systems: DOS, WIN, Windows
    NT
$747
Fundamental and technical analysis,
expert system, neural network. Create
your own neural trading systems using
technical and fundamental analysis.
User controls transfer functions, learning rules, etc. Has double-precision
math. Limited only by your computer's memory and hard-disk size.
Scientific Consultant Services, Inc.
20 Stagecoach Road
Selden, NY 11784
516-696-3333

OMNITRADER*
System: WIN
$595. Demo available.
Covers stocks, bonds, and mutual
funds. Technical analysis, expert system. Performs technical analysis automatically and gives the user clear
trading signals. Uses its adaptive reasoning model to learn from experience; it continually tests and evaluates
its trading techniques to find the best
systems for your securities. Has automatic trend lines, candlestick patterns,
and support-resistance levels. Includes
a game feature to help you learn. This
is a unique program: no experience

required for systems testing since the program figures out which system works well for a particular security.

Nirvana Systems, Inc.
3415 Greystone Drive, Ste. 205
Austin, TX 78731
800-880-0338; 512-345-2566

ONE DAY AT A TIME*
System: DOS
$395

Covers stocks, options, and futures. Technical analysis package, including: RSI, DMI, ADXR, ADX, MACD, Fibonacci retracement lines, Bollinger bands, commodity channel index, moving averages, and more.

Trend Research Ltd.
5615 McLeansville Road
McLeansville, NC 27301
919-292-1402

PEERLESS INTERMEDIATE-TERM
    GENERAL MARKET TIMING SYS-
    TEM
Systems: DOS, WIN
$198

Covers stocks and mutual funds. Technical analysis. Forecasts the intermediate-term and long-term direction of the stock market. Data on the Dow go back to 1987, though older data are available for additional cost. Gives automatic buy and sell signals. There is extensive information on market timing in the manuals, and each signal from 1965 is discussed. Update manually or on-line.

Tiger Investment Software
5631 La Jolla Boulevard
La Jolla, CA 92037
619-459-8577

PERSONAL ANALYST*
System: MAC
$395

Covers stocks, bonds, futures, mutual funds, and options. Charting program. Allows the user to lay out charts with up to sixteen indicators each, including Japanese candle sticks, point and figure, bar charts, and more.

Trendsetter Software
P.O. Box 6481
Santa Ana, CA 92706
800-825-1852; 714-547-5005

PERSONAL HOTLINE*
System: MAC
$595

Covers stocks, bonds, futures, mutual funds, and options. Technical analysis. Performs all charting functions of Personal Analyst, plus includes an expert system to analyze charts. Notifies user of charts that need closer attention.

Trendsetter Software
P.O. Box 6481
Santa Ana, CA 92706
800-825-1852; 714-547-5005

POINTSAHEAD!*
System: DOS
$149

Covers stocks, bonds, and futures. Charting and technical analysis program. Includes forty different technical indicators, displays three graphs simultaneously, includes other convenient features.

Small Investor's Software Company
138 Ocean Avenue
Amityville, NY 11701
800-829-9368; 516-789-9368

POWERTRADER*
System: WIN
$595

Covers stocks, mutual funds, and futures. Charting software, reads Meta-Stock, Worden Brothers, AIQ, CSI,

and ASCII formats. Performs various types of technical analysis to give the user trading signals. Also overlays charts and lets user simulate a portfolio and track performance.
Nirvana Systems
3415 Greystone Drive
Suite 205
Austin, TX 78731
800-880-0338; 512-345-2545

PROFESSIONAL ANALYST*
System: MAC
$395
Covers stocks, bonds, futures, mutual funds, and options. An upgraded version of Personal Analyst. Some additions include the display of headlines on bottom of screen, personal trade tracking, and visual alert levels that are displayed on charts. Several new technical analysis tools are also included.
Trendsetter Software
P.O. Box 6481
Santa Ana, CA 92706
800-825-1852; 714-547-5005

PROFESSIONAL BREAKOUT SYS-
TEM
System: DOS
$385. Demo available.
Covers stocks, bonds, and mutual funds. Gives buy/sell signals for stocks and indexes. Full charting ability and has a proven mechanical trading method. Filters and confirms the trades for the mechanical method by using a volatility breakout system with charting and technical analysis. Shows the profitability of the built-in volatility system; allows testing of user's trading systems or ideas. Has seventeen indicators and a trading report.
New High Co.
Road #2
Riverhead, NY 11901

800-643-8950; 516-722-5407;
516-722-5409

QUOTEEXPRESS
Systems: DOS, WIN, OS/2
$290
Covers stocks, bonds, mutual funds, futures, and options. End-user software for DTN data feed. Gives quotes, charts, and has a scrolling ticker at bottom of screen. Stores incoming data on hard drive so as not to use much RAM.
Integrated Financial Solutions, Inc.
1049 S.W. Baseline
Suite B-200
Hillsboro, OR 97123
800-729-5037; 503-640-5303

RATIOS
System: DOS
$30
Covers stocks. Fundamental analysis. Calculates ratios including ROA, ROE, inventory turnover, net operating margin, and more.
Dynacomp, Inc.
178 Phillips Road
Webster, NY 14580
800-828-6772
716-265-4040

RELEVANCE III—ADVANCED MAR-
KET ANALYSIS*
System: DOS
$795
Covers stocks, bonds, mutual funds, futures, and options. Scans up to fifty markets nightly and screens out trading opportunities based on Gann, Andrews, Fibonacci, RSI, and other technical indicators. Has a simulation mode and a nine-page trading-plan summary for each market.
Relevance III, Inc.

4741 Trousdale Drive, Ste. One
Nashville, TN 37220
615-333-2005

RIGHT TIME*
System: DOS
$499
Covers stocks (futures available for an additional cost). A computerized trading system based on volume-price, support-demand, and global market trends.
T.B.S.P. Inc.
610 Newport Center Drive, Ste. 830
Newport Beach, CA 92660
714-721-8603

SMARTRADER*
Systems: DOS, WIN
$349
Covers stocks, bonds, mutual funds, futures, and options. Charting program for the experienced technician, feeds off spreadsheet data. Allows user to create custom formulas and backtest against historical data. Multiple data issues can be studied at once.
Stratagem Software International, Inc.
520 Transcontinental Drive, Ste. B
Metairie, LA 70001
800-779-7353; 504-885-7353

SSG COMBINED
System: DOS
$189. Demo $5.
Covers stocks. Fundamental analysis. Full-featured program that covers the NAIC (National Association of Investors Corporation) method of analyzing stocks. Has three levels: basic, intermediate, and advanced. User may adjust revenue and earnings per share trends. Screens stocks using any of twenty parameters including industry,

total return, etc. Create stock groups. Has a pop-up notes section for each company to store user comments. Has on-line help. Update on-line.
National Association of Investors Corporation (NAIC)
P.O. Box 220
Royal Oak, MI 48068
810-583-6242

STOCK INVESTOR
Systems: DOS, WIN
$99/yr.
Covers stocks and bonds. Fundamental analysis, database. Allows user to screen over 7,000 stocks. Includes 200 financial variables, and lets users input their own variables.
Media General Financial Services
301 East Grace Street
Richmond, VA 23219
800-446-7922; 804-649-6587

STOCK PROPHET*
System: DOS
$995
Covers stocks, bonds, mutual funds, futures, and options. Provides preprocessing and postprocessing required for BrainMaker. Includes more than thirty indicators for preprocessing and combines multiple indicators into a single clear indication of the price trend. Allows user to test models.
Future Wave Software
1330 S. Gertuda Avenue
Redondo Beach, CA 90277
310-540-5373

STOCK WATCHER
System: MAC
$195
Covers stocks, mutual funds, and options. Technical analysis, charting. High-resolution charting software.

Displays numerous technical indicators.

Micro Trading Software, Inc.
Box 175
Wilton, CT 06897
203-762-7820

SUPERCHARTS*
System: WIN
$250. CD-ROM data bank also
  available. Demo available.
Covers stocks, bonds, and mutual funds. Technical analysis. Has an object-oriented interface, so every item on a chart can be manipulated. Unlimited number of chart windows may be displayed at once. Has over eighty indicators and thirteen drawing tools. Also has animated drawing tools. Create custom indicators and formulas with English-like statements. Contains a systems builder and systems tester. Has an Optimization Results Spreadsheet for easier viewing of systems testing. Utilizes shortcut menus, online help, and detailed commentary on what an indicator is saying at a given time (which helps to teach technical analysis). Update on-line.

Omega Research, Inc.
Omega Research Building
9200 Sunset Drive
Miami, FL 33173-3266
800-556-2022; 305-270-1095

SYSTEM WRITER PLUS*
System: DOS
$975
Covers stocks, bonds, mutual funds, and options. User-friendly system allowing user to devise and test his own trading system. After testing performance, five-, ten-, and-twenty-year charts are prepared automatically.

Omega Research, Inc.

Omega Research Building
9200 Sunset Drive
Miami, FL 33173-3266
800-556-2022

TECHNICAL ANALYSIS SCANNER*
System: DOS
$249. Demo $5.
Covers stocks, futures, and mutual funds. Technical analysis. Analyzes and screens stocks and mutual funds. Has over sixty technical indicators. Also tracks positions. Creates specialized reports. Tests trading systems.

Flexsoft
7172 Regional Street, #276
Dublin, CA 94568
510-829-9733

TECHNICAL INVESTOR
System: DOS
$245
Covers stocks, options, and commodities. Technical analysis, database. Program can store daily historical prices for up to forty years on 2,500 different securities. Also has charting capabilities with technical indicators.

Savant Software, Inc.
120 Bedford Center Road
Bedford, NH 03110
800-231-9900; 603-471-0400

THE TECHNICAL SELECTOR
System: DOS
$145
Covers stocks. Technical analysis. An optional filter for use with Technical Investor, listed above. Analyzes studies to select stocks that exhibit bullish or bearish tendencies.

Savant Software, Inc.
120 Bedford Center Road
Bedford, NH 03110
800-231-9900; 603-471-0400

THE TECHNICIAN*
System: DOS
$249. Demo $5.
Covers indexes. Technical analysis.
Helps you time the market. Calculates
over 100 indicators from three categories: momentum, monetary, and
investor sentiment. User can create
custom indicators. Contains a systems
tester. Has a straightforward and clean
interface, so keystrokes are kept to a
minimum. Comes with a free database
of data going back to 1979. Update
manually or on-line.
Equis International, Inc.
3950 S. 700 East, Suite 100
Salt Lake City, UT 84107
800-882-3040; 801-265-8886

TECHNIFILTER PLUS*
System: DOS
$399
Covers stocks, bonds, mutual funds,
futures, and options. Uses historical
data to back-test buy/sell strategies.
Compatible with data from Dow
Jones Market Analyzer Plus, Meta-
Stock, Telechart 2000, Compu Trac,
and AIQ.
RTR Software
19 W. Hargett Street, Ste. 204
Raleigh, NC 27601
919-829-0786

TICKERWATCHER*
System: MAC
$195–$595
Covers stocks. Monitors an unlimited
number of real-time or delayed
quotes. Tracks historic data and displays charts.
Linn Software, Inc.
3199 Hammock Creek Court
Lithonia, GA 30058
404-929-8802

TIGER MULTIPLE STOCK SCREEN-ING AND TIMING SYSTEM*
System: DOS
$895
Covers stocks. Uses Worden Brothers
data to update 500 stocks nightly.
Proprietary formulas are then used to
create a ranking of the 500 stocks. A
short-term timing scan is run against
the top and bottom stocks and sets of
printed recommendations are prepared
on the most bullish and bearish stocks.
Tiger Investment Software
P.O. Box 9491
San Diego, CA 92169
619-459-8577

TIMER/TIMER PROFESSIONAL*
System: DOS
$350; $450 for professional
Covers indexes. Monitors markets and
tries to recognize tops and bottoms of
market cycles using seven indicators.
Professional version shows a log scale
comparison of three U.S. markets.
Tools for Timing
11345 Highway 7, #499
Minnetonka, MN 55305
800-325-1344

TRADER'S MONEY MANAGER
System: DOS
$399
Covers stock simulation. Uses Monte
Carlo simulation to analyze the track
record of any trading system and computes probabilities for reaching stated
goals. Calculates minimum amount of
capital required for a stated trading
strategy.
Commodity Systems, Inc. (CSI)
200 W. Palmetto Park Road
Boca Raton, FL 33432
800-274-4727; 407-392-8663

TT CHARTBOOK*
System: WIN
Free to subscribers of the Technical Tools database. Data service is $25/month and up.
Covers stocks, bonds, and mutual funds. Technical analysis. The program is designed to feel more like a chartbook than a computer program. The user creates his own chartbooks for easy access. Historical data ordering and daily updating are one seamless operation. Contains dozens of indicators and functions. Create and test systems. Utilizes an optimization feature. Very intuitive product; many traders are able to use it without reading the manual. Has on-line help with hypertext. The chief engineer is Ed Seykota, a very successful trader.
Technical Tools
980 N. Federal Highway, Ste. 304
Boca Raton, FL 33432
800-231-8005; 407-361-9567

U.S. EQUITIES ONFLOPPY
System: DOS
$55–$995 depending on updates
Covers stocks. Fundamental analysis. Covers over 6,000 domestic stocks. Has over 200 statistics per stock. View the stock with a fifty-two-week and sixty-month graph. Examine balance sheet information and company information. Screen and rank based on your own criteria, including custom formulas. You may even weight your favorite criteria.
Morningstar
225 W. Wacker Drive
Chicago, IL 60606
800-876-5005; 312-696-6000

THE VALUE LINE INVESTMENT SURVEY FOR WINDOWS
System: WIN—CD-ROM or floppy

$595/yr—1,700 stocks; $995/yr.— 5,000 stocks
Covers stocks. This service replicates the hard-copy *Value Line* reports (CD version only) as well as do screens of stocks by 200 search fields. The subscription includes monthly updates and a weekly on-line update service.
Value Line Investment Survey for Windows
220 E. 42nd Street
New York, NY 10017-5891
800-535-9648

VALUE/SCREEN
System: DOS
$465/yr. 2-month trial $59.
Covers stocks. Fundamental analysis. Contains information on about 1,600 stocks as well as a portfolio manager. Employs fifty-two screening variables including Value Line's timeliness, safety, and technical ranks. Has market data (e.g. yearly high-low, P-E ratio), historical data (sales, debt ratio), growth projections, and more. Gives detailed reports, statistical summaries and analyses. Update by disk or on-line.
Value Line Publishing
711 Third Avenue
New York, NY 10017
800-654-0508; 212-687-3965

WALL STREET WATCHER
System: MAC
$495
Covers stocks, options, and commodities. Technical analysis. Charting software with over twenty technical indicators. Includes moving averages, RSI, MACD, and more.
Wall Street Watcher
Box 175
Wilton CT 06897
203-762-7820

WAVE WISE SPREADSHEET FOR WINDOWS*

System: WIN
$150
Covers stocks, bonds, futures, and mutual funds. Combines a spreadsheet with stock market charting. Allows the user to perform Elliot wave analysis, cycle analysis, Fibonacci retracements, and "what if" analysis.
Jerome Technology, Inc.
P.O. Box 403
Raritan, NJ 08869
908-369-7503

WINDOWS ON WALL STREET PRO*

System: WIN
$249; $149 for nonpro version. Demo available.
Covers stocks, bonds, and mutual funds. Technical and fundamental analysis. Utilizes dozens of indicators, a powerful formula builder, and the ability to display different kinds of windows at once such as a chart, a spreadsheet, and on-line research. Contains a "Personal Investment Assistant" that performs repetitive tasks such as printing analyses, download-ing quotes, and executing applications. Edits data easily using a spreadsheet. Has a systems tester, a systems builder, and on-line help. Update on-line.
Marketarts, Inc.
P.O. Box 850922
Richardson, TX 75085
214-235-9594

3D FOR WINDOWS*

System: WIN
$199. Demo available.
Covers stocks, bonds, and mutual funds. Technical analysis, expert system. Displays the profitability of seven indicators in 3-D. User determines the best system by looking for the smoothest intersection on the 3-D surface. Does not perform optimization. Indicators include stochastics, RSI, MACD, double moving averages, parabolic stop and reverse, band pass, and CCI.
Mesa
P.O. Box 1801
Goleta, CA 93116
800-633-6372; 805-969-6478

On-Line Services

On-line services provide market information such as prices, news, historic data, and miscellaneous facts related to the securities markets. Much of the data will be applicable to bonds, mutual funds, and commodities as well. Services may be provided on a dial-up basis through a computer modem, or they may be delivered through dedicated media such as cable TV lines or satellite linkup.

ACCESS CUSTOM FINANCIAL SYSTEM*

System: DOS
$49.95
Quote service. Has historic quotes and daily updates customized to the user. Stock data goes back ten years, and futures data goes back 25 years.
$25; Updates via disk or modem.
Prophet Software Corp.
3350 W. Bayshore, #106
Palo Alto, CA 94303
800-772-8040

ACCURON
System: DOS
$129.95
Historical database, includes information on stocks, mutual funds, bonds, futures, commodities, and indexes.
National Computer Network
1929 N. Harlem Avenue
Chicago, IL 60635

AMERICA ONLINE
Systems: DOS, WIN, MAC
$9.95/month and up
Assorted services. News (general, business, economic, company); quotes (stock, mutual fund); financial statement data; on-line brokerage; software library for downloading.
America Online
8619 Westwood Center Drive
Vienna, VA 22182
800-827-6364; 703-448-8700

ANALYST WATCH ON THE INTERNET
Consists of three separate services on the Internet from Zacks Investment Research:
DAILY E-MAIL PORTFOLIO ALERTS
Systems: Requires an e-mail account and an Internet account.
$15/month; $11/month for *Analyst Watch* subscribers. $22.50 for 3-month trial to all three services.
Provides all earnings estimate revisions from analysts and all changes in buy/hold/sell recommendations. Also provides Zacks Performance Ranks. Has new story headlines, news wire stories, earnings per share information, and dividend information. Compare your portfolio and stocks versus the S&P 500.
ZACK COMPANY REPORTS

Systems: Requires an e-mail account and an Internet account.
$15/month; $11/month for *Analyst Watch* subscribers. $22.50 for 3-month trial to all three services.
Provides eight-page research reports on 5,000 stocks. Includes earnings estimates, next earnings report date, company overview, and buy/hold/sell recommendations.
ZACKS CUSTOM EQUITY SCREENS
Systems: Requires an e-mail account and an Internet account.
$15/month; $11/month for *Analyst Watch* subscribers. $22.50 for 3-month trial to all three services.
Screens 5,000 stocks using eighty-one investment ratios that Zacks has found to be effective.
Zacks Investment Research
155 N. Wacker Drive
Chicago, IL 60606
800-399-6659

ARGUS ON-LINE
Systems: DOS, Windows
$75/yr. plus $1.50/minute
Low-cost, on-line Argus and Vickers reports on 400 companies and forty industries. Includes market commentary, economic outlook, and stock analysis. Also has screening capabilities.
Argus Research Corporation
17 Battery Place, 18th Floor
New York, NY 10004
212-425-7500

CADENCE UNIVERSE ONLINE
Systems: DOS, WIN, MAC
$100 plus $55/hour
On-line access to CDA's database of bank, insurance company, mutual fund, and investment advisers. Has

data on returns for comparison analysis.

CDA Investment Technologies, Inc.
1355 Piccard Drive
Rockville, MD 20850
800-833-1394; 301-975-9600

CDA/INVESTNET
Systems: DOS, WIN, MAC
$50 plus $1.50/minute
Tracks insider trading, and reports within twenty-four hours of release by the SEC. User can enter a watch list for tracking. Covers 10,000 securities. Also available through Dow Jones News Retrieval and BMI.
CDA/Investnet
3265 Meridian Parkway, Ste. 130
Ft. Lauderdale, FL 33331
800-243-2324

CNBC ON DEMAND
Stock research reports via fax. Call twenty-four-hour line and request reports on desired companies. Reports include historical price charts, stock reports, industry reports, and headlines from Standard & Poor's, First Call consensus earnings estimates, Business Wire press releases, and research from Argus Research and Vickers Insider Trading.
800-706-CNBC

COMPUSERVE
Systems: DOS, WIN, OS2, MAC
$8.95/month and up
News (general, business, economic, company); quotes (stock, bond, mutual fund); financial statement data; SEC filings; analyst reports; technical analysis; fundamental analysis; mutual fund screening; on-line brokerage. A general on-line service that also covers finance. Has over 1,700 products/

services. Up to twelve years of price history on over 160,000 securities. Covers over 1,900 mutual funds. Company reports and earnings estimates from S&P, Value Line, Disclosure, and I/B/E/S. Investors Forum is a discussion group with on-line support for popular software.
Compuserve, Inc.
5000 Arlington Center Boulevard
Columbus, OH 43220
800-848-8199; 614-529-1349

COMSTOCK
System: DOS
$750 plus $420/month
Provides real-time quotes on stocks, mutual funds, bonds, and commodities. Includes market data and news wire service. Charting is also available.
Standard & Poor's Information Group
670 White Plains Road
Scarsdale, NY 10583
800-431-5019

CSI DATA RETRIEVAL SERVICE
Systems: DOS, WIN
$39 plus $11/month
Historical quotes on domestic stocks, mutual funds, futures, and commodities. Updated daily.
Commodity Systems, Inc.
200 W. Palmetto Park Road
Boca Raton, FL 33432
800-274-4727; 407-392-8663

DATA CONNECTIONS
System: DOS
$85 plus $65/month
Daily and historical price data on stocks, mutual funds, futures, and options. Available via modem or diskette.

Genesis Financial Data Services
411 Woodman Court
Colorado Springs, CO 80919
800-808-3282; 719-260-6111

DATA RETRIEVER
System: DOS
$45
Communications software for use
with Dial/Data. Retrieves historical
and current price data for stocks, mutual funds, indexes, and futures.
Time Trend Software
337 Boston Road
Billerica, MA 01821
508-529-3246

DATALINK
System: DOS
$89
Collects price data on stocks, futures,
and indexes. Transfers data into analysis programs and spreadsheets; can also
save data to disk.
Integrated Financial Solutions,
Inc.
1049 S.W. Baseline, Ste. B-200
Hillsboro, OR 97123
800-729-5037

DATANET
Systems: DOS, WIN
$100/6 months
Designed for users of CableSoft's
Livewire software. Has historic price
information on 14,000 stocks. Also in-
cludes on-line software upgrades.
Cablesoft
530 W. Ojai Avenue
Ojai, CA 93023
805-646-0094

DIAL/DATA*
System: DOS. (Data works with
MAC, but compatible with only
four programs.)

$35 connection fee
$15/month plus fees
Provides daily or historical price data;
covers all U.S., Canadian, and Euro-
pean exchanges. Has very high quality
data. Quotes (stock, bond, mutual
fund); technical and fundamental stock
screening; mutual fund screening.
Dial/Data
56 Pine Street
New York, NY 10005
800-275-5544

DIALOG
Systems: Any communications
software
$125–$230
Database with financial data on over
2.5 million companies. Includes a
search function for turning up data on
a specific request.
Dialog Information Services, Inc.
3460 Hillview Avenue
Palo Alto, CA 94304
800-334-2564

DIALOG QUOTES AND TRADING
Systems: Any communications
software
$45 plus $0.60/minute
Provides twenty-minute-delayed
quotes on stocks, mutual funds, and
options. Has on-line brokerage services available. Also has portfolio management features.
Dialog Information Services, Inc.
3460 Hillview Avenue
Palo Alto, CA 94304
800-334-2564

DOW JONES NEWS RETRIEVAL—
PRIVATE INVESTOR EDITION*
Systems: DOS, WIN, MAC
$29.95/month and up
News (general, business, economic,
company); quotes (stock, bond, mu-

tual fund); financial statement data; analyst reports; technical/fundamental analysis; mutual fund screening; insider trading data. Access articles from *Barron's, The Wall Street Journal,* the *Financial Times*, and hundreds of other business publications. Access U.S. and international news wires, press releases, and abstracts of analysts' reports. Track insider activity on 8,000 companies. Obtain historical quotes dating back to 1981. Read transcripts of the PBS program *Wall Street Week.* Access financial and statistical data on 6,200 companies with Media General and Standard & Poor's. Contains technical analysis reports on over 4,500 stocks. Has Zacks earnings estimates and an encyclopedia.
Dow Jones News Retrieval
P.O. Box 300
Princeton, NJ 08543
800–815–5100; 609–520–4641

DOW JONES NEWS RETRIEVAL— TECHNICAL ANALYST EDITION
Systems: DOS, WIN, MAC
$39.95/month and up
Quotes (stock); historical data; stock screening. Receives daily quotes on over 200,000 securities; has twenty years of pricing history. Compare the performance of different stocks over specific periods. Has stock screening.
Dow Jones News Retrieval
P.O. Box 300
Princeton, NJ 08543
800–815–5100; 609–520–4641

DOWNLOADER*
Systems: DOS, WIN
$195 start–up, plus $69/month
Quotes (stocks, mutual funds, bonds, futures, commodities, options). Data collection program for end-of-day

prices to be used with MetaStock or compatible programs.
Equis International
3950 S. 700 East, Ste. 100
Salt Lake City, UT 84107

DTN SPECTRUM
Systems: Stand–alone system
  compatible with DOS and
  MAC. Uses cable TV or satel-
  lite.
$295 plus $63/month and up
News (business, economic, company); quotes (stock, bond, mutual fund). Provides commentary and information on the debt markets and stock markets. Charts indexes with technical indicators. Also shows fundamental data along with company news. Has weather information. Offers many elective services. Magnify feature doubles the size of the print. Can be used as a stand-alone system or be hooked up to a computer. Compatible with many software titles. Similar to DTN Wall Street, but Spectrum is in color.
Data Transmission Network Cor-
  poration (DTN)
9110 W. Dodge Road, Ste. 200
Omaha, NE 68114
800–485–4000; 402–390–2328

DTN WALL STREET*
Systems: Stand–alone system
  compatible with DOS and
  MAC. Uses cable TV or satel-
  lite.
$295 plus $38/month and up
News (business, economic, company); quotes (stock, bond, mutual fund). Provides commentary and information on the debt markets and stock markets. Offers many elective services. Can be used as a stand-alone system or be hooked up to a computer. Compatible with many software titles.

Data Transmission Network Corporation (DTN)
9110 W. Dodge Road, Ste. 200
Omaha, NE 68114
800-485-4000; 402-390-2328

EDGAR [ELECTRONIC DATA GATHERING, ANALYSIS & RETRIEVAL]
Available on Internet: http://www.sec.gov/edgarhp.htm
Free
Covers corporate filings with the Securities and Exchange Commission. The SEC now requires all publicly held companies to file their financial statements, annual reports (10-K), quarterly reports (10-Q), and other mandated documents electronically. These are captured on the SEC-sponsored EDGAR database and are available at no charge to investors and other interested parties. *Note*: There are other private vendors who are retrieving and reselling EDGAR data for a fee.

ENCORE
System: WIN
$169 plus $12–$80/month
Gives quotes and news on stocks, commodities, mutual funds, and options. Has charting capabilities.
Telemet America, Inc.
325 First Street
Alexandria, VA 22314
800-368-2078

FREE FINANCIAL NETWORK (FFN)*
Systems: DOS, WIN, MAC
No start-up or access fees. Quote fees vary from $0.30/day and up.
News (general, business, economic); quotes (stock, mutual fund); analyst reports; technical analysis; software library for downloading. Information includes quotes, financial magazines, newsletters, investment roundtables, and forums. Vendors can rent sections on FFN.
Micro Code Technologies
220 E. 54th Street, #12-J
New York, NY 10022
212-838-6324

MARKET CENTER*
System: DOS. Uses cable TV, FM, or satellite.
$397 plus $59/month and up
News; quotes (stock, bond, mutual fund); technical analysis; fundamental data; portfolio management; weather information; alerts. Employs a "Superquote" page to view all information on a particular symbol. Automatically puts an asterisk by your symbol when a news story concerns that security. Contains price and volume alerts. Has technical analysis and information on earnings, dividends, etc. Portfolio manager updates your investments every five seconds.
Bonneville Market Information (BMI)
3 Triad Center, Ste. 100
Salt Lake City, Utah 84180
800-255-7374

MONEY CENTER
System: DOS
$880 plus $475/month
Real-time quote service, covering stocks, commodities, and bonds. Also includes news wire services. Allows users to create own charts and export data to Lotus spreadsheets.

Knight-Ridder Financial
75 Wall Street, 23rd floor
New York, NY 10005
800-433-8930; 212-269-1110

PC QUOTE 6.0 FOR WINDOWS ON THE INTERNET
System: Windows 95
$75–$300/month
Real-time quotes through the Internet covering stocks, options, and futures. News retrieval capability. Create charts on historic prices as well as many technical indicators. Windows format allows several charts to be viewed simultaneously with quotes.
PC Quote, Inc.
300 S. Wacker Drive, Ste. 300
Chicago, IL 60606
800-225-5657; 312-913-2800;
http://www.pcquote.com

PERSONAL INVESTING ONLINE SERVICE
Systems: DOS, WIN, MAC, OS2. Requires modem.
No access charges, downloading fees, or monthly fees.
News (general, business, economic, company); financial statement data; analyst reports. Research and analyze over 7,300 stocks and 2,100 mutual funds. Has relative strength rankings, volume analyses, and more. Provides market summaries and earnings reports. Has an investor forum.
Small Investor's Software Company
138 Ocean Avenue
Amityville, NY 11701
800-829-9368; 516-789-9368

PRODIGY
Systems: DOS, MAC, WIN. Requires modem.

$14.95/month and up. Call for a free trial.
A general on-line service that also covers finance. News (general, business, economic, company); quotes (stock, bond, mutual fund); financial statement data; analyst reports; technical and fundamental analysis; software library for downloading; mutual fund screening.
Prodigy Services Company
445 Hamilton Avenue
White Plains, NY 10601
800-776-3449; 914-993-8000

QUOTE MONKEY
System: WIN
$19.95/month. Quotes over 10,000 a month are at $0.001 each.
Historical quotes; stocks (NYSE, AMEX, NASDAQ, and bulletin board), options, futures, Canadian stocks. A low-cost historical quote database, updated monthly. Compatible with MetaStock, Super Charts, and Windows on Wall Street. Database can be accessed via modem and a toll-free phone number.
Primate Software Inc.
1440 N. Harbor Boulevard
Fullerton, CA 92835
714-879-8023

REALTICK III*
System: WIN
$150/month, including data server
Quotes (stocks, bonds, futures, options, and mutual funds). A charting program for Windows, performs technical analysis, and displays news. Also links to Microsoft Excel.
Townsend Analytics, Ltd.
100 S. Wacker Drive, Ste. 1506
Chicago, IL 60606
800-827-0141; 312-621-0141

REUTERS MONEY NETWORK*
Systems: DOS, WIN, MAC
$25 plus monthly fees of $13 and
up. 1-month trial available.

News (general, business, economic, company); quotes (stock, mutual fund); financial statement data; earnings estimates; on-line brokerage; technical and fundamental stock screening; mutual fund screening. Provides news, financial planning/asset allocation guidance, analysis and screening, and quotes. Gives specific suggestions for mutual funds, CDs, and money markets. Sources include Reuters, Dow Jones, *Money, The Wall Street Journal,* CNBC, S&P, Morningstar, and various newsletters. Has a personal news-clipping service available. Has historical charts, alerts, and portfolio management.

Reality Technologies, Inc.
2200 Renaissance Boulevard
King of Prussia, PA 19406
800-346-2024; 610-277-7600

SIGNAL*
Systems: DOS, WIN, MAC. Uses
cable TV, FM, or satellite.
$145 and up, plus $60/month and
up.

Quotes (stock, bond, mutual fund). Tracks over 90,000 securities and indexes. Compatible with over 100 software titles. Historical data go back to 1978. Has many optional services including Dow Jones News Service Headlines, Zacks Earnings Surprise Reports, Vickers Stock Research Corporation, and Sports Service.

Data Broadcasting Corporation
1900 S. Norfolk Street
P.O. Box 5979
San Mateo, CA 94402
800-367-4670; 415-571-1800

S&P COMSTOCK*
Systems: DOS, WIN, MAC. Uses
modem, satellite, or cable.
$230/month and up

News (general, business, company); quotes (stock, bond, mutual fund); financial statement data; technical analysis; analyst reports. This is a very comprehensive system that covers dozens of markets and exchanges all over the world. Flexible system that may interface with over sixty different software providers and data vendors. Interfaces with Microsoft Word and Excel. Has real-time portfolio management and analysis.

Standard & Poor's
600 Mamaroneck Avenue,
5th Floor
Harrison, NY 10528
800-431-5019

STOCK INVESTOR
Systems: DOS, WIN
$99/yr. for AAII Members; $150/
yr. for nonmembers

An on-line database containing fundamental financial data on over 8,000 companies. Allows user to look up, analyze, and screen for companies meeting specific criteria on over 250 variables. Includes I/B/E/S consensus earnings estimates. Updated quarterly.

American Association of Individual Investors
625 N. Michigan Avenue, Ste.
1900
Chicago, IL 60611
312-280-0170

STREETSMART*
System: WIN
$59

Quotes (stocks, mutual funds, futures); financial news. Tracks prices for user-selected securities, with a one-year historical price database. Also has news from Dow Jones News Retrieval Service. Has programmable price and news alerts.

Charles Schwab and Company, Inc.
101 Montgomery Street
Department S
San Francisco, CA 94104
800-334-4455; 415-627-7000

TELECHART PROFESSIONAL
System: WIN, Requires CD-ROM.
$195 plus $49/month
Quotes (stock, mutual fund); technical analysis. Very similar to Telechart 2000, but this comes with a CD-ROM database that covers ten years of history. Has the usual technical indicators as well as proprietary indicators such as time-segmented volume, money stream, and balance of power. User may create custom formulas using plain English and screen stocks using custom screens. Has arithmetic and logarithmic chart scales. User may organize stocks into groups. Has automatic stock splits.

Worden Brothers, Inc.
4905 Pine Cone Drive
Durham, NC 27707
800-776-4940

TELECHART 2000*
System: DOS
$29 plus $19.80/month. One-month trial available.
Quotes (stock, mutual fund); technical analysis. Has the usual technical indicators as well as proprietary indicators such as time-segmented volume, money stream, and balance of power. User may create custom formulas using plain English and screen stocks using custom screens. Has arithmetic

and logarithmic chart scales. User may organize stocks into groups.

Worden Brothers, Inc.
4905 Pine Cone Drive
Durham, NC 27707
800-776-4940

TELEMET ORION*
System: WIN
$400/month and up
Quotes (stock, bond, mutual fund); news (economic, business, company); fundamental and technical analysis; portfolio management. Contains market summary windows, price/volume alerts, and a real-time portfolio manager. Has twenty-six technical indicators with up to ten years of historical data. Fundamental information includes financial statement data, key ratios, insider trading data, etc. Has optional services such as Dow Jones News.

Telemet America, Inc.
325 First Street
Alexandria, VA 22314
800-368-2078; 703-548-2042

TELERATE*
Systems: Stand-alone system; runs WIN
Price dependent on level of service, call for quote.
Quotes, real-time stocks, bonds, mutual funds, futures, and options; news, all financial news. Technical and fundamental analysis. High-powered trading system, covering quotes and Dow Jones news. Covers government securities, international government securities, money markets, foreign exchange, swaps and derivatives, corporate bonds, energy, municipal bonds, commodities, equities, futures, options, and world equity markets.

**Dow Jones Telerate
Harborside Financial Center
600 Plaza Two
Jersey City, NJ 07311
800-334-3813; 201-938-5500**

TELESCAN ANALYZER*
System: DOS
$199 plus $45/month and up
News (general, business, economic,
company); quotes (stock, bond, mutual fund); financial statement data;
SEC filings; analyst reports; earnings
estimates; technical and fundamental
analysis; mutual fund screening.
Covers over 74,000 stocks, mutual
funds, industry groups, and indexes.
Has up to twenty years of historical
data. Has over eighty technical and
fundamental indicators. User can test
buy/sell signals with its profit tester
and stock optimizer. Provides earnings
reports, Zacks earnings estimates, insider trading, and company fact sheets.
Sources include S&P, Morningstar,
and SEC Online.
**Telescan, Inc.
10550 Richmond Avenue, Ste. 250
Houston, TX 77042
800-324-8246; 713-952-1060**

TELESCAN INVESTOR'S PLATFORM
System: WIN
**$349 ($199 without screening soft-
ware) plus $10/month and up**
News (general, business, economic,
company); quotes (stock, bond, mutual fund); financial statement data;
SEC filings; analyst reports; earnings
estimates; technical and fundamental
analysis; mutual fund screening.
Basically a Windows version of Telescan Analyzer with a few additions.
Covers over 74,000 stocks, mutual
funds, industry groups, and indexes.
Information up to twenty years back.

Has over eighty technical and fundamental indicators. User can test buy/
sell signals with its profit tester and
stock optimizer. Provides earnings reports, Zacks earnings estimates, insider
trading, and company fact sheets.
Sources include S&P, Morningstar,
and SEC Online. Has Internet access.
**Telescan, Inc.
10550 Richmond Avenue, Ste. 250
Houston, TX 77042
800-324-8246; 713-952-1060**

TRACK/ONLINE*
**Systems: WIN, DOS. (Data works
with MAC, but software is not
compatible with MAC.)**
$195 plus $200/month and up
News; quotes (stock, bond, mutual
fund). Very comprehensive information service that provides quotes,
news, and optional services such as
historical graphs, fundamental research, and over twenty news sources.
Has optional third-party databases including Zacks Earnings Estimates,
Vickers Institutional Holdings, and
Morningstar Mutual Funds.
**Track/Online
56 Pine Street
New York, NY 10005
800-367-5968**

TRADELINE
Systems: DOS, WIN, MAC
Price varies, call for quote.
Quotes (stocks, bonds, mutual funds,
options, and futures), stock screening,
and technical analysis. Provides stock
price and financial information for a
universe of over 200,000 securities.
Allows user to define screens and cus-
tomize reports. Also available through
Dow Jones News Retrieval and Dow
Jones Market Monitor.

IDD Information Services
Two World Trade Center,
18th Floor
New York, NY 10048
212-323-9107

System: WIN
$24.95/month and up. Demo
available.

Quotes (stock, mutual fund). Contains over 120,000 symbols in its database. Uses special compression techniques through fast data lines so users can download data quickly. Uses the usual technical indicators and capabilities, but it also has its own method called "The Right Time Study." It uses current volume strength theory, moving average analysis, and market direction to generate signals. User may also view raw quotes and sort them as well. Employs "what if" analysis so the user can plan ahead. Has on-line trading and an optional recommendation service.

T.B.S.P. Inc.
610 Newport Center Drive
Ste. 830
Newport Beach, CA 92660
714-721-8603

Systems: DOS, WIN. Uses cable
TV, FM, or satellite.
$495 plus $59/month and up

News; quotes (stock, bond, mutual fund); technical analysis; alerts; weather information. Contains over 150,000 symbols. A powerful real-time program that maintains over 1,000 intraday charts with over 2,300 bars per chart. Can split the screen into sections so the user can view charts, studies, tools, and text at one time. Includes a systems tester. Utilizes bar charts, Japanese candlesticks, point and figure, and line charts. Employs price, indicator, and news alerts. Has on-line help.

Bonneville Market Information
(BMI)
3 Triad Center, Ste. 100
Salt Lake City, UT 84180
800-255-7374

$1.50 per report and up

Gives you instant access by fax to current financial reports. Available reports include S&P Stock Reports, S&P Industry Reports, and S&P News Headlines. Also has First Call Earnings Estimates Reports, Business Wire Press Releases, Lipper Mutual Fund Reports, and Argus Company Reports. Also has Vickers Insider Trading Reports and historical price charts.

650 Madison Ave., 23rd Floor
New York, NY 10022
800-222-6925

Chapter 5

INVESTING IN BONDS

In comparison to stocks, bonds are simpler and more straightforward investment vehicles. This is due primarily to the contractual, closed-end nature of bonds. When you buy a bond, you have loaned a stated amount of money to the bond's issuer. This amount is the *par value* of the bond, also referred to as the *principal* amount of the money you have loaned. The length of the loan you are making is clearly stated in the bond's terms of the loan, also referred to as its *indenture*. The date at which the loan terminates is the *maturity* date. If you hold the bond to maturity, you will receive that stated amount of money, no more and no less. In the interim you will receive *interest* at predetermined intervals, usually every six months. The amount of interest is clearly stated in the bond's indenture. The interest rate of the bond is called its *coupon*.

So you see, buying a bond enters you into a contractual agreement that has a beginning and an end, with entitlements (interest) in between. When the day of the contract's termination arrives (maturity date), that bond ceases to exist. It dies. The same issuer could create and sell another bond for the same length of time and at the same rate of interest, but it would have a different maturity date and, in the legal sense, it is another bond altogether.

Contrast this with investment in the common stock of a company. As long as the company survives in its existing legal form, that is, it does not go out of business or combine with another entity to form a new company, the stock survives. Stocks are traded today for companies that have been in business for over 100 years. Recall that stock ownership is an equity relationship and one that is open-ended. You the investor either elect to be a shareholder in the company, or you don't.

There is no meaningful contractual relationship as there is with a bond. For example, corporate management is under no legal obligation to pay common shareholders periodic cash payments (dividends), whereas the bond issuer has the legal obligation to pay interest when due and in the amount indicated in the bond indenture. Failure to pay interest results in *default*, and it creates massive legal hassles for the issuer. Consequently, bond issuers avoid defaults at all costs.

As we saw in the now familiar Figure 3–1 (page 32), bond returns are considerably lower than the returns on stocks. It should now be apparent why this is the case. Assuming that the issuer is creditworthy and will not default, the only *uncertainty* facing the bond investor is what the fluctuation in interest rates will be while he is the holder of his bond. Since bond values fluctuate inversely with interest rate levels (bonds decline in value as interest rates rise, and vice versa), his concern is that the bonds will depreciate in value. But the bondholder has a safety net, right? It's called the bond's maturity date, and on that date the investor gets all of his money back, irrespective of what is happening to interest rates in general.

Contrast this again with the stockholder. The common stockholder has many more uncertainties confronting her. The multitude of positive or negative factors that impact a company will impact the valuation of that company's stock as well. These could include changes in the U.S. or world economies, changes among its competitors, or technological developments, just to name a few. Because the common stockholder is faced with so much more uncertainty, the valuation of her investment is determined much more by human psychology than is the bond investment. Hence, stocks are subject to the wild swings of human emotions that we've mentioned before: *fear* and *greed*. Conversely, you get lower returns and lower volatility with bonds than with stocks simply because bonds are not as subject to human mood swings as are stocks.

While many professionals and amateurs like to trade bonds aggressively in order to capture fluctuations in price caused by interest rate moves, and some do this quite successfully, let us proceed here under the premise that bonds are to be used as the stabilizer of your portfolio. If you want to rock and roll with swinging trade strategies, do it with stocks, not bonds.

BOND ANALYSIS

Here are the only things you really need to know about a bond:

- Issuer
- Bond rating
- Interest rate
- Maturity date
- Call provisions
- Insurance

Knowing the *issuer* is imperative since you are lending money to that entity. Governments, both foreign and U.S., are big issuers of bonds. They have to be in order to operate under the massive budget deficits with which they all live. Governments do not issue stock (although maybe it should be considered), so bonds and short-term debt instruments are the means for them to function financially. In the U.S. such issuers include the federal government (U.S. Treasury securities), federal agencies (Federal National Mortgage Association, Federal Home Loan Bank, Federal Farm Credit System, and others), state governments, and city and county governments. Bringing up the rear in bond issuance are corporations.

The *bond rating* of any issuer is a vital criterion in bond selection. As with stock analysis, you could spend many hours picking apart an issuer's balance sheet and cash flow statements to ascertain their creditworthiness. All a bondholder cares about is the issuer's ability to pay the interest in the amount agreed upon and at the date due, *plus* the ability to repay the principal amount of the bond on the maturity date. Like stocks, there are firms that perform the required analysis. Four rating services rate almost every publicly traded bond: Moody's Investor Service, Standard & Poor's Corporation, Duff & Phelps Credit Rating Company, and Fitch Investors Service. All four services analyze the issuers, and from this analysis they create a rating in letter form. This rating is then monitored on an ongoing basis by the services to detect financial changes in the issuer that help or injure their existing rating. Below is a matrix of the ratings issued by each of the four services.

TABLE 5-1
BOND RATINGS

Moody's	S&P	Duff & Phelps	Fitch
Aaa	AAA	AAA	AAA
Aa1	AA+	AA+	AA
Aa2	AA	AA	A
Aa3	AA−	AA−	BBB
A1	A+	A+	BB
A2	A	A	B
A3	A−	A−	
Baa1	BBB+	BBB+	
Baa2	BBB	BBB	
Baa3	BBB−	BBB−	

The triple-A rating is the highest rating, as you might guess, and they depreciate from there. The ratings for each of these services extend below the lowest rating shown. We recommend that you invest only in bonds with an A− or A3 rating, or better, at the time of purchase. Leave the B- and C-grade bonds to the professionals managing junk-bond mutual funds. Remember, you own bond investments because you want the lower risk and reduced volatility they afford, as well as the cash flow from them. There is no need to take on unnecessary risk by buying lower-quality credit issues.

The *maturity date* is the date that the principal will come due, and the issuer will send you a check for the par value amount of the bonds you own. Short-term instruments of less than one-year maturity at issuance are technically not bonds. They are usually called Treasury bills (if issued by the U.S. Treasury), certificates of deposit (banks and thrift institutions), or commercial paper (usually corporations), among others. Bonds or notes are typically issued with a maturity of two years or longer. Maturities at issuance can go out to thirty years. Some bonds have longer maturities (100-year bonds have been sold by several issuers in recent years). If you want to guarantee your bond portfolio's value out at some point in time that correlates to an anticipated event, say college for your children, you could buy a long-term bond with a maturity date matching or approximating that event's occurrence.

The *interest rate* on a bond is always stated in annual percentage terms and is referred to as the coupon or coupon rate. The interest on your bond is usually paid to you at six-month intervals, with one payment date corresponding to the month and day of the month that the bond matures in some future year. Some bonds, called *zero-coupon bonds*, do not pay interest at all during the bond's lifetime. Instead you pay a deeply discounted price for the bond and receive only the par value of the bond when it matures, or when you sell the bond to someone else. For example, if you bought a $10,000 par value ten-year zero-coupon bond with a yield of 7.2 percent, you would pay $5,000 for the bond. When the bond matures in ten years you will receive a check for $10,000. The difference between what you paid and what you receive at maturity or when you sell it is the interest.

There is a relationship between interest rates and maturity dates. More often than not, the farther away the maturity date is, the higher the interest rate on the bond will be. The logic of this is that there is some risk in the longer time frame; that is, the amount of uncertainty increases as the time horizon moves further out. In a rational world, investors should be compensated for taking on additional risk of any kind; hence, the higher interest rate for longer maturities. The graphical representation of the time-yield relationship is commonly referred to as the *yield curve*.

A yield curve plots the years left until the bond matures on the bottom axis, and the yield scale on the left axis. As we stated above, usually the yield curve has an upward or positive slope, as yields rise with the longer period until the bond matures. There are periods of time, however, when the yield curve slopes downward to the right. This is called an *inverted yield curve*. In this situation, the inverted curve reflects short-term interest rates that are higher than long-term interest rates. These situations are relatively rare, but they occur when the overall rate of inflation is high and/or the Federal Reserve is itself raising rates in an effort to squelch inflation and slow the economy when it is growing at a high rate that is contributing to inflation. Some readers may recall the late 1970s and early 1980s when short-term rates approached 20 percent and the thirty-year Treasury bond yielded about 14 percent; this was the ultimate in inverted yield curves.

Call provisions afford the issuer of the bond the opportunity to buy the bond back from the investor, usually at a prespecified date and price. The act of repurchasing the bond is termed a *call*. The price specified in the bond indenture is almost always at par value or greater, although this "call price" may be more or less than the investor originally paid for the bond. An issuer cannot foresee the circumstances, at the time of the bond's issuance, that render it to their advantage to exercise the call option. Nevertheless, because it is their option, and not the investor's option, it is never implemented to the investor's benefit.

An issuer would call the bonds when, at the call provision date, it could reissue new bonds at a lower interest rate. In other words, the yield curve is lower than when the bonds were issued, and the issuer is trying to lower their borrowing costs. For you the investor, the attractive bonds you now own could not be replaced with the proceeds from the call. Since bonds are always called at or near par value, you would have to go out and pay more than par for different bonds that have the same interest rate you now enjoy. However, like it or not, the bonds you have are being taken away from you by the call. Conversely, if rates were higher than at issuance, there is no incentive to issue new bonds that would raise their borrowing costs, so no call would occur. Under this scenario you are "stuck" with unattractive bonds, probably valued at a loss. Stated another way, callable bonds are a "heads they win, tails you lose" proposition. The ounce of prevention is easy. Do not invest in bonds with a call provision. *Buy only noncallable bonds.*

Bond *insurance* applies to municipal bonds, which we'll discuss in detail next. There are four major municipal bond insurers: MBIA, AMBAC, FGIC, and FSA. The insurers guarantee that the investor will receive all the interest that is due and the principal owed them upon maturity. Bonds that carry insurance have a triple-A rating. This insurance, and that rating, result in 10 to 20 basis points' lower yield to the investor. Although all of these bond insurers are on solid financial ground, if you are looking for insured bonds it is a good idea to invest in bonds that have an A rating on their own, without any insurance. This lowers the likelihood that the insurance will ever be activated.

MUNICIPAL BONDS

Municipal bonds are bonds issued by nonfederal governmental bodies and agencies: states, counties, cities, and other authorities contained within these, such as school districts and water districts. The vast majority of these bonds enjoy the feature that the interest paid from them is not subject to federal income taxes. The interest may or may not be subject to state and local income taxes. Such bonds are often called "tax-free" or "tax-exempt" bonds, although one must not assume that a municipal bond is exempt from taxation. These days a number of municipalities issue bonds that are fully taxable, and they pay interest rates in accordance with the taxable bond yield curve.

In assessing a municipal bond, one must scrutinize the purpose of the bond proceeds. This is done by studying the preliminary prospectus (also referred to as the official statement, or OS) available from the issuer at the time of the bond's offering to the public. Prospectuses can be obtained from the lead underwriters of the offering or they can be retrieved through the EDGAR system (page 138). Again, the bond rating agencies will have done most of the homework for you on municipal bonds, so pay close attention to those ratings. Be comfortable with both the purpose of the proceeds from the bond sales and the sources of the cash flow that will provide the payment of principal and interest. Bonds backed by the taxing authority of a government body are the safest, since the issuer's constituents can have their taxes increased to pay the bond's interest and principal. This concept may sound loathsome to many investors, but remember the issuer's constituents are the people benefiting from your money that is being loaned to their state, county, or city. Sooner or later they have to pay for the facilities that have been financed on credit.

An example of a municipal bond to be wary of is one where the municipality is in partnership with a private venture to develop land for some specific use. Using housing as an example, if a housing subdivision is developed using municipal financing, and the houses do not sell after all the money has been spent on streets, sewers, and other improvements, the prospects of the bondholder's receiving all the interest and principal that is due them drops considerably. Bonds like this are not likely to be highly rated nor will they carry bond insurance. For this reason, we recommend that investors look only at noncallable issues that are rated A or higher *and* carry insurance. The peace of mind afforded by insurance is well worth the 10 to 20 basis points of yield that it costs.

Not every investor will benefit from using tax-exempt bonds. Only those investors in a tax bracket high enough to warrant municipal bonds should consider them. And of course, you would never use tax-exempt municipals in retirement accounts like IRAs, which already have tax-exempt status. Many people have an aversion to paying taxes. I have seen a number of investors who were in a lower tax bracket that did not justify the use of municipal bonds. Nevertheless, they bought them anyway, just on the rationale that they would not be giving money to the government. They had difficulty grasping the concept that if they bought taxable bonds and paid a small tax on the interest, they would have more money left after paying those taxes than they would receive in municipal bond interest.

So who *would* benefit from the use of municipal bonds? The operative number to work with in making that determination is the investor's *marginal tax rate*. This is different from the "average tax rate" that the investor pays. So do not divide the taxes you paid last year by your adjusted gross income and believe that this is your marginal tax rate. If someone prepares your tax return for you, call them and request the marginal tax rate from them. To determine the marginal tax rate yourself, refer to last year's federal income tax return and the instruction book that came with it. Contained in the latter are the tax tables from which your tax liability was calculated. Cross-reference your tax liability with the table. The table will indicate at what percentage each additional dollar of income will be taxed. That percentage is your marginal tax rate.

Now you need to insert the marginal tax rate into a simple equation that calculates the *taxable equivalent yield* of a municipal bond you may be considering. You need to know two yield numbers, one for the municipal bond you are considering and the other the yield of a taxable bond with the same maturity. If you are looking at a ten-year muni bond, find the yield, in the newspaper or from the broker through which you'll buy the bond, of the ten-year Treasury note. The taxable equivalent yield (TEY) is calculated as follows:

$$\text{TEY} = \frac{\text{Municipal Bond Yield}}{1 - \text{Marginal Tax Rate}}$$

As an example, assume you are contemplating investing in a ten-year municipal bond that yields 5 percent and your marginal tax rate is 31 percent. Inserting those numbers into the formula results in 5 ÷ (1 − 0.31), or 5 ÷ 0.69. This amounts to a 7.25 percent taxable equivalent yield. If the ten-year Treasury note yields 7.25 percent or greater, invest in the Treasury. Otherwise, the municipal bond will generate the greater amount of after-tax income. To clarify, let us look at the comparison in reverse. The 0.69 number is the percent retained after the tax has been paid, sometimes referred to as the *tax retention rate*. When you apply that to the 7.25 percent Treasury note yield, you get a yield just above 5 percent; hence, any Treasury yield less than 7.25 percent would result in *less* after-tax income than that provided by the municipal bond.

Two caveats must be considered in this analysis. First, we have previously considered only federal taxes in calculating taxable equivalent yield. If you are subject to state and local income taxes, the marginal tax rates for these liabilities must be added. So the tax retention rate falls and the taxable equivalent yield rises. In the example above, a 4 percent marginal *state* income tax added to the 31 percent federal marginal tax rate drops the tax retention rate to 0.65 (1 − 0.35). The TEY then rises to 7.69 percent from 7.25 percent. The second thing to remember is that the taxable equivalent yield analysis applies only to the analysis of bonds being purchased at par. Bonds bought above or below par value make the after-tax determination of yields and rate of return more complex because a capital gain or capital loss results when the bond is sold or held to maturity. The calculation resulting from gain or loss requires a computer program or specially programmed bond calculator. Some of the software highlighted in the Resource Guide of this chapter will accomplish this task. Otherwise, any broker you deal with who has the capability to trade bonds can make those calculations for you prior to executing a bond purchase on your behalf.

BUILDING A BOND PORTFOLIO

A pertinent question to ask at this point is, "What discount brokers will trade bonds for me?" The good news is that every discount broker listed in Chapter 2, (pages 16–18) *except* E*TRADE, has the ability to trade bonds for clients. If you know you will be investing heavily in bonds, and you know what type of bonds you will require (municipal bonds, for instance), check this out with the prospective discount broker over the phone before submitting the account application. If you will be investing in both stocks and bonds, and you are uncertain about one broker's bond trading capability but comfortable with another broker's bond desk, split your portfolio so that stocks are traded with the broker of first choice there, and have the bonds traded with another broker. This is one of the few situations that would justify splitting your assets apart, so go ahead and do it if it seems appropriate.

Unlike stock investing, which has spawned newsletters numbering in the hundreds, bond investing is covered by very few newsletters. Part of the reason for this is the limited life of individual bonds, with new bonds constantly being issued and existing bonds maturing. This environment is not conducive to a newsletter covering and recommending individual bonds. Newsletters that do cover the bond market tend to treat it in the broad sense, as in forecasting changes in the direction of interest rates, the shape of the yield curve, and perhaps on what range of maturities investors should be focused. In selecting individual bonds, you will be on your own, so to speak. Fortunately, the intense analytical work has already been done by the rating agencies. Following a few simple tenets, which follow, you can construct an effective bond portfolio with your own efforts.

We have already mentioned some of the bond investment criteria you should employ:

- Buy only bonds rated A3, A−, or better.
- Buy only noncallable bonds.
- If buying municipal bonds, look for those that are insured.

In constructing a bond portfolio, here are some additional elements to consider:

- If buying taxable bonds, use a mix of different bonds such as Treasury bonds, federal agency bonds, and corporate bonds.
- Invest in maturities out to ten years.
- Ladder maturities over the ten-year maturity horizon.
- Plan on holding the bonds to maturity, selling bonds only to raise needed cash or if the bond's rating drops below A3 or A−.

To expand on these points, the first three criteria urge you to invest in high-quality bonds that will create a minimal amount of risk or volatility for you, the investor. Remember, you want bonds to be the low-risk investments in your portfolio. Thus, buy only highly rated bonds that cannot be called away from you by the issuer, and if you should invest in municipal bonds, look first for the insured issues. If using taxable bonds, feel free to mix them up among different types. Despite the quest for low risk, do not believe you are doing yourself a favor by investing only in Treasuries. You are short-changing your rate of return in the process. Create a mixture of the three main types of coupon bonds. Avoid investing in GNMA and other mortgage-backed or asset-backed securities. Reserve zero-coupon bonds of any type for use in IRA accounts or in children's education funds. In short, for most portfolios you should stay with "plain vanilla" investments.

Unless you have identified a year in the distant future, one in which something in particular will occur (here we go with college and retirement again), we recommend that you invest in bonds maturing only as far out as ten years. In today's environment of relatively flat yield curves with single-digit returns, there is little incentive or reward to invest beyond ten years. If each additional maturity year beyond ten does not generate at least 10 basis points (100 basis points = 1.00 percent) of incremental yield per year, you are not being adequately compensated for the additional time risk and potential interest rate risk. Finally, within this ten-year time frame, create what is called a ladder of maturities. This simply means that you are buying bonds whose maturities correspond to each of the years in your time horizon.

To clarify this, if you are investing $100,000 in bonds with maturities as long as ten years, you attempt to buy ten bonds, each being $10,000 in par value. Look for bonds that mature each year, beginning one year hence, until there is a bond maturing in each year of the ten years going forward. This is a very sound strategy, especially for individual investors who may not be comfortable moving bonds back and forth frequently between different years, trying to capture swings in the yield curve. The laddering approach has the strength that it benefits the bond investor when yields are rising and protects them when yields are falling. Consider in the above-mentioned hypothetical $100,000 portfolio that, as a bond matures each year, the strategy is to reinvest those monies out ten years in time, maintaining the moving ten-year time horizon in the process. Since at least one bond is maturing every year, the investor is able to capture an upswing in yields by buying a bond with a higher yield than the bond that just matured. Likewise, if yields are falling, a lower-yielding bond may have to be purchased, but the coupons of the other bonds will be as high or higher than the new bond, thus helping to maintain the yield of the overall portfolio.

Let us assume in the $100,000 bond portfolio the following allocation of bonds by type of issuer: treasuries—$40,000; agencies—$30,000; corporate bonds—$30,000. An example of the laddering structure of the portfolio would be: Treasuries—years 2, 4, 6, 8; agencies—years 1, 3, 9; corporate bonds—years 5, 7, 10. The bond market is similar in structure to the over-the-counter stock market, with no central trading floor for most bond issues. Instead, the bond market consists of the electronically linked group of bond dealers who collectively make the market in bonds. Finding a list of Treasury and agency bonds is easy; they are shown in the daily business newspapers, sorted by maturity. The Treasuries and agency bonds can be identified in the newspaper, and the appropriate maturities selected. Buying the bonds is simply a matter of calling your discount broker's bond desk and placing an order to buy $10,000 par value (or whatever amount is appropriate in your case) of the particular bond. The broker will purchase them from a bond dealer who handles that issue and will charge you a commission, just as in a stock trade.

Locating and buying corporate bonds (and municipal bonds, if those are the issues you need) may be a little more time-consuming. Some corporates are listed in the daily business newspapers, near the Treasury and agency bond listings. Hundreds of other corporate bonds, and all municipal bonds that trade, are not listed there. Corporate and municipal bonds do not trade very actively. They tend to be purchased and held by investors. Therefore, if you buy a corporate or municipal bond that has already been issued, it is accomplished almost by accident. It means that an investor somewhere decided to sell part or all of his holding of the bond, or type of bond, that you just happened to be looking for. While locating such bonds can seem impossible to you, it is relatively easy for your discount broker to find them. There are several electronic "bulletin boards" where bond dealers post the quantity and price of issues they are trying to sell. Your broker's bond-trading desk will have access to these and will shop around looking for the right issue and the right price for you.

The discussion above has focused on the *secondary market* for bonds, that is, the market for bonds that have already been issued into the market and are now freely trading. The new-issue bond market is also an excellent source of investments as well. It requires a little more diligence on the part of the investor. Watch the daily business newspapers in the section indicating new offerings of all types of securities. There will be brief articles describing new bond offerings and there may even be a calendar. Official-looking announcements may also appear, referred to as "tombstones." After seeing an issue that may be right for you, call any office of the lead underwriter listed in the announcement and request a prospectus. The prospectus will outline for you the purpose of the money borrowed, the issuer's financial statements, the credit ratings by the rating services, and any special provisions, such as call features. When you have satisfied yourself that this is a suitable bond investment, contact the discount broker's bond-trading desk and describe the issue. The trader will be able to identify it and try to locate the quantity desired in the secondary market.

The shortcut to locating bonds in the secondary market is simply to call the bond trader and tell him the parameters of the bonds you want:

- Issuer or type of issuer
- Rating of issue
- Amount of bonds
- Price limitation; for example, par value or less
- Desired year of maturity
- Insurance, if applicable

The bond trader then scans the databases of bonds put up for sale by other investors until he finds one or more issues that meet your requirements. He then executes the transaction for you, adding on a fee or commission for his efforts. These fees will vary from $25 to $100 or more per bond traded. Although you should scrutinize such fees to see that they're reasonable, do not get overly aggressive about shopping around for the best bond-fee deal, as you might otherwise do with stock commissions. You will be doing far fewer bond trades than you will stock trades, if you trade both vehicles, so the bond fee will be absorbed or amortized over a longer period of time than stock commissions would be. In other words, if you pay $100 for a bond that you expect to hold for five years, it will have an insignificant impact on that bond's rate of return over the expected holding period. When you enter your order with the broker, do so with the "all or none" stipulation. Otherwise, the broker may take two or more separate trades to fill your order, and you incur two or more broker fees or commissions.

DIRECT INVESTMENT IN TREASURY SECURITIES

Until technology and government regulations allow otherwise, buying and selling bonds, like buying and selling stocks, must be done through a broker, bond dealer, or other licensed intermediary. There is a program, however, that enables individual investors to invest directly with the Federal Reserve Banks to buy U.S. Treasury securities without paying any fees or commissions. The exception to that statement is that the Fed imposes a $25 annual fee on accounts in excess of $100,000. The program is called Treasury Direct. Money is deposited in Treasury Direct accounts with the Federal Reserve to buy specific issues at auction. You cannot just deposit money and place orders for outstanding securities; this program is specifically designed to facilitate the auctions of Treasury securities, which occur regularly. Table 5-2 outlines the securities, auction schedules, and minimum investment amounts.

In payment, bills must be purchased with a cashier's check or certified personal check. Uncertified personal checks can be used to buy notes and bonds. After a

---

TABLE 5-2

TREASURY AUCTION SCHEDULE

ISSUE	AUCTION PERIODS	MINIMUM $
90- and 180-day bills	Monday of every week	$10,000
One-year bills	Every four weeks on a Thursday	$10,000
Two- and five-year notes	Monthly, usually during third week	$ 5,000
Three-year notes	February, May, August, November	$ 1,000
Ten-year notes	February, May, July, August, October, November	$ 1,000
Thirty-year bonds	February, August, November	$ 1,000

purchase is made, a confirmation of the transaction is mailed to you. All trades are book entry; no certificates are mailed. No statements are sent to you, and you cannot sell the securities through Treasury Direct. Whether you hold ninety-day bills or thirty-year bonds, they remain in the Treasury Direct account until maturity. Upon maturity the principal is wired to a bank account designated by you. In the interim, interest is wired to that account as well. If you anticipate selling the securities prior to maturity, you must do so through your discount broker. This requires that the securities be transferred to the broker, which takes several weeks. The Resource Guide at the end of this chapter lists the offices of the Federal Reserve, which can be contacted to learn more about the Treasury Direct program.

YIELD TO MATURITY

The single best measure for an investor to use in evaluating how a particular bond is being priced relative to other bonds is *yield to maturity*. Yield to maturity is the rate of return on a bond that is bought and held to maturity, expressed in an annualized basis. This is often different from the current yield, which was described in Chapter 3, Asset Allocation. Current yield is the annual cash flow from an asset divided by that asset's current market price. So a $10,000 bond with a 7 percent coupon rate and selling at a price of $99 (that's 0.99 × $10,000, or $9,900) has a current yield of 7.07 percent ($700 ÷ $9,900). The *yield to maturity* of that bond, if it was to mature one year hence, would be approximately 8.08 percent (7.07% + [$100 ÷ $9,900]). Thus, yield to maturity not only accounts for a bond's current yield, but it also captures any appreciation in value ($100 in the example), or depreciation, as the case may be, from one point in time until the bond matures. For a bond selling at par value, the current yield and the yield to maturity are the same value. Bonds selling below par (a *discount*) will have a yield to maturity greater than current yield. Bonds selling above par (a *premium*) will have a yield to maturity less than the current yield. Table 5-3 below depicts these relationships.

For illustrative purposes and to explain the concept concisely, the example above showed the yield to maturity to be the current yield with the discount added on for the one year left until the bond matures. While that representation

---

TABLE 5-3[6]

Price of the Bond	Relationship
Selling at Par	Coupon Rate = Current Yield = Yield to Maturity
Selling at a Discount	Coupon Rate < Current Yield < Yield to Maturity
Selling at a Premium	Coupon Rate > Current Yield > Yield to Maturity

---

[6]Frank J. Fabozzi and Irving M. Pollack, *The Handbook of Fixed Income Securities*, 2nd ed. New York: Dow Jones Irwin, 1987.

is correct, accurately calculating yield to maturity must be done with a bond calculator or bond software. Once you know the yield to maturity for a particular issue, you can compare that issue to others to see if it makes sense to hold the bond you have, or to sell it and buy a comparable bond that has a higher yield to maturity. Rather than being adept at calculating yield to maturity, the investor simply needs to understand its relevance and to be aware of its use in comparing two or more bonds.

One aspect of bond investment that can give the novice investor some apprehension is buying bonds at a premium to par (above par). The philosophical difficulty for some investors is they know that, when the bond matures, it will be worth less than they paid for it. Investing in an asset with the guarantee that it will be worth *less* in the future is contrary to common sense. This, again, is where the yield-to-maturity concept comes into play. If a bond is valued above par, at a premium, it implicitly means that the coupon attached to that bond is higher than coupons on bonds being issued at that time. So owning those bonds affords you a special privilege, one for which you have to pay a bonus price. The greater cash flow from the higher coupon will offset the decline in your initial investment. This is why yield to maturity is the key measure of value for bonds.

SUMMARY

At the beginning of this chapter we said that bonds were simpler and more straightforward than stocks. Hopefully, the myriad of details about bonds that have been discussed in the chapter have not nullified that statement. Just realize that the elements you need to know are:

- Issuer
- Bond rating
- Interest rate
- Maturity date
- Call provisions
- Insurance
- Yield to maturity

Create a laddered portfolio of noncallable bonds, with maturities out to ten years, that are rated A3 or A− or better. If municipal bonds are beneficial to your after-tax income, buys bonds with the same criteria above, and add bond insurance as a sweetener. Structure the portfolio ladder so that bonds are continuously maturing at regular intervals. Roll the maturing bonds out to the end of your portfolio horizon. Following these procedures will provide you with a bond portfolio that will satisfy your cash-flow needs with relatively little risk.

RESOURCE GUIDE
INVESTING IN BONDS

Newsletters

Many newsletters that deal with stock investing will also give some attention to the bond market as well. We recommend that you scan the Resource Guide in Chapter 4, Investing in Stocks, to identify these newsletters.

BOND FUND REPORT

Statistical analysis. Covers bond mutual funds. Commentary on interest rates, the bond market, and bond mutual funds. Detailed performance analysis of hundreds of bond mutual funds.
$1,095/yr. Weekly
IBC/Donoghue, Inc.
P.O. Box 9104
Ashland, MA 01721-9104
800-343-5413

CALIFORNIA MUNICIPAL BOND ADVISOR

Covers bonds and bond funds. Fundamental analysis. Gives charts and analysis of California municipal bonds. Also analyzes California municipal bond funds.
$125/yr. Monthly
1750 E. Arenas Road, Ste. 25
Palm Springs, CA 92262
619-320-7997

JUNK BOND REPORTER

Covers bonds. Fundamental analysis. Features news items relevant to junk bonds. Includes statistics on a bellwether group of junk bonds chosen by the editor.
$645/yr. Weekly
American Banker—Bond Buyer
The Thomson Publishing Corp.
P.O. Box 30240

Bethesda, MD 20824
800-733-4371; 301-654-5580

MOODY'S BOND SURVEY

Covers municipal bonds, corporate bonds, government bonds. Technical analysis. Includes statistical information such as ratings changes, offering calendar, and preferred-stock yield averages.
$1,175/yr. Weekly
Moody's Investors Service
99 Church Street
New York, NY 10007
212-553-0437

MUNI WEEK

Covers bonds. Fundamental analysis. Has analysis of muni market and government issues that affect municipal bonds, such as municipal budgets, pending legislation, and issuers bringing bonds to the market.
$525/yr. Weekly
American Banker—Bond Buyer
One State Street
New York, NY 10004
800-367-3989; 212-803-8200

MUNICIPAL BOND BOOK

Covers bonds. Fundamental analysis. Gives debt ratings on municipal bond issuers.
$1,135/yr. Bimonthly
Standard & Poor's

25 Broadway
New York, NY 10004
212-208-8000

**WASHINGTON BOND & MONEY
  MARKET REPORT**
Covers government and municipal
bonds and Treasuries. Fundamental
analysis. Commentary on interest
rates, the economy, money supply,
Federal Reserve, and international
politics.
$325/yr. Biweekly
1545 New York Avenue N.E.
Washington, DC 20002
800-345-2611; 202-526-9664

Books

ALL ABOUT BONDS
Esme Faerber. Probus, 1993.
$19.95 ISBN: 1-55738-437-1
Explains the bond market environment and how it interacts with the
economy. Describes the different types
of bonds and what to look for in evaluating them. Also covers bond mutual
funds.

THE BOND BOOK
Annette Thau. Irwin Professional,
  1994.
$22.95 pbk. ISBN: 1-55738-809-1
This book fills the gap between bond
books aimed at professionals and those
aimed at the novice, which are usually
too simplistic. This book is aimed at
the novice, but the information is
more substantial than in most other
bond books. The author covers everything from Treasury securities to junk
bonds; discusses the risks and
opportunities in bond investing; and
she tells the reader where to find information.

THE COMPLETE BOOK OF BONDS
Donald R. Nichols. Dearborn Financial, 1989.
$12.95 ISBN: 0-79310-089-5
A thorough primer on investing in
bonds. Shows the technical aspects of
government and corporate bonds,
why interest rates fluctuate, and how
and where to use bonds to achieve
your investment objectives.

GETTING STARTED IN BONDS
Michael C. Thomsett. John Wiley
  & Sons, 1991.
$17.95 pbk. ISBN: 0-471-52479-4
This nontechnical book has plenty of
examples that make bonds under-
standable. Topics range from the simple T-bill and savings bond to the
more complex municipal bond and
junk bond. Author explains the risks
and rewards of fixed-income investing, and discusses putting bonds into
your asset allocation mix.

**THE HANDBOOK OF MUNICIPAL
  BONDS**
Susan C. Heide, Robert A. Klein,
  and Jess Lederman. Irwin Professional, 1994.
$85.00 ISBN: 1-55738-577-7
This is a detailed reference source that
is quite technical. In addition to covering the elements of municipal bond
credit analysis, there is lengthy treatment of the role of derivatives in professional portfolio management.

HOW MUNICIPAL BONDS WORK
Robert Zipf. New York Institute
  of Finance, 1995.

$15.95 pbk. ISBN: 0-13-122656-8
A thorough treatment of the municipal bond market, describing the types of bonds, types of municipal issuers, bond insurance, and analysis of issues. For those who know they should invest in munis, this is a good place to start.

MUNICIPAL BOND PORTFOLIO MANAGEMENT

Frank J. Fabozzi, T. Dessa Fabozzi, and Sylvan G. Feldstein. Irwin Professional, 1994.
$80.00 ISBN: 1-55623-672-7
Written for professional managers, the book delves into the different types of municipal bonds and their features. Describes credit analysis techniques and elements of portfolio construction.

THE PERSONAL INVESTOR'S COMPLETE BOOK OF BONDS

Donald R. Nichols. Dearborn Financial, 1990.
$23.95 hc ISBN: 0-88462-627-X
$12.95 pbk. ISBN: 0-7931-0089-5
Covers CDs, treasury securities, municipal bonds, corporate bonds, and more. Also suggests how to use bonds in saving for retirement and other financial goals.

STANDARD & POOR'S STOCK AND BOND GUIDE

McGraw-Hill, updated annually.
$24.95 pbk.
Reference book. Enlarged and annualized version of S&P's monthly stock and bond guides. Contains data on 14,000 stocks, bonds, mutual funds, and annuities.

Software

BOND BUYER FULL TEXT
Systems: Any communications software
$45 plus $2.50/minute
Covers bonds. An on-line version of *The Bond Buyer* and *Credit Markets*. Provides daily coverage of government and Treasury securities, financial futures, corporate bonds, and mortgage securities. Also reports on fiscal and economic policy.
Dialog Information Services, Inc.
3460 Hillview Avenue
Palo Alto, CA 94304
800-334-2564; 415-858-3785

BOND PORTFOLIO
Systems: WIN, MAC. Requires Excel.
$25
Covers bonds. Calculates yield to maturity, yield to first call, duration, and more. Tracks your bond portfolio and provides a summary of your portfolio.
Baarns Publishing
11150 Sepulveda Blvd., Dept. D
Mission Hill, CA 91345
800-377-9235; 818-837-1441

BOND PORTFOLIO MANAGER
Systems: DOS, WIN, MAC
$89
Covers bonds. Tracks market value of each bond and the entire portfolio. Also tracks duration, convexity, reward-risk indicators, the interest payment date, and unrealized gains/losses. Helps you decide which to consider swapping/selling. Reports by creditworthiness and date of maturity. Also has housekeeping data, including a

bond's location, serial number, and transaction broker.

Larry Rosen Company
7008 Springdale Road
Louisville, KY 40241
502-228-4343

BOND SHEET
System: DOS
$149
Covers bonds. Bond calculator. Includes bond-swap module.
Emerging Market Technologies
1230 Johnson Ferry Road, Ste. F-1
Marietta, GA 30068
404-973-2300

BOND SMART
Systems: DOS, WIN
$175/month
Covers bonds. Software for managing, accounting, and tracking bonds in one or more portfolios. Also does calculations.
Wall Street Consulting Group
89 Millburn Avenue
Millburn, NJ 07041
201-762-4300

BOND-TECH'S BOND CALCULATOR
System: DOS
$49
Covers bonds. Handles a wide variety of notes, bonds, money markets, odd first and last coupon securities. Compares the relative value of different securities. Can compute the yield, bond equivalent, CD equivalent yield, duration, and more. Computes horizontal returns; can modify standard conventions. Has context-sensitive help and a tutorial. Menu-driven and has mouse support. Contains a built-in indexed database management system.
Bond-Tech Inc.
P.O. Box 192

Englewood, OH 45322
513-836-3991

BOND VALUE
System: DOS
$65
Covers bonds. Calculates present values of bonds and compares to required rate of return to find bonds for purchase consideration. Covers all kinds of bonds.
Resource Software International, Inc.
330 New Brunswick Avenue
Fords, NJ 08863
201-738-8500

BONDCALC
System: DOS. Requires math co-processor.
$2,900 and up. Demo available.
Covers bonds. Constructs the cash flows for all types of fixed-income securities. Has after-tax, leveraging, and multicurrency capabilities. Covers private placements, commercial mortgages, esoteric high-yield bonds, emerging market debt, convertibles, and more. Portfolio calculations are based on all underlying cash flows. Analyzes the equity portion of a convertible security using artificial intelligence. Contains 100 analytical graphs and reports. Performs swap analysis, matrix pricing, and more. Has context-sensitive help, shortcuts to minimize keystrokes, and pop-up windows. Very comprehensive program.
Bondcalc Corporation
295 Greenwich Street, #3B
New York, NY 10007
212-587-0097

BONDS
System: DOS
$395

Covers bonds. Portfolio management system for bonds. Includes bond calculator.

Emerging Market Technologies
1230 Johnson Ferry Road, Ste. F-1
Marietta, CA 30068
404-973-2300

BONDSEYE
System: DOS
$65
Covers bonds. Calculates bond and money market instruments data, including yield to maturity/call, price from yield, swap analysis, duration, accrued interest, future value, etc. Performs convertible bond analysis. Has an extensive manual with many examples. Calculations are 100% guaranteed.
Ergo, Inc.
1419 Wyant Road
Santa Barbara, CA 93108
800-772-6637; 805-969-9366

BONDSHEET
System: DOS
$95. Demo available.
Covers bonds. Calculates current yield and yield to maturity. Swap analysis tells you whether to trade one bond for another. Utilizes a convenient spreadsheet layout for entering parameters. Bond price can be calculated from a yield. Has a contextual help feature.
Ones & Zeros
708 W. Mt. Airy Avenue
Philadelphia, PA 19119
800-882-2764; 215-248-1010

BOND$MART
System: DOS
$395
Covers bonds. Calculates yield to maturity, CD equivalent yield, Macauley

duration, horizon duration, price volatility of reinvested rate to yield. Works on all kinds of bonds using the Securities Industry Association (SIA) standard as a default, but users can program their own calculations. Can export data to spreadsheet for further analysis.
Portside Market
10926 Adare Drive
Arlington, VA 22032
703-425-2275

THE COMPLETE BOND ANALYZER
Systems: DOS, MAC
$89
Covers bonds. Calculates purchase price given yield to maturity (and vice versa), yield to call, accrued interest, modified duration, and spot rates.
Larry Rosen Company
7008 Springdale Road
Louisville, KY 40241
502-228-4343

GLOBAL TRADER CALCULATOR
System: DOS
$195. Demo $20.
Covers bonds. Calculates domestic and foreign fixed-income securities. Calculates yield to maturity, yield to call, average life, accrued interest, and more. Has a yield swap analysis function. Saves and recalls over 200 swaps and individual security calculations.
ADS Associates, Inc.
23586 Calabasas Road, Ste. 200
Calabasas, CA 91302
800-323-4666; 818-591-2371

INTEX BOND CALCULATIONS
Systems: DOS, WIN. Requires
Excel or Lotus 1-2-3.
$495–$995. Demo available.
Covers bonds. Has seventeen essential bond functions, including calculations

of yield, price, duration, and more within Excel or Lotus. Functions can be added with a simple keystroke. Can handle odd coupon bonds and sinking-fund bonds. Basic to advanced version available, including an international version.

Intex Solutions, Inc.
35 Highland Circle
Needham, MA 02194
617-449-6222

MICROCOMPUTER BOND PROGRAM
Systems: DOS, MAC
$59.95
Covers bonds. Estimates yields and prices of fixed-income securities under many assumptions.

Dynacomp, Inc.
178 Phillips Road
Webster, NY 14580
800-828-6772; (716) 265-4040

PER% SENSE
System: DOS
$100–$175. Demo available.
A full-featured, flexible financial calculator that is easy to use. Helps you figure out whether to refinance a mortgage, whether to finance a car or pay cash, how much you should be saving for retirement, etc. Calculates internal rate of return, valuation of a payment stream, loan amortization, valuation of annuities and life insurance policies, and more. Has over three dozen example problems fully set up; put your numbers in to find the answer. Has extensive hypertext help.

Ones & Zeros
708 W. Mt. Airy Avenue
Philadelphia, PA 19119
800-882-2764; 215-248-1010

On-Line Services

Some of the on-line services that deal with stock investing also provide bond quotes and other bond market information. Refer to the Resource Guide in Chapter 4, Investing in Stocks, for a description of the following services.

Accuron	Money Center
Comstock	Prodigy
Dial/Data	Realtick III
Dow Jones News	Signal
Retrieval	S&P Comstock
Downloader	Telemet Orion
DTN Spectrum/	Telerate
DTN Wall	Telescan
Street	Track/Online
EDGAR	Tradeline
Market Center	Vista RT

Chapter 6

INVESTING IN MUTUAL FUNDS

Mutual funds have been around for decades in one form or another and with one name or another. Despite this longevity, mutual funds have really come into their own in just the last ten years. They are *the* investment of choice in the United States right now. At the end of 1995, over $2.82 trillion were invested in 5,761 U.S. mutual funds. Currently, net new cash inflows into stock mutual funds exceed $20 billion *each month*. Why this incredible interest in mutual funds? Part of the answer lies with the structure and advantages of using mutual funds.

STRUCTURE OF MUTUAL FUNDS

A mutual fund is simply a large pool of money, invested by many diverse parties, that is in turn invested by a professional portfolio manager(s) into individual securities. The pool of money is divided into small units, called *shares*, which are bought and sold just like shares of common stock. Mutual funds can be subdivided into two categories: 1) *open-end funds* 2) *closed-end funds*.

Open-end mutual funds issue new shares as new money is invested into the pool. The number of shares that can be issued is theoretically unlimited. The price of open-end fund shares, referred to as *net asset value* (NAV), is the aggregate market value of the securities held in the fund, divided by the number of shares issued. Open-end mutual funds can be bought and sold in fractional shares.

Closed-end mutual funds issue a limited number of shares, just as a company does with common stock. And like common stock, closed-end shares are traded through a full-commission or discount broker, for which you pay a commission. Closed-end funds typically trade at a discount to their NAV, and for this reason, some investors view them as bargains. The fallacy of this reasoning is that they always trade at a discount, and although the discount can rise and fall during different intervals, there is no profit potential from the discount itself.

There are two types of open-end mutual funds: 1) *load funds* 2) *no-load funds*. A "load" is a pseudonym for the commission or sales charge levied against the investor who buys load fund shares. The commission goes to whomever sold the fund: broker, commission-based financial planner, or any designated sales agent. The commission is taken from the initial amount invested, meaning that you only get to earn a return on the amount left after the commission is paid. Thus, if you invest $10,000 in a fund with a 4 percent load, only $9,600 is actually invested on your behalf. That's a lot to pay for . . . well, whatever it is that load fund salespeople say it is you're receiving for that charge.

You may recall, in Chapter 4, Investing in Stocks, that stock selection was really a process of elimination. So it is with mutual funds also, and the time has come to do some eliminating. We regard commissions and sales loads as unnecessary expenses to be incurred, so the discussion of mutual funds that follows is limited to *no-load open-end mutual funds*. Eliminate closed-end funds and load funds from consideration in your search and analysis of mutual funds.

> *Invest only in no-load open-end mutual-funds*

ADVANTAGES OF MUTUAL FUNDS

By pooling a large amount of dollars and allocating that pool of dollars among a large number of securities (be it stocks, bonds, cash instruments, convertible securities, mortgages, or whatever the fund invests in), an investor is able to invest small amounts of money in a variety of assets that he otherwise could not feasibly invest in. Envision trying to invest the $2,000 annual contribution to your individual retirement account (IRA) in individual stocks or bonds. To create a diversified portfolio of twenty stocks, you would be investing $100 in each stock, and that includes $20 or more per trade for discount brokerage commissions. Now, one could certainly do this, but your portfolio's rate of return would be abysmal. You could also invest the whole amount in one stock, but you would not have a well-diversified portfolio and you would subject your account to considerable risk. How easy, cost effective, and advantageous to your portfolio it is simply to purchase $2,000 of a certain mutual fund, or even to put $1,000 into two mutual funds.

Speaking of diversification, this is another great advantage of using mutual funds. Typically, funds invest in literally hundreds of securities. That means company-specific risk has been eliminated from the portfolio's returns, and with the exception of specialized funds that invest in a particular industry, industry-specific risk has been eliminated also. You do not need hundreds of stocks in a stock fund, or hundreds of bonds in a bond fund, to achieve diversification. Studies have shown that most of the greatest amount of nonmarket risk is eliminated with twelve to twenty different issues representing a broad group of industries or sectors of the economy. Thus, unless you have a portfolio sufficient in size to buy positions in at least a dozen securities, buying mutual funds will be more beneficial to your portfolio's risk profile.

Mutual funds also simplify the investment process. Think of all the securities research, data evaluation, broker searches, and trading that has been discussed in the previous chapters. Mutual funds perform those functions for the investor, and more. Mutual funds do it all for you. All you have to do is pick up the phone and buy or sell the mutual fund shares.

Another advantage of investing in mutual funds is that it is the same as hiring a fee-only investment professional. For a fee, the mutual fund manager brings together the many resources needed to invest wisely, then adds to them the judgment and wisdom of seasoned investment decision making. Most professional money managers, financial planners, and bank trust departments have a minimum size of portfolios that they will manage, usually some amount in excess of $100,000. Investing in a mutual fund enables you to receive comparable investment expertise for a portfolio as small as $1,000. Of course, you will not receive the personalized services from the mutual funds that you do from the other service providers: statements detailing security holdings, meetings with your portfolio manager, attention to your specific needs and requirements, among other things. Nevertheless, mutual fund investing still enables you to hire many different money managers with varying investment styles and philosophies, something that only institutional investors or very wealthy individuals could do otherwise.

TYPES OF MUTUAL FUNDS

The various types of mutual funds are outlined below.

Stock Funds

- Aggressive growth
- Growth
- Growth and income
- International stock
- Index
    - Large capitalization
    - Midsize capitalization
    - Small capitalization

Balanced Funds

Bonds Funds

- Domestic
- International/global
- Convertible
- High yield (junk)
- Tax-exempt

Money Market Funds

Stock Funds

Reviewing each type of fund briefly, *aggressive growth* funds employ a strategy of investing primarily, though not exclusively, in small-capitalization and mid-cap stocks. Some of the investments may be initial public offerings. There is often a high level of *turnover* in the portfolio; that is, stocks are frequently bought and sold, and a particular stock may not remain in the portfolio for a long period of time. Aggressive funds, properly managed, typically provide the highest rates of return, and they also display the most volatility. These are best suited for investors with a long-term horizon and for use in children's accounts in which the money will not be needed for some time.

Growth and *growth and income* funds invest in a broader range of stocks, including large-cap issues paying cash dividends. Turnover in these portfolios is usually lower than aggressive funds, and the portfolio's volatility is less as well. These are good funds to be owned by investors whose time horizon is down to five years or less, or by investors who want capital appreciation in the portfolio but also need cash flow. A very similar investment objective could invoke the use of *balanced* funds. Balanced funds invest in both common stocks and bonds. Because bonds exhibit significantly less volatility than stocks, these funds are useful to investors who want both capital appreciation and cash flow but want to assume less risk than an all-stock fund incurs.

Looking at some other stock funds, *international stock* funds invest in stocks of non-U.S. companies, either through American Depository Receipts (ADRs) traded in the U.S. or invested directly through offshore stock exchanges. The convention is that a fund that invests in both U.S. and non-U.S. stocks is a *global* fund, while an international fund invests solely in non-U.S. stocks. Investors have used international/global funds more and more in recent years. Their attraction is that they provide opportunities for capital appreciation in foreign markets, and they also have historically had movements in directions that counteracted market moves in U.S. stocks. In the process, the overall volatility of the portfolio can be smoothed somewhat. Although there are different styles of international/global fund management, most funds are structured along geographic lines. The portfolio manager allocates monies to those countries that are likely to perform the best. Some funds even invest exclusively in one country or a group of countries in one region.

The last category of stock funds comprises *index* funds. These portfolios seek either to replicate a specific stock index, such as the S&P 500, or to at least closely approximate the rate of return of such an index. Index funds bring to the individual investor the same investment strategy that institutional investors, like pensions plans and endowment funds, have been employing for over twenty years. That strategy engenders the notion that active stock portfolio management will not produce rates of return in excess of the returns of the market averages. Hence, the investor can save the hassle and expense of actively managed funds by using index funds.

Balanced Funds

These are exactly what they sound like: mutual funds that seek to build a portfolio balanced with stocks, bonds, and cash equivalents. In other words the portfolio manager of these funds makes the asset allocation decisions we pondered in Chapter 3, Asset Allocation. The investor who buys balanced funds has delegated the asset allocation decision to that fund manager. The concern investors should have is that the fund manager is making the asset allocation decisions without the benefit of knowing the investor's objectives, risk tolerance, constraints, or life stage. As such, these funds should only be used in certain situations. One such situation might be where the investable funds are limited in size and creating a diversified portfolio of mutual funds is impractical. In all other cases, investors should consider using balanced funds as one component of the entire portfolio which utilizes other types of mutual funds or individual securities.

Bond Funds

As you can see, there are quite a few different bond funds in which one can invest. *Domestic* funds encompass investments in taxable government bonds (U.S. Treasury securities and federal agency securities), corporate bonds, or some combination of the two. *International* bond funds invest overseas, again either in foreign government securities, bonds of foreign companies, or a hybrid fund containing both types. International bond portfolio managers are likely to focus their attention not only on the economic climate of the individual countries as their international stock counterparts do, but they will also look at interest-rate spreads with U.S. yields, and the magnitude and direction of currency fluctuations in relation to the dollar. As with international stock mutual funds, the manager of an international bond mutual fund should have some physical presence in the countries, or at least the region, in which the investments are being made. In this way the manager is not "flying blind."

Convertible funds invest in debentures and preferred stock that are convertible into common shares according to some formula spelled out in the convertible's indenture. Proponents of convertible investing state that these securities offer the best features and performance of both bonds and stocks. They provide an above-average income stream through the coupon interest or preferred dividends. As the underlying stock (the stock into which the convertible is exchangeable) rises in value, the price of the convertible rises also. In theory, these securities have a lower volatility than the underlying stocks, appreciating less than the stocks in rising markets and depreciating less than the underlying stocks in declining markets.

High-yield funds invest in high-yield bonds, commonly referred to as "junk bonds." The delineation of a junk bond according to its rating varies somewhat, but for purposes of this discussion, it refers to corporate bonds having a rating of BB or A+ or less from the rating agencies. For both convertible funds and high-yield funds, portfolio managers structure their portfolio with diversification by industry group. In fact, their style of management is closely aligned with that of stock fund managers. They invest in companies that are enjoying a turnaround in profitability or that already have good earnings momentum, in an effort to capitalize on the trend. In addition to capturing interest rate moves, the manager invests in companies that are likely to have an upgrade in their credit rating in the relevant future. Thus, both convertible and high-yield funds are equivalent to investing in stock funds; the only difference is that the vehicles used are considered debt securities.

Tax-exempt funds invest in tax-free municipal bonds. While many tax-exempt funds invest in a wide range of state and municipal jurisdictions, more and more of these funds are specializing their funds on a state-by-state basis. The primary reason for this is that a number of states allow exemption from state income taxes for the interest earned by legal residents of those states on the bonds issued by jurisdictions within their borders. For example, California residents do not pay state income tax (which can range up to a 9.5 percent marginal tax rate) on interest earned from qualified bonds issued by any municipal agency within California. A number of other states have this feature as well, although some large states (like Illinois) do not afford their residents this feature. For residents of states offering the tax exemption, this can be a consideration that overrides the fact that bonds from other states may offer a yield advantage and perhaps a better credit rating.

Money Market Funds

These are the final type of mutual funds, and they probably require the least explanation. Money market funds are the most homogenous of all mutual funds because of the limited types of securities in which they invest. Due to the requirement that the value of each fund unit remain fixed at $1.00 each and every day, this restricts the investments to instruments that themselves have little or no fluctuation in value: certificates of deposit from banks, commercial paper issued by corporations, and banker's acceptances, as well as many other types of private and government issued securities.

Generally speaking, money market funds are the investment vehicle over which investors will have, or will need, the fewest options from which to choose. For instance, if you have your investments at Deep Discount Brokers, Inc., and they have a choice of three money market funds from the ABC Fund family, you are probably restricted to using one or more of those funds in your account. The only work you need to do is to satisfy yourself that the fund options are suitable for you financial needs. Money market fund alternatives at discount brokers usually include a plain vanilla taxable money market fund, a taxable fund invested only in government securities, and one or more tax exempt money market funds. The latter may include funds from the larger states with hefty state tax rates (New York and California, for example) that afford the exemption of its income from state income taxes. If you reside in one of those states, follow the same appraisal you would do for tax exempt bonds or tax exempt bond funds.

RESEARCHING AND SELECTING MUTUAL FUNDS

Like stock and bond analysis, investment in mutual funds requires some homework on the part of the investor. And, also like stock and bond analysis, the process of researching mutual funds does not have to be the laborious operation that many people make it. Again, there are research services that will rescue the investor from analytical tedium and overkill. Before jumping to these, let's review the basic elements that an investor should investigate before (and after, for that matter) investing in a mutual fund.

Reading a Mutual Fund Prospectus

When you telephone a mutual fund company to inquire about investing in a particular mutual fund, one of the things they will send you is a prospectus for the fund. We discussed prospectuses for new bond offerings in the previous chapter. Likewise, when new stock is sold to the public, a prospectus is issued that describes the company, the size and purpose of the offering, and the risks involved. Mutual fund prospectuses serve the same purpose as those, even if the product described is different. Among the items about which the prospectus informs the investor or potential investor are: 1) the fund philosophy and objective; 2) the fund manager and his background; 3) the fund's investment performance; 4) the fund's expenses; 5) the risk factors related to the fund. Coincidentally, these are the five elements the investor needs to evaluate in analyzing mutual funds.

Mutual fund prospectuses are quite uniform in format, partly because of SEC-mandated content and partly because mutual funds are very homogenous. The primary distinctions between mutual funds are: a) the securities that are bought and sold; b) the people who are managing the portfolio and their philosophy; and c) the expenses attendant to the fund. At the beginning of the prospectus will appear sections like "The Fund" and "Investment Objective and Policies." These will describe where the fund is managed and when the fund was formed, and include a detailed description of the types of securities that are used or may be used in the portfolio. An elaboration on policies will be included if leverage (buying securities with borrowed funds) is used, if short sales (selling stock you don't own in anticipation of the stock's decline in price) are employed, and if derivatives (primarily put and call options) are utilized. The philosophy of the fund manager will be disclosed here as well, although it will certainly not appear in bold typeface, and you may have to hunt for it. The primary thing to be alert for is any disparity between the fund's apparent style of management and the fund's professed objective. An example of this would be a growth fund that has invested or expects to invest in convertible securities. These are good assets for balanced funds or growth-and-income funds, but they are not exceptional growth vehicles.

Other headings in the prospectus will include Portfolio Turnover and Investment Risks. Portfolio turnover refers to the percentage of a portfolio's holdings sold during a twelve-month period. In some growth portfolios, turnover may exceed 100 percent; that is, all of the securities that are in the portfolio today will, in theory, not be there twelve months from now. High turnover in and of itself is not good or bad. What matters most is whether the manager is achieving a satisfactory rate of return. When securities are liquidated, capital gains and losses will result. Presumably the manager is making money for the fund shareholders, so there are likely to be capital gains distributed. If the shares are held in an account where gains are subject to tax, this may be a concern to the investor. In IRAs and other nontaxable accounts, this is not an issue.

The Investment Risk section of the prospectus is primarily legal "boilerplate" designed to ensure that the prospective investor has been apprised that there are risks involved with investment in the shares. Most of the risks outlined have to do with the market fluctuations, volatility in the value of certain holdings, the risk of using short sales, futures and options, and leverage. Additional risks may be simply that the manager will do a poor job of managing the portfolio. All of these are standard admonitions. However, if you're looking through five prospectuses, trying to select one fund to buy, and you read verbiage that outlines risks above and beyond those mentioned here, this is a good excuse to disqualify that fund from consideration.

To learn more about the managers of the funds, look for a heading such as Management of the Fund or Investment Adviser. If they do not outline the portfolio manager's pedigree, it will at least tell how long he has been in the investment business (and perhaps in what positions and with what company) and how long he has managed the particular fund that you're considering. The main thing to be aware of is that the manager has had sufficient experience with the type of fund in which you are considering investing your money. To think of it another way, would you hire that individual as a money manager or financial planner to manage your assets outside of a mutual fund? If you cannot say yes to that question, then move on to considering the next fund.

The expenses associated with the fund are detailed in a Fee Table. These are generally divided into two categories: Shareholder Transaction Expenses and Annual Fund Operating Expenses. *Shareholder transaction expenses* are sales load charges. These should be ZERO because you are investing in no-load funds. *Annual fund operating expenses* are expressed as a percentage of the average net assets in the fund. These expenses include:

- *Management fees*—the portfolio manager's fee for running the portfolio. These should range between 1 and 2 percent.
- *12b-1 fees*—these are fees paid to discount brokers or other third parties who are instrumental in marketing the fund's shares. By regulatory fiat, these fees cannot exceed 0.75 percent, or 75 basis points, of the net asset value.
- *Service fees* are similar to the 12b-1 fees and are payable to brokers for client services rendered to fund shareholders; these should not exceed 25 basis points.

In addition to the above expenses, there may some miscellaneous expenses, such as interest, that are chargeable to the fund.

The measure that mutual fund investors need to know is something called the *expense ratio*. This ratio is the sum of all the expenses charged to the fund, expressed as a percentage of the NAV (net asset value). Equity mutual funds and balanced mutual funds usually have the highest expense ratios, some exceeding 4 percent. The median range of expense ratios among equity funds and balanced funds is approximately between 1 and 2.5 percent. Total rate of return for mutual funds is calculated *before* expenses are factored. That is why the expense ratio is an important number; you must subtract that ratio from the return in order to determine the net return, which is the accurate measure of performance. Having said this, do not go overboard and begin selecting funds on the basis of expense ratios alone, and there are those who do just that. If a fund is surpassing the returns of other funds, with comparable objectives, by 3 percent, but its expense ratio is 1 percent higher than that of the other funds, it is still the best fund to invest in, is it not? So pay attention to expense ratios, but do not allow them to control your decision making.

Speaking of performance, another section or sections will be Annual Total Return and perhaps Management's Discussion of Fund Performance for the previous year. Related to these will be information contained in the Financial Highlights section. The latter will account for the change in NAV from one year to the next, and it may do this for a number of years going back as well. The section will also show the derivation of the rate of return and an accounting of all the expenses and the expense ratio, again over some period of time. Obviously, these are important data that will be key variables in your evaluation of a fund, so pay close attention to this information and collate it in a manner (spreadsheet format, for example) that facilitates easy comparison with the other funds being examined.

Other sections in the prospectus deal with a variety of topics that are probably not crucial to your analysis of the fund. They contain information that is more useful after you have decided to invest in the fund. These include the procedures for purchasing and selling shares, the treatment of capital gains and dividends distributed, certain shareholder services that may be available, and probably account application forms. Equipped with the information in the prospectus, you will be able to make an informed judgment on a mutual fund investment. You may also want to utilize additional tools to make your deliberations more thorough and time efficient.

MUTUAL FUND RESEARCH SERVICES

With the emergence of mutual funds as the fastest-growing type of investment vehicle in the United States, a new branch of investment research has evolved. There are now companies that specialize their research products around mutual funds. Most of these research companies are independent and not affiliated with full-commission brokers or with mutual fund families. As such, they can provide an unbiased evaluation of funds and their performance. So while you could spend hours wading through a pile of prospectuses and creating your own worksheets to compare two or more funds against one another, there are books, newsletters, software, and on-line services that will do most of the work for you. You need only decide for yourself the types of funds that are appropriate for your investment objectives and begin screening them according to your criteria.

One of the most comprehensive sources of mutual fund analysis is furnished by Morningstar, Inc., a privately held research firm based in Chicago. Although they have branched into stock analysis and variable annuity analysis in recent years, Morningstar's forte remains the analysis of mutual funds. Morningstar issues its research on over 5,700 mutual funds using various media, from printed reports to CD-ROM software. Among other items of information, each of its reports on an individual fund contains the following:

- Biography of portfolio managers
- Fund performance in table and chart formats
- Commentary on fund performance
- Largest holdings in the fund
- Style boxes that graphically depict the fund's objective
- Tax analysis showing how taxes have affected returns
- Star ratings that determine risk-adjusted returns and assign ranking to each fund
- Fees and expenses

Having access to this and much more information in a format that allows easy comparison for a number of funds facilitates thorough independent analysis of funds. The software versions of Morningstar's data make the task even less time-consuming. Morningstar's trademark are the star ratings, which rank funds from one star to five, with five stars being the highest rating. The star ratings are derived from their analysis of both performance (rate of return) and risk (standard deviation), factors we described in earlier chapters. The fund's risk score is subtracted from its return score, and that number is plotted in a bell-shaped distribution curve. The funds in the top 10 percent receive a five-star rating. Those in the next 22.5 percent area of the curve receive a four-star rating, and so it goes down to the lowest 10 percent, which earn the one-star rating.

The process of selecting mutual funds is similar to that for selecting stocks, as examined in Chapter 4, Investing in Stocks. It is really a process of elimination. Being the astute investor you now are, you can probably guess what's coming next. Using the star rating criteria, as an example, you could eliminate all funds ranked less than five stars. This narrows down the field of candidates to the top 10 percent of their respective universes based on risk-adjusted return. You can then focus on the specific characteristics of a particular fund, like fund expenses and investment objectives, to evaluate if it belongs in your portfolio. Software published by Morningstar and other vendors makes this screening even more time-efficient. You can quickly screen all funds in a database by any number of criteria, and choose from among those funds that come up on the screen. From there, you are well on your way toward building a mutual fund portfolio that's just right for you.

CREATING YOUR MUTUAL FUND PORTFOLIO

As we learned in Chapter 3, Asset Allocation, before you can actually begin to invest and to build your portfolio, you have to establish your investment objectives. Once you have done this, decide which types of funds will achieve those objectives. To assist you in this, refer to Table 6-1 below.

TABLE 6-1

INVESTMENT OBJECTIVES AND MUTUAL FUND CATEGORIES

GROWTH	*BALANCED*	*INCOME*
Aggressive Growth	Aggressive Growth	Growth and Income
Growth	Growth	International Stock
International Stock	Growth and Income	Index
Index	International Stock	Balanced
	Index	Bond
	Balanced	
	Bond	

We omitted money market funds from the table, as it goes without saying that whatever cash is not permanently invested will reside in money market funds. Those investors having a "balanced" objective obviously have the most latitude in what they can invest. It should be emphasized that *an investor should own at least two mutual funds, but no more than six to eight.* The reason for this is that the funds themselves diversify away most, if not all, nonmarket risk because each fund is invested in a multitude of securities. Thus, if you own too many mutual funds, you will not be receiving the benefit of extraordinary performance that one or two funds might enjoy; it will have been diluted by the less spectacular results of other funds you might have.

Looking at some hypothetical allocations by fund category for each of the three objectives in Table 6-1, assume you are going to invest 20 percent of your portfolio in each of five funds. For the "aggressive" objective you may want to put 20 percent in an international stock fund and another 20 percent in an index fund. The remaining 60 percent can be apportioned among three funds, using at least one aggressive growth fund and possibly all three. In looking at the various aggressive growth and growth funds, you should look for those with different investment philosophies from the others; for example, one that uses a value-oriented approach in stock selection and another that uses a high-rate-of-earnings growth approach.

The "balanced" objective has many alternatives that can be pursued. Again, using five funds, a good strategy would be to buy two or three equity funds and two or three bond funds. If you steer the allocation toward bonds, consider using an aggressive growth fund as one of the two stock funds employed. The type of bond fund to be used will depend on the account type and your marginal tax rate. At the risk of needless repetition, use only taxable bond funds in tax-advantaged accounts like IRAs and 401k accounts. (We'll talk more about bond funds in a moment.) If you want to take the easy way out, you can always invest in different balanced funds, and let the fund portfolio managers do the asset allocation for you.

For the "income" objective you will want to steer the allocation toward bond funds. However, that does not mean you should abandon equity funds altogether. As we concluded in Chapter 3, Asset Allocation, even retired people who need the cash flow to live on should invest at least 20 percent of their assets in equities. A sound strategy here might be to invest 60 percent of the portfolio in three bond funds, 20 percent in a balanced fund, and the remaining 20 percent in one of the equity funds.

Once you've decided on the objective that serves you best and the allocation among types of funds that will optimize the results for that objective, you're ready to begin the search for the right funds in each of the fund categories. Visualize, if you will, the search we are about to begin, using a computer screening program like the Morningstar software referred to earlier. Since the search will be similar for any of the three investment objectives, let's look at the "aggressive" objective to preview the screening process. Recall that we agreed to the following strategy for that objective: index fund—20 percent; international stock fund—20 percent; aggressive growth funds—60 percent. We can quickly dispense with the index fund search; there are relatively few index funds in existence and their performance is within 20 basis points of each other. Pick the one you like best and go with it.

Next, let's find the international stock fund that suits our needs. First select the international stock funds that cover the world, outside the U.S. Your other funds will cover the U.S. stocks adequately, so there is no benefit to using additional mutual funds that will invest more in the U.S. Next, single out the no-load funds. Third, find all funds that are rated five stars, or an equivalent rating for the highest performance record if you are using another fund-rating system. At this point you have reduced a universe of international stock funds that total in the hundreds to perhaps ten. From here you should examine and compare the historic performance over three-year, five-year, and ten-year time periods. If one or two funds have been around for ten years and others have not, go for the funds with longer track records. When you have narrowed the choices down to two or three funds, it's time to obtain and study prospectuses on each fund. The final selection will hinge on non-numeric factors that you discern in the prospectus: research capabilities in the different countries in which the fund invests, the portfolio manager's tenure with that fund or similar funds, the total expense ratios for each fund, to name a few things. With this information in hand, you should be able to decide on one international stock fund that you want to own.

The procedure for finding the aggressive growth and growth funds is essentially identical. The bad news is that there are many more of these funds than there are international stock funds, presently over 1,000 aggressive growth and growth funds. The good news for our hypothetical fund search is that you are looking for three funds, not just one. When you have narrowed the field down to ten funds or less, you can readily afford to be more subjective and less statistical in eliminating those last seven candidates. Here is where you will want to pay more attention to investment philosophy and try to differentiate one fund's philosophy from the others. The goal will be to select three funds, putting 20 percent of the portfolio into each, that have their own special angle: growth criteria or value criteria; high portfolio turnover or low portfolio turnover; use of leverage or unleveraged positions. As with the international stock fund search, or any fund search, you should request and study a prospectus on each fund being considered before reaching a final decision.

Our discussion of research sources for mutual funds has focused on rating services and software for screening different fund criteria. As with stock investing, however, there are a number of reputable newsletters that specialize in mutual fund selection. To identify these and to compare their track records, the *Hulbert Financial Digest* is once again a good place to start. Focus on those letters or advisory services that take a long-term approach in their recommendations, as opposed to those fund-timing letters that move you in and out of funds within a few months. For the latter, there is no solid evidence that short-term moves in and out of funds produce superior results. In fact, many funds penalize short-term investors for selling fund shares that have been held less than some specified time period, such as ninety days. These penalties will be detrimental to your rate of return and impair your investment program. Look for newsletters that 1) have been in publication for more than five years, 2) have an above-average performance track record, and 3) do not have a history of high turnover of funds in any given year.

A FEW WORDS ABOUT BOND FUNDS

Recall in the discussion of bonds in Chapter 5, bond investments were described as closed-end contractual arrangements. The contract has a beginning and an end (maturity date), and in between you are entitled to interest on the investment. When you buy mutual fund shares that invest in bonds, you own a totally different vehicle than you do if you simply buy a bond on your own. The reason is simple. For the broad majority of bond mutual funds, there is no maturity date. As when you own a stock or a stock fund, the investment is an open-ended arrangement. As long as you want to hold the fund shares, they're yours.

Why does this matter? As we said in the chapter dealing with bonds, the attraction of bonds is the cash flow one receives and, more important, the lower volatility (risk) they afford. Irrespective of Federal Reserve policy, the shape of the yield curve, or the direction of interest rates, when a bond is about to mature and return principal to the investor, the bond's price moves toward par value. Maturing bonds provide the investor the opportunity to reinvest the principal at higher interest rates, circumstances permitting. Theoretically, bond mutual funds do not afford you that reinvestment opportunity.

It is true that the mutual fund portfolio manager does have the opportunity to reinvest maturing bonds. She also can shorten and lengthen the average maturity in the portfolio according to what she perceives will happen in the credit markets. The potential problem is that if she is lengthening maturities when your circumstances dictate a shortening of maturities, you have relinquished control of an important policy tool. This can be especially painful if the portfolio manager places her bets on one strategy, and the strategy is wrong. In the process, the calming effect that bonds otherwise have on a portfolio is compromised if not lost with bond funds because the fund itself doesn't mature. It continues on. You're the loser.

We'll stop short of rejecting bond mutual funds altogether. For those who have convinced themselves that they need bonds, and they have a small amount of money to invest there, bond mutual funds may be the only way to go. Those investors should weigh these thoughts:

- Talk yourself out of bond funds and into stock funds.
- If you absolutely need bonds, buy several small blocks through a discount broker or the Treasury Direct program.
- If you feel compelled to buy a bond mutual fund, look for one with a targeted maturity year.

Regarding the last point, there have emerged in recent years some mutual funds that target a specific year in the future, buying only bonds that mature in the specified year. At that time the funds liquidate and pay out to the shareholders, just as a maturing bond would do. This may be the best mutual fund vehicle for investors in these circumstances.

For those investors who have a larger sum of money to invest in bonds, I suggest you forsake bond mutual funds and invest directly in individual bonds. Refer back to Chapter 5, Investing in Bonds or ahead to Chapter 7, Working With Fee-Only Professionals. If working on your own and using a discount broker becomes cumbersome, you may want to hire and work with a fee-only money manager, financial planner, or bank trust department. They are knowledgeable on these investments and have the resources to shop around for bonds that are best suited for your portfolio.

BUYING MUTUAL FUNDS THROUGH A DISCOUNT BROKER

One of the sections contained in the mutual fund prospectus is an account application, which the investor can complete and mail with a check to the fund distributor. If you were to invest in only one mutual fund, or perhaps just a few funds within the same family of funds, this might be a satisfactory arrangement. However, if you do own or expect to own mutual funds from a variety of different issuers, you are creating an administrative nightmare for yourself (and your significant others, if something should happen to you) by having the funds' custodians hold the shares. Using our five-fund hypothetical portfolio, the consequence of having your five-fund portfolio split among the five separate mutual fund companies is that you will receive five statements of your holdings, you will receive five confirmations of any purchases and sales you make, and at year-end you will receive five tax summaries of dividends, interest, and capital gains. Before long you will be buried under a pile of mutual fund paperwork. In addition this setup makes for confusion and errors, and it becomes very easy to lose or misplace a statement or confirmation.

So what's the alternative? Open an account with a discount broker and buy and sell mutual funds through that account. The funds are treated like any other security by the broker. You simply deposit cash, or the mutual fund shares if they are held by the fund custodian, and direct any purchases or sales through the discount broker's trading desk. The broker will issue trade confirmations with each transaction. You will receive periodic statements of your mutual fund holdings. The broker will collect dividends, if you have not directed that they be reinvested in additional fund shares, and sweep the money into a money market fund. At year-end, the broker issues a tax information statement to assist you in your tax return preparation. Another feature that many discount brokers offer is check-writing privileges. In short, using a discount broker as the medium for your mutual fund investments simplifies the whole process for you. And as you remember, keeping things simple is our objective here.

Discount brokers have the capability to trade thousands of mutual funds. There may be some mutual fund companies that are not equipped to have their shares traded through a third party such as a broker. That's fine, because those fund companies have just given you a reason to eliminate them from consideration. With the hundreds of top-quality funds available through the discount broker, you do not need to compromise this feature in order for your investment program to succeed.

Like trading stocks or bonds, the broker is usually compensated with a commission when a mutual fund transaction is executed. Within the last few years, several discount brokers have initiated programs to buy and sell mutual funds for their clients without charging them a commission. These are commonly referred to as "no transaction fee" (NTF) programs. If the brokerage firm is not receiving a commission, how is it compensated in an NTF program? Recall in our discussion of mutual fund expenses earlier in this chapter, there was something called a 12b-1 fee. These are fees assessed to all fund shares, whether the fund issuer holds them or a broker holds them, that compensate third parties for marketing and distributing the fund shares. The discount brokerage that trades and holds your shares receives the 12b-1 fee, and that is how it is compensated. So you see, you as a fund shareholder pay this fee anyway; you may as well receive something in return by using a discount broker that has an NTF program.

A typical NTF program will have several dozen fund families, each with anywhere from one to thirty funds. For example, Jack White & Company's NTF program currently has over 700 mutual funds from which to choose. With NTF programs of that size, no investor will have difficulty in finding five or six quality funds for his portfolio. If you decide to adhere to an NTF program at one of the discount brokerages, you obviously limit yourself to the funds it has available in the program. The good news is that funds that participate in an NTF program with one broker usually are part of another discount broker's NTF plan as well. Hence, it is doubtful that you will face the dilemma of wanting five funds only available through three different brokers. You should also understand that, if you wish, you can invest in other mutual funds that are outside the NTF program. The same broker buys them and charges you a commission. You should not hesitate to purchase non-NTF mutual funds in this fashion if you believe such external funds will enhance your portfolio and its returns. The most important point is that you have a well-structured mutual fund portfolio, with the funds housed at a single location to maximize your control over them.

Repeating the theme of previous chapters, you have enough information here to make mutual fund selections that will provide you with excellent investment returns. The guidance you don't need, however, is the advice of a salesperson who will steer you into mutual funds that feature hefty sales charges or commissions. No amount of "expertise" they might lend to your decision making would justify the current expense or future returns you may forgo.

Since mutual funds are being peddled today by a host of purveyors, in addition to stockbrokers, we should identify these other sales agents as well. Insurance salespeople push mutual funds to insurance clients, either for IRAs, 401k plans, and other qualified retirement accounts, or as add-ons to tax-deferred annuities they may be selling. Banks are the latest entrants into the mutual fund sales craze. The lobbies of bank branches now have a person called a "financial adviser" or some other euphemism for "salesperson." He loves to snag walk-in customers and sell one or more of the bank's proprietary mutual funds. He is also given a list, by the bank branch manager, of those clients who have account balances high enough, or certificates of deposit (CDs) maturing soon enough, that they feel they can contact and convince to buy their mutual funds. Some bank customers buy these funds under the belief that they are insured up to $100,000 in value, as the CDs and other bank accounts are. *Mutual funds sold by banks are not insured for any amount.* So when you next receive a phone call from someone at your bank selling you mutual funds, you'll know how they picked you. While the bank's funds may or may not have sales loads, the fact remains that they are trying to move your money into the funds for a reason: someone in the bank hierarchy receives some or all of the management fee of the mutual funds. Thus, ulterior motive may once again supercede prudent investment decisions.

With the basic input provided by this chapter you can browse the Resource Guide that follows and either look for books that will treat the intricacies of mutual funds in more detail, or you can head straight for the newsletters and rating services that can guide you through the information maze and assist you in building your mutual fund portfolio.

To summarize the basic tenets of mutual fund investing:

- Buy only no-load open-end mutual funds.
- Buy top-ranked mutual funds (five stars).
- Create a portfolio of five or six funds, with risk-return profiles commensurate with your investment objective.
- Centralize your mutual fund portfolio at one discount broker, taking advantage of their NTF program where possible.
- Avoid mutual fund salespeople. Do your own research, fund buying, and fund selling.

RESOURCE GUIDE
INVESTING IN MUTUAL FUNDS

Magazines and Periodicals

Because of the popularity of mutual fund investing today, many of the magazines listed in the Resource Guides in Chapters 3 and 4 will also have sections that deal with mutual funds. The following publications are dedicated exclusively to mutual funds.

MUTUAL FUND MAGAZINE
General-interest magazine for mutual fund investors. Profiles specific funds and fund managers. Covers the outlook for the economy and the markets.
$14.97/yr. Monthly
The Institute for Econometric Research
2200 S.W. 10th Street
Deerfield Beach, FL 33442
800-442-9000

The following are charting services that are sent to subscribers on a frequent basis, either weekly or quarterly.

CHARTCRAFT QUARTERLY (MUTUAL FUNDS) P&F CHARTBOOK
Covers mutual funds. Technical analysis. Includes all mutual funds covered by *Weekly Mutual Funds Breakout Service* (see next entry). Covers two-to-four year period, showing buy and sell signals.
$104/yr. Quarterly
Chartcraft, Inc.
30 Church Street

P.O. Box 2046
New Rochelle, NY 10801
914-632-0422

CHARTCRAFT WEEKLY MUTUAL FUNDS BREAKOUT SERVICE
Covers mutual funds. Technical analysis. Contains P&F charts of mutual funds. Includes buy/sell signals and breakouts.
$154/yr. Weekly
Chartcraft, Inc.
30 Church Street
P.O. Box 2046
New Rochelle, NY 10801
914-632-0422

FUND PERFORMANCE CHARTBOOK
Covers mutual funds. Technical analysis. Includes over 100 mutual fund charts, comparing performance to S&P 500.
$25/issue. Quarterly
Wellington Financial Corporation
6600 Kalanianole Highway,
Ste. 114C
Honolulu, HI 96825-1299
800-992-9989

Newsletters

The following newsletters deal exclusively with mutual fund research and recommendations. Those that have been rated by the Hulbert Financial Digest *are signified by* **HR.**

Many other newsletters that cover other areas, like stock investing, will also deal with mutual funds. To identify these letters, scan the Resource Guide in Chapter 4, Investing in Stocks.

5-STAR INVESTOR

Covers mutual funds. Includes articles that affect mutual funds. Helps fund investors construct a mutual fund portfolio. Explains techniques for analyzing funds. Has focus on top performing funds and other select funds, and editorials on other market subjects.
$65/yr. Monthly
Morningstar
225 W. Wacker Drive
Chicago IL 60606-1228
800-876-5005; 312-696-6000

ALL-STAR FUNDS

Fundamental and technical analysis. Covers mutual funds (stock and bond) and market timing. Has hotline. The aggressive model portfolios aim to outperform the NASDAQ index with less risk; they also rotate among sectors and investment styles. Uses relative strength and momentum. The moderate model portfolios aim to outperform the S&P 500 index with less risk; has tactical asset allocation of funds with low correlation levels and superior risk-adjusted performance. Every recommendation is tracked each month. Three model portfolios use no-load funds, and the other three use Fidelity funds.
$249/yr. Monthly—HR
P.O. Box 203427
Austin, TX 78720
800-299-4223; 512-219-1183

THE CHARTIST MUTUAL FUND TIMER

Technical analysis. Covers mutual funds and market timing. Uses a pro-

prietary model to time the market. Invests in aggressive growth mutual funds and money market funds. Is always 100% invested in only one category, either stocks or money market. The Actual Cash Account model portfolio is very similar to an actual portfolio started in 1988. Includes the views of leading investment advisers.
$100/yr. Monthly—HR
P.O. Box 758
Seal Beach, CA 90740
310-596-2385

CZESCHIN'S MUTUAL FUND OUTLOOK AND RECOMMENDATIONS

Covers mutual funds. Fundamental analysis. Includes at least three model portfolios, and has stock market commentary.
$147/yr. Monthly
Agora, Inc.
824 E. Baltimore Street
Baltimore, MD 21202
301-234-0691

DOHMEN MUTUAL FUND STRATEGY

Covers mutual funds. Fundamental and technical analysis. Makes specific buy and sell recommendations on funds and fund sectors.
$140/yr. Monthly
Bert Dohmen-Ramirez
Wellington Financial Corp.
6600 Kanalianole Highway, 144-C
Honolulu, HI 96825
800-992-9989; 808-396-2220

DONOGHUE'S MONEY FUND DIRECTORY

Lists money funds, includes name, ten-

year performance, expense rates, total assets, minimum investments.
$27.95/yr. Annual
IBC/Donoghue Inc.
290 Elliot Street
Box 91004
Ashland, MA 01721-9104
508-881-2800

DONOGHUE'S MONEY FUND REPORT

Covers mutual funds. Fundamental analysis. Includes weekly statistics and analysis on money funds such as seven- and thirty-day yields, average maturity, and valuation methods.
$195/yr. Weekly
The Donoghue Organization
290 Eliot Street
Box 91004
Ashland, MA 01721-9104
800-343-5413; 508-429-5930

DONOGHUE'S MONEYLETTER

Covers mutual funds. Fundamental analysis. Gives strategies for high-interest money market investments, also lists top-performing money market funds.
$89/yr. Bimonthly
The Donoghue Organization
290 Eliot Street
Ashland, MA 01721-9104
800-343-5413; 508-429-5930

EQUITY FUND OUTLOOK

Fundamental and technical analysis. Covers mutual funds (stock) and market timing. Emphasizes the skill of the fund manager in bull and bear markets (risk/reward ratio). Has model portfolios. Also covers promising new mutual funds.
$115/yr. Monthly—HR
P.O. Box 1040

Boston, MA 02117
617-397-6844

FACTS ON THE FUNDS

Mutual funds. A list of mutual funds and their assets/portfolios.
$195/yr. Quarterly
Vickers Stock Research Corp.
226 New York Avenue
Huntington, NY 11743
516-423-7710

FABIAN'S DOMESTIC INVESTMENT RESOURCE

Technical analysis. Covers mutual funds (stock) and market timing. Has hotline. Their goal is to capture 80 percent of a bull market gain. The mutual fund timing is purely mechanical. The essence of the system is that a signal is generated when their mutual fund composite index and the Dow both cross their thirty-nine-week moving average. Usually there is one switch per year.
$179/yr. Monthly—HR
P.O. Box 2538
Huntington Beach, CA 92647
800-950-8765

FAST TRACK FUNDS

Technical analysis. Covers mutual funds. Gives advice on selecting mutual funds and switching between funds and money market investments. Has hotline.
$107/yr. Monthly—HR
5536 Temple City Boulevard
Temple City, CA 91780

FIDELITY INSIGHT

Fundamental analysis. Covers Fidelity mutual funds (stock and bond). Has hotline. The editor is a former executive with Fidelity Investments. He is a

long-term investor who takes less risk than the market. Has model portfolios.
$99/yr. Monthly—HR
Mutual Fund Investors Association
P.O. Box 9135
Wellesley Hills, MA 02181
800-444-6342

FIDELITY INVESTMENTS MUTUAL FUND GUIDE
Covers mutual funds. Fundamental analysis. Compares performance of Fidelity funds to other funds with thirteen- and thirty-nine-week moving averages.
$89/yr. Monthly
Fidelity Publishing
82 Devonshire Street, R25A
Boston, MA 02109-3614
617-726-6027

FIDELITY MONITOR
Fundamental and technical analysis. Covers Fidelity mutual funds (stock and bond). Has four model portfolios. The income model aims for 8 percent per year with one-third the risk of the S&P 500 index. The growth and income model aims for 11 percent per year with 65 percent of the risk of the S&P 500. The growth model aims for 15 percent per year with the same risk as the S&P 500; this portfolio is always fully invested. The Select System uses a quantitative approach and invests in sector funds; this is the most volatile of the four model portfolios.
$96/yr. Monthly—HR
P.O. Box 1294
Rocklin, CA 95677
800-397-3094

THE FIDELITY SELECT ADVISOR
Covers mutual funds. Fundamental analysis. Makes buy, sell, or hold recommendations. Has model portfolio.

$89/yr. Monthly
New Wave Publishing
15073 92nd Street
Elk River, MN 55330
612-241-0520

FUND EXCHANGE
Technical analysis. Covers mutual funds (stock and bond) and market timing. Has hotline. Gives market signals and has many model portfolios. Also has articles about market timing.
$125/yr. Monthly—HR
1200 Westlake Avenue North
Ste. 700
Seattle, WA 98109
800-423-4893; 206-285-8877

FUND KINETICS
Technical analysis. Covers Fidelity mutual funds (stock). "Fund Kinetics" is a computer-based system that ranks 100 Fidelity mutual funds. One way to use the newsletter is to invest only in the top-rated fund. Another method is to invest in the top few funds. Has model portfolios.
$175/yr. Weekly—HR
2841 23rd Avenue West
Seattle, WA 98199
800-634-6790

FUND WATCH
Bills itself as "The Official Guide to High-Performance Mutual Funds." Includes charts of selected mutual funds.
$80/yr. Monthly
The Institute for Econometric Research
3471 N. Federal Highway
Ft. Lauderdale, FL 33306
800-442-9000

FUNDLINE
Covers mutual funds. Technical and

fundamental analysis. Includes investment strategies and a proprietary analysis formula. Specializes in the Fidelity
Select Funds. Includes telephone hotline.
$127/yr. Monthly—HR
David H. Menashe and Company
P.O. Box 663
Woodland Hills, CA 91365
818-346-5637

GLOBAL INVESTING
Covers ADRs and mutual funds. Fundamental analysis. Gives readers advice
on investing internationally on the
NYSE using ADRs and international
funds.
$245/yr. Monthly—HR
Agorot Ltd.
1040 First Avenue, Ste. 305
New York, NY 10022
800-388-4ADR

GRAPHIC FUND FORECASTER
Technical analysis. Covers Fidelity and
Invesco mutual funds (stock). Has
hotline. Their goal is to have a gain
each month while using a low-risk
strategy. Uses relative strength, Bollinger bands, moving averages, and other
tools. Contains model portfolios.
$129/yr. Monthly—HR
6 Pioneer Circle
P.O. Box 673
Andover, MA 01810
800-532-2322

GROWTH FUND GUIDE
Covers mutual funds. Fundamental
and technical analysis. Includes market
information and a model portfolio of
no-load funds.
$89/yr. Monthly—HR
Growth Fund Research, Inc.
Box 6600

Rapid City, SD 57709
800-621-8322; 605-341-1971

IBC'S MONEYLETTER
Fundamental analysis. Covers bonds
and mutual funds (stock and bond).
Provides asset allocation advice and
model portfolios (including a Fidelity
portfolio and a Vanguard portfolio).
Also has commentary on the bond
market.
$127/yr. Biweekly—HR
IBC Financial Data
290 Eliot Street
P.O. Box 9104
Ashland, MA 01721
800-343-5413

IBC'S MONEY MARKET INSIGHT
Fundamental analysis. Gives yields on
over 1,000 money market funds, for
the past month and trailing twelve
months. Ranks funds by fund category. Commentary on the money
markets.
$675/yr. Monthly—HR
IBC—Financial Data
290 Eliot Street
P.O. Box 9104
Ashland, MA 01721
800-343-5413

IBC'S RATED MONEY FUND RE-
PORT
Fundamental analysis. Rates money
market funds. Provides fund profiles,
including current yields and historic
returns.
$695/yr. Monthly—HR
IBC Financial Data
290 Eliot Street
P.O. Box 9104
Ashland, MA 01721
800-343-5413

INCOME FUND OUTLOOK
Fundamental analysis. Covers mutual funds and closed-end funds (bond and money market). Has hotline. Analyzes the bond and money markets. Has yield forecasts and total return projections. Gives risk ratings and recommendations of what to buy or avoid. Features the highest-yielding federally insured money market accounts and CDs.
$100/yr. Monthly—HR
The Institute for Econometric Research
2200 S.W. 10th Street
Deerfield Beach, FL 33442
800-442-9000

INVESTECH MUTUAL FUND ADVISOR
Technical analysis. Covers mutual funds (stock and bond) and market timing. Included when you subscribe to *InvesTech Market Analyst* (see entry in "Stocks" newsletter section). Has model portfolio.
$160/yr. Every 3 weeks—HR
2472 Birch Glen
Whitefish, MT 59937
800-955-8500; 406-862-7777

THE MANAGED ACCOUNT ADVISOR
Covers mutual funds. Technical analysis. Makes specific recommendations, includes hotline.
$144/yr. Monthly
Zin Investment Services
7 Switchbud Place, #192-312
The Woodlands, TX 77380
713-363-1000

MORNINGSTAR INVESTOR
Has articles on investment ideas and strategies, including interviews with financial planners and other investment ideas. Also includes the "Morningstar 500," a listing of 500 mutual funds along with their investment objective, rating, NAV, trailing twelve-month yield, total returns, bear market ranking, and more.
$79/yr. Monthly
Morningstar
225 W. Wacker Drive
Chicago, IL 60606
800-876-5005; 312-696-6000

MORNINGSTAR MUTUAL FUNDS
Fundamental analysis. Covers mutual funds (stock and bond). This is an investment resource more than a newsletter. Covers 1,500 mutual funds with one page devoted to each fund. Each page includes statistics and graphs to help readers learn a fund's strengths and weaknesses. Each report has up to 500 statistics covering twelve years. Discusses a fund's style of investing, performance, holdings, risk, and more. Has information on the manager and derivatives. Has written analyst evaluations.
$395/yr. Biweekly—HR
Morningstar
225 W. Wacker Drive
Chicago, IL 60606
800-876-5005; 312-696-6000

MORNINGSTAR NO-LOAD FUNDS
Fundamental analysis. Covers mutual funds (stock and bond). This is an investment resource more than a newsletter. Covers over 650 no-load mutual funds with one page devoted to each fund. Each page includes statistics and graphs to help readers learn a fund's strengths and weaknesses. Each report has up to 500 statistics covering twelve years. Discusses a fund's style of investing, performance,

holdings, risk, and more. Has information on the manager and derivatives. Has written analyst evaluations.
$145/yr. Monthly
Morningstar
225 W. Wacker Drive
Chicago, IL 60606
800-876-5005; 312-696-6000

MORNINGSTAR ONDEMAND
Morningstar will fax or mail you single reports on mutual funds. Each page includes statistics and graphs to help readers learn a fund's strengths and weaknesses. Each report has up to 500 statistics covering twelve years. Discusses a fund's style of investing, performance, holdings, risk, and more. Has information on the manager and derivatives. Has written analyst evaluations.
$5 per report
Morningstar
225 W. Wacker Drive
Chicago, IL 60606
800-876-5005; 312-696-6000

MUTUAL FUND FORECASTER
Fundamental analysis and charts of mutual funds. Has telephone hotline and fax updated every Tuesday and Friday evening. Includes fund directory and performance ratings. Makes fund recommendations and includes follow-up on recommendations.
$187/yr. Monthly—HR
The Institute for Econometric Research
3471 N. Federal Highway
Ft. Lauderdale, FL 33306
800-442-9000

MUTUAL FUND INVESTING
Covers mutual funds and asset allocation. Fundamental analysis. Gives general market advice, includes

performance ratings of funds and specific recommendations.
$179/yr. Monthly—HR
Phillips Publishing, Inc.
7811 Montrose Road
Potomac, MD 20854
800-722-9000

THE MUTUAL FUND LETTER
Fundamental analysis. Covers mutual funds (stock and bond). The goal is to take moderate risk to obtain gains of 12 to 20 percent. The letter has a "Family Focus" section which focuses on one mutual fund family. Also has a section of funds that are "In the Spotlight"; these funds are broken down by asset allocation, holdings by industry, ten largest holdings, turnover rate, etc. Has model portfolios.
$149/yr. Monthly—HR
The Mutual Fund Letter
12514 Starkey Road
Largo, FL 34643
800-326-6941

MUTUAL FUND STRATEGIST
Fundamental and technical analysis. Covers mutual funds (stock and bond) and market timing. Has hotline. Their goal is to preserve capital by being in mutual funds during advances and being in cash during periods of high risk. The growth and sector model portfolios have about 1.3 round trips per year. The aggressive portfolio may switch several times per month.
$149/yr. Monthly—HR
P.O. Box 446
Burlington, VT 05402
802-425-2211

MUTUAL FUND TECHNICAL TRADER
Fundamental and technical analysis. Covers mutual funds and closed-end funds (stock). Screens over 3,500

funds to find the consistent performers. Then they select the top thirty to
fifty funds that should do well over
the next one to three years. They
closely watch world markets to identify major turning points in countries
and industries. Has model portfolios.
$139/yr. Monthly—HR
P.O. Box 4560
Burlington, VT 05406
802-658-5500

NO-LOAD FUND ANALYST
Covers mutual funds. Fundamental
analysis. Includes feature articles on financial markets, a thorough review of
selected funds. Has four model portfolios.
$195/yr. Monthly—HR
L/G Research, Inc.
4 Orinda Way, Ste. 230-D
Orinda, CA 94563
800-776-9555

THE NO-LOAD FUND INVESTOR
Fundamental analysis. Covers mutual
funds (stock and bond). Covers over
700 no-load and low-load mutual
funds each month. Has model portfolios. Their goal is to grow "steadily
and safely."
$99/yr. Monthly—HR
P.O. Box 318
Irvington-on-Hudson, NY 10533
800-252-2042; 914-693-7420

**NOLOAD FUND*X
Fundamental analysis. Covers mutual
funds (stock and bond). Rates over
700 major no-load mutual funds and
recommends that readers select the top-
rated funds in each category. Turnover is high because fund leadership
changes often.
$75/yr. Monthly—HR
235 Montgomery Street, Ste. 662

San Francisco, CA 94104
800-323-1510

NO-LOAD MUTUAL FUND SELEC-
TIONS AND TIMING NEWS-
LETTER
Fundamental and technical analysis.
Covers mutual funds. Gives advice on
market timing and fund selection. Includes three model portfolios of no-
load funds: 1) a "sector portfolio,"
based entirely on the Fidelity Select
Funds; 2) an "asset allocations" portfolio that trades among domestic
and international stock, bond funds,
and precious-metal funds; and 3) an
"equity intermediate term" portfolio,
based on only the U.S. equities market.
$180/yr. Monthly—HR
Investment Selections and Tim-
ing, Inc.
1120 Empire Central Place
Dallas, TX 75247
800-800-6563

NO-LOAD PORTFOLIOS
Covers mutual funds. Technical and
fundamental analysis. Focuses on a
buy-and-hold strategy for investing in
mutual funds. Has a market timing
model, which includes technical and
fundamental indicators. Has telephone
hotline.
$69/yr. Monthly—HR
8635 W. Sahara, Ste. 420
The Lakes, NV 89117

PETER ELIADES' STOCK MARKET
CYCLES
Technical analysis. Covers mutual
funds (stock) and market timing. Has
hotline. Mr. Eliades uses technical
analysis with an emphasis on market
cycles. He uses long-term and short-
term market timing. Has two model

portfolios, one for the Fidelity Select Funds and one for Rydex funds.
$252/yr. Every 3 weeks
P.O. Box 6873
Santa Rosa, CA 95406
800-888-4351; 707-579-8444

SECTOR FUND CONNECTION
Covers mutual funds. Technical analysis. Includes mutual fund trading and timing methods.
$35/yr. Monthly
8949 La Riviera Drive
Sacramento, CA 95826
916-363-2055

THE SECTOR FUNDS NEWSLETTER
Covers mutual funds. Technical analysis. Has three model portfolios. One portfolio is comprised of Benham bond funds, another of Fidelity Funds Plus, and there is a third, miscellaneous fund portfolio.
$157/yr. Every 2 Weeks—HR
P.O. Box 270048
San Diego, CA 92198
619-748-0805

SOUND MIND INVESTING
Covers mutual funds. Fundamental analysis. Includes global and domestic business news, and general personal finance news.
$59/yr. Monthly—HR
Pryor and Associates
2337 Glen Eagle Drive
Louisville, KY 40222
502-426-7420

SWITCH FUND ADVISOR
Covers mutual funds and asset allocation. Technical analysis. Uses interest rates and investor sentiment to determine market trends, and makes recommendations on either stock or

money market funds based on these trends.
$195/yr. Bimonthly
Physiconomics, Inc.
P.O. Box 368
Norwalk, CA 90651
800-676-5424

SWITCH FUND TIMING
Covers stocks and mutual funds. Fundamental analysis. Offers strategies on market timing for long-term investors.
$89/yr. Monthly—HR
P.O. Box 25430
Rochester, NY 14625
716-385-3122

TELOFUND INVESTMENT FUND
Covers Vanguard and Fidelity mutual funds. Fundamental and technical analysis. Telephone hotline which uses computer model to make mutual fund switch recommendations.
$250/yr. Monthly
1355 Peachtree Street N.E.,
Ste. 1280
Atlanta, GA 30309
800-828-2219; 404-881-6221

TRENDS IN MUTUAL FUND ACTIVITY
Covers mutual funds. Statistical data. Includes investment objective, sales, and inventory for all mutual funds.
$225/yr. Monthly
Investment Company Institute
1600 M Street N.W., Ste. 600
Washington, DC 20036
202-326-5800

UNITED MUTUAL FUND SECTOR
Covers mutual funds. Fundamental analysis. Gives performance compari-

sons and specific recommendations on mutual funds.
$130/yr. Biweekly
Babson-United Investment Advisors, Inc.
101 Prescott Street
Wellesley Hills, MA 02181
617-235-0900

THE VALUE LINE MUTUAL FUND SURVEY
Analyzes and reports on 2,000 stock and bond funds.
$295/yr. Biweekly—HR

Value Line Publishing
711 Third Avenue
New York, NY 10017
800-633-2252; 212-687-3965

WEBER'S FUND ADVISOR
Covers mutual funds. Fundamental and technical analysis. Gives commentary on the market and other news affecting mutual funds.
$135/yr. Monthly
P.O. Box 3490
New Hyde Park, NY 11040
516-466-1252

Books

ALL ABOUT BOND FUNDS
Werner Renberg. John Wiley & Sons, 1995
$19.95 pbk. ISBN: 0-471-31195-2
Discusses how to evaluate and select bond mutual funds. Shows how to measure potential volatility. Gives historic performance for select funds.

ALL ABOUT MUTUAL FUNDS
Bruce Jacobs. Probus, 1994.
$19.95 ISBN: 1-55738-807-5
Extensive descriptions of the different types of funds, how to begin investing, fund allocation strategies, and more. Includes study-guide questions after each chapter.

BOGLE ON MUTUAL FUNDS
John C. Bogle. Dell, 1994.
$25.00 hc ISBN: 1-556-23860-6
$12.95 pbk. ISBN: 0-440-50682-4
John Bogle, founder of The Vanguard Group (the largest no-load mutual fund company), shows how to invest in mutual funds. He covers equity funds, fixed-income funds, and asset

allocation. He also discusses risk versus reward, indexing strategies, and tax consequences. The reader is shown not only how to invest but also how not to invest. The fixed-income discussion is superior to that of most books on mutual funds.

BUSINESS WEEK GUIDE TO MUTUAL FUNDS
McGraw-Hill, 1995.
$14.95 pbk. ISBN: 0-07-035216-X
Covers over 1,800 mutual funds and also explains how to choose which funds are right for you. Topics range from load fund variations to which funds are best for IRAs and 401(k) plans.

THE DIRECTORY OF MUTUAL FUNDS
The Investment Company Institute, annual edition.
$8.50 pbk.
A catalog of several thousand mutual funds, categorized by investment objective. Includes information like ad-

dresses, phone numbers, sales loads and expenses, minimum investment requirements, and other details.

GETTING STARTED IN MUTUAL FUNDS

Alan Lavine. John Wiley & Sons, 1994.
$16.95 pbk. ISBN: 0-471-57694-8
The author begins by explaining what mutual funds are and how they work. He shows how commissions (if any), expenses, and fees can affect your investment. Then he shows you how to choose funds that are right for your goals and risk/comfort level.

THE HANDBOOK FOR NO-LOAD FUND INVESTORS

Sheldon Jacobs. Irwin Professional, 1995.
$40.00 ISBN: 0-7863-0435-9
Looks at 2,000 no-load and direct-marketed low-load funds. Provides ten-year performance data. Gives information about funds, including how to contact funds for prospectuses and how to buy shares.

HOW MUTUAL FUNDS WORK

Albert J. Fredman and Russ Wiles. New York Institute of Finance, 1993.
$15.95 pbk. ISBN: 0-13-012501-6
Explains the basics of mutual fund investing and how to read a prospectus. Describes different types of mutual funds and how to evaluate them. Offers some portfolio management strategies.

HOW TO BUY MUTUAL FUNDS THE SMART WAY

Stephen Littauer. Dearborn Financial, 1993.
$16.95 pbk. ISBN: 0-79310-478-5
Deals with the strategies of how to use mutual funds to achieve financial goals. Covers some tax-planning issues of funds and the use of funds in retirement plans. Offers advice on record keeping; includes some forms and worksheets.

THE INDIVIDUAL INVESTOR'S GUIDE TO LOW-LOAD MUTUAL FUNDS

American Association of Individual Investors, 1995.
$24.95 pbk. ISBN: 0-942641-64-7
A comprehensive reference book that provides information on hundreds of no-load and low-load mutual funds.

MORNINGSTAR MUTUAL FUND 500

Irwin Professional, 1996.
$35.00 ISBN: 0-7863-0539-8
Directory of 500 open-end mutual funds, showing Morningstar star rankings, investment philosophies, and historical data.

MUTUAL FUND BUYER'S GUIDE

Norman G. Fosback. Irwin Professional, 1995.
$17.95 pbk. ISBN: 1-55738-808-3
Provides summary data on 1,700 funds, including performance and expenses. Offers advice on how to evaluate a fund.

THE MUTUAL FUND ENCYCLOPEDIA

Gerald W. Perritt. Dearborn Financial, 1995.
$35.95 pbk. ISBN: 0-7931-1310-5
Contains profiles of over 3,400 mutual funds. Has information not usually included in most books, including detailed information on fund objectives and strategies, what types of investments are preferred by the fund's management, and more.

MUTUAL FUNDS FOR DUMMIES
Eric Tyson. IDG Books, 1995.
$16.99 pbk. ISBN: 1-56884-226-0
The title says it all! Author discusses
what mutual funds are, how to choose
great funds and avoid the losers, and
much more. He even discusses how to
read a fund's statement, a fund's annual report, and yes, even how to read
a fund's wonderful prospectus.

Software

*An asterik (*) indicates that the product was mentioned in the 1995 Readers' Choice
Awards,* Technical Analysis of STOCKS & COMMODITIES™ *magazine (Bonus Issue
1996). Contact:*

Technical Analysis, Inc.
4757 California Avenue S.W.
Seattle, WA 98116-4499
Phone: 206-938-0570
Fax: 206-938-1307
http://www.traders.com/
mail@traders.com

**CDA HYSALES FOR MUTUAL
FUNDS**
System: WIN
$695
Hypothetical software for mutual
funds. Includes information on 4,000
mutual funds and sixty-two indexes
for the past fifteen years.
CDA Investment Technologies
1355 Piccard Drive
Rockville, MD 20850
800-232-2285

**CDA/WIESENBERGER MUTUAL
FUND PERFORMANCE**
System: WIN
Call for price.
On-line database of mutual funds. Includes data, such as rate of return, net
asset value, load and risk factors. Gives
hypothetical analysis of fund performance. Also available via diskette.
CDA Investment Technologies
1355 Piccard Drive

Rockville, MD 20850
800-232-2285

CLOSED-END FUNDS ONFLOPPY
System: DOS
$45–$195 (depending on updates)
Covers over 520 closed-end funds.
User may screen and rank funds based
on 111 criteria. Graph one fund versus
another or against a benchmark. Has
information on risk, return, and pre-
miums/discounts. Also covers sector
weightings, manager information, and
up to ten years of data. Update by
disk.
Morningstar
225 W. Wacker Drive
Chicago, IL 60606
800-876-5005; 312-696-6000

FUND MASTER TC
System: DOS
$289. Demo $5.
Create up to twenty mutual fund
portfolios. Emphasizes market timing
combined with mutual fund selection.
Ranks mutual funds based on relative
strength. Also has a built-in spreadsheet dedicated to investment analysis.
Choose from simple indicators such as
percent change to complex user-
defined equations. A portfolio manager is built in, so there is no need to
switch between programs. Employs

time-weighted rate of return. Adjusts for dividends and capital gains. Provides tax information with two keystrokes. Utilizes full-featured charting with moving averages, trend channels, and different scales (arithmetic, log, or percent). Menu-driven. Update manually or on-line.

Time Trend Software
337 Boston Road
Billerica, MA 01821
508-250-3866

FUNDGRAF
System: DOS
$100. Demo $10.
Covers stocks and mutual funds. Screens and graphs the best-performing funds of a period (up to 260 weeks). Superimposes different funds for direct comparison. Semilog and linear plotting. Moving averages determine buy and sell signals. Update manually, from update disks, or on-line. Can also be used for stocks.

Parsons Software
1230 W. 6th Street
Loveland, CO 80537
303-669-3744

FUNDSCOPE
System: DOS
$25/month–$300/yr.
FundScope is a mutual fund database covering over 5,000 funds and several indexes. Search by fund name, objective, expense ratio, beta, yield, etc. Displays total return and returns for various periods. Also has fund telephone numbers, ticker symbols, minimum purchase requirements, and more. Ten-year graphs may be displayed as well as moving averages (which give buy/sell signals). Sort by objective, alpha, and reward-risk ratios. Scattergrams can also be generated. Superimpose one fund's graph

onto another. Perform hypothetical studies based on deposits and withdrawals, buy-and-hold strategies, and switching strategies. Calculates internal rate of return. Allows for the grouping of funds. Has context-sensitive help.

American River Software
1523 Kingsford Drive
Carmichael, CA 95608
916-483-1600

FUNDS-ON-LINE
System: DOS
$125 plus $25/month
A software and on-line database combination that compares about 300 mutual funds and gives buy/sell signals using technical analysis. Also has mutual fund screening.

Mutual Fund On-Line Data
1 San Marcos Avenue
San Francisco, CA 94116
800-831-7777

FUNDWATCH
System: DOS
$40
Covers stocks, bonds, and mutual funds. Evaluates and compares investments, including mutual funds, stocks, bonds. Shows graphs, moving averages, yields.

Dynacomp, Inc.
178 Phillips Road
Webster, NY 14580
800-828-6772; 716-265-4040

FUNDWATCH PLUS
Systems: DOS, WIN
$29
Covers stocks and mutual funds. Tracks groups of up to 100 funds. Allows comparison of funds, stocks, and indexes. Uses moving averages and other technical tools. Shows volatility and risk-adjusted performance. Calculates annualized rates of growth, distributions, and total return.

Hamilton Software, Inc.
6432 E. Mineral Place
Englewood, CO 80112
800-733-9607; 303-770-9607

INVESTORS FASTTRACK*
System: DOS
$288/yr.
An on-line service that helps you
choose mutual funds. Updates information daily. Full-color charts and buy/
sell signals are given. Also has commentary and mutual fund screening.
Investors Fasttrack
P.O. Box 77577
Baton Rouge, LA 70879
800-749-1348

**INVESTOR'S GUIDE AND MUTUAL
FUND DIRECTORY**
System: DOS
$99/yr.
Program contains information on no-
load mutual funds. Also includes as-
sorted investment information.
**The Association of No-Load
Funds Mutual Fund Education
Alliance**
1900 Erie Street, Ste. 120
Kansas City, MO 64116
816-471-1454

MONOCLE
System: WIN
**$149; $249 with trading system.
Demo available. 1-month trial
$9.95.**
Covers over 1,000 mutual funds. Easy
to use and comprehensive. Uses technical analysis to help you screen, buy,
and sell mutual funds. You may also
screen based on return, beta, alpha,
and other criteria. Comes with its
own trading systems. Has on-line
help. Update by disk or on-line.
Manhattan Analytics, Inc.

912 Manhattan Avenue, 2nd Floor
Manhattan Beach, CA 90266
800-251-3863; 310-374-2142

MUTUAL FUND DECISION AIDE
System: DOS. Requires Lotus
1-2-3.
$49
Allows you to evaluate performance
from any past year (up to twelve years
ago) to the present. Lets you see the
variations in return, before and after
taxes and load fees. This allows a more
direct comparison of different funds.
Update data manually.
V. A. Denslow and Associates
4151 Woodland Avenue
Western Springs, IL 60558
708-246-3365

MUTUAL FUND EDGE
System: DOS
$265
An add-on product for Telescan's
Mutual Fund Edge. Allows searches
on mutual funds.
Emerging Market
1230 Johnson Ferry Road, Ste. F-1
Marietta, GA 30068
404-973-2300

MUTUAL FUND EXPERT
System: DOS
$95/yr.
Database package, contains 100 pieces
of information on over 3,500 mutual
funds. Allows user to screen for funds
that meet his criteria. Also has data on
thirty-four market indexes for comparison purposes.
**Alexander Steele Systems Tech-
nologies**
12021 Wilshire Boulevard, Ste. 407
Los Angeles, CA 90025
800-678-3863

MUTUAL FUND INVESTOR
System: DOS
$295. Demo $25.

Covers stocks, bonds, and mutual funds. Tracks mutual funds and other securities. Compares fund-to-fund performance between any two dates. Perform hypothetical studies based on deposits and withdrawals, buy-and-hold strategies, and switching strategies. Sophisticated portfolio management includes monthly profit/loss reports, cost basis, total commissions paid, internal rate of return, asset allocation, etc. Also cross-references portfolios, reports current value and average cost basis. Two-year daily and ten-year weekly graphs may be displayed. Uses moving averages for buy/sell signals. Has context-sensitive help. Update manually or on-line.

American River Software
1523 Kingsford Drive
Carmichael, CA 95608
916-483-1600

MUTUAL FUND MANAGER
System: DOS
$49. Demo $5.

Maintains complete annual records including distributions and redemptions. Has three performance reports including weekly reports (gain/loss, net asset value, comparisons to market indexes), performance reports (performance analysis, moving averages, exclusive "beta-predicted performance"), and portfolio distribution analysis (percent of net asset value by fund and fund type, composite beta of portfolio). Update manually.

Denver Data, Inc.
Meridian One, Ste. G-126
9785 Maroon Circle
Englewood, CO 80112
303-790-7327

MUTUAL FUNDS ONDISC
System: DOS. Requires CD-ROM drive.
$295–$795 (depending on updates). Demo $5.

Has the most detailed information on mutual funds available. Covers over 5,700 mutual funds with statistics, written analyses (on 1,500 funds), and Morningstar's own analytical tools. Allows the user to rank and screen mutual funds based on ninety-four criteria. Graph one fund versus another fund or against a benchmark. Learn about a fund's style of investing, the manager, the fund's sector weightings, and much more. Allows the user to see how a portfolio would have performed over time. Has up to eighteen years of historical data and 700 statistics per fund. Has a tutorial.

Morningstar
225 W. Wacker Drive
Chicago, IL 60606
800-876-5005; 312-696-6000

MUTUAL MAX
System: WIN. Works with Morningstar, Quicken, Managing Your Money, and Simply Money.
$40

Mutual MAX shows your asset allocation in more detail; MAX looks at a fund by its allocation in U.S. equities, U.S. bonds, U.S. cash, and foreign holdings that are reported by Morningstar. Has different asset allocation targets to suit different risk and return levels. Has fund screening and more detailed information about funds you are interested in. Comes with a database of fifty large U.S. mutual funds. Update on-line.

Advisor Software, Inc.
P.O. Box 2338

Orinda, CA 94563
800-738-6369; 510-253-5090

PRINCIPIA
System: WIN
$45–$195 (depending on updates)
Covers over 6,000 mutual funds. Has up to ninety-eight categories of information including rating statistics, return information, risk measurements, investment style, fees/expenses, and more. Rank and screen funds based on your criteria. Compare one fund to another or against a benchmark. Create customized reports.
Morningstar
225 W. Wacker Drive
Chicago, IL 60606
800-876-5005; 312-696-6000

**QUARTERLY LOW-LOAD MUTUAL
   FUND UPDATE ON DISK**
Systems: DOS, MAC
$50
Quarterly disk contains 100 criteria for 1,000 low-load and no-load funds. Performance data go back up to ten years. Includes expense ratio, turnover, fees, and more. Includes their quarterly newsletter on mutual funds.
American Association of Individual Investors
625 N. Michigan Avenue,
   Ste. 1900
Chicago, IL 60611
312-280-0170

VALUE LINE FUND ANALYZER
System: WIN. CD-ROM version
   available.
**$295–395. Demo available. 2-
month trial $50.**
Access data on over 3,600 mutual funds with data updated monthly by disk (or weekly if user updates on-line). Has factor analysis, hypothetical investments, and commentary on funds. Sort and filter funds on over 100 criteria including expenses, sector allocation, and risk. Has reports and customized graphs.
Value Line Publishing, Inc.
220 E. 42nd Street
New York, NY 10017
800-284-7607; 212-907-1500

YOUR MUTUAL FUND SELECTOR
System: WIN. CD-ROM version
   available.
$30. Updates extra.
Charts the performance of a fund against the performance of the market. Gives information from Morningstar such as a fund's star rating, minimum investment, size of the fund, and more. Screen through over 1,000 funds. Walks you through questions such as your risk level.
Quicken Investment Services, Inc.
2650 E. Elvira, Ste. 100
Tucson, AZ 85706
800-781-5999

On-Line Services

Almost all the on-line services shown in the Resource Guide in Chapter 4 have services that deal with mutual fund investing. Refer to those pages for more information.

Chapter 7

WORKING WITH FEE-ONLY
PROFESSIONALS

The entire focus of the preceding chapters has been to show you that you do not need the services of a commission-based stockbroker, or any other salesperson for that matter, in order to invest your money successfully and attain your financial goals. You should have a better understanding of how to define your financial goals, how to establish an asset allocation strategy that will move you toward those goals, and finally, how to go about investing in the primary financial assets: stocks, bonds, and mutual funds. Without forsaking any of the content of those chapters, we now want to change focus entirely away from self-investing, and discuss how you can use the services of a fee-only professional.

As the term implies, fee-only investment professionals provide a variety of financial services for a fee, rather than a commission. The significance of a fee as opposed to a commission, of course, is that the advice these professionals render is more likely to be unbiased in nature. The response from commission-based vendors to this notion is usually along the lines that a fee-only provider collects a fee, whether or not he has made money for the client, and therefore the fee-only service provider will take a more cavalier attitude toward the client and his portfolio. And the fee-only professional's rejoinder to this is that he is likely to add more value to the client's portfolio operating the way he does rather than going through the stockbroker's "busywork" of creating trades that are not necessary and using investment instruments that are not appropriate for the client. Let's end this joust by proclaiming two irrefutable doctrines:

■ The fee-only adviser has no ulterior motive in making investment transactions for clients. The transaction, by itself, does not affect the fee-only professional's income.

■ The fee-only adviser has the same vested interest as that of the client: to make the portfolio grow in value. It is the *outcome* of the transaction that determines whether the fee-only professional benefits from it.

To clarify these points, the fee-only adviser typically charges his fee as a percentage of the value of the assets he manages. Thus, if the client's portfolio rises in value, the adviser is rewarded with a higher fee. If the portfolio declines in value, that is, he loses money for the client, the adviser is penalized with a lower fee. So you see, the fee-only adviser's motivation is not in making a buy or sell transaction but in making a transaction that is appropriate for the account circumstances and that is most likely to make money for the client.

One last bit of semantics before we move on. Some professionals, generally financial planners, refer to themselves as "fee-based" service providers. This is a separate and distinct classification from fee-only providers. Fee-based planners may charge a fee for some services, but they may then receive income from commissions for other services. For instance, the planner may charge a fee for preparing a financial plan for her client. The fee may be a fixed charge or it could be based upon an hourly rate. Then, if the planner is hired to manage the client's portfolio, the planner's compensation will revert back to receiving commissions on insurance products or mutual funds sold to the client. You should be aware of this distinction, and avoid confusion by ensuring that the professional you engage in service is a *fee-only professional*.

WHY USE A FEE-ONLY ADVISER?

After devoting the content of this book so far to independent investment decision making, one may wonder why there is any discussion at all about using an investment professional. We've just freed ourselves from the stockbroker and learned how to build our own investment portfolios. Why do we now want to turn to another investment pro? Let's address the issue from several different angles. First, at some point there will come a time when you will be unwilling or unable to attend to your own portfolio. The circumstances could be the time demands of your profession or a prolonged absence from market information due to a lengthy vacation. Or the day could simply come when your portfolio has grown to the point where you would be more comfortable having someone looking at it all the time, rather than the three hours per week that you are able to dedicate to the responsibility.

Secondly, when the time comes that you want professional assistance, you must be aware of the fee-only service providers who will give you the best advice, based on market conditions and your circumstances, and not based on a commission structure for the products at hand. The worst thing you could do, knowing what you've learned so far, is to turn back to the commission-based broker or financial planner for investment guidance. Yet you'd be surprised how many people do just that. I have seen more than a few investors, even wealthy investors with seven-figure and eight-figure portfolios, turn to or return to full-commission stockbrokers, primarily because they were not aware of the alternatives available in the form of fee-only advisers. Incredible but true. And this is why we shall explore the fee-only investment professionals with whom you can work.

The three groups of fee-only service providers are:

- Money managers
- Financial planners
- Trust departments

MONEY MANAGERS

This group of fee-only advisers actually uses different names for their services, in addition to *money manager*. These include *investment adviser* or *registered investment adviser, financial adviser*, and *investment manager*. The term we'll use for the duration of this discussion is *registered investment adviser*, or RIA. To avoid any confusion, RIA is not a professional designation, as CPA is in the accounting profession. The "registered" part refers to the formality and legality of a money manager who registers with the Securities and Exchange Commission (SEC) as a registered investment adviser. The SEC requires registration of those investment professionals who, for monetary compensation, give advice, make recommendations, issue reports, and furnish analyses on securities. Although individuals may register as RIAs, typically it is an advisory firm that has the registration. Those individuals who work for the registrant advisory firm are listed under the firm's registration document, known as Form ADV.

The registration with the SEC does not convey any level of competence, just as having a valid driver's license does not imply that the license holder is a good driver. It simply indicates that the RIA is licensed with the federal government to transact business as an investment adviser. In addition to registration with the SEC, most states require that any RIA registered under the guidelines of the SEC must also register in their state, if the RIA has clients there or solicits new clients there. Thus, regulatory scrutiny over RIAs comes from many sets of eyes. While remaining in compliance with these regulatory agencies can be burdensome to the money managers, it is a benefit to you since the RIAs must be attentive to regulatory requirements that are designed to protect the investor. As you will see in reviewing Form ADV, RIAs and their employees are subjected to much closer examination than are stockbrokers.

RIAs are required by law to provide to a client a copy of Form ADV—Part II when that client signs a contract with them. Each year thereafter, as long as they are still a client, the money manager must *offer* to provide an updated copy of Form ADV—Part II or a comparable "brochure" that contains the same information. The ADV is fairly user-friendly, at least as government documents go. Your eyes may begin to glaze over if you study it for too long, but we'll highlight for you some of the more pertinent details the ADV contains.

The ADV will describe what types of services the money manager provides, for what types of clients these services are rendered, what the fee schedule is, how fees are determined, and when fees are collected. The ADV asks the RIA to describe the specific types of securities he or the firm uses. For example, if the money manager uses futures and options in managing portfolios, this will be stated in the form so that you are aware of the fact. The types of investment analysis that the adviser uses are described. The ADV explains the commissions that your account will be charged on securities transactions. Yes, you still have to pay commissions on trades, but because the adviser does not receive the commissions, his investment decisions on your behalf will not be influenced by them. Since you are dealing with a fee-only adviser, the boxes checked on the ADV should indicate that trades are done through unrelated third-party brokers at commission rates per share that are comparable to those of a discount broker. If you see anything other than this arrangement, such as commissions going to the RIA from a related brokerage firm, turn and run, don't walk, out the money manager's door.

Form ADV—Part II contains several schedules that are very informative since they deal with the people of the RIA. This is of the utmost importance, because when you hire a money manager, or any service provider for that matter, you are really hiring the people who will deliver that service. Schedule A shows who the people are who actually own and/or control and manage the RIA, if it is incorporated. If the organizational structure is a partnership, Schedule B is presented. For other types of structure, Schedule C is used. These schedules show the person's title or status with the RIA, how much of the company they own, and what their Social Security number and/or CRD number is. The CRD number is an identification number issued by the National Association of Securities Dealers (NASD). With it you can contact the NASD and check to see if the person has run afoul of the NASD or SEC in the past.

Schedule D follows, and it deals with each and every person in the RIA firm that is directly or indirectly involved with the management of your money. Among the items it displays are: 1) CRD and Social Security numbers; 2) education from secondary school through college or graduate school; 3) business background, including all employers for previous ten years, and the start dates, end dates, and positions with each employer; 4) professional examinations, designations, and licenses earned and the dates these were received; and 5) legal or administrative proceedings such as lawsuits, injunctions, penalties, suspensions, and so on, arising from previous conduct. In summary, Schedule D, and the entire ADV for that matter, tells you everything you would want to know, or ought to know, about the people working with you in managing your assets.

If the SEC has a credo, it is "Full Disclosure." What an RIA can and cannot do and how it conducts business is bound by certain guidelines. The ADV is designed and monitored by the SEC so that all customers of the RIA are aware of what the firm is doing. The result is that there will be no surprises. If you've worked with a stockbroker in the past, were you provided this amount of information? Not even close. Having the information presented to clients and prospective clients in the form of an official document filed with an agency of the federal government is what makes working with RIAs so appealing to investors. No surprises. Sure, a pamphlet from a brokerage firm can include inflated résumés and marketing hype, but until it's contained in an official document, it's not official.

When you hire an RIA to manage your money, you will execute a contract that outlines the terms of service, what the fee will be, what the objectives of the account are, how the contract is terminated, and other details. Similar contracts are usually executed if you are hiring a financial planner or a trust department. Although this varies from one relationship to another, when you sign this contract with the fee-only adviser, you are delegating to him and his agents a "limited power of attorney." This means that the adviser can initiate transactions on your behalf without seeking your approval beforehand, but the adviser does not have access to the funds himself.

Many investors are confused about who has possession, or *custody*, of their assets, who is making the investment decisions, and who is acting as broker in transactions. So let's clarify the parties and what their functions are. The RIA makes investment decisions on your behalf. When he buys a stock for your portfolio, he contacts a broker that either he or the client has chosen. In the legal sense, the RIA has been granted *limited power of attorney* by the investor. Generally, stocks and bonds and other financial assets are held at one of two places: 1) a brokerage account, or 2) a bank trust department. If the custodian is the broker (make that a discount broker), it will do the trade and will settle the trade. Remember, trade settlement is the exchange of cash for securities between the broker and the custodian, and in this instance, the broker and the custodian are one and the same. The RIA should never handle cash or securities. When the custodian is a bank, the broker settles the trade with the bank through the following procedure:

- RIA concludes trade with the broker.
- RIA notifies bank of trade details (affirmation).
- Broker sends notice of trade to both the RIA and bank (confirmation).
- Bank compares affirmation and confirmation for any discrepancies.
- When affirmation and confirmation are a match, trade is settled.

The functions of a custodian, either a broker or a bank, are to:

- Receive cash deposits from client.
- Disburse cash to wherever the client directs.
- Settle securities transactions that have been initiated by the RIA.

- Receive dividends and interest and invest those monies into the account's money market fund.
- Provide the client with a statement that accounts for the assets held.
- Provide client with year-end tax information on dividends, interest, and capital gains realized during the year.

To ensure there is no misunderstanding, the "client" referred to above is the investor, not the RIA. An investor who hires an RIA enters into a separate contractual agreement with the custodian. The client can use a custodian of his choosing, or the RIA can recommend one with which there is already a working relationship. If the custodian selected is a broker (a discount broker to be sure), they may do the actual buying and selling of securities as well. I say "may" because brokers will also settle trades done through other brokers, for a fee, of course.

Custodians are compensated through fees and/or brokerage commissions. As we just said, brokers acting as custodians are compensated primarily through the stock, bond, or mutual fund trades done through their trading desk. In the case of some mutual funds, the broker may collect a 12b-1 fee, which was discussed in Chapter 6, Investing in Mutual Funds. When the custodian is a bank, the compensation is exclusively through fees. A typical fee arrangement is composed of two parts: 1) a base fee, which is either a flat fee or a percentage of the account's market value; 2) a transaction fee for each trade that is done in the account. Base fees vary among custodians, but the typical yearly fee today should be about 10 basis points, or 0.10 percent of the account's value, with the proviso of a minimum annual fee. The transaction fees range from $15 to $30 per trade. Fees are calculated and paid at three-month intervals.

Fee-only money managers charge their fees in one of two ways: 1) a percentage of assets being managed, or 2) a flat fee. Like the custodians, money managers often have a minimum annual fee they charge, and they may have a minimum account size they will handle as well. The percentage fees charged by money managers start at 1 percent of the portfolio's value. They then scale down from there depending on the asset mix (stocks, bonds, and cash) and the size of the portfolio. Portfolios with a higher percentage of bonds and cash will pay a lower fee in order to maintain a competitive rate of return. Likewise, larger portfolios are assessed a smaller percentage fee because of the economies of scale in managing large portfolios.

As said before, your money manager (or financial planner, if you are using one) should not have custody of your assets or access to them through the custodian. I encountered a money manager several years ago whose firm had custody of its clients' securities. The RIA's office was located in the same building as a bank. The client's securities were in physical form (that is, pieces of paper rather than the usual electronic book entries) and they were placed in safe-deposit boxes. This practice may sound secure, but it poses incredible risk for certificates to be lost or placed in the wrong boxes and for dividends and interest payments to be lost, or for stock splits to be overlooked. And when it comes time to sell a stock or bond, what a nightmare it would be to get the pieces of paper to the broker and avoid failed trades. No, all of these functions are better done by a professional custodian that has your securities within its dominion and in electronic book entry form.

Having cited the exception above, the vast majority of money managers and financial planners do not want custody of assets. When RIAs do act as custodian, they subject themselves to a whole new level of heightened scrutiny by regulators, for obvious reasons. Consequently, most RIAs will not even accept a check from a client to deposit with the custodian into the client's account; to do so is tantamount to taking custody of the client's assets.

Among the functions a good money manager will provide clients are:

- Assisting client in formulating investment objectives
- Reviewing existing assets, rebalancing and reallocating portfolio
- Researching, selecting, purchasing and selling securities
- Reviewing custodian statements for accuracy and completeness
- Issuing his own client statements that include rate of return
- Having periodic meetings to review the client's objectives and review the progress being made toward those objectives

One of the most valuable services any fee-only adviser furnishes clients is assisting them in the formulation of their investment objectives. As you saw in Chapter 3, Asset Allocation, this is no small task. It is made easier, however, by having an RIA's unbiased opinion and the input of someone who sees a wide array of investors and their financial programs. The process may include your completing a detailed questionnaire, or it could mean simply a verbal interview. All this input will be valuable to you and to the money manager in establishing a financial game plan. More important, the money manager should make clear to you that your objectives are reasonable and attainable, and that the objectives and the portfolio allocations are reviewed and revised when they need to be.

We've already touched on the trading relationship between the RIA and the broker. Again, if you request that the account be domiciled at a particular discount broker, this should work for almost any money manager. The larger discount brokers have special groups that deal exclusively with money managers and financial planners. If the broker you choose does not have the capability of working with your money manager, or if the money manager states that she cannot work well with that particular broker, choose another broker or consider having custody at a bank.

Most bank trust departments that sell custody services are able to work with almost any RIA. One advantage to the money manager, and hence an advantage to the client, of using a bank as custodian is that it frees up the money manager to use more than one broker in doing the trades in an account. The manager can shop the trade for best price execution, and the manager can usually obtain a per-share commission rate that is lower than that of the discount broker that might otherwise be used. All of this adds up to better and cheaper execution of clients' trades, which in turn bolsters the realized rate of return.

Speaking of rate of return, one of the greatest features an RIA affords clients is a scorecard of the portfolio's progress. All good money managers will have the capability to compute the portfolio's rate of return on a monthly basis. Both the client and his manager will receive a statement, usually every month, from the custodian. The RIA has his own portfolio accounting system, and the custodian statement is used as a cross-check for such details as receipt of dividends and interest, as well as the details of trades done during the statement period. With this information in the manager's hands, an accurate rate of return can be calculated. Those returns can then be linked with returns of previous months to ascertain the rate of return for certain periods of time, such as previous calendar years or since the manager assumed responsibility for the portfolio. With this information in hand, you are able to track the progress your manager is making in achieving your investment objectives. No retail stockbroker will provide you with the feature of rate-of-return calculation, at least not on accounts over which he has discretion. And if you think about it, rate of return is the most important piece of information you as a client can receive. It's "the bottom line," as they say.

Communication is a vital part of any human relationship, and so it is with the money manager–client relationship. When possible, meetings should be arranged at regular intervals, at least twice a year. These face-to-face encounters ensure that client and manager are in sync with each other's thinking. Some geographic proximity between client and manager is helpful, though not necessary, in this regard. Providing this level of service is difficult for a portfolio manager (that is, the person actually managing your portfolio, the principal or employee of the RIA itself) if they have more than about thirty relationships for which they are responsible. A portfolio manager could easily handle multiple portfolios for each relationship, bringing his management capacity up to sixty or eighty portfolios. Hence, your search for an RIA should include small money managers in addition to larger service providers, as the smaller managers can provide a greater level of personal service.

FINANCIAL PLANNERS

Since we are discussing fee-only *investment* professionals, our primary concern with financial planners is in the context of investment services, not just financial planning services. However, we do want to highlight the planning services they provide as well, so you are aware of the advantages planners afford their clients.

Most of the early financial planners were reconstituted stockbrokers and insurance salespeople. The financial planning community is still heavily populated with these types. Accustomed to making their living from sales commissions, those planners continue to receive their compensation from the sale of insurance policies, annuities, and mutual funds, with an occasional limited partnership thrown in for good measure. The sales of all these products are wrapped up in the package labeled "Financial Plan." As you know, our focus here is exclusively on fee-only financial planners. You may recall that "fee-based" planners may provide services for both a fee and commissions on products sold. Do not be confused; you want to deal solely with fee-only planners. Later in the chapter I'll show you where to go to locate fee-only financial planners.

There are approximately 20,000 registered investment advisers in the U.S., and there are over 100,000 financial planners. Many financial planners are RIAs, although it is uncertain exactly how many planners are registered. It is safe to say that those planners who are registered derive most, if not all, of their income from fees. Many financial planners tend to be sole practitioners, or at most they may have five or six professionals in a group. With the technology and the services available to planners today, there is no compelling reason for them to be in a large-group environment. As I'll discuss later in the chapter, there are advantages to working with a small firm, be it a financial planner or a money manager. While money managers are *specialists* in the art and the science of portfolio management, good financial planners are *generalists,* with expertise in many areas of personal finance. Among the different services they provide are:

- Preparing a financial statement of the client's assets
- Creating a cash-flow budget
- Helping to organize important papers and placing them in safe-deposit box
- Counseling on estate planning strategies
- Advising on wills and trusts
- Apprising client of insurance needs: life, health, and disability
- Suggesting ways of reducing current and future income taxes
- Assisting in quantifying financial goals: college, retirement, and so on
- Implementing financial plan through investment program

How deeply the planner will engage in each of these elements depends on his education, training, credentials, and experience. For example, some planners have law degrees, and with these people you could feel quite comfortable having a will or a trust created. The planner without the law degree will surely know several attorneys, who he can recommend to provide that service. The same can be said for accountants to whom clients may be referred. There are some planners who do not want to be involved in the investment process and will refer clients to money managers.

The great majority of financial planners who do the actual investing for their clients do so through mutual funds. As generalists, the time demands of performing the financial planning and consulting functions do not leave them sufficient time to be researching individual securities. It's far more time-efficient for them to employ one of the fund evaluation services and invest according to their analyses. As we indicated from the previous chapter, mutual fund investing is every bit as rewarding as buying and selling individual securities. Nevertheless, those investors who require or prefer a portfolio filled with twenty to thirty stocks, rather than five or six quality mutual funds, will want to look for a planner who invests in individual issues or a planner who refers financial planning clients to a money manager for the actual investing.

For those financial planners who invest the portfolios themselves, either in mutual funds or individual securities, the level of service should be the same as that of money managers. To recap, these services are:

- Assisting client in formulating investment objectives
- Reviewing existing assets, rebalancing and reallocating portfolio
- Researching, selecting, purchasing, and selling securities (or mutual funds)
- Reviewing custodian statements for accuracy and completeness
- Issuing his own client statements that include rate of return
- Having periodic meetings to review the client's objectives and review the progress being made toward those objectives

These planners should be registered with the SEC and the appropriate state regulatory agencies as RIAs. They will offer you, or you should request if they don't offer, a copy of Form ADV—Part II. Study the ownership structure of the firm and the backgrounds of the service providers. Pay attention to the fee structure of the financial planner. In a sense, planners have two types of services they are offering: 1) financial planning, and 2) investment management. As such, it is likely that there will be two separate fees, one for each service. In this way, those clients who have had a financial plan developed by the planner but who want to manage the assets themselves (or have another party manage them) will pay only for the financial planning services. Financial planning fees are either fixed, or the clients are billed by the hour. Fixed fees usually start at $500 and can range up to several thousand dollars. Hourly fees typically begin at $100 per hour, often with a minimum number of billable hours factored into the contract. Investment management fees are comparable to fees charged by money managers, often starting at 1 percent of the portfolio value, and scaling downward from there. Like money managers, a minimum annual fee and/or a minimum account size is often expected by the planner. There are some planners who bill an hourly rate for investment management services, in lieu of the percentage-of-assets method usually employed. Again, this rate regularly begins at $100 per hour and moves up. We recommend you use planners who utilize the percentage-of-assets methodology in fee calculation. It ensures that your fee is not being padded with hours spent researching securities, doing trades, and performing other functions that are being done for all clients, not just you. It also guarantees that his agenda and yours are one and the same: to make money for you and to not lose money.

If the financial planner is going to manage your assets, the service should be comparable to that of a money manager. The notable exception to this is that many financial planners confine their investment selections to mutual funds, whereas most money managers buy and sell individual securities. Beyond this, the financial planner you hire should provide you with, among other things, periodic statements that include rate-of-return calculations. Since the planners are often involved with tax planning and perhaps tax preparation, they will also be good about providing clients with yearly interest and dividend reports as well as a capital gain and loss report. With proper oversight on the client's part, engaging a good financial planner can yield a lot of service from the one-stop service provider.

TRUST DEPARTMENTS

Bank trust departments are, as the name implies, usually stand-alone departments or subsidiaries of banks. Not all banks have trust departments, and not all trust companies (bank trust departments are often separate corporations) are part of a bank. There are trust companies that are not affiliated with another financial institution. While money managers and financial planners share many similarities, bank trust departments are in a class by themselves. This is because they have something the other two fee-only professionals do not have: trust powers. Trust powers are conveyed to banks by regulatory authorities, thus allowing those institutions to act as *corporate trustees*. Any mentally competent adult can act as a trustee; it's done every time someone creates a living trust for himself or his family. Likewise, individuals who are money managers or financial planners could act as trustees for their clients (through most will not). But only a bank or other institution that has been granted trust powers can act as a corporate trustee. The significance of this is the broader level of service that the trust department offers those clients who require a corporate trustee. Beyond that, their services look like those of the money manager or financial planner.

People create trusts in order to ensure that their assets are handled in the fashion that the trustor, or grantor of the trust, wishes them to be handled. Trusts also help to minimize estate taxes and avoid the process known as probate. Probate can tie up the disposition of one's estate for years; it subjects the estate to an additional layer of legal expenses; and it opens one's wealth to potential public scrutiny because the probate court documents are a matter of public record. Whether to use a trust and what types of trusts are available are topics beyond the purview of this book. Consult with an attorney conversant in trusts and estate planning, with a financial planner, or with a bank trust officer about these topics.

If you create a trust while you are living, you (and your spouse) are typically the trustee of the trust, that is, the person who is legally in charge of trust matters. When the last of the living trustees dies or becomes incompetent, a successor trustee must be able to step in immediately so that the trust's duties are not neglected. The successor trustee can be anyone that, literally, you can trust. Good friends or close relatives can fill the bill, but they'll do a satisfactory job only if they have some degree of knowledge of such matters. Even then, there are many disadvantages to using these people. Mentally insert your own friends and relatives into this position, knowing you're no longer around, and see what unpleasant images come to mind.

The advantages of using a corporate trustee to handle your trust matters are:

- It has knowledgeable professionals who perform these services all the time.
- As an institution, the trust company will outlive even the successor trustees and will be there to execute the trust's instructions.

Envision your assets, after your death, being administered by another party (the trustee) on behalf of your spouse and your children and grandchildren. Summon into your imagination the worst scenarios that might be played out. These could include your spouse's being seduced into giving the assets away to a charity or a bad business venture, leaving nothing for your children or grandchildren. Or perhaps you have kids who will scream and holler that they can't wait for the surviving spouse's death for their inheritance; they need it now so they can open their own record store or fingernail salon, instead of going to college. If these sound like fanciful scenarios, you'd better believe they can happen, as well as much worse things. A well-written trust can prevent these outcomes from occurring, or at least the trust can delay them from happening in the hope that a loose thinking screw will get tightened. But a well-written trust is nearly worthless without a knowledgeable and strong-willed trustee to enforce the trust's provisions. Whoever acts as trustee has to be able to say "no" repeatedly to requests and proposals that go beyond the boundaries of the trust document. Picture your friend or loved one acting as trustee and being under assault by the various parties, some of whom have a close personal relationship with that person. This makes it even harder to say "no." If the visions I've described here make you uneasy, then you want a corporate trustee to act as successor trustee on your trust. Doing so will spare your friend or loved one a lot of grief.

With all this talk about trusts, we must point out that trust departments also handle the same types of accounts that money managers and financial planners handle: agency accounts. Agency accounts are simply those accounts in which the client has hired someone (money manager, financial planner, or trust department) to act as his *agent* in managing his investments. There is no legal document that contains instructions for the disposition of assets upon one's death. Having discussed the trust department's unique characteristics as trustee, let's examine their investment services in order to make a one-on-one comparison with money managers and financial planners.

Most trust departments are much larger than the average money manager or financial planner. Because of this size factor, trust departments have quite a few committees. These committees establish policies such as asset allocation, and they create a list of securities from which the portfolio managers, who actually buy and sell on behalf of individual accounts, can draw investment ideas. With the many legal issues that trust departments must handle, many of the professionals on their staffs are lawyers. All of this legal talent can have a moderating effect on the willingness of the portfolio managers to take risks, even reasonable risks. What results is portfolio strategy that can be conservative, perhaps to a fault. The portfolio managers who personally handle the accounts may have from 150 to 300 portfolios, sometimes more, for which they are responsible. With that many portfolios to monitor, it is impossible to pay too close attention to any one portfolio.

These factors, along with the sheer size of most trust departments, have resulted in trust departments' being characterized as slow-moving behemoths that generate sub-par investment performance. Such generalities are trivial. Nevertheless, those investors who favor a quick and nimble approach to their investments and a high level of personalized service are more likely to find that capability with a small fee-only professional rather than a trust department.

Unlike RIAs, trust departments are exempt from registration with the SEC as investment advisers. This may seem curious to you, since trust departments perform many of the same functions that RIAs do. Trust departments are not left unattended, however. They are supervised by the Office of the Comptroller of the Currency, OCC for short, which is an agency of the U.S. Treasury Department. The OCC does a very thorough job of overseeing trust departments in all facets of their operations. From the standpoint of an investor who is doing some research into the backgrounds of fee-only professionals, it is difficult to find out anything about the backgrounds of trust department employees, beyond what the company management wants you to know. Recall that RIAs must divulge all personnel who are directly or indirectly involved with investment management, and those persons' backgrounds are shown in complete detail. Not so with the trust department. You are taking it on management's faith that the people who will manage your assets are well-educated, well-trained, experienced, and credentialed professionals. With the scrutiny accorded them by the OCC, it is doubtful that any critical information would knowingly be falsified by a trust department's management. On the other hand, there is simply not the quantity of information provided to trust department clients and prospective clients as there is provided to RIAs' clients and prospects, through Form ADV. Beyond personnel, the client is left unaware of any security law violations or civil litigation in which the trust department may be involved. Form ADV contains all of this information, and it is readily available through the registered investment adviser from whom you request it. In addition, there is a phone number at NASD (shown in the Resource Guide at the end of the chapter) that you can call to inquire about an RIA's registration status, and whether or not there have been any regulatory problems with the adviser or the firm's personnel. With a trust department, again, this information and that form of inquiry does not exist.

Let's now review the trust department's investment services:

- Assisting client in formulating investment objectives
- Reviewing existing assets, rebalancing and reallocating portfolio
- Researching, selecting, purchasing and selling securities or investing in the bank's commingled trust funds
- Issuing client statements
- Providing custody of client assets
- Having periodic meetings to review the client's objectives and reviewing the progress being made toward those objectives
- Issuing year-end tax information

These functions may sound very similar to the services provided by money managers and financial planners, but there are some differences. To begin with, the trust department acts as custodian on its own accounts, so the whole process of receiving two sets of statements and reconciling one against the other is eliminated. For the client, it merely means that there won't be a lot of paper piling up on the desk. Another difference is in the investment vehicles that can be put into clients' accounts. Many trust departments have their own mutual funds, and they may also have "in-house mutual funds" called commingled trust funds (CTFs). CTFs look and feel like mutual funds except they are available only to trust clients of that particular institution. With this slight difference, banks are able to invest in just about anything that an RIA can invest in. Many banks, especially the larger ones, have in recent years established their own mutual funds or families of mutual funds. In addition to selling these to the general public, the trust departments may use these funds in clients' accounts in lieu of CTFs. When the mutual funds are used in managed accounts, clients need to be aware that the banks collect mutual fund fees as well as the account management fees. There are prohibitions against "double-dipping," or collecting dual fees. Consequently, some of the mutual fund fees may be rebated to the client. This may still result in higher fees than might otherwise be assessed if individual assets are used in the trust account, rather than mutual fund shares. For instance, if the normal account management fee is 1 percent of assets, and the mutual fund expense ratio is also 1 percent of assets, the bank would be required to rebate part of the mutual fund fee. If that rebate amounts to 80 basis points (it could be more or less), that still results in an effective fee structure of 1.2 percent of assets, an above-average fee structure.

Two more differences should be pointed out, both of which relate to the account statements issued to clients. First, statements from trust departments can be less timely than those of other service providers. Having worked for two of the largest trust departments in the country, I can say that both had a policy of issuing quarterly statements to clients, rather than monthly statements as most RIAs do. This may be good policy if you're trying to save paper, but it is not good client communications policy. The apparent cause of this condition is the number of accounts that the typical trust department services. These can amount to thousands of accounts, and even with high-speed computers, it takes that long for the statements to be prepared, printed, and mailed. In recent years I have seen progress made on this limitation, as statements from the bank custodians we use are arriving earlier than in the past.

The other deficiency is that most trust department statements do not calculate and present rate of return. This remains the case today for most trust statements I am privy to seeing. Once again, size and numbers of accounts are important factors in this regard. Still, with computer software that is available today, even for microcomputers that the smaller RIAs would have, this seems as if it would be a feature that could be easily programmed into the banks' mainframe computer systems. However, it is not.

One further difference is that the bank, acting in its capacity as custodian of the assets, issues the year-end tax information, including Form 1099. While RIAs can usually generate the basic tax information that shows interest, dividends, and capital gains and losses, only a custodian can issue a 1099, which has to be sent to the Internal Revenue Service.

Turning to fees, the fees charged by trust departments are somewhat similar to those of financial planners, at least in structure if not in amount. The one difference for banks is that their fees include the custody charge, whereas the clients of money managers and financial planners have to pay an additional custody charge. The RIAs adjust their fees, however, so that they remain competitive with those of banks. Fees are charged as a percentage of assets, like the RIAs' fees are assessed, starting at 1 percent. Fees are collected quarterly, just as they are for the RIAs. Banks usually have a minimum annual fee, and they almost always have a minimum account size they require to open an account with them. The latter number varies from bank to bank, of course, but it has been creeping up in the last ten years to about $250,000 of investable assets required to open a trust account or agency account with a trust department. Smaller accounts are simply not profitable enough to make it worth their while. One consequence of these rising minimums is that small money managers and financial planners, who know how to manage portfolios under $250,000 in size, and do so profitably for themselves, have built up their businesses serving that segment of the investment market.

The trust department charges additional fees to cover services beyond the basic level of service. Such services include establishing the account, assisting with re-registration of assets into the trust, and the management of certain nonliquid assets, like real estate.

SELECTING A FEE-ONLY PROFESSIONAL

Now that we've reviewed the three types of fee-only advisers, let's walk through the selection process. Here are some criteria that you should use:

- Work with a professional who is geographically close to you.
- Select a service provider who specializes in accounts like yours.
- Choose a firm according to organization structure and philosophy.
- Select people to work with who are experienced and credentialed.

Since communications are key to a good working relationship with your adviser, *work with one who is geographically near you.* What "near" is varies from person to person and place to place. "Near" could be two blocks from your office or two hundred miles from your home. The relevant factor is that it is close enough that you and the adviser can meet face-to-face on a regular basis. Phone chats are nice, but they are no substitute for periodic meetings. Personal meetings help to solidify the working relationship in a way that teleconferencing cannot. Also, if the sudden and unexpected need to meet arises, it can be done with minimal delay and inconvenience. Your service provider should be willing and able to come to you for a meeting at a time and location that are handy for you. After all, *you* are the client, and providing service to the client is why these people exist.

Another important criterion is having an adviser who *specializes in accounts like yours*. If you have a $100,000 portfolio and you open an account with a service provider whose assets are primarily in large pension plans, your account may fall through the cracks. No respectable RIA or trust department would intentionally short-change a client on servicing an account. However, larger accounts demand more attention, and consequently, they may provide a distraction from other, smaller portfolios. Look for firms whose account base includes a lot of accounts that are similar in type and in size to yours.

It is important to find a firm whose *organization structure and philosophy* are consistent with the type of service you are looking for. For example, some investors find it to their advantage to deal with the owner of a firm. These clients would want a small firm whose owners are the service providers. Others may want the security or image of dealing with a large institution. Pay attention to the philosophy of the adviser as well. If what you want is a well-constructed mutual fund portfolio for your IRA rollover, don't waste your time meeting with a small-capitalization growth stock manager, no matter how good their reputation is.

Make certain, regardless of what type of firm you decide to work with, that those who will actually work on your account are *people who are experienced and well credentialed*. As we said earlier, a money manager, financial planner, or trust department does not provide the service to your account, individual people in those firms provide the service. As such, the service given your portfolio is only as good as the people delivering that service. So make sure you know who the people are who will handle your individual account, what their education is, and what experience they have.

The criteria discussed above are somewhat general in scope. Let's look at more specific items to include in your search.

■ *Inquire of friends or business associates about fee-only professionals they use.* There is no substitute for selecting a service provider who has already worked with someone you know, especially if the someone is a person whose opinion you respect. These people could be friends, relatives, your accountant, or your attorney. By no means should the process end with this step, but it is a great place to start.

■ *Identify a service provider in your area through a directory or professional association.* For money managers, try looking through *Nelson's Directory of Investment Managers*, a description of which is contained in the Resource Guide at the end of this chapter. Another resource for conducting a search for a money manager is the Investment Council Association of America (ICAA). You can contact them at 212-344-0999, and they will send you a list of their member firms. For trust departments, there is a listing of every trust company in the U.S. contained in

Appendix B, located in the back of this book. The listings are in alphabetical order, and because there are hundreds of trust companies indexed, there are too many to show addresses and phone numbers. However, if you peruse the list and identify the names geographically near you, you can obtain that information through telephone Directory Assistance. For financial planners, contact the National Association of Personal Financial Advisers (NAPFA) at 888-FEE-ONLY. NAPFA is a national organization of financial planners that, unlike the other financial planner associations, is restricted in membership to fee-only planners. When you call the number above, after giving them some information about yourself and where you live, you will be provided with a list of fee-only financial planners located in your area. After identifying several different advisers, set up an appointment to meet with the principals of the firm or the investment officer who would manage your assets.

■ *Ask for a copy of Form ADV—Part II from a money manager or financial planner.* Scrutinize the firm's services as presented on the ADV to ensure they are in keeping with what you need. Pay close attention to the personnel listed in Schedule D. Match names from Schedule D with the people you meet at the firm. It can occur that the names with the pedigree credentials are located at another office, and they will never meet you or manage your funds. In the case of a trust department, they will not have a Form ADV, so you should request a listing of employees that contains the equivalent information that Schedule D contains.

■ *Examine a sample client statement.* Find out how often statements will be sent to you. Make sure that the rate-of-return calculation is part of each and every statement. If you have special reporting needs, such as a running total of realized gains and losses during the year, see if they can accommodate you (be reasonable with your request, however).

■ *Inquire about what brokers are used on stock and bond trades, and what commission rate is charged per share.* The maximum amount that should be charged per share on trades is $0.10, with a lower limit being $0.06 per share. Depending on trade size, these commissions will be higher than those of many of the deep-discount broker commission schedules shown in Chapter 2, Discount Brokers and Their Services. Don't let this bother you. Most of the deep-discount brokers do not work with RIAs, so this is one of the costs of using a money manager or financial planner. Remember, though, that commission expenses have a different relevance when working with an RIA or trust department. First, you know that the commissions are not driving investment decisions. Second, you are having the rate of return calculated for your portfolio, and commissions will, if excessive, drag down performance. Hence, there is an incentive for the RIA or trust department to try to keep commissions at a minimum.

■ *Ask the prospective adviser for at least one client referral.* Although most clients do not want the intrusion of having someone call them to ask about an adviser, any fee-only professional investor is bound to have one or two clients who are willing to do this. Ask questions that you yourself would be willing to answer if the roles were reversed; in other words, avoid questions about the person's own situation or their portfolio. Typical questions might include:

- Is the adviser meeting the expectations you had when you first hired them?
- Did the adviser counsel you in the beginning of the relationship about your needs, objectives, and tolerance for risk?
- Is the adviser accessible when you want to talk on the phone?
- Are you working with the same portfolio manager you had when you started with them, or are you being shuffled around from manager to manager?
- How often do you meet face-to-face with your adviser?
- Do they call you to set up meetings or do you have to contact the adviser?
- When you meet, do you meet with your portfolio manager or do they substitute a contact person who is not a portfolio manager?
- How often are account statements sent to you? Are they accurate and complete? Do they include rate-of-return figures?

Don't bother asking about performance because the response, in the unlikely event you're given one, will be a number that is relative to their objectives and risk tolerance. These two things may not be the same as yours, a fact that renders the answer meaningless. You may think of additional questions along the same lines as those above. Bear in mind that a) if the person is still a client of the adviser, she is by definition satisfied with the adviser's service, and b) the adviser is not going to refer you to a client who might say anything negative. Still, you will either receive positive affirmation about the adviser, or conversely you may glean hidden dissatisfaction through the nuance of some answer. In any event, this is a worthwhile exercise to go through with *each* adviser you are considering.

■ *Ask advisers to describe their investment philosophies.* Take points away if they cannot explain their philosophy in 100 words or less, or if they simply refer you to their marketing brochure or Form ADV. Included in that explanation should be how much flexibility there is to address your specific needs. Avoid advisers who have a "one size fits all" approach to asset allocation or security selection.

■ *Review their fee schedules.* Make sure you understand how the scale of percentage fees declines as your portfolio rises in value. There should be no hidden fees or charges. It will be most beneficial when you can compare the fee schedules from several RIAs and trust departments. As with any type of service you are shopping for, never select the lowest-priced provider and don't hire the most expensive.

■ *Ask how many relationships your portfolio manager is responsible for.* A desirable number is fewer than twenty. Remember we're talking about relationships here, not number of portfolios. A number between twenty and thirty is marginally acceptable. And anything above thirty suggests a portfolio manager who is overburdened. Unless you are bringing in a very large portfolio (well above $1 million), your account may not receive the attention it should.

■ *When reviewing people who will manage your assets, look for CFAs and CFPs. Chartered financial analysts* (CFAs) are professionals in the investment field who have passed a three-exam series that rigorously covers a variety of topics: accounting, quantitative analysis, economics, securities valuation, portfolio management, ethical and professional standards. Money managers and trust departments usually have CFAs on their staff. The CFA program is administered by the Association for Investment Management and Research (AIMR). To verify the CFA status of a prospective adviser, contact AIMR at 800-892-4258.

Certified financial planners (CFPs) are financial planners who have passed a comprehensive examination administered by the Certified Financial Planner Board of Standards. The Board accredits those people who have passed the CFP program and it also handles and reviews complaints from the public regarding CFPs. The CFP program is a comprehensive course of study culminating in an examination that covers various topics related to the overall financial planning process: financial planning, insurance, investments, tax planning, retirement planning and employee benefits, estate planning. The Board of Standards has a toll-free number to call if you want to verify the certification of a particular planner: 888-CFP-MARK.

To put these designations in perspective, if you are working with a money manager or a trust department, you want to look for those that have CFAs working with you on your account. If you are working with a financial planner, you want to select one with a CFP designation. The best configuration in looking at financial planners are those who have both CFA and CFP designations. It indicates that they are as well versed in investment analysis and portfolio management as they are in the areas of financial planning. Keep in mind that selecting advisers having the CFA and/or CFP designations is no *guarantee* of superior service or investment performance, but these designations suggest that the practitioners holding them are serious about their profession and want to be on the leading edge of the art and the science of investments and financial planning. Investors should also contact the Securities and Exchange Commission or the appropriate government office of the state in which you live or the state in which the adviser is located (see the Resource Guide). In so doing, you can find out if the adviser is in fact registered with those agencies and if they have had any compliance or regulatory infractions.

Earlier in the chapter I mentioned the significance of the size of the firm that you may want to hire. The decision to go with a large firm versus a smaller firm is a personal one. There are no hard and fast rules to follow, but you should consider the following concepts. Some people find great comfort in using very large service providers, of any kind of service. The usual reasons relate to the perception that service will be superior. That's why the service provider got to be so big, right? Well, remind yourself of that the next time you are standing in a long line at a bank, waiting for a live teller. More often than not, there is an inverse relationship between the caliber of service and the size of the service provider. In looking for someone to handle your investments, you do not want to be stuck at the end of the long line, as you are in that bank lobby. You want an investment adviser (even if it's a trust department) who not only wants your business, but *needs* your business. You want an adviser who will do whatever it takes to get your business, keep your business, and have you send even more business to them. In short, you should give serious consideration to using a smaller fee-only advisory firm. They can give more attention to your portfolio, and they will be more flexible in meeting your needs than a large institution. For impersonal services, like custody, go ahead and use the large bank or broker if it makes you feel good. For hands-on personalized service, stick with the small fee-only advisers.

I conclude this chapter with the following thought for you. In most situations and during most periods of time, you are perfectly capable of managing your own investment portfolio, assisted only by the principles and the resources outlined in previous chapters of this book. There may be times, however, when you will feel the need to fall back on professional guidance to fill some need or area of expertise with which you are uncomfortable. Resist the temptation to fall back on a commission-based stockbroker, either the one you worked with in the past or one who cold-calls you in the future in hopes of finding you at a vulnerable period. The fact is that you might be perfectly comfortable managing your $50,000 IRA rollover, but you may not be that comfortable managing a $500,000 family trust that carries more responsibility and requires more complex decision-making. In this case you may seek a fee-only professional to work with you on the trust, keeping the IRA rollover in your own capable hands. Also remember, like kissing the full-commission stockbroker goodbye or changing discount brokers, you can, at will, change investment advisers or cease using them altogether.

The Resource Guide for this chapter will elaborate on some government agencies and associations that may be helpful in identifying the fee-only professional who is right for you.

RESOURCE GUIDE
FEE-ONLY PROFESSIONALS

Directories

AMERICAN BANKERS ASSOCIATION DIRECTORY OF TRUST BANKING

Provides information on over 3,000 trust institutions. Gives basic information plus listing of key trust officers, assets managed, account types, commingled funds.
$295
American Bankers Association
1120 Connecticut Avenue N.W.
Washington, DC 20036
202-663-5000

DIRECTORY OF REGISTERED INVESTMENT ADVISORS

Lists name, address, fax number, SEC number, date of registration, asset information, key people and titles, and investment strategies.
$325/yr. Annual
Money Market Directories
320 E. Main Street
Charlottesville, VA 22902-5234
804-977-1450

NELSON'S DIRECTORY OF INVESTMENT MANAGERS

Listings of money management firms, including addresses, phone numbers, key personnel, investment approaches, assets managed, and fees. Updated annually.
$495
Nelson's Publications
One Gateway Plaza
Port Chester, NY 10573
800-333-6357

Industry Associations

Association for Investment
  Management & Research
  (AIMR)
P.O. Box 3669
Charlottesville, VA 22903-0668
800-892-4258
Verify CFA certification of an
  individual.

Certified Financial Planner Board
  of Standards
1660 Lincoln Street, Ste. 3050
Denver, CO 80264
888-CFP-MARK
Verify CFP designation of an
  individual.

National Association of Personal
  Financial Advisers (NAPFA)
1130 Lake Cook Road, Ste. 150
Buffalo Grove, IL 60089
(800) 366-2732
(888) FEE-ONLY

Get listing of fee-only financial
  planners near you.

National Association of Securities
  Dealers (NASD)
P.O. Box 9401
Gaithersburg, MD 20898-9401
301-590-6500

Check on status of RIAs.

Federal Government Agencies

Department of the Treasury
13th and C Streets S.W.
Washington, DC 20228
202-622-2000

U.S. Securities and Exchange
  Commission
450 5th Street N.W.
Washington, DC 20549
202-272-7450

State Government Agencies

Alabama
Securities Commission
RSA Plaza
770 Washington Avenue
Montgomery, AL 36130
205-242-2984

Alaska
Department of Commerce
Division of Banking and
  Securities
333 Willoughby, 9th Floor SOB
P.O. Box 110807

Juneau, AK 99811-0807
907-465-2521

Arizona
Securities Division
Corporation Commission
1300 W. Washington
Phoenix, AZ 85007
602-542-4242

Arkansas
Arkansas Securities Department
Heritage West Building, 3rd Floor

201 East Markham
Little Rock, AR 72201
501-324-9260

California
Securities Commissioner
Department of Corporations
3700 Wilshire Boulevard
Los Angeles, CA 90010
916-445-8200

Colorado
Division of Securities
Department of Regulatory
   Agencies
1560 Broadway, Ste. 1450
Denver, CO 80203
303-894-2320

Connecticut
Department of Banking,
   Securities
260 Constitution Plaza
Hartford, CT 06103
203-240-8299

Delaware
Division of Securities
Department of Justice
State Office Building
820 N. French Street, 8th Floor
Wilmington, DE 19801
302-577-2515

District of Columbia
Securities Commission
450 5th Street N.W., Ste. 821
Washington, DC 20001
202-626-5105

Florida
Office of Comptroller
Department of Banking and
   Finance
The Capitol, Plaza Level
Tallahassee, FL 32399
904-488-9805

Georgia
Office of the Secretary of State
Business Services and Regulation
2 Martin Luther King, Jr. Drive
802 West Tower
Atlanta, GA 30334
404-656-2894

Hawaii
Department of Commerce and
   Consumer Affairs
1010 Richards Street
P.O. Box 40
Honolulu, HI 96813
808-586-2744

Idaho
Department of Finance
Securities Bureau
700 W. State Street
Boise, ID 83720-0031
208-334-3313

Illinois
Office of the Secretary of State
Securities Department
900 S. Spring Street
Springfield, IL 62704
217-782-2256

Indiana
Office of the Secretary of State
Securities Division
302 W. Washington Street
Room E111
Indianapolis, IN 46204
317-232-6690

Iowa
Securities Division
Insurance Department
Lucas Stone Office Building
Des Moines, IA 50319
515-281-4441

Kansas
Kansas Securities Commission

618 S. Kansas Avenue, 2nd Floor
Topeka, KS 66603
913-296-3307

Kentucky
Financial Institutions Department
477 Versailles Avenue
Frankfort, KY 40601
502-573-3390

Louisiana
Office of Financial Institutions
Commissioner of Securities
8660 United Plaza, 2nd Floor
Baton Rouge, LA 70809
504-925-4660

Maine
Department of Professional and
   Financial Regulation
Securities Division
State House Station 121
Augusta, ME 04333
207-624-8551

Maryland
Division of Securities
200 St. Paul Street, 20th Floor
Baltimore, MD 21202-2020
301-576-6360

Massachusetts
Massachusetts Securities Division
John W. McCormack Building
1 Ashburton Place, Room 1701
Boston, MA 02108
617-727-3548

Michigan
Department of Commerce
Corporation and Securities
   Bureau
6546 Mercantile Way
Lansing, MI 48909
517-334-6213

Minnesota
Department of Commerce
Securities Division
133 E. Seventh Street
St. Paul, MN 55101
612-296-6325

Mississippi
Office of the Secretary of State
P.O. Box 136
202 N. Congress Street, Ste. 601
Jackson, MS 39201
601-359-6364

Missouri
Office of the Secretary of State
Harry S. Truman State Office
   Building
600 West Main Street, 2nd Floor
Jefferson, MO 65101
314-751-4136

Montana
Office of State Auditor
126 N. Sanders, Room 270
Helena, MT 59604
406-444-2040

Nebraska
Department of Banking and
   Finance
Bureau of Securities
1200 N Street, Ste. 311
P.O. Box 95006
Lincoln, NE 68509
402-471-3445

Nevada
Department of State
Securities Division
555 E. Washington Avenue,
Ste. 5200
Las Vegas, NV 89101
702-486-2452

New Hampshire
Department of State

Bureau of Securities Regulation
State House Room 204
Concord, NH 03301
603-271-1463

New Jersey
Bureau of Securities
Department of Law and Public
    Safety
153 Halsey Street
Newark, NJ 07102
201-504-3600

New Mexico
Securities Division
Regulation and Licensing
    Department
725 St. Michaels Drive
Santa Fe, NM 87501
505-827-7140

New York
Department of Law
Bureau of Investor Protection and
    Securities
120 Broadway, 23rd Floor
New York, NY 10271
212-416-8200

North Carolina
Securities Division
300 N. Salisbury Street, Ste. 301
Raleigh, NC 27603
919-733-3924

North Dakota
Securities Commissioner
State Capitol
600 East Boulevard Avenue,
5th Floor
Bismarck, ND 58505
701-328-2910

Ohio
Division of Securities
Department of Commerce,
3rd Floor

2 Nationwide Plaza
Columbus, OH 43215
614-466-3440

Oklahoma
Oklahoma Department of
    Securities
First National Center
120 N. Robinson, Ste. 860
Oklahoma, OK 73102
405-235-0230

Oregon
Department of Finance and
    Corporate Securities
21 Labor and Industries Building
Salem, OR 97310
503-378-4387

Pennsylvania
Securities Commission
Eastgate Office Building
1010 N. Seventh Street, 2nd Floor
Harrisburg, PA 17102
717-787-8061

Puerto Rico
Office of the Commissioner of
    Financial Institutions
Central Europa Building, Ste. 600
1492 Ponce de Leon Avenue
San Juan, PR 00909
809-723-3131

Rhode Island
Department of Business
    Regulation
Securities Division
233 Richmond Street, Ste. 232
Providence, RI 02903
401-277-3048

South Carolina
Department of State
Securities Division
1205 Pendleton Street, Ste. 501

Columbia, SC 29201
803-758-2744

South Dakota
Division of Securities
118 W. Capitol Avenue
Pierre, SD 57501
605-773-4823

Tennessee
Securities Division
Department of Commerce and
Insurance
Volunteer Plaza, 6th Floor,
Ste. 680
500 James Robertson Parkway
Nashville, TN 37219
615-741-2947

Texas
State Securities Board
P.O. Box 13167
Austin, TX 78711
512-305-8300

Utah
Department of Commerce
Securities Division
160 E. 300 South
P.O. Box 45808
Salt Lake City, UT 84145
801-530-6600

Vermont
Department of Banking,
Insurance, and Securities
Securities Division
89 Main Street
Drawer 20
Montpelier, VT 05620
802-828-3420

Virginia
State Corporation Commissioner

Division of Securities and Retail
Franchising
1300 E. Main Street, 9th Floor
Richmond, VA 23219
804-371-9610

Virgin Islands of the United States
Corporations and Trade Names
Division
Office of the Lieutenant Governor
P.O. Box 450
St. Thomas, VI 00801
809-774-2991

Washington
Department of Financial
Institutions
Securities Division
210 11th Street S.W.
Third Floor West
P.O. Box 9033
Olympia, WA 98507
360-902-8760

West Virginia
Securities Division
Office of the State Auditor
State Capitol Building
Room W-118
1900 Kanawha Boulevard East
Charleston, WV 25305
304-558-2257

Wisconsin
Office of the Commissioner of
Securities
101 E. Wilson Street, 4th Floor
Madison, WI 53702
608-266-3414

Wyoming
Secretary of State
State Capitol Building
Cheyenne, WY 82002
307-777-7370

Chapter 8

INVESTMENT

PERFORMANCE

H umans are enthralled and captivated by performance, and we don't just mean investment performance now. People love to watch the performance of a great athlete in action. They enjoy watching an exceptional performance by a gifted actor or actress. And even those who don't spend time watching auto racing can be awed by the 200-plus mph speeds of today's high-performance race cars. So it's no wonder that, given the chance to measure the performance of investments, people can develop expectations that exceed reality, or at least they exceed the necessity of the moment. In this chapter we want to reiterate the *rate of return* concept and differentiate it from *performance*. We also want to provide guidelines for investors to formulate performance standards that are relevant to their own situation.

RATE OF RETURN VERSUS PERFORMANCE

Rate of return is an arithmetic calculation. It is an *absolute* measure of an investment's profitability (appreciation in value and/or income generated) to an investor during a given time frame. *Performance* is a *relative* measure, comparing rates of return between two or more investments or indexes of investment groups. Each of these measures has its use. The trouble starts when investors confuse the two or use them in the wrong contexts.

To employ a car analogy, you could buy a street-legal Porsche 911 Turbo today that could reach a top speed of 180 mph; that is the *absolute* measure of its speed. Turning to its *relative* speed, it could blow off the racetrack any other street-legal car that is silly enough to race you. On the other hand, if you were silly enough to race against an Indy-class car, they would blow you and your little Porsche off the track. It's all relative, isn't it? What seems like a good vehicle to accomplish one goal is not that great for achieving another. The worst scenario happens when that vehicle is misused for its intended task. If you hopped into the Porsche and ran it up to 160 mph on your way to the store to buy a carton of milk, there's a high probability you would crash and burn. So let's park the Porsche in the garage before we do any more damage.

Individual investors need to monitor the rate of return on their investments. They do not need to focus on the relative performance of their investments. They do not have to ignore relative performance totally, but when they fixate on performance they may begin making decisions that are inappropriate for their situation. The result: They crash and burn. This is one of the recurring problems of investors who have relied on full-commission stockbrokers or other commission-based practitioners for investment advice. A common sales ploy is to show investors how their stocks or mutual funds are lagging on some index. The solution to this problem, of course, is the product or service that they intend to sell. In reality the investor may not even have a problem because a) the return on the stocks or mutual funds may be doing just what they were intended to do, and b) the index against which the investments are being measured may be totally inappropriate for the client's objectives. Before pursuing the issue of performance any further, let's review the rate-of-return calculations.

RATE OF RETURN REVISITED

As we discussed in Chapter 3, Asset Allocation, *rate of return* is the expression in percentage terms of the reward to the investor for buying and holding a particular investment. When a portfolio of two or more securities is involved, you can determine the rate of return for the entire portfolio. Doing so helps investors to keep score of how their investment is doing. And remember, these are *absolute* calculations, even though the result is a percentage. Recall that rate of return comprises two parts: 1) appreciation or depreciation of the assets' value; and 2) the income or yield derived from the assets.

If a stock, a bond, or an entire portfolio of stocks and bonds rose 7 percent in value over the course of a year and had a yield of 5 percent during that year, a rough approximation of the rate of return would be 12 percent. A more precise calculation would begin with the change in value of the portfolio plus the income derived from the portfolio during the year (both in total dollars, not percentages), divided by the value of the portfolio at the beginning of the time period. For example, a portfolio that started the year with a value of $52,000 has its assets appreciate $4,800 and receives $1,100 in dividends and interest. The sum of the increase in value, $5,900, divided by the $52,000 beginning value, results in a percentage rate of return amounting to 11.35 percent ($5,900 ÷ $52,000). If you knew that the ending value of the portfolio at year-end was $57,900 ($52,000 + $5,900), you could take a shortcut with the following formula: [($57,900 ÷ $52,000) − 1] × 100. Either method gets you to the same answer of an 11.35 percent rate of return. That equation again is:

[(Value at END of Period ÷ Value at BEGINNING of Period) − 1] × 100

If you have a portfolio in which you make no new deposits nor do you make any withdrawals (an IRA or IRA rollover, for instance), this is *the* way to calculate ROR. Things become troublesome, however, when you have a portfolio in which you are making periodic contributions and/or withdrawals. Unless those contributions or withdrawals are made on the very first day of the period or the very last day of the period, the equation cannot be used as it is described above. Since you are comparing the end value against the beginning value, any deposit to or withdrawal from the portfolio distorts the end value. Remember we are not trying to measure how much the portfolio is worth at the end of the period. We are trying to determine how *profitable* the investments have been.

For dynamic accounts where money is flowing into and out of the portfolio, you must use the *time-weighted rate of return* calculation. The basic concept of the time-weighted rate of return is to break the large time period, usually a year, into subperiods. Each subperiod is defined by the day money is added to the account or the day when money is withdrawn from the account. Within each of those subperiods, the ROR calculation is the same as the equation above. Let's review another example to illustrate how time-weighted ROR is calculated, and we'll keep the example unrealistically simple.

The beginning value remains the same as the previous example: $52,000. On April 1 an addition of $6,000 is made to the account. The portfolio is valued the day prior to the addition and the rate of return is calculated for the three-month subperiod. The ending value on March 31 is $55,000, and the rate of return for the subperiod becomes: [($55,000 ÷ $52,000) − 1] × 100 = 5.77 percent. Enter April 1 and there is now a new beginning value for the second subperiod: $55,000 + $6,000 = $61,000. Now "fast-forward" to year-end. The ending value of the second subperiod is $64,200, and the ROR for this subperiod is: [($64,200 ÷ $61,000) − 1] × 100 = 5.25 percent. So here you are with rates of return calculated for two subperiods; what do you do now? No, you don't add them together, but you do "link" them together in the following manner, denoting the two subperiods as "a" and "b": {[(1 + ROR_a) × (1 + ROR_b)] − 1} × 100. So the numbers work out to: ([1.0577 × 1.0525] − 1) × 100 = 11.32 percent rate of return for the year. This return is very close to the first example, even though the ending value is considerably higher here, due to the $6,000 addition to the portfolio.

We did not go through these exercises so investors could consume hours of their time toiling with such calculations. It is important, however, that you know and understand the basic concepts of rate-of-return calculation. Our methodology above is quite simplistic but still fairly accurate. More precise calculations, employing different equations but the same principles, can be done with any number of computer software programs. We recommend a review of software in the Resource Guide to Chapter 4.

These examples should convey that rate of return is not determined by how much money is in the portfolio, how much is added to the portfolio, or how much money is withdrawn from the portfolio. Rate of return measures, during some time period, the profitability of an investment or portfolio of investments relative to where the investment or the portfolio started at the beginning of that time period. However, by stating profitability in relative terms (through percentages), ROR invites comparisons between different types of investments. This is where you begin to enter the netherworld of *performance*, a place that can be enlightening, but also scary and dangerous.

PERFORMANCE

Once upon a time, "good investment performance" meant you were exceeding inflation and probably the yield on Treasury bills. Everyone knew that bonds would provide a higher return than the T–bills, with almost no additional risk. They also knew that investing in stocks, regarded as a "risky" strategy until about thirty years ago, was the best way to ensure wealth accumulation over long periods of time.

As the 1970s emerged, money managers and trust departments that catered to large institutional investors such as pension and profit-sharing plans began to market themselves more aggressively. One of the simplest and most straightforward ways of differentiating themselves from their competitors was to select a benchmark for the type of investment service they were promoting, and show how they had exceeded that benchmark over selected time periods.

The Standard & Poor's 500 (S&P 500) index became, and remains today, the benchmark of choice for most players, because it represents a large number of stocks across a broad range of industries. Since then there have arisen several other indexes with 2,000 stocks or 6,000 stocks, covering small-cap companies as well as the large stocks. Also appearing on the scene was a new subindustry: investment consultants. These practitioners perform the task of gathering rate-of-return information from professional investors, categorizing it into any number of pigeon-holes, collating the returns, and creating a matrix of *performance* that is provided to the institutional investors (pension plans, profit-sharing plans, insurance companies, endowments, foundations, among others). This structure of analysis and accountability soothes the nerves of those who are responsible for the management. Professional investors are managing the monies on a day-to-day basis, and there are other experts, the consultants, who are keeping an eye on the professional investors and monitoring their investment returns. When the returns slip below the benchmark, that money manager is fired and replaced with another whose returns have exceeded the benchmark, at least in the recent past.

This notion of performance, and the measurement and evaluation of it, brings to mind an incident from a number of years ago. Prior to his making a presentation to a group of portfolio managers and securities analysts, the chief executive officer of a Fortune 500 company was conversing with a group of attendees. At the time, I worked for a very large bank trust department as an analyst, so I did not need to explain what it was I did or for whom I did it. Another attendee, a portfolio manager who owned a small, start-up money management firm, was introducing himself and trying to characterize his firm. The CEO asked the question, "When you market your firm, on what basis do you sell yourself to a prospective client?" Without a moment of hesitation, the money manager's response was, "We sell ourselves by our people, our organizational structure, and our investment philosophy. We don't sell *performance* because *performance* can be fabricated." To this the CEO responded, "You're the first person I've heard answer that question correctly."

Now, at the time this occurred I was not a portfolio manager; I was an investment analyst. And I worked for a large organization; I did not have my own money management firm. Nevertheless, the incident rang true in my mind, and it has stayed with me ever since. Performance numbers can be and are fabricated or contrived, all the time. If not by outright miscalculation, performance can be enhanced by changing around the time period being measured. And so-called composites (groups of accounts lumped together to create an index of performance) can be manipulated by including better-performing accounts and omitting the underperformers. The notable exception to this is that mutual fund performance can be assured to be accurate, because each fund is one portfolio which is valued daily. There is no opportunity for manipulation.

Institutional investors need to play the performance number game. It is how their world has come to be defined. And because they have the assistance from the consultant community, they will have a fairly accurate picture of the returns that their managers and other managers are generating. Moreover, these institutional investors have objectives that are defined by rates of return. For example, a pension plan will have an unfunded future liability that requires they earn no less than, let's say, 8 percent per year. If they do not match that, they have to ante up a larger contribution for that year to make up the difference.

In contrast, individual investors do not have to play the performance number game. Their objectives are, or should be, defined by their life stage goals. You need $100,000 in ten years for the child's college education. Or you need $850,000 in savings in twenty years to live comfortably after retirement. Along the way, good performance should be based on whether your portfolio made reasonable progress during the year. If it does not one year, you should assume that it will be compensated for the next, but only if you maintain your strategy. If two or three consecutive years go by with insufficient growth, then it's time to reassess your strategy. The problem is that people get impatient and hastily make changes, often ill-advised changes. As an illustration of this, you only have to look at 1994 and 1995.

In 1994, bond returns were negative and stock returns were marginally positive, with the S&P 500 up about 1.3 percent. Three-month Treasury bills earned 4.2 percent during the year, making them the highest-returning asset group. So the impatient investor during 1994 could easily have rationalized selling his stocks and going into cash instruments. Had he done so, however, he would have missed all or part of the explosive move in stocks during 1995, when the S&P 500 rose over 37 percent! The investor who did not forsake stocks ended with an 18 percent compounded annual return for the two years, even though he felt he was in quicksand during year one. Considering that the long-term return for the S&P 500 is 10.5 percent per year, the two years combined provided a return that is 7.5 percent in excess of that average. There is a valuable lesson there for investors to learn.

The epilogue to the story relates to those investors and money managers who did not match or exceed the S&P 500 return in 1995. There were many stories in the financial news media of mutual fund managers and other prominent money managers who had earned returns of "only" 24 percent or 28 percent or 34 percent, well below the S&P 500 return of 37 percent. In the context of a measure that has risen at a 10.5 percent annual rate over many decades, 24 percent, 28 percent, and 34 percent returns are pretty good. In fact, if you think about it long enough, it sounds almost idiotic to say that those returns are deficient. You, as an informed investor, need to resist being sucked into this line of reasoning. Beating the S&P 500 may be a laudable accomplishment, but it should not be the investment objective.

As for the bond investor, most do not have easy access to bond market indexes. As an alternative to finding and using an index, they can simply select a Treasury note, listed in the bond section of the financial newspapers, which matches the maturity of their own bonds. They can easily track the monthly movement in the price of the bond, calculating rates of return for the bond by 1) comparing the beginning and ending values, just like the ROR examples above, and 2) adding in the amount of the yield accrued during that interval. On the latter factor, a quarterly determination of return would involve taking the annual *yield* (not the coupon, but the coupon divided by the price at the beginning of the period) and adding that to the percentage change in the price of the bond during the time interval measured. Even this may be more work than is necessary. You invested in bonds to begin with, because you were assured that a) you would receive every dollar of principal that you originally invested upon maturity, and b) you would receive interest at a predetermined rate and at predetermined intervals. Unless the bond is subject to a deterioration in creditworthiness that jeopardizes either of those elements, you know what your return will be over time. You should not be concerned about price fluctuations in the meantime.

The points to be drawn from this discussion are:

■ Performance based solely upon comparative rate-of-return computations is (with the stated exception of mutual funds) subject to the vagaries of calculation and interpretation.

■ Therefore, performance for the individual investor should be redefined along the lines of progress made toward that investor's investment goals.

One last point, regarding market benchmarks,

■ When selecting a benchmark, and you do need them at times, stay with a simple benchmark for the asset group, even if your particular investments are not a perfect match with those of the benchmark. If you're investing in stocks, use the S&P 500, and forget those 2,000 stock indexes and foreign stock indexes with strange initials. If your investments don't measure up to something as simple as the S&P 500, perhaps you should change your investments.

When you see printed advertisements today for investment products and services that are selling rate-of-return statistics, you will see a caption or a legend that reads something like this: "Past performance is no guarantee of future results." You should now have a better understanding of what that caption means, literally and figuratively. Literally, it's a warning that says you can look at these numbers, but they're essentially meaningless as regards the future unknown. Figuratively, it is the admonition to you the investor to keep focused on your true objectives and not to become preoccupied by short-term results.

RESOURCE GUIDE
INVESTMENT PERFORMANCE

Books

Most investment textbooks will treat the calculation of rate of return. Managing Investment Portfolios *is among those. For a more philosophic discussion of setting objectives and measuring performance, along the lines discussed in this chapter, read* Investment Policy.

INVESTMENT POLICY
Charles D. Ellis. Irwin Professional, 1993.
$35.00 ISBN: 1-55623-088-5
The formulation of investment strategies is the topic of the book. It provides an unusual but very appropriate way for investors to set their investment objectives both with themselves and their investment advisers.

MANAGING INVESTMENT PORTFOLIOS: A DYNAMIC PROCESS

John L. Maginn and Donald L. Tuttle. Warren, Gorham and Lamont, 1990.
$50.00 ISBN: 0-7913-0322-5
Comprehensive textbook covering many investment topics from contributing investment professionals. Areas include fundamentals of portfolio management, determining investment objectives and constraints, asset allocation, portfolio construction, and more.

Chapter 9

CAVEAT INVESTOR

A t this point you should have a good feeling about being able to make appropriate investment decisions on your own behalf, unencumbered by the biased recommendations and unsuitable investment products and services being peddled by the full-commission stockbroker, and you have a wealth of information to assist you in achieving your financial objectives. Perhaps most important, you should be able to overcome the fear that grips many investors and compels them to rely on the advice of a commission-based salesperson. Before leaving you to pursue your investment program, there are a number of suggestions and warnings I'd like to offer.

BEFORE INVESTING IN VARIABLE ANNUITIES, SCRUTINIZE THE DETAILS.

Variable annuities have become a very hot product in recent years, being aggressively pushed by stockbrokers, insurance salespeople, and commission-based financial planners. The sales pitch to investors is the tax-deferral feature they possess. Typically, you invest in one or more mutual funds from a menu, and the interest and gains from those funds accrue to you but they are not taxable until the annuity matures.

Few people look forward to paying taxes, especially if there is a way to legally defer taxable income and capital gains. Tax deferral is a powerful sales tool in selling annuities. The unattractive features of these instruments include:

- They have sizable front-end sales commissions, which explains why they are so popular with salespeople.
- You are locked in to the instrument for the duration of its maturity. If you have to liquidate the annuity before maturity, you get the double-whammy: 1) you pay an early withdrawal penalty, and 2) all gains and income that have been deferred become taxable.
- Your choice of investment (mutual funds) options is limited. It is possible that the ability to invest in other mutual funds that would generate higher returns would more than offset the tax-savings feature of the annuity.

The comments about the perceived tax advantages of annuities driving the decision to tie up a chunk of one's money in an illiquid asset leads into the next caveat.

DO NOT BASE YOUR INVESTMENT DECISIONS ON TAX CONSEQUENCES.

Have you ever owned a stock on which you had a large unrealized capital gain? Did you defer selling some or all of the stock because you did not want to pay taxes on the transaction? If you have done much investing, at one time or another you have gone through this mental exercise. If you are honest with yourself, you will realize that paying a tax is the "price of success." Think about it. You have a profit on an investment! Except in the most unusual circumstances, after you sell the security at a profit and pay the tax on the gain, you will still have more money than you did before making the investment. If saving taxes is your main priority, perhaps you should structure your investment philosophy to *lose* money each year on your investments, say $3,000, so that you can use the loss to reduce your taxable ordinary income.

Now we're not suggesting you totally abandon tax considerations; we just don't think taxes should direct your policy and paralyze you into inaction. For instance, if you are three weeks away from having held a profitable stock for twelve months, unless something very wrong is happening to the stock, you should defer the sale for at least three weeks. That way you avail yourself of the 28 percent maximum capital gains tax rate. Likewise, if you are within a few weeks of the year-end, you would defer the sale in order to push the realized gain into the next tax year. In less obvious situations, you run the risk of coming out a net loser by not taking some profits. Remember, if you have a five-point profit on a stock at the moment of deliberating to sell or not sell, and if you are in the 31 percent tax bracket, the stock only has to drop 1½ points to offset your perceived tax savings. So if selling an asset seems appropriate for other reasons, don't let taxes override those judgments.

UNLESS YOU ARE AN EXPERIENCED TRADER AND AN EXPERT MARKET TECHNICIAN, STAY AWAY FROM DERIVATIVE SECURITIES.

These include options and futures, called derivatives because their value is *derived* from the prices and price movements of other securities and commodities. Users of specific commodities, be they interest rates or pork bellies, need to use futures and options to control the risk of their enterprises. You don't need to assume their risks for them, which is what you do when you get on the other side of them in a derivatives trade. These are marketed as "get rich quick" investments, but as usual, the ones getting rich are the salespeople selling them and the floor traders on the commodity exchanges trading them. If to "get rich quick" is your objective, you stand a much better chance at the blackjack tables in Atlantic City or Las Vegas.

DO NOT INVEST ON THE BASIS OF "TIPS" AND RUMORS, EVEN FROM PEOPLE YOU KNOW AND TRUST.

Even experienced professional investors can get sucked into this trap. Don't let it happen to you. It is one thing to invest according to the advice of others if those people have a record of reasonable success in their recommendations. It is quite another thing to invest according to a rumor or even according to one's impressions. A classic example occurred a few years ago when someone approached me, knowing I was a professional investor, and inquired about a biotech company. I happened to know something about the company: It was a developmental-stage company, meaning it had no products, little revenue, and it was a one-product company, *if* it ever received approval on a new drug it was testing. The stock was selling in the high twenties at the time, and I stated that if it did not receive regulatory approval on its prospective drug, it would become a $10 stock. When I asked why he was interested, he pointed out that he had had a chance casual meeting with the company's CEO. My acquaintance was impressed with his knowledge and personality, and decided to invest in the stock. The bottom line was that within six months of that conversation, approval of the drug was denied and the stock sold off to $4 per share. Enough said.

BEWARE OF INVESTING IN FOREIGN STOCKS.

Foreign investing has come into vogue in recent years, being sold on the bases that 1) there are opportunities for growth companies in other countries that far surpass the U.S., and 2) foreign stock markets do not trade in sync with the U.S. market, hence, foreign investments lower your portfolio's volatility (risk). Neither point is worth disputing. However, having had to follow several Japanese companies when I was an investment analyst, I know firsthand how difficult it is to get a firm grip on the markets, cultures, and characteristics of foreign companies. If you do not have reliable and trustworthy people situated in the countries in which you invest, people who will act as analysts familiar with local markets, you are flying blind. You may think you know what's going on, but you don't. Look at how how many sophisticated investors were caught flat-footed with Mexico's currency crisis in 1995. If you feel you must invest offshore, do so through one or more no-load mutual funds that invest in foreign markets. The funds' managers should have the critical mass in place to have their analysts in each country in which they invest. And only invest in funds that diversify by many different countries, where the manager select the countries in which they will invest. In other words, do not buy funds that invest exclusively in one country.

AVOID WRAP-FEE ACCOUNTS.

Wrap-fee accounts have grown at an incredible rate in recent years. And why not? The client invests his money, through a brokerage firm, in an account that the broker then allocates among money managers. The broker thus becomes an ersatz consultant, moving the client's money here and there in accordance with good or bad "performance." This is a classic case of how a fixation on performance can muddle decision making. The primary problems with these programs are:

- They are very expensive. Fees start at 3 percent of the account value. That fee is divided as follows: money manager—1 percent; brokerage firm—1 percent; stockbroker—1 percent. Beyond the amount involved, there is something distasteful about the broker and his employer collecting two-thirds of an exorbitant fee for doing almost nothing.
- There is no proof they produce satisfactory results for clients, especially after factoring in the high fees involved.

Brokers, who are the people supervising wrap-fee accounts, have a short-term trading mentality. That is how they've made their livelihood. What happens here is that a manager who goes six months without superlative rates of return is terminated and another manager selected who happens to be hot at the moment.

Responsible consultants know that a money manager needs, and deserves, three to five years to verify his capability. The result for the client is that he is moved from the underperforming money manager, who will resume reporting good rates of return shortly thereafter. The account is moved to the "hot" manager, whose style may deteriorate, if only temporarily, resulting in additional poor performance for the account. Wrap-fee accounts are nothing more than an oasis where the dinosaurs (full-commission brokers) have stopped to drink at the fee-only investment management waterhole, on their journey to extinction.

ATTENTION READERS

There are many products and services shown in the Resource Guide sections in this book. We cannot endorse any products or services in the book. To do so would compromise its objectivity and its usefulness to the reader. If you are interested in seeing a listing of the books, periodicals, software, on-line services, and the discount brokers that the author has personally used, you may receive a copy by sending a check for $2.95 to cover postage-and-handling costs and made payable to Rios Del Mar. Mail this along with your address to:

Rios Del Mar
P.O. Box 3069
Del Mar, CA 92014-3069

Allow 4–6 weeks for delivery.

APPENDIX A:
COMPANIES WITH DIVIDEND
REINVESTMENT PLANS

A

AAR Corp.   (NYSE:AIR)

Abbott Laboratories   (NYSE:ABT)

Acme-Cleveland Corp.   (NYSE:AMT)

ADAC Laboratories   (NASDAQ:ADAC)

Aetna Life and Casualty Co.   (NYSE: AET)

AFLAC, Inc.   (NYSE:AFL)

Air Products & Chemicals, Inc.   (NYSE: APD)

Albany International Corp.   (NYSE:AIN)

Albemarle Corp.   (NYSE:ALB)

Alcan Aluminium Ltd   (NYSE:AL)

Alco Standard Corp.   (NYSE:ASN)

Allegheny Ludlum Corp.   (NYSE:ALS)

Allegheny Power System, Inc.   (NYSE: AYP)

Allergan, Inc.   (NYSE:AGN)

Allied Group, Inc.   (NASDAQ:ALGR)

AlliedSignal, Inc.   (NYSE:ALD)

ALLTEL Corporation   (NYSE:AT)

Aluminum Company of America (NYSE:AA)

Amcast Industrial Corp.   (NYSE:AIZ)

AMCORE Financial, Inc.   (NASDAQ: AMFI)

Amerada Hess Corp.   (NYSE:AHC)

American Brands, Inc.   (NYSE:AMB)

American Business Products, Inc. (NYSE:ABP)

American Colloid Company (NASDAQ:ACOL)

American Electric Power Co.   (NYSE: AEP)

American Express Co.   (NYSE:AXP)

American Filtrona Corp.   (NASDAQ: AFIL)

American General Corp.   (NYSE: AGC)

American Greetings Corp.   (NASDAQ: AGREA)

American Health Properties, Inc. (NYSE:AHE)

American Heritage Life   (NYSE:AHL)

American Home Products Corp. (NYSE:AHP)

American Industrial Properties REIT (NYSE:IND)

American Real Estate Partners, LP (NYSE:ACP)

American Recreation Centers, Inc. (NASDAQ:AMRC)

American Water Works Co., Inc.
(NYSE:AWK)

Ameritech Corp.   (NYSE:AIT)

Amoco Corp.   (NYSE:AN)

AMP, Inc.   (NYSE:AMP)

AmSouth Bancorp.   (NYSE:ASO)

AmVestors Financial Corp.   (NYSE:
AMV)

Angeles Mortgage Investment Trust
(ASE:ANM)

Angeles Participating Mortgage Trust
(ASE:APT)

Angelica Corp.   (NYSE:AGL)

Anheuser-Busch Cos., Inc.   (NYSE:
BUD)

Aon Corp.   (NYSE:AOC)

Apache Corp.   (NYSE:APA)

Aquarion Co.   (NYSE:WTR)

ARCO Chemical Co.   (NYSE:RCM)

Armstrong World Industries, Inc.
(NYSE:ACK)

Arnold Industries, Inc.   (NASDAQ:
AIND)

Arrow Financial Corp.   (NASDAQ:
AROW)

Arvin Industries, Inc.   (NYSE:ARV)

ASARCO, Inc.   (NYSE:AR)

Ashland Coal, Inc.   (NYSE:ACI)

Ashland, Inc.   (NYSE:ASH)

ASR Investments Corp.   (ASE:ASR)

Asset Investors Corp.   (NYSE:AIC)

Associated Banc-Corp.   (NASDAQ:
ASBC)

AT&T Corp.   (NYSE:T)

Atlanta Gas Light Co.   (NYSE:ATG)

Atlantic Energy, Inc.   (NYSE:ATE)

Atlantic Richfield Co.   (NYSE:ARC)

Atmos Energy Corp.   (NYSE:ATO)

Avery Dennison Corp.   (NYSE:AVY)

Avnet, Inc.   (NYSE:AVT)

Avon Products, Inc.   (NYSE:AVP)

B

Baker Hughes, Inc.   (NYSE:BHI)

Baldwin Technology Company, Inc.
(ASE:BLD)

Ball Corp.   (NYSE:BLL)

Baltimore Gas and Electric Co.   (NYSE:
BGE)

Banc One Corp.   (NYSE:ONE)

Bancorp Hawaii, Inc.   (NYSE:BOH)

Bancorp New Jersey, Inc.   (NASDAQ:
BCNJ)

BancorpSouth, Inc.   (NASDAQ:BOMS)

Bandag, Inc.   (NYSE: BDG)

Bando McGlocklin Capital
Corp.   (NASDAQ:BMCC)

Bangor Hydro-Electric Co.   (NYSE:
BGR)

Bank of Boston Corp.   (NYSE:BKB)

Bank of Granite Corp.   (NASDAQ:
GRAN)

Bank of New York Co., Inc.   (NYSE:
BK)

Bank South Corp.   (NASDAQ: BKSO)

BankAmerica Corp.   (NYSE: BAC)

Bankers First Corp.   (NASDAQ:SNKF)

Bankers Trust New York Corp.   (NYSE:
BT)

Banknorth Group, Inc.   (NASDAQ:
BKNG)

BanPonce Corp.   (NASDAQ:BPOP)

Banta Corp.   (NASDAQ:BNTA)

Banyan Short Term Income Trust   (ASE:
VST)

Bard, C. R. Inc.   (NYSE:BCR)

Barnes Group Inc.   (NYSE:B)

Barnett Banks, Inc.   (NYSE:BBI)

Bausch & Lomb, Inc.   (NYSE:BOL)

Baxter International, Inc.   (NYSE:BAX)

Bay State Gas Co.   (NYSE:BGC)

Bay View Capital Corp.   (NASDAQ:
BVFS)

BayBanks, Inc.   (NASDAQ:BBNK)

BB&T Financial Corp.   (NASDAQ:
BBTF)

BCE, Inc.   (NYSE:BCE)

Beckman Instruments, Inc.   (NYSE:
BEC)

Becton, Dickinson and Company
(NYSE:BDX)

Bedford Property Investors, Inc.   (NYSE:
BED)

Bell Atlantic Corp.   (NYSE:BEL)

BellSouth Corp.   (NYSE:BLS)

Bemis Co., Inc.   (NYSE:BMS)

Beneficial Corp.   (NYSE:BNL)

Berkshire Gas Co.   (NASDAQ:BGAS)

Berkshire Realty Company, Inc.
(NYSE:BRI)
Bethlehem Steel Corp. (NYSE:BS)
Bindley Western Industries, Inc. (NYSE:
BDY)
Birmingham Steel Corp. (NYSE:BIR)
Black Hills Corp. (NYSE:BKH)
Block (H & R) Inc. (NYSE:HRB)
Blount, Inc. (ASE:BLT.A)
BMJ Financial Corp. (NASDAQ:SMJF)
Boatmen's Bancshares, Inc. (NASDAQ:
BOAT)
Bob Evans Farms, Inc. (NASDAQ:
BOBE)
Boddie-Noell Properties (ASE:BNP)
Boise Cascade Corp. (NYSE:BCC)
Boston Bancorp (NASDAQ:SBOS)
Boston Edison Co. (NYSE:BSE)
Bowater, Inc. (NYSE:BOW)
Bradley Real Estate Trust (ASE:BTR)
Brady (W. H.) Co. (NASDAQ:
BRCOA)
Braintree Savings Bank (The)
(NASDAQ:BTSB)
Briggs & Stratton Corp. (NYSE:BGG)
Bristol-Myers Squibb Co. (NYSE:BMY)
British Airways PLC (NYSE:BAB)
British Petroleum Co. PLC (NYSE:BP)
Brooklyn Union Gas Co. (NYSE:BU)
Brown-Forman Corp. (NYSE:BF.B)
Brown Group, Inc. (NYSE:BG)
Browning-Ferris Industries, Inc. (NYSE:
BFE)
Brunswick Corp. (NYSE: BC)
Brush Wellman, Inc. (NYSE:BW)
BSB Bancorp, Inc. (NASDAQ:BSBN)
BT Financial Corp. (NASDAQ:BTFC)
Burnham Pacific Properties, Inc.
(NYSE:BPP)

C

Cabot Corp. (NYSE:CBT)
Cadmus Communications Corp.
(NASDAQ:CDMS)
California Bancshares, Inc. (NASDAQ:
CABI)
California Financial Holding Company
(NASDAQ:CFHC)

California Water Service Co. (NYSE:
CWT)
Callaway Golf Co. (NYSE:ELY)
Campbell Soup Co. (NYSE:CPB)
Canadian Pacific Ltd. (NYSE:CP)
Capstead Mortgage Corp. (NYSE:
CMO)
Carlisle Companies, Inc. (NYSE:CSL)
Carolina First Corp. (NASDAQ:
CAFC)
Carolina Freight Corp. (NYSE:CAO)
Carolina Power & Light Co. (NYSE:
CPL)
Carpenter Technology Corp. (NYSE:
CRS)
Cascade Natural Gas Corp. (NYSE:
CGC)
Caterpillar, Inc. (NYSE: CAT)
Cathay Bancorp, Inc. (NASDAQ:
CATY)
CBI Industries, Inc. (NYSE:CBI)
CBS, Inc. (NYSE: CBS)
CBT Corp. (NASDAQ:CBTC)
CCB Financial Corp. (NASDAQ:
CCBF)
Cedar Fair L.P. (NYSE:FUN)
Centerbank (NASDAQ:CTBX)
Centerior Energy Corp. (NYSE:CX)
Central & South West Corp. (NYSE:
CSR)
Central Fidelity Banks, Inc. (NASDAQ:
CFBS)
Central Hudson Gas & Electric Corp.
(NYSE:CNH)
Central Louisiana Electric Co., Inc.
(NYSE:CNL)
Central Maine Power Co. (NYSE:CTP)
Central Vermont Public Service Corp.
(NYSE:CV)
Centura Banks, Inc. (NYSE:CBC)
Century Telephone Enterprises,
Inc. (NYSE:CTL)
Champion International Corp. (NYSE:
CHA)
Charter One Financial, Inc. (NASDAQ:
COFI)
Chase Manhattan Corp. (NYSE:CMB)
Chemed Corp. (NYSE:CHE)
Chemical Banking Corp. (NYSE:CHL)

Chemical Financial Corp. (NASDAQ: CHFC)

Chesapeake Corp. (NYSE:CSK)

Chesapeake Utilities Corp. (NYSE: CPK)

Chester Valley Bancorp, Inc. (NASDAQ:CVAL)

Chevron Corp. (NYSE:CHV)

Chiquita Brands International, Inc. (NYSE:CQB)

Chittenden Corp. (NASDAQ:CNDN)

Chrysler Corp. (NYSE:C)

Chubb Corp. (NYSE:CB)

Church & Dwight Co., Inc. (NYSE: CHD)

CIGNA Corp. (NYSE:CI)

CILCORP, Inc. (NYSE:CER)

Cincinnati Bell, Inc. (NYSE:CSN)

Cincinnati Financial Corp. (NASDAQ: CINF)

Cincinnati Milacron, Inc. (NYSE:CMZ)

CINergy Corp. (NYSE:CIN)

Citicorp (NYSE:CCI)

Citizens Bancorp (NASDAQ:CIBC)

Citizens Banking Corp. (NASDAQ: CBCF)

Clarcor, Inc. (NYSE:CLC)

Cleveland-Cliffs, Inc. (NYSE:CLF)

Clorox Co. (NYSE:CLX)

CML Group, Inc. (NYSE:CML)

CMS Energy Corp. (NYSE:CMS)

CNB Bancshares, Inc. (NYSE:BNK)

Coca-Cola Bottling Co. Consolidated (NASDAQ:COKE)

The Coca-Cola Company (NYSE:KO)

Coca-Cola Enterprises, Inc. (NYSE: CCE)

Colgate-Palmolive Co. (NYSE:CL)

Colonial BancGroup, Inc. (NYSE:CNB)

Colonial Gas Co. (NASDAQ:CGES)

Columbia Gas System, Inc. (NYSE:CG)

Comerica, Inc. (NYSE:CMA)

Commerce Bancorp, Inc. (NASDAQ: COBA)

Commercial Assets, Inc. (ASE:CAX)

Commercial Intertech Corp. (NYSE: TEC)

Commonwealth Energy System (NYSE: CES)

Community Bank System, Inc. (ASE: CTY)

Compass Bancshares, Inc. (NASDAQ: CBSS)

Computer Associates Int'l, Inc. (NYSE: CA)

COMSAT Corp. (NYSE:CQ)

ConAgra, Inc. (NYSE:CAG)

Connecticut Energy Corp. (NYSE: CNE)

Connecticut Natural Gas Corp. (NYSE: CTG)

Connecticut Water Service, Inc. (NASDAQ:CTWS)

Conrail, Inc. (NYSE:CRR)

Consolidated Edison Co. of New York (NYSE:ED)

Consolidated Natural Gas Co. (NYSE: CNG)

Consolidated Papers, Inc. (NYSE:CDP)

Consumers Water Co. (NASDAQ: CONW)

Cooper Industries, Inc. (NYSE:CBE)

Copley Properties, Inc. (ASE:COP)

CoreStates Financial Corp. (NYSE:CFL)

Corning, Inc. (NYSE:GLW)

CPC International, Inc. (NYSE:CPC)

CPI Corp. (NYSE:CPY)

Cracker Barrel Old Country Store (NASDAQ:CBRL)

Crane Co. (NYSE:CR)

Crestar Financial Corp. (NYSE:CF)

Crompton & Knowles Corp. (NYSE: CNK)

CRSS, Inc. (NYSE:CRX)

CSX Corp. (NYSE:CSX)

Cummins Engine Co., Inc. (NYSE: CUM)

Cyprus Amax Minerals (NYSE:CYM)

D

D & N Financial Corp. (NASDAQ: DNFC)

Dana Corp. (NYSE:DCN)

Dauphin Deposit Corp. (NASDAQ: DAPN)

Dayton Hudson Corp. (NYSE:DH)

Dean Foods Co. (NYSE:DF)

Deere & Company (NYSE:DE)

Delmarva Power & Light Co.   (NYSE: DEW)

Delta Air Lines, Inc.   (NYSE:DAL)

Delta Natural Gas Co., Inc.   (NASDAQ: DGAS)

Deposit Guaranty Corp.   (NASDAQ: DEPS)

Detroit Edison Co.   (NYSE:DTE)

Dexter Corp.   (NYSE:DEX)

The Dial Corp   (NYSE:DL)

Diebold, Inc.   (NYSE:DBD)

Dime Bancorp, Inc.   (NYSE:DME)

Dominion Resources, Inc.   (NYSE:D)

Donaldson Co., Inc.   (NYSE:DCI)

Donnelley (R. R.) & Sons Co.   (NYSE: DNY)

Dow Chemical Co.   (NYSE:DOW)

Dow Jones & Co., Inc.   (NYSE:DJ)

DPL, Inc.   (NYSE:DPL)

DQE   (NYSE:DQE)

Dresser Industries, Inc.   (NYSE:DI)

Du Pont, (E. I.) de Nemours & Co.   (NYSE:DD)

Duke Power Co.   (NYSE:DUK)

Duracell International, Inc.   (NYSE: DUR)

Duriron Co., Inc.   (NASDAQ:DURI)

DVI, Inc.   (NYSE:DVI)

E

E-Systems, Inc.   (NYSE:ESY)

E'Town Corp.   (NYSE:ETW)

Eastern Co.   (ASE:EML)

Eastern Enterprises   (NYSE:EFU)

Eastern Utilities Associates   (NYSE:EUA)

Eastman Chemical Company   (NYSE: ENN)

Eastman Kodak Co.   (NYSE:EK)

Eaton Corp.   (NYSE:ETN)

Ecolab, Inc.   (NYSE:ECL)

EG&G, Inc.   (NYSE:EGG)

Elco Industries, Inc.   (NASDAQ:ELCN)

EMC Insurance Group, Inc.   (NASDAQ:EMCI)

Emerson Electric Co.   (NYSE:EMR)

Empire District Electric Co.   (NYSE: EDE)

Energen Corp.   (NYSE:EGN)

EnergyNorth, Inc.   (NYSE:EI)

Engelhard Corp.   (NYSE:EC)

Enron Corp.   (NYSE:ENE)

Enserch Corp.   (NYSE:ENS)

Enserch Exploration Partners Ltd.   (NYSE:EP)

Entergy Corp.   (NYSE:ETR)

Equifax, Inc.   (NYSE:EFX)

Equitable Companies, Inc.   (NYSE:EQ)

Equitable Resources, Inc.   (NYSE:EQT)

Essex County Gas Company   (NASDAQ:ECGC)

Ethyl Corp.   (NYSE:EY)

Evergreen Bancorp, Inc.   (NASDAQ: EVGN)

Exxon Corp.   (NYSE:XON)

F

F & M Bancorp   (NASDAQ:FMBN)

F & M National Corp.   (NYSE:FMN)

Fay's, Inc.   (NYSE:FAY)

Federal-Mogul Corp.   (NYSE:FMO)

Federal National Mortgage Association   (NYSE:FNM)

Federal Paper Board Co., Inc.   (NYSE: FBO)

Federal Realty Investment Trust   (NYSE: FRT)

Federal Signal Corp.   (NYSE:FSS)

Ferro Corp.   (NYSE:FOE)

Fifth Third Bancorp   (NASDAQ:FITB)

Figgie International, Inc.   (NASDAQ: FIGI)

FINA, Inc.   (ASE:FI)

Financial Trust Corp.   (NASDAQ:FITC)

First American Corp.   (NASDAQ: FATN)

FirstMerit Corp.   (NASDAQ:FMER)

First Bank System, Inc.   (NYSE:FBS)

First Chicago Corp.   (NYSE:FCN)

First Citizens Bancshares, Inc.   (NASDAQ:FCNCA)

First Colonial Group, Inc.   (NASDAQ: FTCG)

First Colony Corporation   (NYSE:FCL)

First Commerce Corp.   (NASDAQ: FCOM)

First Commercial Corp.   (NASDAQ: FCLR)

First Commonwealth Financial Corp. (NYSE:FCF)

First Empire State Corp. (ASE:FES)

First Federal Capital Corp. (NASDAQ: FTFC)

First Fidelity Bancorp. (NYSE:FFB)

First Financial Holdings, Inc. (NASDAQ:FFCH)

First Harrisburg Bancor, Inc. (NASDAQ:FFHP)

First Michigan Bank Corp. (NASDAQ: FMBC)

First Midwest Bancorp, Inc. (NASDAQ: FMBI)

First Mississippi Corp. (NYSE:FRM)

First National Bancorp (ASE:FNH)

First Northern Savings Bank (NASDAQ:FNGB)

First of America Bank Corp. (NYSE: FOA)

First Security Corp. (NASDAQ:FSCO)

First Tennessee National Corp. (NASDAQ:FTEN)

First Union Corp. (NYSE:FTU)

First Union Real Estate Investments (NYSE:FUR)

First Virginia Banks, Inc. (NYSE:FVB)

First Western Bancorp, Inc. (NASDAQ: FWBI)

Firstar Corp. (NYSE:FSR)

Firstbank of Illinois Co. (NASDAQ: FBIC)

Fleet Financial Group, Inc. (NYSE:FLT)

Fleming Companies, Inc. (NYSE:FLM)

Florida Progress Corp. (NYSE:FPC)

Florida Public Utilities Co. (ASE:FPU)

Flowers Industries, Inc. (NYSE:FLO)

Fluor Corporation (NYSE:FLR)

Food Lion, Inc. (NASDAQ:FDLNA)

Ford Motor Co. (NYSE:F)

Fort Wayne National Corp. (NASDAQ: FWNC)

Foster Wheeler Corp. (NYSE:FWC)

Fourth Financial Corp. (NASDAQ: FRTH)

FPL Group, Inc. (NYSE:FPL)

Franklin Resources, Inc. (NYSE:BEN)

Freeport-McMoRan, Inc. (NYSE:FTX)

Fuller (H. B.) Co. (NASDAQ:FULL)

Fulton Financial Corp. (NASDAQ: FULT)

G

Gannett Co., Inc. (NYSE:GCI)

GATX Corp. (NYSE:GMT)

GenCorp, Inc. (NYSE:GY)

General Electric Co. (NYSE:GE)

General Housewares Corp. (NYSE: GHW)

General Mills, Inc. (NYSE:GIS)

General Motors Corp. (NYSE:GM)

General Public Utilities Corp. (NYSE: GPU)

General Re Corp. (NYSE:GRN)

General Signal Corp. (NYSE:GSX)

Genuine Parts Co. (NYSE:GPC)

Georgia-Pacific Corp. (NYSE:GP)

Giant Food, Inc. (ASE:GFS.A)

Giddings & Lewis, Inc. (NASDAQ: GIDL)

Gillette Co. (NYSE:G)

GoodMark Foods, Inc. (NASDAQ: GDMK)

Goodrich (B. F.) Co. (NYSE:GR)

Goodyear Tire & Rubber Co. (NYSE: GT)

Gorman-Rupp Co. (ASE:GRC)

Goulds Pumps, Inc. (NASDAQ:GULD)

Grace (W. R.) & Co. (NYSE:GRA)

Graco, Inc. (NYSE:GGG)

Grand Metropolitan PLC (NYSE:GRM)

Great Southern Bancorp, Inc. (NASDAQ:GSBC)

Great Western Financial Corp. (NYSE: GWF)

Green Mountain Power Corp. (NYSE: GMP)

Grow Group, Inc. (NYSE:GRO)

GTE Corp. (NYSE:GTE)

Guardsman Products, Inc. (NYSE:GPI)

H

Hancock Holding Company (NASDAQ:HBHC)

Handleman Co. (NYSE:HDL)

Handy & Harman (NYSE:HNH)

Hanna (M. A.) Co. (NYSE:MAH)

Hannaford Brothers Co. (NYSE:HRD)

Hanson PLC   (NYSE:HAN)

Harcourt General, Inc.   (NYSE:H)

Harland (John H.) Company   (NYSE:JH)

Harley-Davidson, Inc.   (NYSE:HDI)

Harleysville Group, Inc.   (NASDAQ: HGIC)

Harris Corp.   (NYSE:HRS)

Harsco Corp.   (NYSE:HSC)

Hartford Steam Boiler Inspection (NYSE:HSB)

Hartmarx Corp.   (NYSE:HMX)

Haverfield Corp.   (NASDAQ:HVFD)

Hawaiian Electric Industries, Inc. (NYSE:HE)

Health & Retirement Properties Trust (NYSE:HRP)

Health Care REIT, Inc.   (NYSE:HCN)

Heilig-Meyers Company   (NYSE:HMY)

Heinz (H. J.) Co.   (NYSE:HNZ)

Hercules, Inc.   (NYSE:HPC)

Hershey Foods Corp.   (NYSE:HSY)

Hibernia Corp.   (NYSE:HIB)

Home Depot, Inc.   (NYSE:HD)

Homestake Mining Co.   (NYSE:HM)

Honeywell, Inc.   (NYSE:HON)

Hormel Foods   (NYSE:HRL)

Houghton Mifflin Company   (NYSE: HTN)

Household International, Inc.   (NYSE: HI)

Houston Industries, Inc.   (NYSE:HOU)

HRE Properties   (NYSE:HRE)

Hubbell, Inc.   (NYSE:HUB.B)

HUBCO, Inc.   (NASDAQ:HUBC)

Huffy Corp.   (NYSE:HUF)

Huntington Bancshares, Inc. (NASDAQ:HBAN)

I

Idaho Power Co.   (NYSE:IDA)

IES Industries, Inc.   (NYSE:IES)

Illinois Tool Works, Inc.   (NYSE:ITW)

Illinova Corp.   (NYSE:ILN)

Imo Industries, Inc.   (NYSE:IMD)

Imperial Bancorp   (NASDAQ:IBAN)

Imperial Holly Corp.   (ASE:IHK)

Imperial Oil Ltd.   (ASE:IMO)

Inco Ltd.   (NYSE:N)

Independence Bancorp, Inc.   (NASDAQ: IBNJ)

Independent Bank Corp.   (NASDAQ: IBCP)

Indiana Energy, Inc.   (NYSE:IEI)

Ingersoll-Rand Co.   (NYSE:IR)

Inland Steel Industries, Inc.   (NYSE: IAD)

Insteel Industries, Inc.   (NYSE:III)

Integra Financial Corp.   (NYSE:ITG)

Intel Corp.   (NASDAQ:INTC)

Interchange Financial Services Corp. (ASE:ISB)

International Business Machines Corp. (NYSE:IBM)

International Flavors & Fragrances   (NYSE:IFF)

International Multifoods Corp.   (NYSE: IMC)

International Paper Co.   (NYSE:IP)

Interpublic Group of Companies, Inc. (NYSE:IPG)

Interstate Power Co.   (NYSE:IPW)

Iowa-Illinois Gas & Electric Co.   (NYSE: IWG)

IPALCO Enterprises, Inc.   (NYSE:IPL)

IRT Property Co.   (NYSE:IRT)

ITT Corp.   (NYSE:ITT)

IWC Resources Corp.   (NASDAQ: IWCR)

J

Jacobson Stores, Inc.   (NASDAQ:JCBS)

Jefferson Bankshares, Inc.   (NASDAQ: JBNK)

Jefferson-Pilot Corp.   (NYSE:JP)

Johnson & Johnson   (NYSE:JNJ)

Johnson Controls, Inc.   (NYSE:JCI)

Joslyn Corp.   (NASDAQ:JOSL)

Jostens, Inc.   (NYSE:JOS)

Justin Industries, Inc.   (NASDAQ:JSTN)

K

K N Energy, Inc.   (NYSE:KNE)

Kaman Corp.   (NASDAQ:KAMNA)

Kansas City Power & Light Co.   (NYSE: KLT)

Keithley Instruments, Inc.   (ASE:KEI)

Kelley Oil & Gas Partners, Ltd. (NASDAQ:KOGC)

Kellogg Co. (NYSE:K)

Kellwood Company (NYSE:KWD)

Kennametal, Inc. (NYSE:KMT)

Kerr-McGee Corp. (NYSE:KMG)

KeyCorp (NYSE:KEY)

Keystone Financial, Inc. (NASDAQ: KSTN)

Keystone Heritage Group, Inc. (NYSE: KHG)

Keystone International, Inc. (NYSE:KII)

Kimberly-Clark Corp. (NYSE:KMB)

Kmart Corp. (NYSE:KM)

Knape & Vogt Manufacturing Company (NASDAQ:KNAP)

Knight-Ridder, Inc. (NYSE:KRI)

Kollmorgen Corp. (NYSE:KOL)

Kranzco Realty Trust (NYSE:KRT)

KU Energy Corp. (NYSE:KU)

Kuhlman Corp. (NYSE:KUH)

Kysor Industrial Corp. (NYSE:KZ)

L

La-Z-Boy Chair Co. (NYSE:LZB)

Laclede Gas Co. (NYSE:LG)

Lafarge Corp. (NYSE:LAF)

Lancaster Colony Corp. (NASDAQ: LANC)

Lance, Inc. (NASDAQ:LNCE)

LG&E Energy Corp. (NYSE:LGE)

Lilly (Eli) & Co. (NYSE:LLY)

Lilly Industries, Inc. (NYSE:LI)

Limited (The), Inc. (NYSE:LTD)

Lincoln National Corp. (NYSE:LNC)

Lincoln Telecommunications Co. (NASDAQ:LTEC)

Liz Claiborne, Inc. (NYSE:LIZ)

Loctite Corp. (NYSE:LOC)

Long Island Lighting Company (NYSE: LIL)

Louisiana Land & Exploration Company (NYSE:LLX)

Louisiana-Pacific Corp. (NYSE:LPX)

Lowe's Companies, Inc. (NYSE:LOW)

Lubrizol Corp. (NYSE:LZ)

Luby's Cafeterias, Inc. (NYSE:LUB)

Lukens, Inc. (NYSE:LUC)

Lyondell Petrochemical Co. (NYSE: LYO)

M

MacDermid, Inc. (NASDAQ:MACD)

Madison Gas & Electric Co. (NASDAQ: MDSN)

Magna Group, Inc. (NASDAQ:MAGI)

Mallinckrodt Group, Inc. (NYSE:MKG)

Manitowoc Company, Inc. (NYSE: MTW)

Manpower, Inc. (NYSE:MAN)

MAPCO, Inc. (NYSE:MDA)

Marion Merrell Dow, Inc. (NYSE: MKC)

Mark Twain Bancshares, Inc. (NASDAQ:MTWN)

Marsh & McLennan Companies, Inc. (NYSE:MMC)

Marsh Supermarkets, Inc. (NASDAQ: MARSA)

Marshall & Ilsley Corp. (NASDAQ: MRIS)

MASSBANK Corp. (NASDAQ:MASB)

Mattel, Inc. (NYSE:MAT)

May Department Stores Company (NYSE:MA)

Maytag Corp. (NYSE:MYG)

McCormick & Co., Inc. (NASDAQ: MCCRK)

McDermott International, Inc. (NYSE: MDR)

McDonald's Corp. (NYSE:MCD)

McGraw-Hill, Inc. (NYSE:MHP)

McKesson Corp. (NYSE:MCK)

MCN Corp. (NYSE:MCN)

MDU Resources Group, Inc. (NYSE: MDU)

Mead Corp. (NYSE:MEA)

Medford Savings Bank (NASDAQ: MDBK)

Media General, Inc. (ASE:MEG.A)

Medtronic, Inc. (NYSE:MDT)

Medusa Corp. (NYSE:MSA)

Mellon Bank Corp. (NYSE:MEL)

Mercantile Bancorp., Inc. (NYSE:MTL)

Mercantile Bankshares Corp. (NASDAQ:MRBK)

Merck & Co., Inc. (NYSE:MRK)

Mercury Finance Company (NYSE: MFN)

Meridian Bancorp, Inc. (NASDAQ: MRDN)

Merrill Lynch & Co., Inc. (NYSE: MER)

Merry Land & Investment Co., Inc. (NYSE:MRY)

Michigan National Corp. (NASDAQ: MNCO)

Mid Am, Inc. (NASDAQ:MIAM)

Mid-America Realty Investments (NYSE:MDI)

Middlesex Water Co. (NASDAQ: MSEX)

Midlantic Corp. (NASDAQ:MIDL)

Midwest Resources, Inc. (NYSE: MWR)

Millipore Corp. (NYSE:MIL)

Minnesota Mining & Manufacturing Co. (NYSE:MMM)

Minnesota Power & Light Co. (NYSE: MPL)

Mobil Corp. (NYSE:MOB)

Mobile Gas Service Corp. (NASDAQ: MBLE)

Modine Manufacturing Co. (NASDAQ: MODI)

Monmouth Real Estate Investment Corp. (NASDAQ:MTA)

Monsanto Co. (NYSE:MTC)

Montana Power Co. (NYSE:MTP)

Morgan (J. P.) & Co. Inc. (NYSE:JPM)

Morrison Knudsen Corp. (NYSE: MRN)

Morton International, Inc. (NYSE: MII)

Motorola, Inc. (NYSE:MOT)

N

Nalco Chemical Co. (NYSE:NLC)

Nash-Finch Co. (NASDAQ:NAFC)

Nashua Corp. (NYSE:NSH)

National City Bancshares, Inc. (NASDAQ:NCBE)

National City Corp. (NYSE:NCC)

National Commerce Bancorp (NASDAQ:NCBC)

National Data Corp. (NYSE:NDC)

National Fuel Gas Co. (NYSE:NFG)

National Penn Bancshares, Inc. (NASDAQ:NPBC)

National Service Industries, Inc. (NYSE: NSI)

National-Standard Co. (NYSE:NSD)

NationsBank Corp. (NYSE:NB)

Nationwide Health Properties, Inc. (NYSE:NHP)

NBD Bancorp, Inc. (NYSE:NBD)

NBSC Corp. (NASDAQ:NSCB)

Neiman-Marcus Group, Inc. (NYSE: NMG)

Nevada Power Co. (NYSE:NVP)

New England Electric System (NYSE: NES)

New Jersey Resources Corp. (NYSE: NJR)

New Plan Realty Trust (NYSE:NPR)

New York State Electric & Gas Corp. (NYSE:NGE)

New York Times Co. (ASE:NYT.A)

Newell Co. (NYSE:NWL)

Niagara Mohawk Power Corp. (NYSE: NMK)

NICOR, Inc. (NYSE:GAS)

NIPSCO Industries, Inc. (NYSE:NI)

Nooney Realty Trust, Inc. (NASDAQ: TI)

NorAm Energy Corp. (NYSE:NAE)

Nordson Corp. (NASDAQ:NDSN)

Norfolk Southern Corp. (NYSE:NSC)

North American Trust, Inc. (ASE: NAM)

North Carolina Natural Gas Corp. (NYSE:NCG)

North Fork Bancorporation, Inc. (NYSE:NFB)

Northeast Utilities Service Co. (NYSE: NU)

Northern States Power Co. (NYSE: NSP)

Northern Telecom Ltd. (NYSE:NT)

Northrop Grumman Corp. (NYSE: NOC)

Northwest Illinois Bancorp, Inc. (NASDAQ:NWIB)

Northwest Natural Gas Co. (NASDAQ: NWNG)

Northwestern Public Service Co.
(NYSE:NPS)
Norwest Corp.   (NYSE:NOB)
NOVA Corporation   (NYSE:NVA)
Novo-Nordisk A/S   (NYSE:NVO)
Nucor Corp.   (NYSE:NUE)
NUI Corp.   (NYSE:NUI)
NYNEX Corp.   (NYSE:NYN)

O

Occidental Petroleum Corp.   (NYSE:
OXY)
Ohio Casualty Corp.   (NASDAQ:
OCAS)
Ohio Edison Co.   (NYSE:OEC)
Oklahoma Gas & Electric Co.   (NYSE:
OGE)
Old Kent Financial Corp.   (NASDAQ:
OKEN)
Old National Bancorp   (NASDAQ:
OLDB)
Old Republic International Corp.
(NYSE:ORI)
Olin Corp.   (NYSE: OLN)
ON Group, Inc.   (NASDAQ:OMGI)
Omnicare, Inc.   (NYSE:OCR)
One Valley Bancorp of West Virginia
(NASDAQ:OVWV)
Oneida Ltd.   (NYSE:OCQ)
Oneok, Inc.   (NYSE:OKE)
Orange & Rockland Utilities, Inc.
(NYSE:ORU)
Orbital Engine Corporation Ltd.
(NYSE:OE)
Otter Tail Power Co.   (NASDAQ:
OTTR)
Outboard Marine Corp.   (NYSE:OM)
Owens & Minor, Inc.   (NYSE:OMI)

P

Pacific Enterprises   (NYSE:PET)
Pacific Gas & Electric Co.   (NYSE:PCG)
Pacific Telesis Group   (NYSE:PAC)
PacifiCorp   (NYSE:PPW)
Paine Webber Group, Inc.   (NYSE:PWJ)
Pall Corp.   (NYSE:PLL)
Panhandle Eastern Corp.   (NYSE:PEL)
Parker Hannifin Corp.   (NYSE:PH)
Paychex, Inc.   (NASDAQ:PAYX)

PECO Energy Co.   (NYSE:PE)
Penney (J. C.) Co. Inc.   (NYSE:JCP)
Pennsylvania Enterprises, Inc.   (NYSE:
PNT)
Pennsylvania Power & Light Co.
(NYSE:PPL)
Pennzoil Co.   (NYSE:PZL)
Pentair, Inc.   (NASDAQ:PNTA)
Peoples Energy Corp.   (NYSE:PGL)
Pep Boys—Nanny, Moe & Jack   (NYSE:
PBY)
PepsiCo, Inc.   (NYSE:PEP)
Perkin-Elmer Corp.   (NYSE:PKN)
Pfizer, Inc.   (NYSE:PFE)
Phelps Dodge Corp.   (NYSE:PD)
Philadelphia Suburban Corp.   (NYSE:
PSC)
Philip Morris Companies, Inc.   (NYSE:
MO)
Phillips Petroleum Co.   (NYSE:P)
Piccadilly Cafeterias, Inc.   (NYSE:PIC)
Piedmont Natural Gas Co.   (NYSE:
PNY)
Pinnacle West Capital Corp.   (NYSE:
PNW)
Pioneer Hi-Bred International, Inc.
(NASDAQ:PHYB)
Pioneer-Standard Electronics, Inc.
(NASDAQ:PIOS)
Pitney Bowes, Inc.   (NYSE:PBI)
Ply Gem Industries, Inc.   (NYSE:PGI)
PMC Capital, Inc.   (ASE:PMC)
PNC Bank Corp.   (NYSE:PNC)
Polaroid Corp.   (NYSE:PRD)
Portland General Corp.   (NYSE:PGN)
Portsmouth Bank Shares, Inc.
(NASDAQ:POBS)
Potlatch Corp.   (NYSE:PCH)
Potomac Electric Power Co.   (NYSE:
POM)
PPG Industries, Inc.   (NYSE:PPG)
Praxair, Inc.   (NYSE:PX)
Premier Industrial Corp.   (NYSE:PRE)
Presidential Realty Corp.   (ASE:PDL.B)
Prime Bancorp, Inc.   (NASDAQ:PSAB)
Procter & Gamble Co.   (NYSE:PG)
Providence Energy Corp.   (ASE:PVY)
Provident Bankshares Corp.   (NASDAQ:
PBKS)

Providian Corp. (NYSE:PVN)
PSI Resources, Inc. (NYSE:PIN)
Public Service Co. of Colorado (NYSE: PSR)
Public Service Co. of North Carolina (NYSE:PGS)
Public Service Enterprise Group, Inc. (NYSE:PEG)
Puget Sound Power & Light Co. (NYSE:PSD)

Q

Quaker Oats Co. (NYSE:OAT)
Quaker State Corp. (NYSE:KSF)
Quanex Corp. (NYSE:NX)
Questar Corp. (NYSE:STR)

R

Ralston Purina Co. (NYSE:RAL)
Raymond Corp. (NASDAQ:RAYM)
Raytheon Co. (NYSE:RTN)
Real Estate Investment Trust of CA (NYSE:RCT)
Regions Financial Corp. (NASDAQ: RGBK)
Reliastar Financial Corp. (NYSE:RLR)
Resource Mortgage Capital Inc. (NYSE: RMR)
Reynolds & Reynolds Co. (NYSE: REY)
Reynolds Metals Co. (NYSE:RLM)
Rhone-Poulenc Rorer, Inc. (NYSE: RPR)
Rite Aid Corp. (NYSE:RAD)
RLI Corp. (NYSE:RLI)
Roadway Services, Inc. (NASDAQ: ROAD)
Roanoke Electric Steel Corp. (NASDAQ:RESC)
Roanoke Gas Company (NASDAQ: RGCO)
Rochester Gas & Electric Corp. (NYSE: RGS)
Rochester Telephone Corp. (NYSE: RTC)
Rockefeller Center Properties, Inc. (NYSE:RCP)
Rockwell International Corp. (NYSE: ROK)

Rollins Environmental Services, Inc. (NYSE:REN)
Rollins, Inc. (NYSE:ROL)
Rollins Truck Leasing Corp. (NYSE: RLC)
Roosevelt Financial Group, Inc. (NASDAQ:RFED)
Rose's Stores, Inc. (NASDAQ:RSTOQ)
Rouse Co. (NASDAQ:ROUS)
RPM, Inc. (NASDAQ:RPOW)
Rubbermaid, Inc. (NYSE:RBD)
Russell Corp. (NYSE:RML)
Ryder System, Inc. (NYSE:R)
Rykoff-Sexton, Inc. (NYSE:RYK)
RYMAC Mortgage Investment Corp. (ASE:RM)

S

Safety-Kleen Corp. (NYSE:SK)
St. Joseph Light & Power Co. (NYSE: SAJ)
St. Paul Bancorp, Inc. (NASDAQ: SPBC)
St. Paul Companies, Inc. (NYSE:SPC)
Salomon, Inc. (NYSE:SB)
Samson Energy Co., LP (ASE:SAM)
San Diego Gas & Electric Company (NYSE:SDO)
Sara Lee Corp. (NYSE:SLE)
Savannah Foods & Industries, Inc. (NYSE:SFI)
SCANA Corp. (NYSE:SCG)
SCEcorp (NYSE:SCE)
Schering-Plough Corp. (NYSE:SGP)
Schwab (Charles) Corp. (NYSE:SCH)
Scientific-Atlanta, Inc. (NYSE:SFA)
Scott Paper Co. (NYSE:SPP)
Seafield Capital Corp. (NASDAQ: SFLD)
Sears, Roebuck & Co. (NYSE:S)
Second Bancorp, Inc. (NASDAQ: SECD)
Security Capital Bancorp (NASDAQ: SCBC)
Seibels Bruce Group, Inc. (NASDAQ: SBIG)
Selective Insurance Group, Inc. (NASDAQ:SIGI)

ServiceMaster Limited
Partnership (NYSE:SVM)

Shawmut National Corp. (NYSE:SNC)

Sherwin-Williams Company (NYSE:
SHW)

Shoreline Financial Corp. (NASDAQ:
SLFC)

Sierra Pacific Resources (NYSE:SRP)

SIFCO Industries, Inc. (ASE:SIF)

Signet Banking Corp. (NYSE:SBK)

Simpson Industries, Inc. (NASDAQ:
SMPS)

Sizeler Property Investors, Inc. (NYSE:
SIZ)

Smith (A. O.) Corp. (NYSE:AOS)

Smucker (J. M.) Co. (NYSE:SJM.A)

Snap-on, Inc. (NYSE:SNA)

Sonat, Inc. (NYSE:SNT)

Sonoco Products Co. (NASDAQ:
SONO)

Sotheby's Holdings, Inc. (NYSE:BID)

South Jersey Industries, Inc. (NYSE:SJI)

Southeastern Michigan Gas Enterprises
(NASDAQ:SMGS)

Southern California Water Co. (NYSE:
SCW)

Southern Co. (NYSE:SO)

Southern Indiana Gas & Electric Co.
(NYSE:SIG)

Southern National Corp. (NYSE:SNB)

Southern New England
Telecommunications (NYSE:SNG)

SouthTrust Corp. (NASDAQ:SOTR)

Southwest Gas Corp. (NYSE:SWX)

Southwest Water Co. (NASDAQ:
SWWC)

Southwestern Bell Corp. (NYSE:SBC)

Southwestern Energy Co. (NYSE:SWN)

Southwestern Public Service Co. (NYSE:
SPS)

Sprint Corp. (NYSE:FON)

SPX Corp. (NYSE:SPW)

Standard Commercial Corp. (NYSE:
STW)

Standard Federal Bank (NYSE:SFB)

Standard Products Co. (NYSE:SPD)

Stanhome, Inc. (NYSE:STH)

Stanley Works (NYSE:SWK)

Star Banc Corp. (NYSE:STB)

State Street Boston Corp. (NASDAQ:
STBK)

Stone & Webster, Inc. (NYSE:SW)

Stride Rite Corp. (NYSE:SRR)

Suffolk Bancorp (NASDAQ:SUBK)

Sumitomo Bank of California
(NASDAQ:SUMI)

Summit Bancorporation (NASDAQ:
SUBN)

Summit Tax Exempt Bond Fund, LP
(ASE:SUA)

Sun Co., Inc. (NYSE:SUN)

Sundstrand Corp. (NYSE:SNS)

SunTrust Banks, Inc. (NYSE:STI)

Supervalu, Inc. (NYSE:SVU)

Susquehanna Bancshares, Inc.
(NASDAQ:SUSQ)

Synovus Financial Corp. (NYSE:SNV)

Sysco Corp. (NYSE:SYY)

T

Talley Industries, Inc. (NYSE:TAL)

Tambrands, Inc. (NYSE:TMB)

TCF Financial Corp. (NYSE:TCB)

TECO Energy, Inc. (NYSE:TE)

Telephone & Data Systems, Inc. (ASE:
TDS)

Temple-Inland, Inc. (NYSE:TIN)

Tenet Healthcare Corp. (NYSE:THC)

Tenneco, Inc. (NYSE:TGT)

Texaco, Inc. (NYSE:TX)

Texas Instruments, Inc. (NYSE:TXN)

Texas Utilities Co. (NYSE:TXU)

Textron, Inc. (NYSE:TXT)

Thomas & Betts Corp. (NYSE:TNB)

Thomas Industries, Inc. (NYSE:TII)

Tidewater, Inc. (NYSE:TDW)

Time Warner, Inc. (NYSE:TWX)

Times Mirror Company (NYSE:TMC)

Timken Co. (NYSE:TKR)

TNP Enterprises, Inc. (NYSE:TNP)

Torchmark Corp. (NYSE:TMK)

Toro Co. (NYSE:TTC)

Total System Services, Inc. (NYSE:TSS)

Transamerica Corp. (NYSE:TA)

TransCanada Pipelines Ltd. (NYSE:
TRP)

Tribune Company (NYSE:TRB)

Trinova Corp. (NYSE:TNV)

True North Communications, Inc. (NYSE:TNO)

TRW, Inc.   (NYSE:TRW)

Twin Disc, Inc.   (NYSE:TDI)

Tyco International Ltd.   (NYSE:TYC)

U

UGI Corp.   (NYSE:UGI)

UJB Financial Corp.   (NYSE:UJB)

Unicom Corp.   (NYSE:UCM)

Union Bank   (NASDAQ:UBNK)

Union Camp Corp.   (NYSE:UCC)

Union Carbide Corp.   (NYSE:UK)

Union Electric Co.   (NYSE:UEP)

Union Pacific Corp.   (NYSE:UNP)

Union Planters Corp.   (NYSE:UPC)

United Bankshares, Inc.   (NASDAQ: UBSI)

United Carolina Bankshares Corp. (NASDAQ:UCAR)

United Cities Gas Co.   (NASDAQ: UCIT)

United Illuminating Co.   (NYSE:UIL)

United Mobile Homes, Inc.   (NASDAQ: UMHI)

U.S. Bancorp   (NASDAQ:USBC)

United States Shoe Corp.   (NYSE:USR)

United States Trust Corp.   (NASDAQ: USTC)

United Water Resources, Inc.   (NYSE: UWR)

UNITIL Corp.   (ASE:UTL)

Universal Corp.   (NYSE:UVV)

Universal Foods Corp.   (NYSE:UFC)

Universal Health Realty Income Trust (NYSE:UHT)

Unocal Corp.   (NYSE:UCL)

UNUM Corp.   (NYSE:UNM)

Upjohn Co.   (NYSE:UPJ)

Upper Peninsula Energy Corp. (NASDAQ:UPEN)

US BANCORP, Inc.   (NASDAQ: UBAN)

USF&G Corp.   (NYSE:FG)

USLICO Corp.   (NYSE:USC)

USLIFE Corp.   (NYSE:USH)

UST Corp.   (NASDAQ:USTB)

UST, Inc.   (NYSE:UST)

US West, Inc.   (NYSE:USW)

USX Corp.—Marathon   (NYSE:MRO)

USX Corp.—U.S. Steel Group   (NYSE: X)

UtiliCorp United, Inc.   (NYSE:UCU)

V

Valley National Bancorp   (NYSE:VLY)

Valley Resources, Inc.   (ASE:VR)

Varian Associates, Inc.   (NYSE:VAR)

Venture Stores, Inc.   (NYSE:VEN)

Vermont Financial Services Corp. (NASDAQ:VFSC)

VF Corp.   (NYSE:VFC)

Vulcan Materials Co.   (NYSE:VMC)

W

Wachovia Corp.   (NYSE:WB)

Walgreen Co.   (NYSE:WAG)

Warner-Lambert Co.   (NYSE:WLA)

Washington Energy Co.   (NYSE: WEG)

Washington Gas Light Co.   (NYSE: WGL)

Washington Mutual Savings Bank (NASDAQ:WAMU)

Washington National Corp.   (NYSE: WNT)

Washington Real Estate Investment Trust (ASE:WRE)

Washington Trust Bancorp, Inc. (NASDAQ:WASH)

Washington Water Power Co.   (NYSE: WWP)

Weingarten Realty Investors   (NYSE: WRI)

Weis Markets, Inc.   (NYSE:WMK)

Wells Fargo & Co.   (NYSE:WFC)

Wendy's International, Inc.   (NYSE: WEN)

Wesbanco, Inc.   (NASDAQ:WSBC)

West Company (The)   (NYSE:WST)

West One Bancorp   (NASDAQ:WEST)

Westamerica Bancorp   (NASDAQ: WABC)

Westcoast Energy Inc.   (NYSE:WE)

Western Resources, Inc.   (NYSE:WR)

Westinghouse Electric Corp.   (NYSE: WX)

Westport Bancorp, Inc.   (NASDAQ: WBAT)

Westvaco Corp.   (NYSE:W)
Weyerhaeuser Co.   (NYSE:WY)
Whirlpool Corp.   (NYSE:WHR)
Whitman Corp.   (NYSE:WH)
WICOR, Inc.   (NYSE:WIC)
Wilmington Trust Co.   (NASDAQ: WILM)
Winn-Dixie Stores, Inc.   (NYSE:WIN)
Wisconsin Energy Corp.   (NYSE:WEC)
Witco Corp.   (NYSE:WIT)
WLR Foods, Inc.   (NASDAQ:WLRF)
WMX Technologies, Inc.   (NYSE: WMX)
Woolworth Corp.   (NYSE:Z)
Worthington Industries, Inc. (NASDAQ:WTHG)
WPL Holdings, Inc.   (NYSE:WPH)
WPS Resources Corporation   (NYSE: WPS)
Wrigley (Wm.) Jr. Co.   (NYSE:WWY)

X

Xerox Corp.   (NYSE:XRX)

Y

Yankee Energy System, Inc.   (NYSE: YES)
York Financial Corp.   (NASDAQ: YFED)

Z

Zero Corp.   (NYSE:ZRO)
Zions Bancorporation   (NASDAQ: ZION)
Zurn Industries, Inc.   (NYSE:ZRN)

Source: *DRIP Investor* newsletter, Hammond, Indiana

APPENDIX B:
TRUST COMPANIES

A

A. G. Edwards Trust Company; Saint Louis, MO

Abbott Bank; Alliance, NE

Acadia Trust, NA; Portland, ME

Ackley State Bank; Ackley, IA

Adams Bank and Trust; Ogalala, NE

Adams County National Bank; Gettysburg, PA

Adirondack Trust Company; Saratoga Springs, NY

Advent Trust Company; Houston, TX

Advest Bank; Hartford, CT

Albany Bank and Trust Company, NA; Chicago, IL

Albert City Savings Bank; Albert City, IA

Albright Title and Trust Company; Newkirk, OK

Alden State Bank; Alden, IA

Alice Bank of Texas; Alice, TX

Allen Bank and Trust Company; Harrisonville, MO

Alton Savings Bank; Alton, IA

Alva State Bank and Trust Company; Alva, OK

Alvin State Bank; Alvin, TX

Amalgamated Bank of Chicago; Chicago, IL

Amalgamated Bank of New York; New York, NY

AmalgaTrust Company, Inc; Chicago, IL

Amarillo National Bank; Amarillo, TX

Amboy National Bank; Old Bridge Township, NJ

Amcore Bank, NA, Rockford; Rockford, IL

AMCORE Trust Company; Rockford, IL

American Bank; Cerro Gordo, IL

American Bank, NA; Saint Paul, MN

American Bank of Commerce; Las Vegas, NV

American Bank of Rock Island; Rock Island, IL

American Bank and Trust Company; Tulsa, OK

American Bank and Trust of Polk County; Lake Wales, FL

American Banking Company; Moultrie, GA

American Guaranty & Trust Company; Newark, DE

American Interstate Bank; Manning, IA

American Marine Bank; Bainbridge Island, WA

American National Bank; Humboldt, NE

American National Bank; Texarkana, TX

American National Bank of Beaver Dam; Beaver Dam, WI

American National Bank of Cheyenne; Cheyenne, WY

American National Bank of Da Kalb County; Sycamore, IL

American National Bank of Florida; Jacksonville, FL

American National Bank of Lawton; Lawton, OK

American National Bank of Texas; Terrell, TX

American National Bank of Vincennes; Vincennes, IN

American National Bank and Trust Company; Danville, VA

American National Bank and Trust Company of Chattanooga; Chattanooga, TN

American National Bank and Trust Company of Chicago; Chicago, IL

American National Bank and Trust Company of Sapulpa, Oklahoma; Sapulpa, OK

American National Bank and Trust Company of Shawnee; Shawnee, OK

American National Trust and Investment Management Company; Muncie, IN

American Savings Bank; Tripoli, IA

American State Bank; Charleston, AR

American State Bank; Lawrenceburg, IN

American State Bank; Sioux Center, IA

American State Bank; Lubbock, TX

American State Bank and Trust Company of Williston; Williston, ND

American State Bank and Trust Company of Dickinson; Dickinson, ND

American Trust Bank; Cumberland, MD

American Trust Bank of West Virginia, Inc.; Keyser, WV

American Trust Company; Lebanon, NH

American Trust and Savings Bank; Dubuque, IA

American Trust and Savings Bank; Lowden, IA

American Trust and Savings Bank of Whiting, Indiana; Whiting, IN

AmericanMidwest Bank and Trust; Melrose Park, IL

AmeriFirst Bank; Sikeston, MO

AmQuest Bank, NA.; Duncan, OK

AmSouth Bank of Alabama; Birmingham, AL

AmSouth Bank of Florida; Clearwater, FL

AmSouth Bank of Tennessee; Chattanooga, TN

Anawon Trust NA; Attleboro, MA

ANB Investment Management and Trust Company; Chicago, IL

Anchor Bank; Myrtle Beach, SC

Anchor State Bank; Anchor, IL

Anderson Brothers Bank; Mullins, SC

Anderson National Bank of Lawrenceburg; Lawrenceburg, KY

Anderson State Bank, Inc; Hemingway, SC

Androscoggin Savings Bank; Lewiston, ME

Anna State Bank; Anna, IL

Apollo Trust Company; Apollo, PA

Arcadia Bank & Trust Company; Kalamazoo, MI

Arkansas Bank; Jonesboro, AR

Arkansas State Bank; Siloam Springs, AR

Arrowhead Bank; Llano, TX

Arvest Trust Company, NA; Rogers, AR

Ashton State Bank; Ashton, IA

Associated Bank Green Bay, NA; Green Bay, WI

Associated Bank Lakeshore, NA; Manitowoc, WI

Associated Bank, NA; Neanah, WI

Associated Trust Company, Inc; Memonronee Falls, WI

Atlantic Trust Company, NA; Washington, DC

Audubon State Bank; Audubon, IA

Austin Bank of Chicago; Chicago, IL

Austin Trust Company; Austin, TX

B

Baker Boyer National Bank; Walla Walla, WA

Baldwin Savings Bank; Baldwin, IA

Ballston Spa National Bank; Ballston Spa, NY

Baltimore Trust Company; Selbyville, DE

Banc One Illinois Investment Management and Trust Group; Evanston, IL

BancBoston Trust Company of New York; New York, NY

BancFirst; Stillwater, OK

Banco Central Hispano—Puerto Rico; Hato Rey, PR

Banco Central Hispano—USA; New York, NY

Banco Popular de Puerto Rico; Hato Rey, PR

Banco Santander Puerto Rico; San Juan, PR

Bancorp Trust Company, NA; Naples, FL

Bangor Savings Bank; Bangor, ME

Bank IV Kansas, NA; Wichita, KS

Bank IV Oklahoma, NA; Tulsa, OK

Bank Leumi Trust Company of New York; New York, NY

Bank Midwest; Armstrong, IA

Bank Midwest of Kansas, NA; Lenexa, KS

Bank of Alma; Alma, MI

Bank of Alton; Alton, IL

Bank of America Alaska, NA; Anchorage, AK

Bank of America Arizona; Phoenix, AZ

Bank of America, NT&SA; San Francisco, CA

Bank of America Nevada; Las Vegas, NV

Bank of America Oregon; Portland, OR

Bank of America Texas, NA; Dallas, TX

Bank of America Trust Company of Florida, NA; Boca Raton, FL

Bank of Ashland, Inc.; Ashland, KY

Bank of Augusta; Augusta, AR

Bank of Benton; Benton, KY

Bank of The Bluegrass and Trust Company; Lexington, KY

Bank of Bluffs; Bluffs, IL

Bank of Bolivar; Bolivar, TN

Bank of Boston—Connecticut; Hartford, CT

Bank of Boston—Florida, NA; Palm Beach, FL

Bank of Boulder; Boulder, CO

Bank of Cabot; Cabot, AR

Bank of Cadiz and Trust Company; Cadiz, KY

Bank of California, NA; San Francisco, CA

Bank of Camden; Camden, TN

Bank of Casey; Casey, IL

Bank of Cave City; Cave City, AR

Bank of Charles Town; Charles Town, WV

Bank of Charleston; Charleston, IL

Bank of Chenoa; Chenoa, IL

Bank of Cherry Creek, NA; Denver, CO

Bank of Clarke County; Berryville, VA

Bank of Cleveland; Cleveland, TN

Bank of Commerce; Idaho Falls, ID

Bank of Commerce; Chanute, KS

Bank of Commerce; Greenwood, MS

Bank of Commerce; Milton-Freewater, OR

Bank of Commerce; Fort Worth, TX

Bank of Commerce and Trust Company; Wellington, KS

Bank of Commerce and Trust Company; Crowley, IA

Bank of Commerce and Trust Company; Saint Francisville, LA

Bank of Crockett; Bells, TN

Bank of Danville and Trust Company; Danville, KY

Bank of Dickson; Dickson, TN

Bank of Doniphan; Doniphan, NE

Bank of Douglas County; Castle Rock, CO

Bank of Dwight; Dwight, IL

Bank of Edwardsville; Edwardsville, IL

Bank of Fayetteville, NA; Fayetteville, AR

Bank of Geneva; Geneva, IN

Bank of Gleason; Gleason, TN

Bank of Guam; Agana, GU

Bank of Halls; Halls, TN

Bank of Hanover and Trust Company; Hanover, PA

Bank of Harlan; Harlan, KY

Bank of Harrisburg; Harrisburg, IL

Bank of Herrin; Herrin, IL

Bank of Hollandale; Hollandale, MS

Bank of Huntingdon; Huntingdon, TN

Bank of Illinois in Normal; Normal, IL

Bank of Kansas; Hutchinson, KS

Bank of Kilmichael; Kilmichael, MS

Bank of Lancaster; Kilmarnock, VA

Bank of Lancaster County, NA; Lancaster, PA

Bank of Madison; Madison, NE

Bank of Marion; Marion, VA

Bank of Maroa; Maroa, IL

Bank of Marshall County; Benton, KY

Bank of Maysville; Maysville, KY

Bank of McCrory; McCrory, AR

Bank of McMechen; McMechen, WV

Bank of Mid-Jersey; Bordentown Township, NJ

Bank of Millbrook; Millbrook, NY

Bank of Mississippi; Tupelo, MS

Bank of Mobile; Mobile, AL

Bank of Mondovi; Mondovi, WI

Bank of Montreal Trust Company; New York, NY

Bank of Mt. Carmel; Mount Carmel, IL

Bank of Nashville; Nashville, TN

Bank of New Albany; New Albany, MS

Bank of New Hampshire; Concord, NH

Bank of New Madrid; New Madrid, MO

Bank of New York; New York, NY

Bank of New York (NJ); West Paterson, NJ

Bank of New York Trust Company; White Plains, NY

Bank of New York Trust Company of California; Los Angeles, CA

Bank of New York Trust Company of Florida, NA; Miami, FL

Bank of Newport; Newport, RI

Bank of North Dakota; Bismarck, ND

Bank of Northern Illinois, NA; Waukegan, IL

Bank of Nova Scotia Trust Company of New York; New York, NY

Bank of Oakfield; Oakfield, WI

Bank of O'Fallon; O'Fallon, IL

Bank of Oklahoma, NA; Oklahoma City, OK

Bank of Oklahoma, NA; Tulsa, OK

Bank of Oklahoma, NA; Dallas, TX

Bank of Orleans; Orleans, IN

Bank of the Ozark; Ozark, AR

Bank of Papillion; Papillion, NE

Bank of Perryville; Perryville, MO

Bank of Pontiac; Pontiac, IL

Bank of Putnam County; Cookeville, TN

Bank of Raleigh, Inc.; Beckley, WV

Bank of Rantoul; Rantoul, IL

Bank of Ripley; Ripley, TN

Bank of San Francisco; San Francisco, CA

Bank of Santa Fe; Santa Fe, NM

Bank of Sharon; Sharon, TN

Bank of Smithtown; Smithtown, NY

Bank of the Southwest; Dodge City, KS

Bank of Springfield; Springfield, IL

Bank of Stockton; Stockton, CA

Bank of Sun Prairie; Sun Prairie, WI

Bank of Sunset and Trust Company; Sunset, LA

Bank of Tallassee; Tallassee, AL

Bank of Tazewell County; Tazewell, VA

Bank of Toccoa; Toccoa, GA

Bank of Tokyo Trust Company; New York, NY

Bank of Trenton and Trust Company; Trenton, TN

Bank of Utah; Ogden, UT

Bank of Verona; Verona, WI

Bank of Waldron; Waldron, AR

Bank of Washington; Washington, MO

Bank of Waukegan; Waukegan, IL

Bank of Webb; Webb, MS

Bank of the West; San Francisco, CA

Bank of West Memphis; West Memphis, AR

Bank of Weston; Weston, MO

Bank of White Sulphur Springs; White Sulphur Springs, WV

Bank of Williamsburg; Williamsburg, KY

Bank of Winona; Winona, MS

Bank of Wolcott; Wolcott, IN

Bank of Yazoo City; Yazoo City, MS

Bank One, Arizona, NA; Phoenix, AZ

Bank One, Bloomington-Normal; Bloomington, IL

Bank One, Champaign-Urbana; Champaign, IL

Bank One, Cleveland, NA; Cleveland, OH

Bank One, Colorado, NA; Denver, CO

Bank One, Dayton, NA; Dayton, OH

Bank One, Indianapolis, NA; Indianapolis, IN

Bank One, Lexington, NA; Lexington, KY

Bank One, Lima, NA; Lima, OH

Bank One, Marietta, NA; Marietta, OH

Bank One Ohio Trust Company, NA; Westerville, OH

Bank One, Peoria; Peoria, IL

Bank One, Portsmouth, NA; Portsmouth, OH

Bank One, Quad Cities, NA; Moline, IL

Bank One, Rockford, NA; Rockford, IL

Bank One, Springfield; Springfield, IL

Bank One, Texas, NA; Dallas, TX

Bank One Trust Company; Akron, OH

Bank One Trust Company, NA; Mansfield, OH

Bank One, Utah, NA; Salt Lake City, UT

Bank One, West Virginia, NA, Huntington; Huntington, WV

Bank One, West Virginia, Wheeling, NA; Wheeling, WV

Bank One, Wisconsin Trust Company, NA; Milwaukee, WI

Bank One, Youngstown, NA; Youngstown, OH

Bank South, NA; Atlanta, GA

Bank and Trust Company; Litchfield, IL

Bank and Trust of Puerto Rico; Hato Rey, PR

BankAmerica National Trust Company; New York, NY

BankAmerica State Trust Company; Los Angeles, CA

BankChampaign, NA; Champaign, IL

BankEast Trust Company; Manchester, NH

Bankers Trust Company; Des Moines, IA

Bankers Trust Company; New York, NY

Bankers Trust Company Connecticut, Ltd; Greenwich, CT

Bankers Trust Company New Jersey Limited; Jersey City, NJ

Bankers Trust Company of California, NA; Los Angeles, CA

Bankers Trust Company of Florida, NA; West Palm Beach, FL

Bankers Trust Company of the Southwest; Houston, TX

BankFirst; Knoxville, TN

BankIllinois Trust Company; Champaign, IL

BankOne of Western Kentucky, NA; Hopkinsville, KY

Bankplus; Belzoni, MS

BANKWEST; Goodland, KS

BANKWEST; Saint Francis, KS

BankWest, Inc.; Pierre, SD

Bannister Bank and Trust; Kansas City, MO

Banterra Bank of West Frankfort; West Frankfort, IL

Bar Harbor Banking and Trust Company; Bar Harbor, ME

Baraboo National Bank; Baraboo, WI

Barbour County Bank; Philippi, WV

Barnett Bank of Southeast Georgia, NA; Brunswick, GA

Barnett Banks Trust Company, NA; Jacksonville, FL

Barnett Banks Trust Company, NA; Pensacola, FL

Barnett Banks Trust Company, NA; Tampa, FL

Barretville Bank and Trust Company; Barretville, TN

Bath National Bank; Bath, NY

Bath Savings Trust Company; Bath, ME

Bath State Bank; Bath, IN

Bay Area Bank & Trust; Houston, TX

Bay Bank & Trust Company; Panama City, FL

BayBank; Burlington, MA

Baylake Bank; Sturgeon Bay, WI

Baylake Bank Kewaunee; Kewaunee, WI

Beacon Trust Company; Chatham, NJ

Beatrice National Bank and Trust Company; Beatrice, NE

Beaver Dam Deposit Bank; Beaver Dam, KY

Belmont National Bank; St. Clairsville, OH

Belvidere National Bank and Trust Company; Belvidere, IL

Beneficial National Bank; Wilmington, DE

Bennington State Bank; Salina, KS

Benton County Savings Bank; Norway, IA

Benton County State Bank; Blairstown, IA

Berkeley Federal Bank and Trust, FSB; Palisades Park, DE

Berkshire County Savings Bank; Pittsfield, MA

Bessemer Trust Company; Woodbridge, NJ

Bessemer Trust Company, NA; New York, NY

Bessemer Trust Company of Florida; Palm Beach, FL

Bethany Trust Company; Bethany, MO

Beverly National Bank; Beverly, MA

Beverly Trust Company; Oak Lawn, IL

Billtmore Investors Bank; Lake Forest, IL

Bippus State Bank; Bippus, IN

Blackhawk State Bank; Beloit, WI

Bloomfield State Bank; Bloomfield, IN

Blue Ball National Bank; Blue Ball, PA

Blue Grass Savings Bank; Blue Grass, IA

Blue Ridge Bank and Trust Company; Kansas City, MO

Bluestem National Bank; Fairbury, IL

Boatmen's National Bank of Texas; Austin, TX

Boatmen's Bank of Iowa, NA; Des Moines, IA

Boatmen's Bank of Kansas; Overland Park, KS

Boatmen's Bank of Mid-Missouri; Columbia, MO

Boatmen's Bank of Southern Missouri; Springfield, MO

Boatmen's Bank of Tennessee; Memphis, TN

Boatmen's First National Bank of Amarillo; Amarillo, TX

Boatmen's First National Bank of Kansas City; Kansas City, MO

Boatmen's National Bank of St. Louis; St. Louis, MO

Boatmen's Trust Company; St. Louis, MO

Boatmen's Trust Company—An Oklahoma Trust Company; Oklahoma City, OK

Boatmen's Trust Company of Arkansas; Little Rock, AR

Boatmen's Trust Company of Illinois; Belleville, IL

Boatmen's Trust Company of Illinois; Quincy, IL

Boone Bank & Trust Company; Boone, IA

Boone County National Bank of Columbia; Columbia, MO

Boone National S&LA, FA; Columbia, MO

Borel Bank & Trust Company; San Mateo, CA

Boston Harbor Trust Company, NA; Boston, MA

Boston Private Bank & Trust Company; Boston, MA

Boston Safe Deposit and Trust Company; Boston, MA

Boston Safe Deposit and Trust Company of California; Los Angeles, CA

Boston Safe Deposit and Trust Company of New York; New York, NY

Boulder Valley Bank & Trust; Boulder, CO

Bow Mills Bank and Trust; Bow, NH

Bradford Investment Services Company, Inc.; Reno, NV

Bradford National Bank of Greenville; Greenville, IL

Bradford Trust Company; Nashville, TN

Brady National Bank; Brady, TX

Braintree Savings Bank; Braintree, MA

Branch Banking and Trust Company; Raleigh, NC

Branch Banking and Trust Company of South Carolina; Columbia, SC

Bremen Bank & Trust Company; St. Louis, MO

Brenton Bank, NA; Des Moines, IA

Brenton Bank, NA; Jefferson. IA

Brewery Park Trust; Detroit, MI

Bridgehampton National Bank; Bridgehampton, NY

Bridgeview Bank and Trust Company; Bridgeview, IL

Bright National Bank; Flora, IN

Brinson Trust Company; Chicago, IL

Britton & Koontz First National Bank; Natchez, MS

Broadway National Bank; San Antonio, TX

Brotherhood Bank and Trust Company; Kansas City, KS

Brown Advisory and Trust Company; Baltimore, MD

Brown Brothers Harriman Trust Company of Florida; Naples, FL

Brown Brothers Harriman Trust Company of Texas; Dallas, TX

Brownsville Bank; Brownsville, TN

Bruning State Bank; Bruning, NE

Bryn Mawr Trust Company; Bryn Mawr, PA

BSB Bank & Trust Company; Binghamton, NY

BT Management Trust Company; Johnstown, PA

Bucktail Bank and Trust Company; Williamsport, PA

Buena Vista National Bank of Chester; Chester, IL

Buffalo Savings Bank; Buffalo, IA

Bunkie Bank & Trust Company; Bunkie, LA

Burke & Herbert Bank and Trust Company; Alexandria, VA

Burlington Bank and Trust; Burlington, IA

Burlington County Bank; Burlington, NJ

Burns National Bank of Durango; Durango, CO

Burt Savings Bank; Burt, IA

Busey Bank of McLean County; Le Roy, IL

C

Calcasieu-Marine National Bank; Lake Charles, LA

Caldwell Bank & Trust Company; Columbia, LA

Caldwell Trust Company; Venice, FL

California Central Trust Bank Corporation; Costa Mesa, CA

Callaway Bank; Fulton, MO

Calumet National Bank; Hammond, IN

Calvert Bank; Calvert City, KY

Cambridge Savings Bank; Cambridge, MA

Cambridge Trust Company; Cambridge, MA

Camden National Bank; Camden, ME

Camelback Trust Company; Scottsdale, AZ

Canaan National Bank; Canaan, CT

Canadian State Bank; Yukon, OK

Canandaigua National Bank & Trust Company; Canandaigua, NY

Canterbury Trust Company, Inc.; Birmingham, AL

Canton State Bank; Canton, IL

Cape Ann Savings Bank; Gloucester, MA

Cape Cod Bank and Trust Company; Hyannis, MA

Capital Bank; Miami, FL

Capital Bank of Cape Girardeau County; Cape Girardeau, MO

Capital Bank of Southwest Missouri; Ozark, MO

Capital Bank & Trust; Clayton, MO

Capital City Trust Company; Tallahassee, FL

Capital Guardian Trust Company of Nevada; Reno, NV

Capitol Bank and Trust; Chicago, IL

Carlinville National Bank; Carlinville, IL

Carlsbad National Bank; Carlsbad, NM

Carolina Commercial Bank; Allendale, SC

Carolina First Bank; Greenville, SC

Carolina Southern Bank; Spartanburg, SC

Carroll Bank & Trust; Huntingdon, TN

Carroll County Bank and Trust Company; Westminster, MD

Carroll County State Bank; Carroll, IA

Carroll County Trust Company of Carrollton, Missouri; Carrollton, MO

Carrollton Bank and Trust Company; Carrollton, IL

Carthage Bank; Carthage, MS

Casey County Bank; Liberty, KY

Catahoula-LaSalle Bank; Jonesville, LA

Cavalry Banking—A Federal Savings Bank; Murfreesboro, TN

Cayuga Savings Bank; Auburn, NY

Centier Bank; Highland, IN

Central Bank; Granite City, IL

Central Bank; Monroe, LA

Central Bank; Savannah, TN

Central Bank; Provo, UT

Central Bank & Trust; Fort Worth, TX

Central Bank and Trust Company; Hutchinson, KS

Central Bank and Trust Company; Lexington, KY

Central Carolina Bank & Trust Company; Durham, NC

Central Fidelity National Bank; Richmond, VA

Central Illinois Bank; Champaign, IL

Central National Bank; Junction City, KS

Central National Bank, Canajoharie; Canajoharie, NY

Central National Bank of Alva; Alva, OK

Central National Bank and Trust Company; Attica, IN

Central National Bank & Trust Company of Enid; Enid, OK

Central Pacific Bank; Honolulu, HI

Central State Bank; Elkader, IA

Central State Bank; Muscatine, IA

Central Trust Bank; Jefferson City, MO

Central Trust & Savings Bank; Geneseo, IL

Central Trust & Savings Bank; Cherokee, IA

Centura Bank; Rocky Mount, NC

Century Bank and Trust; Milledgeville, GA

Century Bank and Trust; Coldwater, MI

Century National Bank and Trust Company; Rochester, PA

Chambersburg Trust Company; Chambersburg, PA

Champaign National Bank; Champaign, IL

Champaign National Bank and Trust; Urbana, IL

Chancellor Trust Company; New York, NY

Chaplin State Bank; Chaplin, IL

Charles Schwab Trust Company; San Francisco, CA

Charter National Bank; Taylor, MI

Charter National Bank—Houston; Houston, TX

Charter State Bank; Beebe, AR

Charter Trust Company; Concord, NH

Chase Manhattan Bank, NA; New York, NY

Chase Manhattan Bank USA, Wilmington, DE

Chase Manhattan Bank of Connecticut, NA; Bridgeport, CT

Chase Manhattan Private Bank (Florida); Palm Beach, FL

Chase Manhattan Trust Company of California, NA; San Francisco, CA

Chelsea Savings Bank; Belle Plaine, IA

Chemical Bank, New York, NY

Chemical Bank Delaware; Wilmington, DE

Chemical Bank, FSB; Palm Beach, FL

Chemical Bank and Trust Company; Midland, MI

Chemical Trust Company of California; San Francisco, CA

Chemung Canal Trust Company; Elmira, NY

Cherokee State Bank; Cherokee, IA

Chesapeake Bank; Kilmarnock, VA

Chicago City Bank and Trust Company; Chicago, IL

Chicago Heights National Bank; Chicago Heights, IL

Chickasha Bank & Trust Company; Chickasha, OK

Chittenden Bank; Burlington, VT

Choate, Hall & Stewart; Boston, MA

Christiana Bank & Trust Company; Greenville, DE

Citibank, NA; New York, NY

Citicorp Trust, NA; Los Angeles, CA

Citicorp Trust, NA; Palm Beach, FL

Citizens Bank; Batesville, AR

Citizens Bank; Marianna, FL

Citizens Bank; Mooresville, IN

Citizens Bank; Leon, IA

Citizens Bank; Sac City, IA

Citizens Bank; Hickman, KY

Citizens Bank; Columbia, MS

Citizens Bank; Farmington, NM

Citizens Bank; Carthage, TN

Citizens Bank; Elizabethton, TN

Citizens Bank; Levelland, TX

Citizens Bank of Central Indiana; Bloomington, IN

Citizens Bank of Chatsworth; Chatsworth, IL

Citizens Bank of Clovis; Clovis, NM

Citizens Bank of Eldon; Eldon, MO

Citizens Bank of Illinois; Effingham, IL

Citizens Bank of Jonesboro; Jonesboro, AR

Citizens Bank of Kansas, NA; Kingman, KS

Citizens Bank of Kentucky; Madisonville, KY

Citizens Bank of Maryland; Laurel, MD

Citizens Bank of Philadelphia, Miss.; Philadelphia, MS

Citizens Bank of Southwest Missouri; Nevada, MO

Citizens Bank & Trust; Carlisle, AR

Citizens Bank & Trust; Shawnee, KS

Citizens Bank & Trust; Hazard, KY

Citizens Bank & Trust; Rock Port, MO

Citizens Bank & Trust Company; Van Buren, AR

Citizens Bank & Trust Company; Covington, LA

Citizens Bank & Trust Company; Hutchinson, MN

Citizens Bank & Trust Company; Louisville, MS

Citizens Bank & Trust Company; Marks, MS

Citizens Bank & Trust Company; Chillicothe, MO

Citizens Bank & Trust Company; Okmulgee, OK

Citizens Bank & Trust Company; Palmerton, PA

Citizens Bank & Trust Company; Torrington, WY

Citizens Bank & Trust Company of Baytown, Texas; Baytown, TX

Citizens Bank & Trust Company of Grayson Co; Leitchfield, KY

Citizens Bank & Trust Company of Jackson; Jackson, KY

Citizens Bank & Trust Company of Paducah; Paducah, KY

Citizens Bank & Trust Company in St. Paul; NE

Citizens Bank & Trust Company; Celina, OH

Citizens & Savings Bank; Flint, MI

Citizens Commercial Trust and Savings Bank of Pasadena; Pasadena, CA

Citizens Deposit Bank & Trust, Inc.; Vanceburg, KY

Citizens Exchange Bank; Fairmount, IN

Citizens and Farmers Bank; West Point, VA

Citizens Federal Bank, FSB; Dayton, OH

Citizens First Bank; El Dorado, AR

Citizens First Bank; Fordyce, AR

Citizens First National Bank; Princeton, IL

Citizens FNB of Storm Lake; Storm Lake, IA

Citizens First State Bank; Walnut, IL

Citizens First State Bank; Hartford City, IN

Citizens-Jackson County Bank; Warrensburg, MO

Citizens National Bank; Charles City, IA

Citizens National Bank; Concordia, KS

Citizens National Bank; Fort Scoff, KS

Citizens National Bank; Athens, TN

Citizens National Bank in Independence; Independence, KS

Citizens National Bank of Albion; Albion, IL

Citizens National Bank of Berkeley Springs; Berkeley Springs, WV

Citizens National Bank of Boone-Stratford; Boone, IA

Citizens National Bank of Elkins; Elkins, WV

Citizens National Bank of Evans City; Butler, PA

Citizens National Bank of Evansville; Evansville, IN

Citizens National Bank of Henderson; Henderson, TX

Citizens National Bank of Hope; Hope, AR

Citizens National Bank of Lebanon; Lebanon, KY

Citizens National Bank of Leesburg; Leesburg, FL

Citizens National Bank of Macomb; Macomb, IL

Citizens National Bank of Meridian; Meridian, MS

Citizens National Bank of Meyersdale; Meyersdale, PA

Citizens National Bank of Milam County; Cameron, TX

Citizens National Bank of Norwalk; Norwalk, OH

Citizens National Bank of Paintsville; Paintsville, KY

Citizens National Bank of Paris; Paris, IL

Citizens National Bank of Southern Pennsylvania; Greencastle, PA

Citizens National Bank of Toluca; Toluca, IL

Citizens National Bank and Trust Company; Port Richey, FL

Citizens & Northern Bank; Wellsboro, PA

Citizens Savings Bank; Anamosa, IA

Citizens Savings Bank; Gilman, IA

Citizens Savings Bank; Hawkeye, IA

Citizens Savings Bank and Trust Company; Nashville, TN

Citizens Savings Bank and Trust Company; Saint Johnsbury, VT

Citizens Security Bank & Trust Company; Bixby, OK

Citizens State Bank; Bald Knob, AR

Citizens State Bank; Petersburg, IN

Citizens State Bank; Williamsport, IN

Citizens State Bank; Clarinda, IA

Citizens State Bank; Marathon, IA

Citizens State Bank; Monticello, IA

Citizens State Bank; Oakland, IA

Citizens State Bank; Pocahontas, IA

Citizens State Bank; Postville, IA

Citizens State Bank; Sheldon, IA

Citizens State Bank; Wyoming, IA

Citizens State Bank; Hugoton, KS

Citizens State Bank; Moundridge, KS

Citizens State Bank; Paola, KS

Citizens State Bank; Marshfield, MO

Citizens State Bank; Corrigan, TX

Citizens State Bank; Woodville, TX

Citizens State Bank, Liberal, Kansas; Liberal, KS

Citizens State Bank of Corpus Christi; Corpus Christi, TX

Citizens State Bank of Dickinson, Texas; Dickinson, TX

Citizens State Bank of Lena; Lena, IL

Citizens State Bank of Milford; Milford, IL

Citizens State Bank of New Castle, Indiana; New Castle, IN

Citizens State Bank of Shipman; Shipman, IL

Citizens State Bank & Trust; Fort Atkinson, WI

Citizens State Bank & Trust Company; Ellsworth, KS

Citizens State Bank & Trust Company; Hiawatha, KS

Citizens State Bank & Trust Company; Woodbine, KS

Citizens Trust Bank; Atlanta, GA

Citizens Trust Company; Coudersport, PA

Citizens Trust Company; Providence, RI

Citizens Union Bank; Shelbyville, KY

Citizens-Union Savings Bank; Fall River, MA

City Bank & Trust; Oklahoma City, OK

City Bank and Trust Company; Jackson, MI

City Bank and Trust Company; McMinnville, TN

City Bank and Trust Company of Moberly; Moberly, MO

City National Bank; Beverly Hills, CA

City National Bank of Baton Rouge; Baton Rouge, LA

City National Bank of Charleston; Charleston, WV

City National Bank of Colorado City; Colorado City, TX

City National Bank of Florida; Miami, FL

City National Bank of Fort Smith; Fort Smith, AR

City National Bank of Pittsburg; Pittsburg, KS

City National Bank and Trust Company; Gloversville, NY

City National Bank & Trust Company of Guymon; Guymon, OK

City National Bank & Trust Company of Lawton, Oklahoma; Lawton, OK

City Savings Bank & Trust Company; De Ridder, LA

City State Bank; Central City, IA

Clay City Banking Co; Clay City, IL

Clay County State Bank; Louisville, IL

Clear Lake Bank and Trust Company; Clear Lake, IA

Clearfield Bank & Trust Company; Clearfield, PA

Cleghorn State Bank; Cleghorn, IA

Cleveland Bank and Trust Company; Cleveland, TN

Cleveland State Bank; Cleveland, MS

Clinton Bank; Clinton, KY

Clinton National Bank; Clinton, IA

Coconut Grove Bank; Miami, FL

Cole-Taylor Bank; Chicago, IL

Collinsville Savings Society; Collinsville, CT

Colonial Bank; Des Peres, MO

Colonial Bank of Greenville; Greenville, TX

Colonial National Bank USA; Claymont, DE

Colorado Bank & Trust Company of La Junta; La Junta, CO

Colorado East Bank Trust; Lamar, CO

Colorado National Bank; Denver, CO

Colorado State Bank of Denver; Denver, CO

Columbia County Farmers National Bank; Bloomsburg, PA

Columbian National Bank & Trust Company; Topeka, KS

Columbian Trust Company; Overland Park, KS

Columbus Bank and Trust Company; Columbus, NE

Columbus Junction State Bank; Columbus Junction, IA

Comerica Bank; Detroit, MI

Comerica Bank—California; San Jose, CA

Comerica Bank—Illinois; Chicago, IL

Comerica Bank—Texas; Dallas, TX

Comerica Bank & Trust, FSB; Boca Raton, FL

Commerce Bank; Bloomington, IL

Commerce Bank; El Dorado, KS

Commerce Bank; Virginia Beach, VA

Commerce Bank, NA; Peoria, IL

Commerce Bank, NA; Hays, KS

Commerce Bank of Kansas City, NA; Kansas City, KS

Commerce Bank, NA; Manhattan, KS

Commerce Bank, NA; St. Louis, MO

Commerce Bank, NA; Springfield, MO

Commerce Bank NA; Cherry Hill, NJ

Commerce Bank of Kansas City, NA; Kansas City, MO

Commerce Bank of St. Joseph, NA; St. Joseph, MO

Commerce Bank and Trust; Topeka, KS

Commerce Bank & Trust Company; Worcester, MA

Commercial Bank; Parsons, KS

Commercial Bank; Middlesboro, KY

Commercial Bank; Salem, OR

Commercial Bank; Mason, TX

Commercial Bank; Whitewater, WI

Commercial Bank of New York; New York, NY

Commercial Bank & Trust Company; Monticello, AR

Commercial Bank & Trust Company; Paris, TN

Commercial Banking and Trust Company; Parkersburg, WV

Commercial National Bank in Nacogdoches; Nacogdoches, TX

Commercial National Bank of Beeville; Beeville, TX

Commercial National Bank of Berwyn; Berwyn, IL

Commercial National Bank of Brady; Brady, TX

Commercial National Bank in Shreveport; Shreveport, LA

Commercial Savings Bank; Carroll, IA

Commercial and Savings Bank of St. Clair County; St. Clair, MI

Commercial State Bank & Trust Company; Hoskins, NE

Commercial Trust Company, Inc.; Hato Rey, PR

Commercial Trust Company of Fayette; Fayette, MO

Commercial Trust & Savings Bank; Storm Lake, IA

Commercial Trust & Savings Bank; Mitchell, SD

Commonwealth Bank & Trust Company; Louisville, KY

Community Bank; Hoopeston, IL

Community Bank; Noblesville, IN

Community Bank; Indianola, MS

Community Bank; Longview, TX

Community Bank; Waco, TX

Community Bank, NA; Olean, NY

Community Bank of Bergen County, NJ; Maywood, NJ

Community Bank of South Carolina; Vamville, SC

Community Bank and Trust; Neosho, MO

Community Bank and Trust Company; Montrose, PA

Community Bank & Trust—Habersham; Cornelia, GA

Community Bank & Trust, NA; Olney, IL

Community Banks, NA; Hazleton, PA

Community Banks of Shelby County; Cowden, IL

Community First National Bank; Fargo, ND

Community First National Bank of Fergus Falls; Fergus Falls, MN

Community First National Bank & Trust Company of Dickinson; Dickinson, ND

Community First State Bank; Docorah, IA

Community First State Bank of Huron; Huron, SD

Community National Bank; Derby, VT

Community Savings Bank; Edgewood, IA

Community State Bank; Avilla, IN

Community State Bank; Brook, IN

Community State Bank; Royal Center, IN

Community State Bank; Ankeny, IA

Community State Bank; Tipton, IA

Community Trust; Sioux Falls, SD

Community Trust Bank; Irvington, IL

Community Trust Bank; Choudrant, LA

Compass Bank; Birmingham, AL

Compass Bank; Dallas, TX

Concordia Bank & Trust Company; Vidalia, LA

Condon National Bank of Coffeyville; Coffeyville, KS

Consolidated Bank and Trust Company; Richmond, VA

Constitution Trust Company; Dover, NH

Continental Bank New York Trust Company; New York, NY

Converse County Bank; Douglas, WY

Cordele Banking Company; Cordele, GA

CoreStates Bank; NA; Philadelphia, PA

CoreStates Bank of Delaware, NA; Wilmington, DE

CoreStates/New Jersey National Bank; Pennington, NJ

Cornbelt Bank & Trust Company; Pittsfield, IL

Corsicana National Bank; Corsicana, TX

Cortland Savings and Banking Company; Cortland, OH

Corydon State Bank; Corydon, IA

Cosmopolitan Bank and Trust; Chicago, IL

Cotton Exchange Bank; Kennett, MO

Country Club Bank, NA; Kansas City, MO

County Bank; Greenwood, SC

County National Bank; Clearfield, PA

Cozad State Bank and Trust Company; Cozad, NE

Crawford County State Bank; Robinson, IL

Crawford County Trust and Savings Bank; Denison, IA

Cresco Union Savings Bank; Cresco, IA

Crestar Bank; Washington, DC

Crestar Bank; Bethesda, MD

Crestar Bank; Richmond, VA

Croghan Colonial Bank; Fremont, OH

Cross County Bank; Wynne, AR

Crossroads Bank; Effingham, IL

Cumberland County Bank; Crossville, TN

Cumberland Valley National Bank & Trust Company; London, KY

Cupertino National Bank; Cupertino, CA

Custer Federal Savings and Loan Association; Broken Bow, NE

Custodial Trust Company; Princeton, NJ

Cynthiana State Bank; Cynthiana, IN

D

Dacotah Bank; Aberdeen, SD

Dacotah Bank—Webster; Webster, SD

Dai-ichi Kangyo Bank of California; Los Angeles, CA

Dai-ichi Kangyo Trust Company of New York; New York, NY

Daiwa Bank Trust Company; New York, NY

Danielson Trust Company; San Diego, CA

Danvers Savings Bank; Danvers, MA

Danville State Savings Bank; Danville, IA

Darby Bank and Trust Co; Vidalia, GA

Dauphin Deposit Bank and Trust Company; Harrisburg, PA

Davis County Savings Bank; Bloomfield, IA

Davis Trust Company; Elkins, WV

De Witt Bank and Trust Company; De Witt, AR

De Witt Bank and Trust Company; De Witt, IA

Decatur Bank and Trust Company; Decatur, IN

DeKalb County Bank and Trust Company; Alexandria, TN

Del Norte Federal Savings and Loan Association; Del Norte, CO

Del Rio Bank and Trust Company; Del Rio, TX

Delaware Charter Guarantee and Trust Company; Wilmington, DE

Delaware County Bank and Trust Company; Delaware, OH

Delaware National Bank of Delhi; Delhi, NY

Delaware Trust Company; Wilmington, DE

Delta National Bank & Trust Company of Florida; Miami, FL

Delta National Bank & Trust Company of New York; New York, NY

DeMotte State Bank; DeMotte, IN

Dent County Bank and Trust Company; Salem, MO

Denver Savings Bank; Denver, IA

Deposit Bank of Carlisle; Carlisle, KY

Deposit Guaranty National Bank; Jackson, MS

Dermott State Bank; Dermott, AR

Deseret Trust Company; Salt Lake City, UT

Deseret Trust Company of California; Los Angeles, CA

Devon Bank; Chicago, IL

Dickinson County Savings Bank; Milford, IA

Dime Bank; Hawley, PA

Diversified Trust Company, Inc.; Memphis, TN

Douglas County Bank; Lawrence, KS

Douglas County Bank and Trust Co; Omaha, NE

Downers Grove National Bank; Downers Grove, IL

Downingtown National Bank; Downingtown, PA

Dreyfus Trust Company; Uniondale, NY

Drovers and Mechanics Bank; York, PA

Du Quoin National Bank; Du Quoin, IL

Dubuque Bank and Trust Company; Dubuque, IA

Duck Hill Bank; Duck Hill, MS

Dukes County Savings Bank; West Tisbury, MA

Dulaney National Bank of Marshall; Marshall, IL

Dumas State Bank; Dumas, AR

DuPage National Bank; West Chicago, IL

Dupont State Bank; Dupont, IN

Durant Bank and Trust Company; Durant, OK

Dyer, Robertson and Lamme Trust Company; Houston, TX

E

Eagle Bank; Williamstown, KY

Eagle Bank and Trust; Little Rock, AR

Earlham Savings Bank; West Des Moines, IA

East Texas National Bank of Palestine; Palestine, TX

Eastern Bank and Trust Company; Salem, MA

Eastern Heights State Bank of Saint Paul; Saint Paul, MN

Eaton National Bank and Trust Company; Eaton, OH

Edgar County Bank and Trust Company; Paris, IL

Effingham State Bank; Effingham, IL

Elberfeld State Bank; Elberfeld, IN

Elgin State Bank; Elgin, IA

Elk Horn Bank and Trust Company; Arkadelphia, AR

Elkton Bank and Trust Company; Elkton, KY

Elliott State Bank; Jacksonville, IL

Elm Hill Trust; Nashville, TN

Elyria Savings and Trust National Bank; Elyria, OH

Emmet County State Bank; Estherville, IA

Empire National Bank of Traverse City; Traverse City, MI

Emporia State Bank and Trust Company; Emporia, KS

Emprise Bank; Wichita, KS

Emprise Bank, NA; Hays, KS

English State Bank; English, IN

Ennis State Bank; Ennis, TX

Enterprise Bank and Trust Company; Lowell, MA

Ephrata National Bank; Ephrata, PA

Equitable Trust Company; Nashville, TN

Evangeline Bank and Trust Company; Ville Platte, LA

Evergreen Bank, NA; Glens Falls, NY

Exchange Bank; Santa Rosa, CA

Exchange Bank and Trust Company; Perry, OK

Exchange National Bank; Marysville, KS

Exchange National Bank of Jefferson City; Jefferson City, MO

Exchange National Bank & Trust Company of Ardmore; Ardmore, OK

Exchange National Bank & Trust Company of Atchison; Atchison, KS

Exchange State Bank; Adair, IA

Exchange State Bank; Collins, IA

Exchange State Bank; Exira, IA

Exchange State Bank; Springville, IA

Exterbank; New York, NY

F

F&M Bank—Hallmark; Springfield, VA

F&M Bank and Trust Company; Tulsa, OK

F&M Bank—Peoples; Warrenton, VA

F&M Bank—Blakeley; Ranson, WV

F&M Bank—Keyser, Inc,; Keyser, WV

F&M Bank—Lancaster; Lancaster, WI

F&M Bank—Martinsburg, Inc.; Martinsburg, WV

F&M Bank—Winchester; Winchester, VA

Factory Point National Bank of Manchester Center; Manchester Center, VT

Fairbank State Bank; Fairbank, IA

Fairfax State Savings Bank; Fairfax, IA

Fairfield National Bank; Fairfield, IL

Fairmount State Bank; Fairmount, IN

Falls City National Bank; Falls City, TX

Farmer City State Bank; Farmer City, IL

Farmers Bank; Greenwood, AR

Farmers Bank; Frankfort, IN

Farmers Bank; Clay, KY

Farmers Bank and Capital Trust Company; Frankfort, KY

Farmers Bank and Capital Trust Company; Versailles, KY

Farmers Bank of Lynchburg; Lynchburg, TN

Farmers Bank of Maryland; Annapolis, MD

Farmers Bank and Trust; Atwood, KS

Farmers Bank and Trust Company; Blytheville, AR

Farmers Bank and Trust Company; Clarksville, AR

Farmers Bank and Trust Company; Magnolia, AR

Farmers Bank and Trust Company; Bardstown, KY

Farmers Bank and Trust Company; Marion, KY

Farmers Bank and Trust Company; Nebraska City, NE

Farmers Bank and Trust Company;
Princeton, KY

Farmers Deposit Bank; Eminence, KY

Farmers Deposit Bank; Middleburg, KY

Farmers and Drovers Bank; Council
Grove, KS

Farmers First Bank; Lititz, PA

Farmers and Mechanics Bank; Galesburg,
IL

Farmers and Mechanics National Bank;
Frederick, MD

Farmers and Merchants Bank; Des Arc,
AR

Farmers and Merchants Bank; Reyno, AR

Farmers and Merchants Bank; Stuttgart,
AR

Farmers and Merchants Bank; Summer-
ville, GA

Farmers and Merchants Bank; Boswell, IN

Farmers and Merchants Bank; Hunter-
town, IN

Farmers and Merchants Bank; Hannibal,
MO

Farmers and Merchants Bank; Imperial,
NE

Farmers and Merchants Bank; Honesdale,
PA

Farmers and Merchants Bank; Huron, SD

Farmers and Merchants Bank; Clarksville,
TN

Farmers and Merchants Bank; Dyer, TN

Farmers and Merchants Bank; Timberville,
VA

Farmers and Merchants Bank; Reedsburg,
WI

Farmers and Merchants Bank; Tomah,
WI

Farmers and Merchants Bank of Carlinville; Carlinville, IL

Farmers and Merchants Bank of Fort
Branch; Fort Branch, IN

F&M Bank of Rochester, Indiana; Rochester, IN

Farmers and Merchants Bank and Trust;
Burlington, IA

Farmers and Merchants Bank and Trust;
Hagerstown, MD

Farmers and Merchants Bank and Trust;
Marinette, WI

Farmers-Merchants Bank and Trust Company; Breaux Bridge, LA

F&M Bank and Trust of Watertown; Watertown, SD

F&M National Bank of Bridgeton;
Bridgeton, NJ

Farmers-Merchants National Bank of Paxton; Paxton, IL

Farmers and Merchants Savings Bank;
Lone Tree, IA

Farmers and Merchants Savings Bank;
Manchester, IA

Farmers and Merchants Savings Bank;
Waukon, IA

Farmers and Merchants State Bank; Lo-
gansport, IN

Farmers and Merchants State Bank; Neola,
IA

Farmers and Merchants State Bank; Win-
terset, IA

Farmers and Merchants State Bank of
Bushnell; Bushnell, IL

F&M State Bank of Virden, Illinois; Virden, IL

F&M Trust Company of Chambersburg;
Chambersburg, PA

F&M Trust Company of Long Beach;
Long Beach, CA

Farmers National Bank of Cynthiana;
Cynthiana, KY

Farmers National Bank of Danville; Danville, KY

Farmers National Bank of Geneseo; Geneseo, IL

Farmers National Bank of Lebanon; Lebanon, KY

Farmers National Bank of Oberlin; Oberlin, KS

Farmers National Bank of Prophetstown;
Prophetstown, IL

Farmers Savings Bank; Fostoria, IA

Farmers Savings Bank; Kalona, IA

Farmers Savings Bank; Martelle, IA

Farmers Savings Bank; Mitchellville, IA

Farmers Savings Bank; Oskaloosa, IA

Farmers Savings Bank; Pierson, IA

Farmers Savings Bank; Princeton, IA

Farmers Savings Sank; Remsen, IA

Farmers Savings Bank, Walford IA

Farmers Savings Bank, West Union, IA

Farmers Savings Bank, Wever, IA

Farmers Savings Bank and Trust—Traer; Traer, IA

Farmers Savings Bank and Trust—Vinton; Vinton, IA

Farmers State Bank; Pittsfield, IL

Farmers State Bank; Brookston, IN

Farmers State Bank; Lagrange, IN

Farmers State Bank; Liberty, IN

Farmers State Bank; Losantville, IN

Farmers State Bank; Mentone, IN

Farmers State Bank; New Ross, IN

Farmers State Bank; Sweetser, IN

Farmers State Bank; Algona, IA

Farmers State Bank; Hawarden, IA

Farmers State Bank; Jesup, IA

Farmers State Bank; Keosauqua, IA

Farmers State Bank; Marcus, IA

Farmers State Bank; Marion, IA

Farmers State Bank; Merrill, IA

Farmers State Bank; Sturgis, KY

Farmers State Bank of Brush; Brush, CO

Farmers State Bank of Fort Morgan; Fort Morgan, CO

Farmer's State Bank of Palestine; Palestine, IL

Farmers State Bank of Sublette; Sublette, IL

Farmers State Bank and Trust Company; Jacksonville, IL

Farmers State Bank and Trust Company; Mount Sterling, IL

Farmers State Bank and Trust Company; Aurora, NE

Farmers State Bank and Trust Company; Lexington, NE

Farmers State Bank & Trust Company of Superior; Superior, NE

Farmers State Savings Bank; Independence, IA

Farmers and Traders Bank of California, MO.; California, MO

Farmers and Traders Savings Bank; Bancroft, IA

Farmers Trust Bank; Lebanon, PA

Farmers Trust Company; Carlisle, PA

Farmers Trust and Savings Bank; Buffalo Center, IA

Farmers Trust and Savings Bank; Spencer, IA

Farmers Trust and Savings Bank; Williamsburg, IA

Farmers Union Bank; Ripley, TN

Fauquier Bank; Warrenton, VA

Federal Trust Bank, a FSB; Winter Park, FL

Federated Bank; Onarga, IL

Fidelity Federal Bank, a FSB; Glendale, CA

Fidelity Management Trust Company; Boston, MA

Fidelity National Bank; Atlanta, GA

Fidelity State Bank; Garden City, KS

Fidelity State Bank and Trust Company; Dodge City, KS

Fidelity Trust Company; Salt Lake City, UT

Fiduciary Trust Company; Boston, MA

Fiduciary Trust Company InterNational; New York, NY

Fiduciary Trust InterNational of California; Los Angeles, CA

Fiduciary Trust InterNational of the South; Miami, FL

Fifth Avenue Trust; New York, NY

Fifth Third Bank; Lexington, KY

Fifth Third Bank; Cincinnati, OH

Fifth Third Bank; Piqua, OH

Fifth Third Bank; Toledo, OH

Fifth Third Bank of Central Indiana; Indianapolis, IN

Fifth Third Bank of Columbus; Columbus, OH

Fifth Third Bank of Northern Kentucky, Inc.; Florence, KY

Fifth Third Trust Co. and Savings Bank, FSB; Naples, FL

Financial Federal Trust and Savings Bank of Olympia Fields; Olympia Fields, IL

First Alabama Bank; Birmingham, AL

First American Bank; Dundee, IL

First American Bank; Fort Dodge, IA

First American Bank; Webster City, IA

First American Bank; Bryan, TX

First American Bank and Trust Company; Athens, GA

First American Bank and Trust Co; Fort Atkinson, WI

First American Bank Valley; Grand Forks, ND

First American Bank West; Minot, ND

First American Bank Wisconsin; Menomonie, WI

First American Trust Company; Santa Ana, CA

First American Trust Company, NA; Nashville, TN

First American Trust Company of Minnesota; Saint Cloud, MN

First Bank; O'Fallon, IL

First Bank; McComb, MS

First Bank; Chesterfield, MO

First Bank; Troy, NC

First Bank; Groveton, TX

First Bank (NA); Milwaukee, WI

First Bank Kansas; Salina, KS

First Bank, NA; Chicago, IL

First Bank, NA; Minneapolis, MN

First Bank of the Americas; New York, NY

First Bank of Arkansas; Jonesboro, AR

First Bank of Berne; Berne, IN

First Bank of Huntingburg; Huntingburg, IN

First Bank of Schaumburg; Schaumburg, IL

First Bank of South Dakota (NA); Sioux Falls, SD

First Bank and Trust; Sullivan, IN

First Bank and Trust; Rock Rapids, IA

First Bank and Trust; Spirit Lake, IA

First Bank and Trust; Beaumont, TX

First Bank and Trust; Cleveland, TX

First Bank and Trust; Menomonie, WI

First Bank and Trust Company; Glidden, IA

First Bank and Trust Company; Cozad, NE

First Bank and Trust Company; Duncan, OK

First Bank and Trust Company; Perry, OK

First Bank and Trust Company of Murphysboro; Murphysboro, IL

First Bank and Trust Company of Princeton, KY; Princeton, KY

First Bank and Trust East Texas; Lufkin, TX

First Bank and Trust of Clarendon; Clarendon, TX

First Bankers Trust Company, NA; Quincy, IL

First Banking Center—Burlington; Burlington, WI

First Bulloch Bank and Trust Company; Statesboro, GA

First Busey Trust and Investment Company; Urbana, IL

First Central State Bank; De Witt, IA

First Charter National Bank; Concord, NC

First Citizens Bank, Hardin County; Elizabethtown, KY

First Citizens Bank, NA; Michigan City, IN

First Citizens Bank of Hohenwald; Hohenwald, TN

First Citizens Bank and Trust Company; Raleigh, NC

First Citizens Bank & Trust Company of South Carolina; Columbia, SC

First Citizens National Bank; Mansfield, PA

First Citizens National Bank of Dyersburg; Dyersburg, TN

First Citizens State Bank; Terre Haute, IN

First Citizens State Bank of Whitewater, Wisconsin; Whitewater, WI

First City Bank; Murfreesboro, TN

First City Bank and Trust Company; Hopkinsville, KY

First Coleman National Bank of Coleman; Coleman, TX

First Colonial Trust Company; Oak Park, IL

First Columbia Bank and Trust Company; Bloomsburg, PA

First Commercial Bank; Birmingham, AL

First Commercial Bank; Chicago, IL

First Commercial Trust Company, NA; Little Rock, AR

First Commonwealth Trust Company; Indiana, PA

First Community Bank; Lynchburg, VA

First Community Bank, Inc.; Bluefield, WV

First Community Bank of Bedford County; Shelbyville, TN

First Community Bank and Trust; Franklin, IN

First County Bank; Stamford, CT

First Dakota National Bank; Yankton, SD

First Exchange Bank; Mannington, WV

First and Farmers Bank of Somerset, Inc.; Somerset, KY

First Farmers Bank and Trust; Converse, IN

First F&M National Bank of Columbia; Columbia, TN

First Farmers State Bank; Sullivan, IN

First Farmers State Bank of Minier; Minier, IL

First Federal Bank of California; Santa Monica, CA

First Federal Savings Bank; Clarksville, TN

First Federal Savings Bank of the Midwest; Storm Lake, IA

First Fidelity Bank, NA; New Haven, CT

First Fidelity Bank, NA; Stamford, CT

First Fidelity Bank, NA; Elkton, MD

First Fidelity Bank, NA; Norman, OK

First Financial Bank of Mississippi County; East Prairie, MO

First Financial Trust Company; Albuquerque, NM

First Financial Trust, NA; Framingham, MA

First Guaranty Bank & Trust Company of Jacksonville; Jacksonville, FL

First Hawaiian Bank; Honolulu, HI

First Independent Bank; Vancouver, WA

First InterNational Bank & Trust; Fargo, ND

First InterNational Bank Northwest Region; Boise, ID

First Interstate Bank Northwest Region; Kalispell, MT

First Interstate Bank Northwest Region; Portland, OR

First Interstate Bank Northwest Region; Seattle, WA

First Interstate Bank of Arizona, NA; Phoenix, AZ

First Interstate Bank of Commerce; Billings, MT

First Interstate Bank of Commerce; Sheridan, WV

First Interstate Bank of Denver, NA; Denver, CO

First Interstate Bank of Nevada, NA; Las Vegas, NV

First Interstate Bank of New Mexico, NA; Santa Fe, NM

First Interstate Bank of Texas, NA; Houston, TX

First Interstate Bank of Utah, NA; Salt Lake City, UT

First Interstate Bank of Wyoming, NA; Casper, WY

First Jacksonville Bank and Trust; Jacksonville, AR

First Kansas Bank & Trust Company; Gardner, KS

First-Knox National Bank of Mount Vernon; Mount Vernon, OH

First Knoxville Rank; Knoxville, TN

First Liberty National Bank; Liberty, TX

First Merchants Bank, NA; Muncie, IN

First Mid-Illinois Bank & Trust, NA; Mattoon, IL

First Midwest Trust Company, NA; Joliet, IL

First NH Investment Service; Manchester, NH

First Nashua State Bank; Nashua, IA

First National Bank; Brewton, AL

First National Bank; Paragould, AR

First National Bank; Searcy, AR

First National Bank; La Jolla, CA

First National Bank; Fort Collins, CO

First National Bank; Chicago Heights, IL

First National Bank; Vandalia, IL

First National Bank; Cloverdale, IN

First National Bank; Kokomo, IN

First National Bank; Missouri Valley, IA

First National Bank; Abilene, KS

First National Bank; Goodland, KS

First National Bank; Orangeburg, SC

First National Bank; Marshall, TX

First National Bank; Waupaca, WI

First National Bank in Alamogordo; Alamogordo, NM

First National Bank in Amboy; Amboy, IL

First National Bank—Ames; Ames, IA

First National Bank in Blytheville; Blytheville, AR

First National Bank in Brookings; Brookings, SD

First National Bank in Cameron; Cameron, TX

First National Bank in Carlyle; Carlyle, IL

First National Bank, Cedar Rapids; Cedar Rapids, IA

First National Bank, Christiansburg, VA; Christiansburg, VA

First National Bank in De Kalb; De Kalb, IL

First National Bank in Fairfield; Fairfield, IA

First National Bank in Graham; Graham, TX

First National Bank in Green Forest; Green Forest, AR

First National Bank—Iowa City, Iowa City, IA

First National Bank in Lamar; Lamar, CO

First National Bank in Le Mars; Le Mars, IA

First National Bank in Manitowoc; Manitowoc, WI

First National Bank in Mansfield; Mansfield, LA

First National Bank in Massillon; Massillon, OH

First National Bank in New Hampton; New Hampton, IA

First National Bank in Newton; Newton, IL

First National Bank in Olney; Olney, IL

First National Bank in Osceola; Osceola, AR

First National Bank in Peru; Peru, IL

First National Bank in Port Lavaca; Port Lavaca, TX

First National Bank in Pratt; Pratt, KS

First National Bank in Robinson; Robinson, IL

First National Bank in Ronceverte; Ronceverte, WV

First National Bank in Sioux Falls; Sioux Falls, SD

First National Bank in Sweetwater, Sweetwater, TX

First National Bank in Taylorville; Taylorville, IL

First National Bank of Abilene; Abilene, TX

First National Bank of Absecon; Absecon, NJ

First National Bank of Anchorage; Anchorage, AK

First National Bank of Artesia; Artesia, NM

First National Bank of Atmore; Atmore, AL

First National Bank of Bar Harbor; Bar Harbor, ME

First National Bank of Barry; Barry, IL

First National Bank of Bay City—A Norwest Bank; Bay City, TX

First National Bank of Beardstown; Beardstown, IL

First National Bank of Berryville; Berryville, AR

First National Bank of Berwick; Berwick, PA

First National Bank of Blue Island; Blue Island, IL

First National Bank of Bluefield; Bluefield, WV

First National Bank of Boston; Boston, MA

First National Bank of Bradford County; Towanda, PA

First National Bank of Brooksville; Brooksville, KY

First National Bank of Brownfield; Brownfield, TX

First National Bank of Bryan; Bryan, TX

First National Bank of Buffalo; Buffalo, WY

First National Bank of Carrollton; Carrollton, KY

First National Bank of Central Illinois; Springfield, IL

First National Bank of Chester; Chester, WV

First National Bank of Chicago; Chicago, IL

First National Bank of Chrisman; Chrisman, IL

First National Bank of Clarksdale; Clarksdale, MS

First National Bank of Cleburne County; Heber Springs, AR

First National Bank of Clifton Forge; Clifton Forge, VA

First National Bank of Clovis; Clovis, NM

First National Bank of Commerce; New Orleans, LA

First National Bank of Conway County; Morrilton, AR

First National Bank of Cortland; Cortland, NY

First National Bank of Crawford County; Van Buren, AR

First National Bank of Crossett; Crossett, AR

First National Bank of Damariscotta; Damariscotta, ME

First National Bank of Danville; Danville, IL

First National Bank of De Witt; De Witt, AR

First National Bank of Decatur; Decatur, IL

First National Bank of Denham Springs; Denham Springs, LA

First National Bank of Dona Ana County; Las Cruces, NM

First National Bank of Dwight; Dwight, IL

First National Bank of Eastern Arkansas; Forrest City, AR

First National Bank of El Campo; El Campo, TX

First National Bank of El Dorado; El Dorado, AR

First National Bank of Eldorado; Eldorado, TX

First National Bank of Elmer; Elmer, NJ

First National Bank of Evergreen Park; Evergreen Park, IL

First National Bank of Farmington; Farmington, NM

First National Bank of Florence; Florence, AL

First National Bank of Fort Smith; Fort Smith, AR

First National Bank of Fort Stockton; Fort Stockton, TX

First National Bank of Fredericksburg; Fredericksburg, PA

First National Bank of Gainesville; Gainesville, GA

First National Bank of Greencastle; Greencastle, PA

First National Bank of Greenville; Greenville, AL

First National Bank of Griffin; Griffin, GA

First National Bank of Hampton; Hampton, IA

First National Bank of Hartford; Hartford, WI

First National Bank of Holmes County; Lexington, MS

First National Bank of Hope; Hope, AR

First National Bank of Hope; Hope, NJ

First National Bank of Houma; Houma, LA

First National Bank of the Hudson Valley; Poughkeepsie, NY

First National Bank of Huntington; Huntington, IN

First National Bank of Huntsville; Huntsville, TX

First National Bank of Hutchinson; Hutchinson, KS

First National Bank of Illinois; Lansing, IL

First National Bank of Ipswich; Ipswich, MA

First National Bank of Jacksonville; Jacksonville, TX

First National Bank of Joliet; Joliet, IL

First National Bank of Kansas; Shawnee Mission, KS

First National Bank of La Grange; La Grange, IL

First National Bank of La Grange; La Grange, TX

First National Bank of Lafayette; Lafayette, LA

First National Bank of Lake Charles; Lake Charles, LA

First National Bank of Lamesa; Lamesa, TX

First National Bank of Lawrence County at Walnut Ridge; Walnut Ridge, AR

First National Bank of Liberal; Liberal, KS

First National Bank of Litchfield; Litchfield, CT

First National Bank of Lockport; Lockport, IL

First National Bank of Long Island; Glen Head, NY

First National Bank of Longmont; Longmont, CO

First National Bank of Magnolia; Magnolia, AR

First National Bank of Maryland; Baltimore, MD

First National Bank of Mayfield; Mayfield, KY

First National Bank of McGehee; McGehee, AR

First National Bank of McGregor; McGregor, TX

First National Bank of McMinnville; McMinnville, TN

First National Bank of Mifflintown; Mifflintown, PA

First National Bank of Mineola; Mineola, TX

First National Bank of Monterey; Monterey, IN

First National Bank of Mount Dora; Mount Dora, FL

First National Bank of Mt. Pulaski; Mount Pulaski, IL

First National Bank of Muscatine; Muscatine, IA

First National Bank of Newman Grove; Newman Grove, NE

First National Bank of North Dakota; Grand Forks, ND

First National Bank of Nowata; Nowata, OK

First National Bank of Oelwein; Oelwein, IA

First National Bank of Ogden; Ogden, IL

First National Bank of Ohio; Akron, OH

First National Bank of Olathe; Olathe, KS

First National Bank of Omaha; Omaha, NE

First National Bank of Oneida; Oneida, TN

First National Bank of Ottawa; Ottawa, IL

First National Bank of Paintsville; Paintsville, KY

First National Bank of Palmerton; Palmerton, PA

First National Bank of Pana; Pana, IL

First National Bank of Pennsylvania; Hermitage, PA

First National Bank of Phillips County; Helena, AR

First National Bank of Pipestone; Pipestone, MN

First National Bank of Platteville; Platteville, WI

First National Bank of Port Allegany; Port Allegany, PA

First National Bank of Portland; Portland, IN

First National Bank of Portsmouth; Portsmouth, NH

First National Bank of Raymond; Raymond, IL

First National Bank of Reidsville; Reidsville, NC

First National Bank of Reynoldsville; Reynoldsville, PA

First National Bank of Rochester; Rochester, NY

First National Bank of St. Marys; St. Marys, WV

First National Bank of San Benito; San Benito, TX

First National Bank of Santa Fe; Santa Fe, NM

First National Bank of Seymour; Seymour, TX

First National Bank of Shelby; Shelby, NC

First National Bank of Shelbyville; Shelbyville, TN

First National Bank of Slippery Rock; Slippery Rock, PA

First National Bank of Smith Center; Smith Center, KS

First National Bank of South Carolina; Holly Hill, SC

First National Bank of South Miami; South Miami, FL

First National Bank of Southwestern Ohio; Hamilton, OH

First National Bank of Springdale; Springdale, AR

First National Bank of Sterling—Rock Falls; Sterling, IL

First National Bank of Sullivan; Sullivan, IL

First National Bank of Talladega; Talladega, AL

First National Bank of Temple; Temple, TX

First National Bank of Three Rivers; Three Rivers, MI

First National Bank of Tullahoma; Tullahoma, TN

First National Bank of Warsaw; Warsaw, IN

First National Bank of Washington; Washington, KS

First National Bank of Waverly; Waverly, IA

First National Bank of Weatherford; Weatherford, TX

First National Bank of West Chester; West Chester, PA

First National Bank of West Point; West Point, GA

First National Bank of West Point; West Point, MS

First National Bank of West Texas; Hale Center, TX

First National Bank of West Union; West Union, IA

First National Bank of Winfield; Winfield, KS

First National Bank of Wynne; Wynne, AR

First National Bank of Wyoming; Laramie, WY

First National Bank of York; York, NE

First National Bank of Zanesville; Zanesville, OH

First National Bank, Torrington; Torrington, WY

First National Bank and Trust; Osawatomie, KS

First National Bank and Trust; Phillipsburg, KS

First National Bank and Trust; London, KY

First National Bank and Trust; Monroe, WI

First National Bank and Trust Company; Louisville, GA

First National Bank and Trust Company; Georgetown, KY

First National Bank and Trust Company; Columbia, MO

First National Bank and Trust Company; Falls City, NE

First National Bank and Trust Company; Minden, NE

First National Bank and Trust Company; Asheboro, NC

First National Bank and Trust Company; Ponca City, OK

First National Bank and Trust Co; Waynesboro, PA

First National Bank and Trust Company; Athens, TN

First National Bank and Trust Company in Aurora; Aurora, NE

First National Bank & Trust Company, Carbondale, Carbondale, IL

First National Bank & Trust Company, Chickasha, Chickasha, OK

First National Bank & Trust Company in Clinton; Clinton, OK

First National Bank & Trust Company in Gibson City; Gibson City, IL

First National Bank & Trust Company in Larned; Larned, KS

First National Bank & Trust Company of Ada; Ada, OK

First National Bank & Trust Company of Ardmore; Ardmore, OK

First National Bank & Trust Company of Baraboo; Baraboo, WI

First National Bank & Trust Company of Beatrice; Beatrice, NE

First National Bank & Trust Company of Beloit; Beloit, WI

First National Bank & Trust Company of Bottineau; Bottineau, ND

First National Bank & Trust Company of Broken Arrow; Broken Arrow, OK

First National Bank & Trust Company of Clinton; Clinton, IL

First National Bank & Trust Company of Corbin; Corbin, KY

First National Bank & Trust Company of Junction City; Junction City, KS

First National Bank & Trust Company of McAlester; McAlester, OK

First National Bank & Trust Company of Miami; Miami, OK

First National Bank & Trust Company of Mountain Home; Mountain Home, AR

First National Bank & Trust Company of Newtown; Newtown, PA

First National Bank & Trust Company of Okmulgee; Okmulgee, OK

First National Bank & Trust Company of Rochelle; Rochelle, IL

First National Bank & Trust Company of the Treasure Coast; Stuart, FL

First National Bank & Trust Company of Vinita; Vinita, OK

First National Bank & Trust Company of Westherford; Weatherford, OK

First National Bank & Trust Company of Williston; Williston, ND

First National Bank & Trust of Syracuse; Syracuse, NE

First National Bank, Valparaiso; Valparaiso, IN

First National Bank in West Memphis; West Memphis, AR

First National Trust Bank; Sunbury, PA

First and Ocean National Bank; Newburyport, MA

First of America Bank—Indiana; Indianapolis, IN

First of America Bank—Indiana; La Porte, IN

First of America Bank—Michigan, NA; Kalamazoo, MI

First of America Trust Company; Peoria, IL

First Ozark National Bank; Flippin, AR

First Parke State Bank; Rockville, IN

First & Peoples Bank, Springfield, Springfield, KY

First & Peoples Bank and Trust Company; Russell, KY

First Premier Bank, NA; Sioux Falls, SD

First Savings Bank of Perkasie; Perkasie, PA

First Security Bank; Searcy, AR

First Security Bank; Batesville, MS

First Security Bank of Bozeman; Bozeman, MT

First Security Bank of Idaho, NA; Boise, ID

First Security Bank of New Mexico, NA; Albuquerque, NM

First Security Bank of Utah, NA; Salt Lake City, UT

First Security Bank of Wyoming; Rock Springs, WY

First Security Bank & Trust; Charles City, IA

First Security Bank and Trust Company; Norton, KS

First Security Bank & Trust of Miles City; Miles City, MT

First Security Savings Bank, FSB; Bloomfield Hills, MI

First Security Trust Company; Boca Raton, FL

First Security Trust Company; Tucumcari, NM

First Security Trust Company of Nevada; Las Vegas, NV

First Source Bank; South Bend, IN

First Springfield Bank & Trust; Illiopolis, IL

First State Bank; Atwood, IL

First State Bank; Mendota, IL

First State Bank; Brazil, IN

First State Bank; Belmond, IA

First State Bank; Britt, IA

First State Bank; Brunsville, IA

First State Bank; Greene, IA

First State Bank; Hawarden, IA

First State Bank; Ida Grove, IA

First State Bank; Manchester, IA

First State Bank; Nora Springs, IA

First State Bank; Riceville, IA

First State Bank; Sioux Rapids, IA

First State Bank; Sumner, IA

First State Bank; Webster City, IA

First State Bank; Junction City, KS

First State Bank; Norton, KS

First State Bank; Holly Springs, MS

First State Bank; Waynesboro, MS

First State Bank; Gothenburg, NE

First State Bank; Scottsbluff, NE

First State Bank; Brownsville, TN

First State Bank; Athens, TX

First State Bank; Celeburne, TX

First State Bank; Dimmitt, TX

First State Bank; Monahans, TX

First State Bank; Spearman, TX

First State Bank; Danville, VA

First State Bank; Barboursville, WV

First State Bank, Bourbon, Indiana; Bourbon, IN

First State Bank, Conrad; Conrad, IA

First State Bank, NA; Odessa, TX

First State Bank of Bayport; Bayport, MN

First State Bank of Beardstown; Beardstown, IL

First State Bank of Bloomington; Bloomington, IL

First State Bank of Covington; Covington, TN

First State Bank of Forrest; Forrest, IL

First State Bank of Gainesville; Gainesville, TX

First State Bank of Gowrie; Gowrie, IA

First State Bank of Harvard; Harvard, IL

First State Bank of Hotchkiss; Hotchkiss, CO

First State Bank of Middlebury; Middlebury, IN

First State Bank of Monticello; Monticello, IL

First State Bank of Porter; Porter, IN

First State Bank of Shelby; Shelby, MT

First State Bank of Stratford; Stratford, TX

First State Bank of Texas; Denton, TX

First State Bank of Thornton, Iowa; Thornton, IA

First State Bank of Uvalde; Uvalde, TX

First State Bank of Warren; Warren, AR

First State Bank Shannon-Polo; Shannon, IL

First State Bank and Trust; Tonganoxie, KS

First State Bank and Trust Company; Albany, GA

First State Bank and Trust Company; Valdosta, GA

First State Bank and Trust Company; Pittsburg, KS

First State Bank and Trust Company; Caruthersville, MO

First State Bank and Trust Company; Carthage, TX

First State Bank and Trust Company; Mission, TX

First State Bank and Trust Company in Cordele; Cordele, GA

First State Bank & Trust Company of Larned; Larned, KS

First State Bank & Trust Company of Shawnee; Shawnee, OK

First Stuttgart Bank and Trust Company; Stuttgart, AR

First Tennessee Bank, NA; Memphis, TN

First Trust Bank; Ontario, CA

First Trust Bank of Shelbyville; Shelbyville, IL

First Trust Company of Montana, NA; Billings, MT

First Trust Company of North Dakota NA; Fargo, ND

First Trust Corporation; Denver, CO

First Trust, NA; St. Paul, MN

First Trust of MidAmerica; Kansas City, MO

First Trust and Savings Bank; Aurelia, IA

First Trust and Savings Bank; Cedar Rapids, IA

First Trust and Savings Bank; Moville, IA

First Trust and Savings Bank; Oxford, IA

First Trust and Savings Bank; Wheatland, IA

First Trust and Savings Bank of Taylorville; Taylorville, IL

First Trust and Savings Bank of Watseka, IL; Watseka, IL

First Trust & Savings Bank, Omida; Omida, TN

First Union National Bank of Florida; Jacksonville, FL

First Union National Bank of Georgia; Decatur, GA

First Union National Bank of Maryland; Rockville, MD

First Union National Bank of North Carolina; Charlotte, NC

First Union National Bank of South Carolina; Greenville, SC

First Union National Bank of Tenneesee; Nashville, TN

First Union National Bank of Virginia; Washington, DC

First Union National Bank of Virginia; Roanoke, VA

First United Bank; Bellevue, NE

First United Bank; Neligh, NE

First United Bank of West Virginia, NA; Piedmont, WV

First United Bank & Trust Company; Holdenville, OK

First United National Bank & Trust; Great Bend, KS

First United National Bank & Trust; Oakland, MD

First Valley Bank; Bethlehem, PA

First Vermont Bank and Trust Company; Brattleboro, VT

First Victoria National Bank; Victoria, TX

First Virginia Bank; Falls Church, VA

First Virginia Bank—Central Maryland; Bel Air, MD

First Virginia Bank—Colonial; Richmond, VA

First Virginia Bank—Commonwealth; Williamsburg, VA

First Virginia Bank—Highlands; Covington, VA

First Virginia Bank—Maryland; Upper Marlboro, MD

First Virginia Bank—Mountain Empire; Damascus, VA

First Virginia Bank—South Hill; South Hill, VA

First Virginia Bank—Southside; Farmville, VA

First Virginia Bank—Southwest; Roanoke, VA

First Virginia Bank of Tidewater; Norfolk, VA

First Western Bank & Trust; Minot, ND

First Western Trust Services Company; New Castle, PA

First Whitney Bank & Trust; Atlantic, IA

Firstar Bank Burlington, NA; Burlington, IA

Firstar Bank Cedar Rapids, NA; Cedar Rapids, IA

Firstar Bank Council Bluffs; Council Bluffs, IA

Firstar Bank Des Moines, NA; Des Moines, IA

Firstar Bank Eau Claire, NA; Eau Claire, WI

Firstar Bank Illinois; Oak Park, IL

Firstar Bank Madison, NA; Madison, WI

Firstar Bank Oshkosh, NA; Oshkosh, WI

Firstar Bank Ottumwa; Ottumwa, IA

Firstar Bank Quad Cities, NA; Davenport, IA

Firstar Bank Sheboygan, NA; Sheboygan, WI

Firstar Bank Sioux City, NA; Sioux City, IA

Firstar Metropolitan Bank & Trust; Phoenix, AZ

Firstar Trust Company; Milwaukee, WI

Firstar Trust Company of Florida, NA; West Palm Beach, FL

Firstar Trust Company of Minnesota; Minneapolis, MN

FirstBank; Texarkana, TX

FirstBank Southwest; Amarillo, TX

FirsTier Bank, NA, Lincoln; Lincoln, NE

FirsTier Bank, NA, Omaha; Norfolk, NE

FirsTier Bank, NA, Omaha; Omaha, NE

FirsTier Bank, NA, Omaha; Scottsbluff, NE

Five Points Bank; Grand Island, NE

Flanagan State Bank; Flanagan, IL

Fleet Bank, NA; Hartford, CT

Fleet Bank—NH; Manchester, NH

Fleet Bank of Maine; Portland, ME

Fleet Bank of Massachusetts; Boston, MA

Fleet Trust Company; Albany, NY

Fleet Trust Company; Rochester, NY

Fleet Trust Company; Providence, RI

Fleet Trust Company of Florida, NA; Naples, FL

Flemington National Bank & Trust Company; Flemington, NJ

Flora Bank & Trust; Flora, IL

FMB Old State Bank; Fremont, MI

FMB—Trust; Holland, MI

FNB Bank, NA; Danville, PA

Fordyce Bank & Trust Company; Fordyce, AR

Fort Madison Bank & Trust Co; Fort Madison, IA

Fort Wayne National Bank; Fort Wayne, IN

Founders National Trust Bank; Naples, FL

Founders Trust Company; Dallas, TX

Founders Trust Personal Bank; Grand Rapids, MI

Fountain Trust Company; Covington, IN

Fowler State Bank; Fowler, IN

Foxboro National Bank of Foxboro; Foxboro, MA

Frances Slocum Bank and Trust Company; Wabash, IN

Francisco State Bank; Francisco, IN

Frank Russell Trust Company; Tacoma, WA

Franklin Bank & Trust Company; Franklin, KY

Franklin County National Bank of Brookville; Brookville, IN

Franklin-Lamoille Bank; Saint Albans, VT

Franklin State Bank & Trust Company; Winnsboro, LA

Franklin Street Trust Company; Chapel Hill, NC

Fredonia State Bank; Nacogdoches, TX

Fremont County Savings Bank; Sidney, IA

Fremont National Bank and Trust Company; Fremont, NE

Friendship State Bank; Friendship, IN

Frontier Bank; Everett, WA

Frost National Bank; San Antonio, TX

Fuji Bank and Trust Company; New York, NY

Fulton Bank; Fulton, KY

Fulton Bank; Lancaster, PA

Fulton County National Bank and Trust Company; McConnellsburg, PA

G

G W Jones Exchange Bank; Marcellus, MI

Galena State Bank & Trust Company; Galena, IL

Garden State Bank; Lakewood, NJ

Garrard Bank & Trust Company; Lancaster, KY

Garrett State Bank; Garrett, IN

Garrison State Bank; Garrison, ND

Gateway State Bank; Clinton, IA

Genesse Valley Trust Company; Pittsford, NY

Geneva State Bank; Geneva, NE

George K Baum Trust Company; Kansas City, MO

George State Bank; George, IA

Gerber State Bank; Argenta, IL

Gering State Bank and Trust Company; Gering, NE

German American Bank; Jasper, IN

Germantown Trust & Savings Bank; Breese, IL

Gibson County Bank; Princeton, IN

Glastonbury Bank & Trust Company; Glastonbury, CT

Glenmede Trust Company; Philadelphia, PA

Glenmede Trust Company of New Jersey, Princeton, NJ

Glens Falls National Bank and Trust Company; Glens Falls, NY

Glenview State Bank; Glenview, IL

Glenwood State Bank; Glenwood, IA

Glenwood Trust Company; Chicago, IL

Goodland State Bank; Goodland, IN

Gorham Savings Bank; Gorham, ME

Gothenburg State Bank & Trust Company; Gothenburg, NE

Grafton State Bank; Grafton, WI

Grand Bank; Grand Rapids, MI

Grand Island Trust Company; Grand Island, NE

Grand National Bank; Waukegan, IL

Grange National Bank/Wyoming County Laceyville; Tunkhannock, PA

Granite Savings Bank and Trust Company; Barre, VT

Grant County Bank; Ulysses, KS

Grant County Deposit Bank; Williamstown, KY

Grant County State Bank; Swayzee, IN

Granville National Bank; Granville, IL

Great Barrington Savings Bank; Great
Barrington, MA

Great Financial Bank, FSB; Owensboro,
KY

GreatBanc Trust Company; Aurora, IL

Green Belt Bank & Trust; Iowa Falls, IA

Green Mountain Bank; Rutland, VT

Greene County Bank; Greeneville, TN

Greenfield Banking Company; Greenfield,
IN

Greenfield Savings Bank; Greenfield,
MA

Greensburg Deposit Bank & Trust Co;
Greensburg, KY

Grinnell State Bank; Grinnell, IA

Groos Bank, NA; San Antonio, TX

Grundy County National Bank; Morris,
IL

Grundy National Bank of Grundy Center;
Grundy Center, IA

Gruver State Bank; Gruver, TX

Guaranty Bank; Mount Pleasant, TX

Guaranty Bank & Trust; Kansas City,
KS

Guaranty Bank & Trust Company; Denver, CO

Guaranty Bank & Trust Company; Venice, FL

Guaranty Bank & Trust Company; Cedar
Rapids, IA

Guaranty Bank & Trust Company; Belzoni, MS

Guaranty Bank & Trust Company;
Oklahoma City, OK

Guaranty National Bank; Gainsville, TX

Guaranty State Bank and Trust Company;
Beloit, KS

Guaranty Trust Company of Missouri;
Clayton, MO

Guardian Trust Company; Los Angeles,
CA

Guardian Trust Company; Topeka, KS

Guthrie County State Bank; Guthrie Center, IA

H

H F Gehant Banking Co; West Brooklyn,
IL

Habersham Bank; Cornelia, GA

Hagerstown Trust Company; Hagerstown,
MD

Hale County State Bank; Plainview, TX

Hamilton Bank of Upper East Tennessee;
Johnson City, TN

Hamlin Bank and Trust Company;
Smethport, PA

Hancock Bank; Gulfport, MS

Hancock Bank of Louisiana; Baton
Rouge, LA

Hancock Bank & Trust Company;
Hawesville, KY

Hannibal National Bank; Hannibal, MO

Hardin County Bank; Savannah, TN

Hardin County Savings Bank of Eldora;
Eldora, IA

Hardware State Bank; Lovington, IL

Hardwick Bank & Trust Company; Dalton, GA

Harleysville National Bank & Trust Company; Harleysville, PA

Harlingen National Bank; Harlingen, TX

Harris Bank Barrington, NA; Barrington,
IL

Harris Bank Naperville; Naperville, IL

Harris Bank Palatine, NA; Palatine, IL

Harris Bank St. Charles; Geneva, IL

Harris Bank Winnetka, NA; Winnetka, IL

Harris Bank Woodstock; Woodstock, IL

Harris Trust Bank of Arizona; Scottsdale,
AZ

Harris Trust Company of Florida; West
Palm Beach, FL

Harris Trust Company of New York;
New York, NY

Harris Trust and Savings Bank; Chicago,
IL

Harrison County Bank; Lost Creek, WV

Harrison Deposit Bank and Trust Company; Cynthiana, KY

Hart County Bank and Trust Company;
Munfordville, KY

Harvard State Bank; Harvard, IL

Haskell National Bank; Haskell, TX

Hastings City Bank; Hastings, MI

Havana National Bank; Havana, IL

Hawaiian Trust Company, Ltd; Honolulu, HI

Hawkeye Bank; Des Moines, IA

Hawkeye Bank; Newton, IA

Hawkeye Bank of Dubuque, NA; Dubuque, IA

Hawkeye Bank of Lyon County; Rock Rapids, IA

Hawkeye Bank of Maquoketa; Maquoketa, IA

Hawkeye Bank of Mount Pleasant; Mount Pleasant, IA

Hawkeye Bank of Vinton; Vinton, IA

Heartland Trust Company; Fargo, ND

Hedrick Savings Bank; Hedrick, IA

Helena National Bank; Helena, AR

Hendricks County Bank and Trust Company; Brownsburg, IN

Herget National Bank of Pekin; Pekin, IL

Heritage Bank, NA; Holstein, IA

Heritage Bank of St. Joseph; Saint Joseph, MO

Heritage Bank and Trust; Racine, WI

Heritage Bank & Trust Company; Darlington, IN

Heritage Federal Bank, FSB; Kingsport, TN

Heritage National Bank; Pottsville, PA

Heritage Trust and Asset Management, Inc.; Grand Junction, CO

Heritage Trust Company; Tinley Park, IL

Heritage Trust Company; Erie, PA

Heritage Trust Company of New Mexico; Taos, NM

Herkimer County Trust Company; Little Falls, NY

Herring National Bank of Vernon; Vernon, TX

Hershey Trust Company; Hershey, PA

Hibernia National Bank; New Orleans, LA

High Point Bank and Trust Company; High Point, NC

Hill-Dodge Banking Company; Warsaw, IL

Hills Bank & Trust Company; Hills, IA

Hillsdale County National Bank; Hillsdale, MI

Hilltop National Bank; Casper, WY

Holladay Bank and Trust; Salt Lake City, UT

Hollidaysburg Trust Company; Hollidaysburg, PA

Holmes County Bank and Trust Company; Lexington, MS

Home Bank and Trust Company; Eureka, KS

Home Federal Bank of Tennesee, FSB; Knoxville, TN

Home National Bank of Arkansas City; Arkansas City, KS

Home National Bank of Thorntown; Thorntown, IN

Home State Bank; Loveland, CO

Home State Bank; Jefferson, IA

Home State Bank; Royal, IA

Home State Bank, NA; Crystal Lake, IL

Home State Bank & Trust Company; McPherson, KS

Home Trust and Savings Bank; Osage, IA

HomeBanc, a Federal Savings Bank; Rockford, IL

Homeland Bank, NA—Waterloo; Des Moines, IA

Homeland Bank, NA—Waterloo; Waterloo, IA

Honesdale National Bank; Honesdale, PA

Horizon Bank; Hot Springs, AR

Horizon Bank, A Savings Bank; Bellingham, WA

Houghton State Bank; Red Oak, IA

Howard Bank, NA; Burlington, VT

Hudson Savings Bank; Hudson, MA

Hudson United Bank; West Orange, NJ

Hudson Valley Bank; Yonkers, NY

Humboldt Trust and Savings Bank; Humboldt, IA

Huntington Banks of Michigan; Birmingham, MI

Huntington National Bank; Covington, KY

Huntington National Bank of Indiana; Indianapolis, IN

Huntington National Bank, West Virginia, NA; Charleston, WV

Huntington Trust Company, NA; Columbus, OH

Huntington Trust Company of Florida, NA; Naples, FL

I

IAA Trust Company; Bloomington, IL

IAI Trust Company; Minneapolis, MN

Iberville Trust & Savings Bank; Plaquemine, LA

IBJ Schroder Bank & Trust Company; New York, NY

Ida County State Bank; Ida Grove, IA

IDS Trust Company; Minneapolis, MN

Illini Bank; Springfield, IL

Illinois State Bank and Trust; East Alton, IL

Imperial Trust Company; Los Angeles, CA

Independence Bank; Independence, OH

Independence Bank of Chicago; Chicago, IL

Indiana Community Bank, SB; Lebanon, IN

Indiana Federal Bank for Savings; Valparaiso, IN

Indiana Lawrence Bank; North Manchester, IN

Indiana State Bank of Terre Haute; Terre Haute, IN

Indiana Trust and Investment Management Co; Mishawaka, IN

Industrial Bank of Japan Trust Company; New York, NY

Integra Investment Services Company, NA; Pittsburgh, PA

International Bank of Commerce; Laredo, TX

InterNational State Bank; Raton, NM

INTRUST Bank, NA; Wichita, KS

Investment Trust Company; Denver, CO

Investors Bank & Trust Company; Boston, MA

Investors Fiduciary Trust Company; Kansas City, MO

Investors Services Trust Company; Overland Park, KS

Investors Trust Company; Wyomissing, PA

Iola Bank and Trust Co; Iola, KS

Iowa Falls State Bank; Iowa Falls, IA

Iowa Savings Bank; Coon Rapids, IA

Iowa Savings Bank; Dike, IA

Iowa State Bank; Algona, IA

Iowa State Bank; Clarksville, IA

Iowa State Bank; Des Moines, IA

Iowa State Bank; Hull, IA

Iowa State Bank; West Bend, IA

Iowa State Bank and Trust Company; Iowa City, IA

Iowa State Bank & Trust Company of Fairfield; Fairfield, IA

Iowa State Savings Bank; Clinton, IA

Iowa State Savings Bank; Creston, IA

Iowa State Savings Bank; Knoxville, IA

Iowa Trust and Savings Bank; Centerville, IA

Iowa Trust and Savings Bank; Emmetsburg, IA

Iowa Trust and Savings Bank; Oskaloosa, IA

Irwin Bank and Trust Company; Irwin, PA

Irwin Union Bank and Trust Company; Columbus, IN

Isabella Bank and Trust; Mount Pleasant, MI

Island National Bank and Trust Company; Palm Beach, FL

Israel Discount Bank of New York; New York, NY

Itasca Bank and Trust Co; Itasca, IL

J

J. P. Morgan California; Los Angeles, CA

J. P. Morgan Delaware; Wilmington, DE

J. P. Morgan Florida Federal Savings Bank; Palm Beach, FL

J & W Seligman Trust Company; New York, NY

Jackson County Bank; Seymour, IN

Jeff Davis Bank and Trust Company; Jennings, LA

Jefferson Bank of Florida; Miami Beach, FL

Jefferson Guaranty Bank; Metairie, LA

Jefferson National Bank; Charlottesville, VA

Jefferson State Bank; San Antonio, TX

Jersey State Bank; Jerseyville, IL

Jim Thorpe National Bank; Jim Thorpe, PA

John Warner Bank; Clinton, IL

Johnson Heritage Trust Company; Racine, WI

Jones National Bank & Trust Company of Seward; Seward, NE

Jonestown Bank and Trust Company; Jonestown, PA

Juniata Valley Bank; Mifflintown, PA

K

Kalamazoo County State Bank; Schoolcraft, MI

Kanaly Trust Company; Houston, TX

Kane County Bank & Trust Co; Elburn, IL

Kansas State Bank; Kansas, IL

Kansas State Bank; Ottawa, KS

Kaw Valley State Bank and Trust Company; Topeka, KS

Kearney State Bank and Trust Company; Kearney, NE

Kelly Field National Bank; San Antonio, TX

Kennett National Bank; Kennett, MO

Kentland Bank; Kentland, IN

Kentucky Bank; Paris, KY

Kentucky Bank & Trust of Greenup County; Russell, KY

Kentucky Home Trust Company; Louisville, KY

Keokuk Savings Bank and Trust Company; Keokuk, IA

Kerndt Brothers Savings Bank; Lansing, IA

Key Bank of Colorado; Denver, CO

Key Bank of Wyoming; Cheyenne, WY

Key Biscayne Bank and Trust Company; Key Biscayne, FL

Key Trust Company; Albany, NY

Key Trust Company; Horsham, PA

Key Trust Company of Alaska; Anchorage, AK

Key Trust Company of Florida; Naples, FL

Key Trust Company of Maine; Portland, ME

Key Trust Company of the Northwest; Tacoma, WA

Key Trust Company of Ohio, NA; Cleveland, OH

Key Trust Company of the West; Boise, ID

Key Trust Company of the West; Ogden, UT

Key Trust Company of the West; Salt Lake City, UT

Key Trust Company of the West; Cheyenne, WY

KeyCorp Shareholder Services, Inc.; Denver, CO

KeyCorp Shareholder Services, Inc.; Dallas, TX

KeyCorp Shareholder Services, Inc.; Houston, TX

Keystone Savings Bank; Keystone, IA

Kilbourn State Bank; Milwaukee, WI

Kingfisher Bank & Trust Co; Kingfisher, OK

Kingsley State Bank; Kingsley, IA

Kikpatrick Pettis Trust Company; Omaha, NE

Kirkwood Bank and Trust Co.; Bismarck, ND

Kleberg First National Bank of Kingsville; Kingsville, TX

Klein Bank; Houston, TX

L

La Porte Savings Bank; La Porte, IN

La Salle National Bank; La Salle, IL

La Salle State Bank; La Salle, IL

Lafayette American Bank and Trust Company; Bridgeport, CT

Lafayette Bank; Lehigh Valley, PA

Lafayette Bank and Trust Company; Lafayette, IN

Laird Nortan Trust Company; Seattle, WA

Lake City Bank; Warsaw, IN

Lake City State Bank; Lake City, IA

Lake County Trust Company; Crown Point, IN

Lake Forest Bank and Trust Company; Lake Forest, IL

Lakeside Bank; Chicago, IL

Lamesa National Bank; Lamesa, TX
Lancaster National Bank; Lancaster, NH
Lapeer County Bank and Trust Company; Lapeer, MI
Laredo National Bank; Laredo, TX
LaSalle National Trust, NA; Chicago, IL
Laurens State Bank; Laurens, IA
Lawrenceburg National Bank; Lawrenceburg, KY
Le Claire State Bank; Le Claire, IA
Le Mars Bank and Trust Company; Le Mars, IA
Leader Federal Bank for Savings; Memphis, TN
League City Bank and Trust; League City, TX
Leavenworth National Bank & Trust Company; Leavenworth, KS
Lebanon-Citizens National Bank; Lebanon, OH
Lebanon Valley National Bank; Lebanon, PA
Ledyard National Bank; Hanover, NH
Lee County Bank and Trust, NA; Fort Madison, IA
Legg Mason Trust Company; Baltimore, MD
Leitchfield Deposit Bank and Trust Company; Leitchfield, KY
Lenox Savings Bank; Lenox, MA
Lewistown Trust Company; Lewistown, PA
Lexington State Bank; Lexington, NC
Lexington State Bank; Lexington, SC
Lexington State Bank and Trust Company; Lexington, NE
Liberty Bank and Trust; Tucson, AZ
Liberty Bank and Trust; Forest City, IA
Liberty Bank and Trust; Woodbine, IA
Liberty Bank and Trust; Gibbsboro, NJ
Liberty Bank and Trust Company; Mayfield, KY
Liberty Bank & Trust Company of Oklahoma City, NA; Oklahoma City, OK
Liberty Bank & Trust Company of Tulsa, NA; Tulsa, OK
Liberty Bank and Trust, NA; Pocahontas, IA

Liberty National Bank of Northern Kentucky; Erlanger, KY
Liberty National Bank and Trust Company; Dickinson, ND
Liberty National Bank & Trust Company of Indiana; New Albany, IN
Liberty National Bank & Trust Company of Kentucky; Louisville, KY
Liberty National Bank & Trust Company of Kentucky; Shelbyville, KY
Liberty State Bank; Liberty, TN
Liberty Trust & Savings Bank; Durant, IA
Lincoln Bank of North Carolina; Lincolnton, NC
Lincoln Bank and Trust Company; Ardmore, OK
Lincoln County Bank; Fayetteville, TN
Lincoln Savings Bank; Reinbeck, IA
Lincoln Trust Company; Englewood, CO
Lincolnland Bank; Dale, IN
Lindell Bank and Trust Company; St. Louis, MO
Linden State Bank; Linden, IN
Lisbon Bank and Trust Company; Lisbon, IA
Little River Bank; Lepanto, AR
Livermore Falls Trust Company; Livermore Falls, ME
Logan County Bank; Lincoln, IL
Longview Bank and Trust Company; Longview, TX
Longview National Bank; Longview, TX
Lorain National Bank; Lorain, OH
LTCB Trust Company; New York, NY
Luana Savings Bank; Luana, IA
Lufkin National Bank; Lufkin, TX
Luzerne National Bank; Luzerne, PA
Lyndonviile Savings Bank and Trust Company; Lyndonville, VT

M

M. S. Bailey & Son, Bankers; Clinton, SC
M&I First National Bank; West Bend, WI
M&I Trust Company of Arizona; Phoenix, AZ
Madison Bank and Trust; Huntsville, AR
Magna Trust Company; Belleville, IL
Mahaska State Bank; Oskaloosa, IA

Mahoning National Bank of Youngstown; Youngstown, OH

Main Line Trust Company; Wayne, PA

Maine Bank and Trust Company; Portland, ME

Manchester Trust Bank; Lakehurst, NJ

Manufacturers Bank and Trust Company; Forest City, IA

Manufacturers and Traders Trust Company; Buffalo, NY

Maquoketa State Bank; Maquoketa, IA

Marengo State Bank; Marengo, IN

Marine State Bank; Marengo, IN

Marine Midland Bank; Buffalo, NY

Marine Trust Company of Carthage; Carthage, IL

Maritime Bank & Trust Company; Essex, CT

Mark Twain Bank; Ladue, MO

Mark Twain Illinois Bank; Belleville, IL

Mark Twain Kansas Bank; Shawnee, KS

Mark Twain Kansas City Bank; Kansas City, MO

Markesan State Bank; Markesan, WI

Marquette Bank of South Dakota NA; Sioux Falls, SD

Marquette National Bank; Chicago, IL

Marquette Trust Company; Rochester, MN

Marshall & Ilsley Trust Company; Milwaukee, WE

Marshall & Ilsley Trust Company of Florida; Naples, FL

Marshall National Bank and Trust Company; Marshall, VA

Mason City National Bank; Mason City, IL

Massachusetts Fidelity Trust Company; Cedar Rapids, IA

MASSBANK for Savings; Lowell, MA

Mauch Chunk Trust Company; Jim Thorpe, PA

Maynard Savings Bank; Maynard, IA

Maywood-Proviso State Bank; Maywood, IL

Mazon State Bank; Mazon, IL

McAllen National Bank; McAllen, TX

McDowell County National Bank in Welch; Welch, WV

McGehee Bank; McGehee, AR

McHenry State Bank; McHenry, IL

McKenzie Banking Company; McKenzie, TN

Mechanics Bank of Richmond; Richmond, CA

Mechanicsville Trust and Savings Bank; Mechanicsville, IA

Mediapolis Savings Bank; Mediapolis, IA

Mellon Bank (DE), NA; Wilmington, DE

Mellon Bank (MD); Bethesda, MD

Mellon Bank, NA; Pittsburgh, PA

Melvin Savings Bank; Melvin, IA

Mercantile Bank, NA; Brownsville, TX

Mercantile Bank of Cape Girardeau; Cape Girardeau, MO

Mercantile Bank of Centralia; Centralia, IL

Mercantile Bank of Flora, NA; Flora, IL

Mercantile Bank of Franklin County; Washington, MO

Mercantile Bank of Illinois, NA; Alton, IL

Mercantile Bank of Joplin, NA; Joplin, MO

Mercantile Bank of Kansas; Prairie Village, KS

Mercantile Bank of Kansas City; Kansas City, MO

Mercantile Bank of Lake of the Ozarks; Eldon, MO

Mercantile Bank of Lawrence; Lawrence, KS

Mercantile Bank of Mt. Vernon; Mount Vernon, IL

Mercantile Bank of Northern Iowa; Waterloo, IA

Mercantile Bank of Plattsburg; Plattsburg, MO

Mercantile Bank of Poplar Bluff; Poplar Bluff, MO

Mercantile Bank of St. Joseph; Saint Joseph, MO

Mercantile Bank of Springfield; Springfield, MO

Mercantile Bank of Topeka, NA; Topeka, KS

Mercantile Bank of Trenton NA; Trenton, MO

Mercantile Bank of West Central Missouri; Sedalia, MO

Mercantile Bank and Trust, FSB; Dallas, TX

Mercantile National Bank of Indiana; Hammond, IN

Mercantile-Safe Deposit and Trust Company; Baltimore, MD

Mercantile Trust Company, NA; St. Louis, MO

Mercantile Trust and Savings Bank; Quincy, IL

Merchants Bank; Vicksburg, MS

Merchants and Farmers Bank; Dumas, AR

Merchants and Farmers Bank; West Helena, AR

Merchants and Farmers Bank; Kosciusko, MS

Merchants and Farmers Bank and Trust Company; Leesville, LA

Merchants & Manufacturers Bank—Ellisville; Ellisville, MS

Merchants and Marine Bank; Pascagoula, MS

Merchants National Bank of Aurora; Aurora, IL

Merchants National Bank of Bangor; Bangor, PA

Merchants National Bank of Fort Smith; Fort Smith, AR

Merchants National Bank of Winona; Winona, MN

Merchants and Planters Bank; Newport, AR

Merchants and Planters Bank; Raymond, MS

Merchants and Planters Bank; NA; Camden, AR

Merchants Trust Company; Burlington, VT

Meridian Bank, New Jersey; Medford, NJ

Meridian Trust Company; Reading, PA

Meridian Trust Company of California; San Francisco, CA

Metcalf State Bank; Overland Park, KS

Metrobank; East Moline, IL

Metropolitan Federal Bank; FSB; Cheyenne, WY

MFC First National Bank; Escanaba, MI

MFC First National Bank; Marquette, MI

MFC First National Bank; Menominee, MI

Miami County National Bank Paola; Paola, KS

Michigan National Bank; Farmington Hills, MI

Mid-America Bank and Trust Company of Lousville; Louisville, KY

Mid-America National Bank of Chicago; Chicago, IL

Mid American National Bank and Trust Company; Toledo, OH

MidCity National Bank of Chicago; Chicago, IL

Mid Penn Bank; Millersburg, PA

Mid-State Bank and Trust Company; Altoona, PA

Mid-Wisconsin Bank; Medford, WI

Middle Tennessee Bank; Columbia, TN

Midland National Bank; Midland, TX

Midlantic Bank NA; Edison, NJ

Midway National Bank of St. Paul; St. Paul, MN

Midwest Heritage Bank, FSB; Chariton, IA

Midwest Trust Company; Overland Park, KS

Midwest Trust Services Inc; Elmwood Park, IL

Mifflinburg Bank and Trust Company; Lewisburg, PA

Milford National Bank and Trust Company; Milford, MA

Milledgeville State Bank; Milledgeville, IL

Milwaukee Western Bank; Milwaukee, WI

Minden Bank and Trust Company; Minden, LA

Minden Exchange/Bank & Trust Company; Minden, NE

Minersville Safe Deposit Bank & Trust Company; Minersville, PA

Minnesota Trust Company of Austin; Austin, MN

Minonk State Bank; Minonk, IL

Mission Bank; Mission, KS

Mission Management and Trust Company; Tucson, AZ

Mitsubishi Bank Trust Company of New York; New York, NY

Mitsubishi Trust and Banking Corporation (USA); New York, NY

Mitsui Trust Bank (USA); New York, NY

Monroe Bank & Trust; Monroe, MI

Monroe County Bank; Bloomington, IN

Montgomery & Traders Bank and Trust Company; Mount Sterling, KY

Monticello Banking Company; Monticello, KY

Moody National Bank of Galveston; Galveston, TX

Moody Trust Company; Portland, OR

Moorhead State Bank; Moorhead, IA

Morgan Guaranty Trust Company of New York; New York, NY

Morgantown Bank and Trust; Morgantown, KY

Morrill and Janes Bank and Trust Company; Hiawatha, KS

Morrill State Bank and Trust Co; Sabetha, KS

Mound City Bank; Platteville, WI

Mount Sterling National Bank; Mount Sterling, KY

Mount Vernon Bank and Trust Company; Mount Vernon, IA

Mount Zion State Bank and Trust; Mount Zion, IL

Mountain States Bank; Denver, CO

Moxham National Bank of Johnstown; Johnstown, PA

Muncy Bank and Trust Company; Muncy, PA

Municipal Trust and Savings Bank; Bourbonnais, IL

N

Napoleon State Bank; Napoleon, IN

National Bank of Alaska; Anchorage, AK

National Bank of Blacksburg; Blacksburg, VA

National Bank of Canton; Canton, IL

National Bank of Commerce; Memphis, TN

National Bank of Commerce of Birmingham; Birmingham, AL

National Bank of Commerce of El Dorado; El Dorado, AR

National Bank of Commerce of Mississippi; Columbus, MS

National Bank of Commerce Trust and Savings Association; Lincoln, NE

National Bank of Delaware County, Walton; Walton, NY

National Bank of Fredericksburg; Fredericksburg, VA

National Bank of the Main Line; Media, PA

National Bank of Malvern; Malvern, PA

National Bank of Mendota; Mendota, IL

National Bank of Monmouth; Monmouth, IL

National Bank of Petersburg; Petersburg, IL

National Bank of Rising Sun; Rising Sun, MD

National Bank of Rockwell City; Rockwell City, IA

National Bank of Royal Oak; Royal Oak, MI

National Bank of South Carolina; Sumter, SC

National Bank of Stamford; Stamford, NY

National Bank and Trust Company; Wilmington, OH

National Bank and Trust Company of Sycamore; Sycamore, IL

National City Bank; Cleveland, OH

National City Bank, Dayton; Dayton, OH

National City Bank, Indiana; Indianapolis, IN

National City Bank, Kentucky; Louisville, KY

National City Bank, Northeast; Akron, OH

National City Bank, Northwest; Toledo, OH

National City Bank of Evansville; Evansville, IN

National City Bank of Minneapolis; Minneapolis, MN

National City Bank, Southern Indiana; New Albany, IN

National City Trust; Columbus, OH

National City Trust Company; West Palm Beach, FL

National Exchange Bank and Trust of Fond du Lac; Fond du Lac, WI

National Grand Bank of Marblehead; Marblehead, MA

National Westminster Bank USA; New York, NY

NationsBank, NA (Carolinas); Columbia, SC

NationsBank of Florida, NA; Tampa, FL

NationsBank of Georgia, NA; Atlanta, GA

NationsBank of Kentucky, NA; Hopkinsville, KY

NationsBank of North Carolina, NA; Charlotte, NC

NationsBank of Tennessee, NA; Nashville, TN

NationsBank of Texas, NA; Dallas, TX

NationsBank of Virginia, NA; Richmond, VA

NationsBank Trust Company, NA; Washington, DC

NationsBank Trust Company of New York; New York, NY

Nazareth National Bank and Trust Company; Nazareth, PA

NBC Bank Rockdale; Rockdale, TX

NBD Bank; Venice, FL

NBD Bank; Evanston, IL

NBD Bank; Detroit, MI

NBD Bank, NA; Indianapolis, IN

NBT Bank, NA; Norwich, NY

Nebraska State Bank & Trust Company; Broken Bow, NE

Nevada State Bank; Las Vegas, NV

New Albin Savings Bank; New Albin, IA

New England Trust Company; Providence, RI

New Farmers National Bank of Glasgow; Bowling Green, KY

New Farmers National Bank of Glasgow; Glasgow, KY

New Haven Savings Bank; New Haven, CT

New Iberia Bank; New Iberia, LA

New London Trust, FSB; New London, NH

New Milford Savings Bank; New Milford, CT

New South Federal Savings Bank; Irondale, AL

New Washington State Bank; New Washington, IN

Newton County Bank; Newton, MS

Newton Trust Company; Newton, NJ

Nippon Credit Trust Company; New York, NY

NLSB; New Lenox, IL

Nodaway Valley Bank; Maryville, MO

North American Trust Company; San Diego, CA

North Carolina Trust Company; Greensboro, NC

North Central Trust Company; La Crosse, WI

North Dallas Bank & Trust Co.; Dallas, TX

North Fork Bank; Mattituck, NY

North Salem State Bank; North Salem, IN

North Shore Bank of Commerce; Duluth, MN

North Shore Trust and Savings; Waukegan, IL

North Side Bank & Trust Company; Cincinnati, OH

North Side State Bank of Rock Springs; Rock Springs, WY

Northern Central Bank; Williamsport, PA

Northern Indiana Trust Company; Fort Wayne, IN

Northern Trust Bank—Lake Forest, NA; Lake Forest, IL

Northern Trust Bank of Arizona, NA; Phoenix, AZ

Northern Trust Bank of California, NA; Los Angeles, CA

Northern Trust Bank of Florida, NA; Miami, FL

Northern Trust Bank of Texas, NA; Dallas, TX

Northern Trust Bank of Vero Beach; Vero Beach, FL

Northern Trust Company; Chicago, IL

Northern Trust Company of New York; New York, NY

Northfield Savings Bank; Northfield, VT

Northumberland National Bank; Northumberland, PA

Northwest Bank; Oklahoma City, OK

Northwest Bank & Trust Company; Davenport, IA

Northwest National Bank; Vancouver,
WA

Northwestern Bank; Chippewa Falls, WI

Northwestern Savings Bank & Trust, FSB;
Traverse City, MI

Northwestern Trust and Investors Advisory Co.; Seattle, WA

Norwalk Savings Society; Norwalk, CT

Norwest Bank Colorado, NA; Boulder,
CO

Norwest Bank Colorado, NA; Brighton,
CO

Norwest Bank Colorado, NA; Colorado
Springs, CO

Norwest Bank Colorado, NA; Denver,
CO

Norwest Bank Colorado, NA; Fort Collins, CO

Norwest Bank Colorado, NA; Grand
Junction, CO

Norwest Bank Colorado, NA; Greeley,
CO

Norwest Bank Colorado, NA; Longmont,
CO

Norwest Bank Illinois, NA; Galesburg, IL

Norwest Bank Indiana, NA; Fort Wayne,
IN

Norwest Bank Iowa, NA; Des Moines, IA

Norwest Bank Minnesota, NA; Minneapolis, MN

Norwest Bank Minnesota North, NA;
Duluth, MN

Norwest Bank Minnesota Southwest, NA;
Marshall, MN

Norwest Bank Nebraska, NA; Omaha,
NE

Norwest Bank New Mexico, NA; Albuquerque, NM

Norwest Bank North Dakota, NA; Fargo,
ND

Norwest Bank South Dakota, NA; Sioux
Falls, SD

Norwest Bank Texas, Kerrville, NA;
Kerrville, TX

Norwest Bank Texas, NA; Lubbock, TX

Norwest Bank Texas Plainview, NA;
Plainview, TX

Norwest Bank Wisconsin, NA; Sheboygan, WI

Norwest Bank Wyoming, NA; Casper,
WY

Norwest Capital Management & Trust
Company; Billings, MT

Norwest Investment Management and
Trust; Scottsdale, AZ

Norwest Trust Company, New York;
New York, NY

Norwest Trust Texas, NA, Wichita Falls;
Wichita Falls, TX

Norwest Trust Texas, Waco, NA; Waco,
TX

O

Oak Brook Bank; Oak Brook, IL

Oakland State Bank; Oakland, IA

Oaks Bank and Trust Company; Dallas,
TX

Oaktree Trust Company; Columbus, NE

Ohio Bank; Findlay, OH

Ohio Company Trust Department; Columbus, OH

Ohio Valley Bank Company; Gallipolis,
OH

Ohio Valley National Bank of Henderson;
Henderson, KY

Oklahoma Bank and Trust Company;
Clinton, OK

Oklahoma National Bank & Trust Company of Chickasha; Chickasha, OK

Old Kent Bank; Elmhurst, IL

Old Kent Bank; Grand Rapids, MI

Old National Trust Company; Evansville,
IN

Old Phoenix National Bank of Medina;
Medina, OH

Old Point National Bank of Phoebus;
Hampton, VA

Old Second National Bank of Aurora;
Aurora, IL

Old Smyrna Trust; Brentwood, TN

Old Stone Trust Company; Providence,
RI

Olney Trust Bank; Olney, IL

Omega Bank, NA; State College, PA

OmniBank; Mantee, MS

OnBank and Trust Co.; Syracuse, NY

One Valley Bank, NA; Charleston, WV

Oneida Savings Bank; Oneida, NY

Oneida Valley National Bank of Oneida; Oneida, NY

Orange County Trust Company; Middletown, NY

OrangeBank; Orange, TX

Oriental Bank and Trust; San Juan, PR

Orrstown Bank; Shippensburg, PA

Ossian State Bank; Ossian, IN

Oswego Community Bank; Oswego, IL

Otoe County Bank & Trust Company; Nebraska City, NE

Overton Bank and Trust, NA; Fort Worth, TX

Owen County State Bank; Spencer, IN

Owensboro National Bank; Owensboro, KY

Ozark Bank; Ozark, MO

P

Pacesetter Bank of Hartford City; Hartford City, IN

Pacesetter Bank of Montpelier; Montpelier, IN

Pacific Bank, NA; San Francisco, CA

Pacific National Bank of Nantucket; Nantucket, MA

Pacific Northwest Trust Company; Portland, OR

Packers Nebraska Bank and Trust Company; Omaha, NE

Paducah Bank and Trust Company; Paducah, KY

Page County State Bank; Clarinda, IA

Palm Beach National Bank & Trust Company; Palm Beach, FL

Palmetto Bank; Laurens, SC

Palmetto State Bank; Hampton, SC

Palos Bank and Trust Company; Palos Heights, IL

Panora State Bank; Panora, IA

Paragon Bank and Trust; Holland, MI

Parish Bank and Trust Company; Momence, IL

Park National Bank; Newark, OH

Park West Bank and Trust Company; West Springfield, MA

Parker Square Bank, NA; Wichita Falls, TX

Pasadena National Trust Company; Pasadena, CA

Peapack-Gladstone Bank; Gladstone, NJ

Pecos County State Bank; Fort Stockton, TX

Pendleton Banking Company; Pendleton, IN

Penn Central National Bank; Huntingdon, PA

Penn Security Bank and Trust Company; Scranton, PA

Pennsville National Bank; Pennsville, NJ

Pennsylvania Fiduciary and Estate Services, Inc.; Lemoyne, PA

Pennsylvania National Bank and Trust Company; Pottsville, PA

Pennsylvania Trust Company; Radnor, PA

Pennyrile Citizens Bank and Trust Company; Hopkinsville, KY

Peoples Bank; Waldo, AR

Peoples Bank; Bridgeport, CT

Peoples Bank; Brownstown, IN

Peoples Bank; Pratt, KS

Peoples Bank; Biloxi, MS

Peoples Bank; Mendenhall, MS

Peoples Bank; Ripley, MS

Peoples Bank; Senatobia, MS

Peoples Bank; Sardis, TN

Peoples Bank, a Federal Savings Bank; Munster, IN

Peoples Bank of Columbus Junction; Columbus Junction, IA

Peoples Bank of Fleming County, Kentucky; Flemingsburg, KY

Peoples Bank of Glen Rock; York, PA

Peoples Bank of Lakeland; Lakeland, FL

Peoples Bank of Mullens; Mullens, WV

Peoples Bank of Murray, Murray, KY

Peoples Bank of Oxford; Oxford, PA

Peoples Bank and Trust; Rock Valley, IA

Peoples Bank and Trust Company; Selma, AL

Peoples Bank and Trust Company; Mountain Home, AR

Peoples Bank and Trust Company; Aurora, CO

Peoples Bank and Trust Company; Indianapolis, IN

Peoples Bank and Trust Company; Sunman, IN

Peoples Bank and Trust Company; McPherson, KS

Peoples Bank and Trust Company; Greensburg, KY

Peoples Bank and Trust Company; Hazard, KY

Peoples Bank and Trust Company; Owenton, KY

Peoples Bank and Trust Company; Minden, LA

Peoples Bank and Trust Company; Tupelo, MS

Peoples Bank and Trust Company of Lincoln County; Troy, MO

Peoples Bank and Trust Company of Madison County; Berea, KY

Peoples Bank & Trust Company of St. Bernard; Chalmette, LA

Peoples Bank and Trust of Pana; Pana, IL

Peoples Banking Company; Findlay, OH

Peoples Banking and Trust Company; Marietta, OH

Peoples Commercial Bank; Winchester, KY

Peoples Federal Savings Bank of DeKalb County; Auburn, IN

Peoples First National Bank & Trust Company; Paducah, KY

Peoples Loan and Trust Bank; Winchester, IN

Peoples National Bank; Kingfisher, OK

Peoples, National Bank of Grayville; Grayville, IL

Peoples National Bank and Trust; Ottawa, KS

Peoples National Bank & Trust Company of Washington; Washington, IN

Peoples Savings Bank; Elma, IA

Peoples Savings Bank; Wellsburg, IA

Peoples Savings Bank of New Britain; New Britain, CT

Peoples State Bank; Bloomington, IN

Peoples State Bank; Elkader, IA

Peoples State Bank; Winfield, IA

Peoples State Bank; Saint Joseph, MI

Peoples State Bank of Francesville; Francesville, IN

Peoples State Bank of Mansfield; Mansfield, IL

Peoples State Bank of Newton, Illinois; Newton, IL

Peoples State Bank and Trust Company; Ellinwood, KS

People's Trust Company; Brookville, IL

Peoples Trust Company; Linton, IN

Peoples Trust Company of Saint Albans; Saint Albans, VT

Peoples Trust and Savings Bank; Boonville, IN

Peoples Trust and Savings Bank; Riverside, IA

Peoples and Union Bank; Lewisburg, TN

Pepperell Trust Company; Biddeford, ME

Perry State Bank; Perry, IA

Petefish, Skiles and Company; Virginia, IL

Phenix-Girard Bank; Phenix City, AL

Phillipsburg National Bank and Trust Company; Phillipsburg, NJ

Piedmont Trust Bank; Martinsville, VA

Pike County Bank; Petersburg, IN

Pilot Grove Savings Bank; Pilot Grove, IA

Pinnacle Bank; Cicero, IL

Pinnacle Bank of the Quad Cities; Silvis, IL

Pinnacle Management and Trust; Houston, TX

Pioneer Bank; Chattanooga, TN

Pioneer Bank and Trust; Ponca City, OK

Pioneer Bank and Trust; Belle Fourche, SD

Pioneer Bank and Trust Company; River Grove, IL

Pioneer Bank and Trust Company; Maplewood, MO

Pioneer Citizens Bank of Nevada; Reno, NV

Pioneer Trust Bank, NA; Salem, OR

Piper Trust Company; Minneapolis, MN

Pitcairn Trust Company; Jenkintown, PA

Plains National Bank of West Texas; Lubbock, TX

Planters Bank; Hawkensville, GA

Planters Bank; Tunica, MS

Planters Bank and Trust Company; Forrest City, AR

Planters Bank and Trust Company; Indianola, MS

Planters Bank and Trust Company of Virginia; Staunton, VA

Planters and Merchants Bank; Gillett, AR

Platte Valley Bank of Missouri; Platte City, MO

Platte Valley State Bank and Trust Company; Kearney, NE

Plymouth Savings Bank; Falmouth, MA

PNC Bank Delaware; Wilmington, DE

PNC Bank, FSB; Tampa, FL

PNC Bank, Indiana, Inc.; New Albany, IN

PNC Bank, Kentucky, Inc.; Louisville, KY

PNC Bank, NA; Pittsburgh, PA

PNC Bank, New England; Boston, MA

PNC Bank, New Jersey, NA; Mount Laurel, NJ

PNC Bank, Ohio, NA; Cincinnati, OH

PNC Trust Company of New York; New York, NY

Pocahontas Federal Savings and Loan Association; Pocahontas, AR

Pocahontas State Bank; Pocahontas, IA

Polk City Savings Bank; Polk City, IA

Pontiac National Bank; Pontiac, IL

Port Gibson Bank; Port Gibson, MS

Port Washington State Bank; Port Washington, WI

Portage National Bank; Portage, PA

Postville State Bank; Postville, IA

Poweshiek County Savings Bank; Brooklyn, IA

Prairie City Bank; Prairie du Chien, WI

Premier Bank, NA; Baton Rouge, LA

Premier Trust Company; Bluefield, VA

Premier Trust Services, Inc.; Freeport, IL

Premier Bank and Trust; Elyria, OH

Primary Bank; Peterborough, NH

Princeton Bank and Trust Company, NA; East Brunswick, NJ

Private Trust Company, NA; Cleveland, OH

PrivateBank and Trust Company; Chicago, IL

Producers Savings Bank; Green Mountain, IA

Provident Bank; Cincinnati, OH

Provident Bank of Kentucky; Alexandria, KY

Provident Savings Bank; Jersey City, NJ

Provident Trust Company; Omaha, NE

Prudential Bank and Trust Company; Atlanta, GA

Pueblo Bank and Trust Company; Pueblo, CO

Pulaski Bank and Trust Company; Little Rock, AR

Pullman Bank and Trust Company; Chicago, IL

Putnam County National Bank of Carmel; Carmel, NY

Putnam Fiduciary Trust Company; Boston, MA

Putnam Trust Company of Greenwich; Greenwich, CT

Q

Quincy State Bank; Quincy, FL

R

R–G Federal Savings Bank; Guaynabo, PR

Raccoon Valley States Bank; Adel, IA

Ramsey National Bank & Trust Company of Devils Lake; Devils Lake, ND

Randall-Story State Bank; Story City, IA

Randolph County Bank; Winchester, IN

Rapides Bank and Trust Company in Alexandria; Alexandria, LA

Rawlins National Bank; Rawlins, WY

Rayne State Bank and Trust Company; Rayne, LA

Reedsburg Bank; Reedsburg, WI

Regions Bank; Fort Walton Beach, FL

Regions Bank of Louisiana; Baton Rouge, LA

Regions Bank of Tennessee; Nashville, TN

Reliance Trust Company; Atlanta, GA

Republic Bank and Trust Company; Louisville, KY

Republic National Bank of New York; New York, NY

Republic New York Trust Company of Florida, NA; Miami, FL

Resource Trust Company; Minneapolis, MN

Resources Trust Company; Englewood, CO

Rhode Island Hospital Trust National Bank; Providence, RI

Richardson County Bank and Trust Company; Falls City, NE

Richfield Bank and Trust Co; Richfield, MN

Richland Trust Company; Mansfield, OH

Riddell National Bank of Brazil, Indiana; Brazil, IN

Ridgefield Bank; Ridgefield, CT

Riggs National Bank of Maryland; Rockville, MD

Riggs National Bank of Virginia; McLean, VA

Riggs National Bank of Washington, DC; Washington, DC

Ripley County Bank; Osgood, IN

Rippey Savings Bank; Rippey, IA

Rittenhouse Trust Company; Radnor, PA

River Forest State Bank and Trust Company; River Forest, IL

River Oaks Trust Company; Houston, TX

Riverway Bank; Houston, TX

Robertson Banking Company; Demopolis, AL

Rochester State Bank; Rochester, IL

Rock Island Bank; Rock Island, IL

Rock Springs National Bank; Rock Springs, WV

Rockefeller Trust Company; New York, NY

Rockland Trust Company; Hanover, MA

Rolfe State Bank; Rolfe, IA

Roxboro Savings Bank, SSB; Roxboro, NC

Royal National Bank of Palestine; Palestine, TX

RoyWest Trust Corp (U.S. Virgin Islands) Ltd; Charlotte Amalie, VI

Rublo Savings Bank of Brighton; Brighton, IA

Rushmore Trust and Savings, FSB; Bethesda, MD

Rushville State Bank; Rushville, IL

Ruthven State Bank; Ruthven, IA

S

S. K. Trust Company; Clearwater, FL

S&T Bank; Indiana, PA

Sabine State Bank and Trust Company; Many, LA

Sac City State Bank; Sac City, IA

Sachem Trust, NA; Guilford, CT

Safety Fund National Bank; Fitchburg, MA

Saint Ansgar State Bank; Saint Ansgar, IA

St. Bernard Bank and Trust Company; Arabi, LA

St. Clair County State Bank; Osceola, MO

St. James Bank and Trust Company; Lutcher, LA

St. Landry Bank and Trust Company; Opelousas, LA

St. Martin Bank and Trust Company; Saint Martinville, LA

St. Marys State Bank; St. Marys, KS

Sakura Trust Company; New York, NY

Salamanca Trust Company; Salamanca, NY

Salem Trust Bank; Winston-Salem, NC

Salisbury Bank and Trust Company; Lakeville, CT

San Benito Bank and Trust Company; San Benito, TX

Sanborn Savings Bank; Sanborn, IA

Sand Ridge Bank; Schererville, IN

Sandy Spring National Bank of Maryland; Olney, MD

Santa Barbara Bank & Trust; Santa Barbara, CA

Santa Monica Bank; Santa Monica, CA

Sanwa Bank California; Los Angeles, CA

Sanwa Bank Trust Company of New York; New York, NY

Saratoga State Bank; Saratoga IN

Savanna State Bank; Savanna, IL

Savings Institute; Mansfield Center, CT

Schuyler State Bank; Rushville, IL

Schuyler State Bank and Trust Company; Schuyler, NE

Scotiabank de Puerto Rico; San Juan, PR

Scott State Bank; Bethany, IL

Scottdale Bank and Trust Company; Scottdale, PA

Scripps Bank; La Jolla, CA

Scudder Trust Company; Salem, NH

Seafirst Bank; Seattle, WA

Seaway National Bank of Chicago; Chicago, IL

Second Bank and Trust; Culpeper, VA

Second National Bank of Saginaw; Saginaw, MI

Second National Bank of Warren; Warren, OH

Secured Trust Corporation; Tyler, TX

Security Bank; Paragould, AR

Security Bank; Marshaltown, IA

Security Bank; Ralls, TX

Security Bank of Amory; Amory, MS

Security Bank of Kansas City; Kansas City, KS

Security Bank and Trust Company; Maysville, KY

Security Bank and Trust Company; Miami, OK

Security Bank and Trust Company; Paris, TN

Security Bank and Trust Company, Decorah; Decorah, IA

Security Bank and Trust Company of Glencoe; Glencoe, MN

Security Capital Bank; Salisbury, NC

Security Federal Savings Bank; Elizabethton, TN

Security First National Bank; Alexandria, LA

Security Investment Management and Trust Company; Phoenix, AZ

Security National Bank of Sioux City, Iowa; Sioux City, IA

Security National Bank and Trust Company; Springfield, OH

Security National Bank and Trust Company of Norman; Norman, OK

Security Savings Bank; Eagle Grove, IA

Security Savings Bank; Ireton, IA

Security Savings Bank; Larchwood, IA

Security Savings Bank; Williamsburg, IA

Security State Bank; Guttenberg, IA

Security State Bank; Hartley, IA

Security State Bank; Independence, IA

Security State Bank; Lake Park, IA

Security State Bank; New Hampton, IA

Security State Bank; Sheldon, IA

Security State Bank; Sutherland, IA

Security State Bank; Scott City, KS

Security State Bank; Farwell, TX

Security State Bank; Centralia, WA

Security State Bank of Pecos; Pecos, TX

Security State Bank and Trust; Fredericksburg, TX

Security State Bank and Trust Company; Polson, MT

Security Trust Company; San Diego, CA

Security Trust and Financial Company; San Antonio, TX

Security Trust and Savings Bank; Storm Lake, IA

Seguin State Bank and Trust Company; Seguin, TX

SEI Trust Company; Wayne, PA

Semper Trust Company; Plymouth Meeting, PA

Sentinel Trust Company; Nashville, TN

Sequatchie County Bank; Dunlap, TN

Shawmut Bank Connecticut, NA; Hartford, CT

Shawmut Bank, NA; Boston, MA

Shawmut National Trust Company; Stuart, FL

Shawmut Trust Company; New York, NY

Shawnee State Bank; Shawnee, KS

Shelby County State Bank; Shelbyville, IL

Shelby County State Bank; Harlan, IA

Shelby County Trust Bank; Shelbyville, KY,

Shelton Savings Bank; Shelton, CT

Shoreline Bank; St. Joseph, MI

Sibley State Bank; Sibley, IA

Signet Trust Company; Richmond, VA

Silsbee State Bank; Silsbee, TX

Simmons First National Bank; Pine Bluff, AR

Simpson County Bank; Franklin, KY

Sioux County State Bank; Orange City, IA

Sloan State Bank; Sloan, IA

Smackover State Bank; Smackover, AR

Smith County State Bank and Trust Company; Smith Center, KS

Smith Trust and Savings Bank; Morrison, IL

Society Bank, Michigan; Ann Arbor, MI

Society National Bank, Indiana; South Bend, IN

Society Trust Company of New York; New York, NY

Solon State Bank; Solon, IA

Solvay Bank; Solvay, NY

Somerset Trust Company; Somerset, PA

Somerville Bank and Trust Company; Somerville, TN

South Branch Valley National Bank of Moorefield; Moorefield, WV

South Chicago Bank; Calumet City, IL

South Holland Trust and Savings Bank; South Holland, IL

South Ottumwa Savings Bank; Ottumwa, IA

South Side National Bank in St. Louis; St. Louis, MO

South Side Trust and Savings Bank of Peoria: Peoria IL

South Story Bank & Trust; Slater, IA

Southern Michigan Bank & Trust; Coldwater, MI

Southgate Trust Company; Shawnee Mission, KS

Southington Savings Bank; Plantsville, CT

Southside Bank; Tyler, TX

SouthTrust Bank of Alabama, NA; Birmingham, AL

SouthTrust Estate & Trust Company, Inc.; Saint Petersburg, FL

SouthTrust Estate and Trust Company of Georgia, NA; Atlanta, GA

Southwest Bank; Bolivar, MO

Southwest Bank; Fort Worth, TX

Southwest Bank and Trust Company of Omaha; Omaha, NE

Southwest Financial Bank and Trust; New Lenox, IL

Southwest Georgia Bank; Moultrie, GA

Southwest Guaranty Trust Company; Houston, TX

Southwest Missouri Bank; Carthage, MO

Southwest National Bank of Pennsylvania; Greensburg, PA

Southwest National Bank of Wichita; Wichita, KS

Soy Capital Bank and Trust Company; Decatur, IL

Spencer County Bank; Santa Claus, IN

Springfield State Bank; Springfield, KY

Springfield Trust Company; Springfield, MO

Springs Valley Bank & Trust Company; Jasper, IN

Standard Bank and Trust; Independence, MO

Standard Bank & Trust Company; Hickory Hills, IL

Star Bank, NA; Cincinnati, OH

Star Bank, NA, Indiana; Richmond, IN

Star Bank, NA, Kentucky; Covington, KY

Star Trust Company; Marion, IN

State Bank; Everly, IA

State Bank; Fenton, MI

State Bank; Fayetteville, NC

State Bank of Alcester; Alcester, SD

State Bank of Arthur; Arthur, IL

State Bank of Ashland; Ashland, IL

State Bank of Auburn; Auburn, IL

State Bank of Bement; Bement, IL

State Bank of Blue Mound; Blue Mound, IL

State Bank of Burnettsville; Burnettsville, IN

State Bank of Cairo; Cairo, NE

State Bank of Chrisman; Chrisman, IL

State Bank of Countryside; Countryside, IL

State Bank of Cross Plains; Cross Plains, WI

State Bank of Geneva; Geneva, IL

State Bank of Graymont; Graymont, IL

State Bank of Hammond; Hammond, IL

State Bank of Herscher; Herscher, IL

State Bank of Jerseyville; Jerseyville, IL

State Bank of the Lakes; Antioch, IL

State Bank of Lawler; Lawler, IA

State Bank of Ledyard; Ledyard, IA

State Bank of Lincoln; Lincoln, IL

State Bank of Lizton; Lizton, IN

State Bank of Markle; Markle, IN

State Bank of Medora; Medora, IN

State Bank of Mount Horeb; Mount Horeb, WI

State Bank of Oxford; Oxford, IN

State Bank of Schaller; Schaller, IA

State Bank of Toledo; Toledo, IA

State Bank of Wapello; Wapello, IA

State Bank of Washington; Washington, IN

State Bank of Waverly; Waverly, IA

State Bank & Trust Company; Nevada, IA

State Bank & Trust Company; Harrodsburg, KY

State Bank & Trust Company; Brookhaven, MS

State Bank & Trust Company; Dillon, MT

State Bank & Trust Company; Defiance, OH

State Bank & Trust Company; San Marcos, TX

State Bank & Trust Company of New Ulm; New Ulm, MN

State Bank & Trust, NA; Tulsa, OK

State Bank & Trust of Kenmare; Kenmare, ND

State Central Bank; Keokuk, IA

State National Bank; El Paso, TX

State National Bank of Frankfort; Frankfort, KY

State National Bank & Trust Company; Wayne, NE

State Savings Bank; Bedford, IA

State Street Bank & Trust Company; Quincy, IL

State Street Bank & Trust Company; Boston, MA

State Street Bank & Trust Company, NA; New York, NY

State Street Bank & Trust Company of California, NA; Los Angeles, CA

State Street Bank & Trust Company of Connecticut, NA; Hartford, CT

State Street Bank & Trust Company of Maryland, NA; Columbia, MD

State Street Bank & Trust Company of New Hampshire, NA; Manchester, NH

Staten Island Savings Bank; Staten Island, NY

Stephenson National Bank and Trust; Marinette, WI

Stephenville Bank and Trust Company; Stephenville, TX

Sterling Bank; Houston, TX

Sterling Bank & Trust, FSB; Southfield, MI

Sterling National Bank & Trust Company of New York; New York, NY

Steuben Trust Company; Hornell, NY

Stillwater National Bank & Trust Company; Stillwater, OK

Stock Yards Bank & Trust Company; Louisville, KY

Stone Fort National Bank; Nacogdoches, TX

Suburban Bank of Barrington; Barrington, IL

Suburban Federal Savings Bank; Cincinnati, OH

Suffolk County National Bank of Riverhead; Southampton, NY

Sulphur Springs State Bank; Sulphur Springs, TX

Sumitomo Bank of California; San Francisco, CA

Sumitomo Bank of New York Trust Company; New York, NY

Sumitomo Trust & Banking Co. (USA); New York, NY

Summit Bank; Summit, NJ

Summit Bank; Johnstown, PA

Sun Bank; Selinsgrove, PA

Sun Bank Capital Management; NA; Orlando, FL

Sun Bank—Miami, NA; Miami, FL

Sun Bank, NA; Orlando, FL

Sun Bank North Central Florida; Ocala, FL

Sun Bank of Volusia County; Daytona Beach, FL

Sun Bank—South Florida, NA; Fort Lauderdale, FL

Sun Bank—Southwest Florida; Fort Myers, FL

Sun Bank—Tallahassee, NA; Tallahassee, FL

Sun Bank—Treasure Coast, NA; Fort Pierce, FL

Sun Bank and Trust Company; Brooksville, FL

Sun Bank—West Florida; Pensacola, FL

Sun Trust Bank of Tampa Bay; Tampa, FL

Sun Trust Bank, West Georgia, NA; Columbus, GA

SunBank—Mid-Florida, NA; Winter Haven, FL

Sunburst Bank; Baton Rouge, LA

Sunburst Bank; Jackson, MS

Sunflower Bank, NA; Salina, KS

Sunstar Bank; Washington, IL

SunTrust Bank Atlanta; Atlanta, GA

SunTrust Bank, East Tennessee, NA; Knoxville, TN

SunTrust Bank, Gulf Coast; Sarasota, FL

SunTrust Bank, Middle Georgia, NA; Macon, GA

SunTrust Banks, North Florida, NA; Jacksonville, FL

Sunwest Bank of Albuquerque, NA; Albuquerque, NM

Sunwest Bank of El Paso; El Paso, TX

Superior National Bank and Trust Company; Hancock, MI

Sussex County State Bank; Franklin, NJ

Swea City State Bank; Swea City, IA

Swisher Trust & Company Savings Bank; Swisher, IA

Synovus Trust Company; Albany, GA

Synovus Trust Company; Americus, GA

Synovus Trust Company; Athens, GA

Synovus Trust Company; Brunswick, GA

Synovus Trust Company; Columbus, GA

Synovus Trust Company; La Grange, GA

Synovus Trust Company; Monroe, GA

Synovus Trust Company; Statesboro, GA

Synovus Trust Company; Thomasville, GA

T

Taintor Savings Bank; New Sharon, IA

Tama State Bank; Tama, IA

Taneytown Bank & Trust Company; Taneytown, MD

Taylor County Bank; Campbellsville, KY

Tell City National Bank; Tell City, IN

Templeton Savings Bank; Templeton, IA

Tennessee Community Bank; Covington, TN

Terre Haute First National Bank; Terre Haute, IN

Terre Haute Savings Bank; Terre Haute, IN

Terrell State Bank; Terrell, TX

Texarkana National Bank; Texarkana, TX

Texas Bank; Brownwood, TX

Texas Bank; Weatherford, TX

Texas Commerce Bank, NA; Houston, TX

Texas Commerce Bank—San Angelo, NA; San Angelo, TX

Texas First Bank; Galveston, TX

Texas Gulf Bank, NA; Lake Jackson, TX

Texas National Bank of Waco; Waco, TX

Texas State Bank; McAllen, TX

Texas State Bank; San Angelo, TX

Third National Bank in Nashville; Nashville, TN

Thumb National Bank and Trust Company; Pigeon, MI

Titonka Savings Bank; Titonka, IA

Today's Trust Company; Freeport, IL

Tokai Trust Company of New York; New York, NY

Tompkins County Trust Company; Ithaca, NY

Toronto-Dominion Bank Trust Company; New York, NY

Torrington Savings Bank; Torrington, CT

Town & Country Bank of Quincy; Quincy, IL

Town & Country Bank of Springfield; Springfield, IL

Toyo Trust Company of New York; New York, NY

Traders National Bank of Tullahoma; Tullahoma, TN

Trans Financial Bank; Pikeville, KY

Tredegar Trust Company; Richmond, VA

Trenton Trust Company; Trenton, MO

Treynor State Bank; Treynor, IA

Tri-City Bank and Trust Company; Bristol, TN

Tri-County Bank & Trust Company; Roachdale, IN

Tri-County Trust Company; Glasgow, MO

Trigg County Farmers Bank; Cadiz, KY

Troy Bank & Trust Company; Troy, AL

Troy Savings Bank; Troy, NY

Trust Bank of the United States; Baton Rouge, LA

Trust Center of America; Bismarck, ND

Trust Company; Saint Joseph, MO

Trust Company Bank of Augusta, NA; Augusta, GA

Trust Company Bank of Northeast Georgia, NA; Athens, GA

Trust Company Bank of Northwest Georgia, NA; Rome, GA

Trust Company Bank of South Georgia, NA; Albany, GA

Trust Company Bank of Southeast Georgia, NA; Brunswick, GA

Trust Company of America; Englewood, CO

Trust Company of Connecticut; Hartford, CT

Trust Company of Georgia Bank of Savannah, NA; Savannah, GA

Trust Company of Illinois; Glen Ellyn, IL

Trust Company of Kansas; Wichita, KS

Trust Company of Kentucky; Ashland, KY

Trust Company of Knoxville; Knoxville, TN

Trust Company of Louisiana; Ruston, LA

Trust Company of Maine, Inc; Bangor, ME

Trust Company of Manhattan; Manhattan, KS

Trust Company of New Jersey; Jersey City, NJ

Trust Company of Oklahoma; Muskogee, OK

Trust Company of Oklahoma; Tulsa, OK

Trust Company of the South; Miami, FL

Trust Company of the South; Burlington, NC

Trust Company of Sterne, Agee and Leach Inc.; Birmingham, AL

Trust Company of Toledo, NA; Holland, OH

Trust Company of Virginia; Richmond, VA

Trust Company of Washington; Bellevue, WA

Trust Company of the West; Los Angeles, CA

Trust Management Inc.; Fort Worth, TX

Trustco Bank; Schenectady, NY

TrustCorp; Great Falls, MT

Trustmark National Bank; Jackson, MS

Tuscola National Bank; Tuscola, IL

Twentieth Street Bank, Inc.; Huntington, WV

Twin City Bank; North Little Rock, AR

U

U.S. Trust Company Limited; New York, NY

U.S. Trust Company of California, NA; Los Angeles, CA

U.S. Trust Company of Connecticut; Stamford, CT

U.S. Trust Company of Florida Savings Bank; Palm Beach, FL

U.S. Trust Company of New Jersey; Princeton, NJ

U.S. Trust Company of the Pacific Northwest; Portland, OR

U.S. Trust Company of Texas, NA; Dallas, TX

UMB Bank, NA; Colorado Springs, CO

UMB Bank, NA; Overland Park, KS

UMB Bank, NA; Kansas City, MO

Union Bank; Los Angeles, CA

Union Bank; Loogootee, IN

Union Bank; Morrisville, VT

Union Bank of Benton; Benton, AR

Union Bank of Illinois; Swansea, IL

Union Bank of Tyler County, Inc.; Middlebourne, WV

Union Bank and Trust; Denver, CO

Union Bank and Trust Company; Monticello, AR

Union Bank and Trust Company; North
Vernon, IN

Union Bank and Trust Company; Straw-
berry Point, IA

Union Bank and Trust Company; Minneapolis, MN

Union Bank and Trust Company; Lincoln, NE

Union Bank and Trust Company; Pottsville, PA

Union Bank and Trust Company; Bowling Green, VA

Union Bank and Trust Company; Evansville, WI

Union Bank and Trust Company of Indiana; Greensburg, IN

Union Colony Bank; Greeley, CO

Union County Bank; Blairsville, GA

Union County National Bank of Liberty;
Liberty, IN

Union National Bank of Macomb; Macomb, IL

Union National Bank of Mount Carmel;
Mount Carmel, PA

Union National Bank of Texas; Laredo,
TX

Union National Bank of Wichita; Wichita, KS

Union National Bank and Trust Company;
Sparta, WI

Union National Bank & Trust Company
of Souderton; Souderton, PA

Union National Mount Joy Bank; Mount
Joy, PA

Union Planters Bank of Northeast Arkansas; Jonesboro, AR

Union Planters Bank of Northwest Mississippi; Clarksdale, MS

Union Planters National Bank; Memphis,
TN

Union Safe Deposit Bank; Stockton, CA

Union Savings Bank; Covington, TN

Union Savings Bank of Danbury; Danbury, CT

Union State Bank; Windfall, IN

Union State Bank; Monona, IA

Union State Bank; Rockwell City, IA

Union State Bank; Clay Center, KS

Union State Bank and Trust Company of
Clinton; Clinton, MO

Union Trust Bank; Union City, IN

Union Trust Company; Ellsworth, ME

UnionBank; Streator, IL

United American Bank of Memphis;
Memphis, TN

United Bank and Trust; Tecumseh, MI

United Carolina Bank; Whiteville, NC

United Carolina Bank of South Carolina;
Greenville, SC

United Citizens Bank and Trust Company;
Campbellsburg, KY

United Community Bank; Chatham, IL

United Community Bank; Ocheyedan, IA

United Counties Trust Company; Cran-
ford, NJ

United Illinois Bank of Southern Illinois;
Benton, IL

United Jersey Bank; Hackensack, NJ

United Missouri Trust Company of New
York; New York, NY

United National Bank; Plainfield, NJ

United National Bank; Beckley, WV

United National Bank; Parkersburg, WV

United National Bank & Trust Company;
Canton, OH

United Nebraska Bank; North Platte, NE

United Southern Bank; Eustis, FL

United States National Bank of Galveston;
Galveston, TX

United States National Bank of Oregon;
Sacramento, CA

United States National Bank of Oregon;
Reno, NV

United States National Bank of Oregon;
Portland, OR

United States National Bank of Oregon;
Seattle, WA

United States Trust Company; Boston,
MA

United States Trust Company of New
York; New York, NY

University Bank & Trust Company; Palo
Alto, CA

USBANCORP Trust Company; Johnstown, PA

Ute State Bank; Ute, IA

V

Valley American Bank and Trust Company; South Bend, IN

Valley Bank; Elk Point, SD

Valley Bank; Sweetwater, TN

Valley Bank and Trust; Cherokee, IA

Valley Bank and Trust; Mapleton, IA

Valley National Bank; Clifton, NJ

Valley View State Bank; Overland Park, KS

Van Horn State Bank of Van Horn; Van Horn, TX

Van Liew Trust Company; Providence, RI

Van Wert National Bank; Van Wert, OH

Vanguard Bank & Trust Company; Fort Walton Beach, FL

Veedersburg State Bank; Veedersburg, IN

Vermillion Valley Bank; Piper City, IL

Vermont National Bank; Brattleboro, VT

Vevay Deposit Bank; Vevay, IN

Victor State Bank; Victor, IA

Victoria Bank and Trust Company; Victoria, TX

Vigil Asset Management Group, Inc; Wausau, WI

Villa Grove State Bank; Villa Grove, IL

Villa Park Trust & Savings Bank; Villa Park, IL

Village Bank and Trust Company; Ridgefield, CT

Vine Street Trust Company; Lexington, KY

Virginia Bank and Trust Company; Danville, VA

Volunteer Bank; Jackson, TN

W

Wachovia Bank of Georgia, NA; Atlanta, GA

Wachovia Bank of North Carolina, NA; Winston-Salem, NC

Wachovia Bank of South Carolina, NA; Columbia, SC

Waggoner National Bank of Vernon; Vernon, TX

Walcott Trust and Savings Bank; Walcott, IA

Walters Bank and Trust Company; Walters, OK

Warren Bank and Trust Company; Warren, AR

Warren-Doynton State Bank; New Berlin, IL

Washington Bank and Trust Company; Franklinton, LA

Washington State Bank; Washington, IA

Washington Trust Bank; Spokane, WA

Washington Trust Company; Westerly, RI

Watseka First National Bank; Watseka, IL

Waukesha State Bank; Waukesha, WI

Waukon State Bank; Waukon, IA

Wayland State Bank; Wayland, IA

Wayne Bank; Honesdale, PA

Wayne Bank and Trust Co.; Cambridge City, IN

Wayne County Bank; Waynesboro, TN

Wayne County Bank & Trust Company; Fairfield, IL

Wayne County National Bank of Wooster; Wooster, OH

Weakley County Bank; Dresden, TN

Weldon State Bank & Trust; Weldon, IL

Wellington Trust Company, NA; Boston, MA

Wells Fargo Bank, NA; San Francisco, CA

Wells Fargo Institutional Trust Company, NA; San Francisco, CA

Wemple State Bank; Waverly, IL

Wesbanco Bank Barnesville; Barnesville, OH

WesBanco Bank Fairmont Inc; Fairmont, WV

WesBanco Bank Kingwood, Inc.; Kingwood, WV

WesBanco Bank Parkersburg; Parkersburg, WV

WesBanco Bank Wheeling; Wheeling, WV

West Alabama Bank and Trust; Reform, AL

West Branch State Bank; West Branch, IA

West Burlington Bank; West Burlington, IA

West Chicago State Bank; West Chicago, IL

West Des Moines State Bank; West Des Moines, IA

West Liberty State Bank; West Liberty, IA

West Michigan National Bank; Manistee, MI

West One Bank, Idaho; Boise, ID

West One Bank, Oregon; Portland, OR

West One Bank, Utah; Salt Lake City, UT

West One Trust Company; Salt Lake City, UT

West One Trust Company, Washington; Seattle, WA

West Suburban Bank; Lombard, IL

West Texas Trust Company; Levelland, TX

Westamerica Bank; Sacramento, CA

Western Bank; Las Cruces, NM

Western Bank; Medford, OR

Western Commerce Bank; Lovington, NM

Western National Bank; Odessa, TX

Western Springs National Bank and Trust; Western Springs, IL

Westport Bank and Trust Company; Westport, CT

WestStar Bank; Bartlesville, OK

White County Bank; Carmi, IL

Whitney National Bank; New Orleans, LA

Whittier Trust Company; South Pasadena, CA

Wilber National Bank; Oneonta, NY

Williamsport National Bank; Williamsport, PA

Williamsville State Bank; Williamsville, IL

Wilmington Trust Company; Wilmington, DE

Wilmington Trust of Forida, NA; Stuart, FL

Wilson Bank & Trust; Lebanon, TN

Wilson & Muir Bank & Trust Company; Bardstown, KY

Wilton Savings Bank; Wilton, IA

Winnsboro State Bank & Trust Company; Winnsboro, LA

Winona National and Savings Bank; Winona, MN

Wood County Trust Company; Wisconsin Rapids WI

Wood and Huston Bank; Marshall, MO

Woodford Bank and Trust Company; Versailles, KY

Woodford County Bank; El Paso, IL

Woodstown National Bank & Trust Company; Woodstown, NJ

Woodway Financial Advisors—A Trust Company; Houston, TX

Woronoco Savings Bank; Westfield, MA

Worth Bank and Trust; Palos Heights, IL

Wyoming Bank and Trust Company; Buffalo, WY

Wyoming County Bank; Warsaw, NY

Wyoming Trust and Management Co.; Gillette, WY

Y

Yasuda Bank and Trust Company, (USA); New York, NY

York Bank and Trust Company; York, PA

York State Bank & Trust Company; York, NE

Z

Zapp National Bank of St. Cloud; Saint Cloud, MN

Zions First National Bank; Salt Lake City, UT

Source: *American Bankers' Association Directory of Trust Banking*

Index of Resource Guide Products and Services

NEWSLETTERS

BOOKS

MAGAZINES & PERIODICALS

ON-LINE SERVICES

SOFTWARE